TRAUMA

Trauma

CONTEMPORARY DIRECTIONS IN TRAUMA
THEORY, RESEARCH, AND PRACTICE

SECOND EDITION

*Edited by Shoshana Ringel
and Jerrold R. Brandell*

 COLUMBIA UNIVERSITY PRESS   NEW YORK

COLUMBIA UNIVERSITY PRESS
Publishers Since 1893
New York   Chichester, West Sussex

cup.columbia.edu
Copyright © 2020 Columbia University Press

Library of Congress Cataloging-in-Publication Data

Names: Ringel, Shoshana, editor. | Brandell, Jerrold R., editor.
Title: Trauma : contemporary directions in trauma theory, research, and practice /
    edited by Shoshana Ringel and Jerrold R. Brandell.
Description: Second edition. | New York : Columbia University Press, [2019] |
    Includes bibliographical references and index.
Identifiers: LCCN 2019015739| ISBN 9780231188869 (hardcover) |
    ISBN 9780231188876 (trade pbk.)
Subjects: LCSH: Post-traumatic stress disorder.
Classification: LCC RC552.P67 T7476 2019 | DDC 616.85/21—dc23
    LC record available at https://lccn.loc.gov/2019015739

Cover design: Milenda Nan Ok Lee
Cover image: Regien Paassen © Shutterstock

CONTENTS

TRAUMA

Introduction

ALTHOUGH THERE HAS BEEN MUCH scholarship devoted to the study of
trauma, the field has continued to expand since the publication of the
first edition of this book, in 2011. From an earlier focus on the interpersonal aspects of trauma, including child abuse and domestic violence,
traumatic experiences have taken on a political and social dimension—
for example, the war on terror and combat trauma associated with it, institutional racism and oppression as shown in police brutality and rates of
incarceration of people of color, school shootings in American public
schools, which are increasingly linked to the problem of bullying, sexual
assault of women, and the plight of refugees and migrants across the globe.
These social and political phenomena have added to the magnitude of traumatic experiences in everyday life, thereby increasing the complexity
of the tasks facing mental health professionals, who deal with the effects of
trauma on a daily basis.

This book will present new developments in the conceptualization
of trauma and trauma-related interventions from diverse clinical perspectives, including cognitive-behavioral therapy, psychodynamic therapy,
mindfulness-based trauma models, and attachment theory. Clinical chapters will focus on various populations and themes associated with trauma,
though by no means all: the use of art therapy with children who have suffered loss and bereavement, the impact of bullying on schoolchildren, the
trauma transgender people experience in their daily lives, cultural and historical trauma among Native Americans, the traumatic history and experiences of incarcerated and formerly incarcerated African American women,

the sequelae of combat trauma on individuals and families, and the impact of trauma-focused clinical practice on the clinician.

Because of its broad scope as well as its emphasis on the application of diverse theoretical viewpoints to a variety of post-traumatic situations, we believe this anthology represents a new and different transtheoretical approach to clinical scholarship on trauma. Indeed, no social work text of which we are aware, and few written by authors with other professional backgrounds, has focused specifically on theoretical and clinical issues associated with trauma.

The book is designed to provide a clear and accessible description of contemporary theoretical perspectives on trauma as well as clinical applications for treatment with a variety of populations, including both research outcomes on the utility of the approach and clinical vignettes to illustrate its usefulness.

1

History and Development of Trauma Theory

DISCUSSION OF MAIN CONCEPTS

▸ SHOSHANA RINGEL

THE RELATIONSHIP BETWEEN TRAUMA and mental illness was first investigated by the neurologist Jean Martin Charcot, a French physician working with traumatized women in the Salpetriere hospital. During the late nineteenth century, a major focus of Charcot's study was hysteria, a disorder commonly diagnosed in women. Hysterical symptoms included sudden paralysis, amnesia, sensory loss, and convulsions. Women constituted the vast majority of patients with hysteria, and at the time the symptoms of hysteria were thought to originate in the uterus. Until Charcot, the common treatment for hysteria was hysterectomy. Charcot was the first to understand that the origin of hysterical symptoms was not physiological but rather psychological in nature, although he was not interested in the inner lives of his female patients. He noted that traumatic events could induce a hypnotic state in his patients and was the first to "describe both the problems of suggestibility in these patients, and the fact that hysterical attacks are dissociative problems—the results of having endured unbearable experiences" (van der Kolk, van der Hart, and Marmar 1996, 50). In Salpetriere, young women who had suffered violence, rape, and sexual abuse found safety and shelter, and Charcot presented his theory to large audiences through live demonstrations in which patients were hypnotized and then helped to remember their trauma, a process that culminated in the abrogation of their symptoms (Herman 1992).

Pierre Janet, a student of Charcot, continued to study dissociative phenomena and traumatic memories. Janet investigated the influence of patients' traumatic experiences on personality development and behavior. He recognized that patients' intense affects were reactions to their perception of traumatic events, and he found that through hypnosis and abreaction, or reexposure to the traumatic memories, patients' symptoms could be alleviated (van der Kolk, McFarlane, and Weisaeth 1996). Janet referred to dissociative phenomena as unconscious fixed ideas, the core of traumatic experiences and reenactments. A primary fixed idea contains the memories, sensory experiences, emotions, and behaviors associated with the trauma. Janet observed that these internal personalities had their own discrete senses of self, developmental stages, and behavioral characteristics and that each held different aspects of the traumatic memory. He believed that it was important to help patients resolve their traumatic memories and integrate them through long-term treatment and a trusting therapy relationship. Janet was also the first to use a phase-oriented approach with his patients (van der Hart 2016).

In his early studies of hysteria (1893–1895), Freud, too, was initially influenced by Charcot and adopted some of his ideas. In the *Studies on Hysteria* ([1893] 1962), co-authored with Josef Breuer, Freud suggested that "we must point out that we consider it essential for the explanation of hysterical phenomena to assume the presence of a dissociation, a splitting of the content of consciousness. The regular and essential content of a hysterical attack is the recurrence of a physical state which the patient has experienced earlier" (Breuer and Freud, 1962, 30, as cited in van der Kolk, McFarlane, and Waisaeth, 1996).

Freud and Breuer termed traumatic dissociation "hypnoid hysteria" and highlighted its relationship to a traumatic antecedent. In 1896, Freud suggested that "a precocious experience of sexual relations . . . resulting from sexual abuse committed by another person . . . is the *specific cause* of hysteria . . . not merely an agent provocateur" ([1896] 1962), 152, italics added; as cited in van der Kolk, McFarlane and Waisaeth, 1996). In the 1880s, Freud and Breuer, as well as Janet, independently concluded that hysteria was caused by psychological trauma. They agreed that unbearable reactions to traumatic experiences produced an altered state of consciousness, which Janet called "dissociation." According to Janet, dissociation manifested in hysterical symptoms (Herman 1992). Putting the emotions into words and reconstructing the past helped alleviate the patients' symptoms.

However, Freud eventually moved from what has been termed "seduction theory" to conflict theory (see chapter 3 for a more detailed discussion of this development), suggesting that it was not memories of external trauma that caused hysterical symptoms but rather the unacceptable nature of sexual and aggressive wishes. What his followers neglected to notice, however, was that although Freud privileged intrapsychic theory and fantasy over external trauma, he did suggest that it was possible for external trauma to influence the patient's state of mind (Diamond 2004). Ferenczi ([1933] 1955) was the only one among Freud's followers who regarded his patients' stories of childhood sexual abuse as veridical recollections, but he remained somewhat of an outsider in the psychoanalytic movement during his lifetime, his theories only gaining favor in the decades following his untimely death in 1933.

Crisis-intervention methods to address traumatic events developed gradually, with the establishment of the first suicide hotline in 1902 in San Francisco. Psychological "first aid" was then further developed in the context of military combat. During World War I, psychiatrists observed how soldiers returned with "shell shock." Psychological first aid was initially conceived as a way to help WWI soldiers overcome their symptoms of uncontrollable weeping and screaming, memory loss, physical paralysis, and lack of responsiveness (Herman 1992). The goal was a short intervention that would help the soldiers recover and return to the front as soon as possible. It was observed that by providing intervention close to the front and soon after deployment, traumatized soldiers were able to overcome their shell shock symptoms and return to active combat duty. In 1923, following World War I, Abram Kardiner started to treat traumatized U.S. war veterans (Kardiner 1941). Like Janet and Freud, he observed the nature of reenactment, a central construct in modern trauma theory, and noted that "the subject acts as if the original traumatic situation were still in existence and engages in protective devices which failed on the original occasion" (1941, 82; also in van der Kolk van der Hart and Marmar 1996, 58). Kardiner also foresaw an important controversy that continues to haunt trauma therapists, that is, whether to bring the traumatic memories into the patient's consciousness or to focus on stabilization (van der Kolk, van der Hart, and Marmar 1996, 58). Whereas earlier trauma theorists blamed the soldiers' symptoms on their poor moral character, Kardiner understood that any man could be affected by the atrocities of war and that the traumatic symptoms were a normal response to an unbearable situation.

Kardiner and his colleague Herbert Spiegel argued that the most powerful intervention against overwhelming terror was "the degree of relatedness between the soldier, his immediate fighting unit, and their leader" (Herman 1992, 25). Consequently, treatment for traumatized soldiers during the Second World War focused on minimizing separation between the soldiers and their comrades and providing brief intervention methods, such as hypnosis. Kardiner and Spiegel warned, however, that cathartic experiences and hypnosis by themselves, without consistent follow-up, were not sufficiently helpful and that unless the traumatic memories were integrated in consciousness, the improvement would not last (Kardiner and Spiegel 1947, in Herman 1992). During World War II, psychiatrists reintroduced hypnosis as a treatment for trauma, and the U.S. Army developed the use of "group stress debriefing" (Shalev and Ursano 1990, cited in van der Kolk, van der Hart, and Marmar 1996, 59).

After World War II, studies on the impact of prolonged stress and trauma on concentration camp survivors coincided with observations of combat stress. Henry Krystal (1968, 1978, 1988) was a psychoanalyst and Holocaust survivor who studied outcomes of prolonged traumatization on concentration camp survivors, observing that "traumatized patients come to experience emotional reactions merely as somatic states, without being able to interpret the meaning of what they are feeling" (van der Kolk, van der Hart, and Marmar 1996, 60). Krystal elaborated on the diagnosis of *alexithymia*, a typical syndrome in chronically traumatized people. He described the effect of trauma on the capacity to experience, identify, and verbalize feelings, as well as physiological needs, and these patients' tendency to somatize affective experiences, their inclination to express themselves in an overly concrete manner, and their lack of capacity to symbolize and dream. McDougall, who also worked with traumatized patients, suggested that it was not the absence of affect that was the issue. Instead, she stated that her patients "were not suffering from an inability to experience or express emotions, but from an inability to contain and reflect over an excess of affective experiences" (McDougall 1989, 94).

Contemporary trauma theory in civilian contexts developed after the 1942 Cocoanut Grove fire in Boston. During that fire, 493 people perished in a nightclub, many of them trampled to death. Following the tragedy, Erich Lindemann, who treated a number of the survivors, observed that they displayed common responses. He began to theorize about normal grief reactions, including preoccupation with lost loved ones, identification with the deceased, expressions of guilt and hostility, disorganization, and somatic complaints (Lindemann 1944). Gerald Caplan, who also worked with survivors of the Cocoanut Grove fire, was the first to systematically describe the components of crisis. He spoke of people being "in a state of crisis when they face an obstacle to important life goals . . . an obstacle that is, for a time, insurmountable by the use of customary methods of problem solving. A period of disorganization ensues, a period of upset, during which many abortive attempts at solution are made" (Caplan 1961, 18). During the same time, Parad was interested in examining the impact of particular types of crises and identified five components that affected victims' abilities to cope with overwhelming life events:

- The stressful event poses a problem which is by definition insoluble in the immediate future
- The problem overtaxes the psychological resources of the family, since it is beyond their traditional problem-solving methods
- The situation is perceived as a threat or danger to the life goals of the family members
- The crisis period is characterized by tension which mounts to a peak, then falls
- Perhaps of the greatest importance, the crisis situation awakens unresolved key problems from both the near and distant past

(Parad and Caplan 1960, 11–12)

During the Vietnam War, soldiers and veterans returned with incapacitating symptoms that often developed into chronic problems affecting their capacity to cope with and function in civilian life. Many of them started to abuse drugs and alcohol, behaved violently toward their partners, or became homeless and unemployable. Lifton and Shatan, who worked with Vietnam veterans, conducted "rap groups" for the veterans, during which they could share their experiences with their comrades and receive validation and support. Lifton and Shatan identified twenty-seven common symptoms of "traumatic neurosis" (Lifton 1973). These symptoms were catalogued based

on Lifton and Shatans' observations of veterans, as well as on their read-
ings of Kardiner and the literature on Holocaust survivors and on victims of accidents, which they compared with clinical records of Vietnam
veterans. Many of these symptoms were later included in the diagnosis of
post-traumatic stress disorder (PTSD) that appeared in the *Diagnostic and
Statistical Manual of Mental Disorders*, third edition (*DSM-III*); they were
also used in panel discussions leading to the inclusion of this diagnosis (van
der Kolk, McFarlane, Weisaeth 1996). Figley (1978) also contributed to the
growing treatment literature on Vietnam veterans, and Shay (1994) made
theoretical contributions to the understanding of the long-term effect of
combat trauma on Vietnam veterans by applying Greek-mythological imagery. In his book *Achilles in Vietnam*, Shay used, for example, the story of
Achilles to anchor his discussion of Vietnam veterans' experiences and psychological wounds. Shay used Homer's story from the *Iliad* as a metaphor
for the "moral injury" that soldiers suffered when they were betrayed by
their commanders and other authority figures, as Achilles felt betrayed by
Agamemnon. The soldiers' subsequent disillusionment contributed to the
unraveling of their character and to their engaging in immoral acts during
combat (such as killing women and children). In later decades, the term
moral injury was applied to veterans' distress regarding acts that violated
their ethical beliefs. These acts were sometimes done through drone attacks and other long-distance strategies, but they still had a deep and lasting effect on the combatants, including nightmares, intrusive thoughts,
depression, and suicidal ideation (Litz et al. 2009).

Along with combat trauma and the trauma of Holocaust survivors,
trauma in the lives of women moved from the private domain of the home
to the public arena as a consequence of the women's movement in the 1970s.
Women's consciousness-raising groups shared common characteristics of the
Vietnam veterans' rap groups in that they were based on open sharing, validation, and support, and they "helped overcome barriers of denial, secrecy
and shame" (Herman 1992, 29). The purpose was not only to provide psychological healing but also to bring about social change in policies and institutions. An epidemiological survey by Diana Russell in the 1980s of over
nine hundred women chosen at random showed that one woman in four
had been raped and one woman in three had been sexually abused in childhood, statistics that were quite shocking insofar as such problems had
been well hidden and denied until that era (Russell 1984). The first rape

crisis center opened in 1971, and a more comprehensive understanding and treatment of domestic violence followed (Herman 1992). Additional contributions to the understanding of types of trauma and their impact were made by Lenore Terr (1979) through her work with children involved in a school-bus kidnapping in Chowchilla, California.

PTSD AND THE *DSM-III*

Psychological trauma and post-traumatic stress disorder were not included in the *DSM* until 1980, soon after returning Vietnam War veterans presented with severe symptoms and clearly needed prolonged psychological services. Advocates for combat veterans and mental health professionals collaborated in bringing these events and their aftermath to public view (Herman 1981, 1992; van der Kolk, McFarlane, and Weisaeth 1996). Together with advocates of battered women, rape victims, and abused children, these clinicians brought their influence to bear on the *DSM-III* committees, and all these groups were included under the diagnosis of PTSD in 1980. Veteran's advocates, mental health professionals, and others working with victims of domestic violence and adult survivors of childhood incest/sexual abuse reported similar symptoms in their traumatized clients. Many had been further victimized owing to social stigma and a lack of understanding of their behavioral, emotional, and cognitive symptoms. In addition to advocating for the acceptance of the PTSD diagnosis, women's advocates opposed the inclusion of certain personality disorders that they regarded as being sexist or culturally biased, such as masochistic and histrionic personality disorders.

The *DSM* diagnosis of PTSD addressed immediate symptoms following combat experiences, rape, domestic violence, and child abuse; symptoms were further categorized along four clusters: intrusive reexperiencing, avoidance, hyperarousal, and hypervigilance, with general symptoms of anxiety and dysphoria in addition (Ford and Courtois 2009). Although the PTSD diagnosis addresses the symptoms of post-trauma stress, it does not focus on causes in a patient's early developmental history, which may include childhood abuse and neglect, nor does it offer a more complex and comprehensive view of psychosocial stressors and daily functioning that exert influence over all areas of adult life.

COMPLEX TRAUMATIC STRESS DISORDER

As stated above, whereas the diagnosis of PTSD included the comprehensive symptoms of trauma, it did not address early antecedents in childhood, the impact on long-term social and professional functioning, and the role of trauma in personality disorders. Herman (1992) was the first to suggest that complex PTSD be included as a new diagnosis that would address the multiple origins of trauma and its effects on all aspects of a person's life. She noted that women with borderline personality disorder were frequently marginalized by mental health professionals who failed to understand the connection between their early experience of sexual abuse and their present personality structure. More recently, Courtois developed the comprehensive diagnosis of complex trauma (Courtois 2004; Ford and Courtois 2009), which she explains as the "inability to self-regulate, self-organize, or draw upon relationships to regain self-integrity" (Ford and Courtois 2009, 17). Complex trauma is "associated with histories of multiple traumatic stressors and exposure experiences, along with severe disturbances in primary care giving relationships" (Ford and Courtois 2009, 18). It can lead to substance abuse, unemployment, and homelessness, and it affects all psychosocial aspects of living. A diagnosis of complex traumatic stress disorder calls for a treatment model that addresses the immediate post-traumatic symptoms, as well as psychosocial counseling, substance abuse treatment, domestic violence interventions, and assistance in improving professional and interpersonal skills as well as in obtaining housing.

DEVELOPMENTAL TRAUMA DISORDER

Along with the recognition of complex traumatic stress disorder and its effects on all aspects of a person's life, van der Kolk (2005) recommended the inclusion of a new diagnosis, which he called "developmental trauma disorder," for children with complex developmental trauma histories. This diagnosis is distinct from other childhood diagnoses such as ADHD, oppositional defiant disorder, and conduct disorder in that it specifically addresses the consequences of early trauma in relation to abuse and neglect. Van der Kolk notes that a study by Kaiser Permanente of 17,337 members revealed that 11 percent reported having been emotionally abused as children, 30.1 percent reported early physical abuse, and 19.9 percent reported sexual abuse (in van der Kolk 2005). This survey shows that childhood abuse is much more common than previously known and that those children deprived of intervention or treatment of early abuse symptoms will likely suffer from behavioral, emotional, and cognitive disturbances for the rest of their lives. In addition, early trauma affects the neurological development of young children, who may be unable to develop the necessary neuronal structures to process information, regulate emotions, and categorize experiences. This can lead to poor impulse control, aggression, difficulty in interpersonal relationships, and poor academic performance because of the child's inability to concentrate. In later development, such children may develop self-harming and substance-abuse disorders in an effort to regulate their emotional arousal, owing to their difficulty in self-soothing and affect regulation. Van der Kolk suggests that multiple exposures to childhood traumas, including "abandonment, betrayal, physical or sexual assaults, or witnessing domestic violence" (2005, 406), can have negative consequences that continue to reverberate throughout childhood, adolescence, and adulthood.

TRAUMA IN CONTEMPORARY LIFE

Traumatic stress has become more prevalent and complex in contemporary American life as a result of the mass trauma of 9/11, the ongoing war against terrorism, police violence against African American men, the refugee crisis, and violence against women, all of which have led to an increased incidence of PTSD and traumatization in the general population. These developments have also led to the addition of new treatment approaches such as mindfulness and mind/body therapies, as discussed in this volume. In the immediate aftermath of 9/11, mental health professionals treated survivors based on the principles of critical-incident stress debriefing (CISD) (Mitchell 1983; Everly and Mitchell 1999). This treatment approach is based on the assumption that encouraging expression of one's thoughts and feelings about the traumatic event soon after it happens will bring about relief and resolution of symptoms (Seery et al. 2008). However, to date there are few data to show that expressing one's thoughts and feelings immediately after trauma is a good way of coping. Although some studies indicate that trauma expression results in better mental health, research has shown that the mean amount of time between the target event and the participant's disclosure was fifteen months, well beyond the limits of early intervention (Fratteroli 2006).

A meta-analysis by van Emmerik, Kamphuis, Hulsbosch, and Emmelkamp (2002) shows that CISD did not significantly improve PTSD and other trauma-related symptoms such as general anxiety and depression. In addition, Sherman, Zanotti, and Jones (2005) found that survivors of 9/11 who chose not to discuss the trauma they experienced showed better mental health outcomes two years after 9/11 than people who chose to express their feelings and discuss their experiences. As a result of these studies, trauma-intervention methods have become less intrusive and are now based on stabilization and on psychosocial, mindfulness-based, and other embodied-treatment approaches (Basham and Miehls 2006; Briere and Scott 2006; Ford and Courtois 2009; Follette et al. 2015; van der Kolk 2014).

As a result of the wars in Iraq and Afghanistan, which have entailed multiple, long deployments for military personnel, the violent deaths of peers, and a high incidence of physiological and psychological trauma, the rates of complex PTSD have been increasing. Complex PTSD affects both soldiers and their families and requires new intervention approaches. Prolonged exposure techniques (Foa 2006; Foa et al. 2005) immediately following the event, although helpful to some patients, have been found to be far too intense for others. Moreover, the treatment drop-out rate is quite high (Basham, personal communication, 2009). A phase-based approach that would include stabilization techniques, education, and social-skills training may be more effective in helping these soldiers integrate their experiences, adapt to civilian life and to their roles in their families, and return to productive lives (Ford and Courtois 2009).

CONTEMPORARY APPROACHES TO TRAUMA

In this second edition, we have included traumatized groups that are less familiar to professional audiences in order to contribute to the dissemination of new knowledge. The emphasis in this book is on clinical interventions with a number of specific communities, such as refugees, war veterans, members of the LGBTQIA+ community, and incarcerated and formerly incarcerated African American women. We have added a chapter on mindfulness-based trauma interventions, approaches that have become more prevalent and that are supported by emerging research studies. These therapies are particularly significant in trauma work, where experiences are frequently stored in nonverbal parts of the brain such as the amygdala, and in sensory and somatic domains. Mind/body-based therapies help clients access traumatic experiences that are not yet available for verbal narration and cognitive reflection. Many clients require processes other than talk therapy to make the material available to their conscious awareness.

Sensorimotor therapy is influenced by several bodies of literature, including mindfulness practice, attachment theory, and neurobiology, particularly Schore's work on affect regulation (2003; 2007) and also by Peter Levine's somatic therapy model (Levine 1997). As discussed in chapter 6, there is emerging research to support its clinical usefulness with traumatized clients. The model focuses on both body and mind, but rather than focusing on verbal and analytical skills, the interaction of thought, feeling, bodily sensation, and movement is emphasized through mindfulness observations of the "here and now." Sensorimotor therapists help clients

> regulate arousal by carefully tracking physical sensations for signs of dysregulation, by asking questions that direct attention to relationships between bodily response and narrative content, by teaching clients to recognize the physical signs that indicate dysregulated or hyperarousal, and by encouraging them to experiment with specific somatic interventions that promote regulation.
>
> (Fisher and Ogden 2009, 317)

The therapist encourages the client to express experience through action and arm and bodily movements, which may be either protective or aggressive in nature. The therapeutic process includes phases of stabilization, memory and emotion work, and finally integration.

Another group of treatments showing promise with traumatized clients is mindfulness-based therapies. Although these have not been specifically developed to address trauma, they have been effective in the management of stress, pain, and chronic and terminal illness. There has been much research on mindfulness-based therapy, which has entered the health care field and is rapidly becoming part of a treatment protocol in hospitals and health care settings. Mindfulness therapies are inspired by Eastern meditation practices, and all share common elements. In addition to dialectical behavioral therapy (DBT), other mindfulness-based therapies have been developed and show promise in the treatment of borderline personality disorder, anxiety, depression, and pain management. To date, these models include DBT (Linehan 1993a, 1993b)—developed for borderline personality disorders—acceptance and commitment therapy (Hayes and Strosahl 2004), mindfulness-based cognitive therapy (Segal, Williams, and Teasdale 2002), and mindfulness-based stress reduction (Kabat-Zinn, 1990, 2003, 2005). We have chosen to include acceptance and commitment therapy (ACT) in this volume, which shows promise with war-related PTSD.

The principles common to all these models include:

- Acceptance of internal experiences as they are, even when difficult, and observing them with curiosity, openness, and compassion
- Integrating mindfulness skills with change-based strategies, which suggests that although there is an attitude of patience and acceptance, there is also an emphasis on teaching skills for change (e.g., affect regulation and social skills)
- Decentering or defusion: observing experiences as transitory mental states, such that the client learns to recognize that thoughts and feelings pass and change, and there is no need to immediately react or identify oneself with what one is thinking and feeling

(Baer and Huss 2008)

The goals of such treatment are increasing awareness of the present-moment experience, including sensations, thoughts, feelings, and environmental stimuli; cultivating an accepting, nonjudgmental stance; reducing symptoms; developing self-exploration and insight; developing wisdom and compassion; and finally, living in accordance with values such as love, compassion, integrity, and honesty (Baer and Huss 2008). Unlike cognitive-behavioral therapy (CBT), mindfulness-based models advocate staying with states of mind, feelings, and physical sensations, rather than using distraction strategies or restructuring thoughts and beliefs (cognitive restructuring). States of mind might include traumatic memories, physical pain and discomfort, negative thoughts, and intense feeling states. The client learns to allow, accept, and welcome mental states and bodily sensations without trying to fix them or change them.

OUTLINE OF THE BOOK

In this book, we will address contemporary developments in the principal theoretical models that deal with trauma, including cognitive-behavioral, psychodynamic, mindfulness-based therapies, and attachment theories. All these models have been used in trauma-informed therapies and have either substantial or emerging bodies of research to support their effectiveness. Although this volume is not intended to comprehensively address all populations and communities affected by various kinds of trauma, we have tried to select groups that the literature has not yet fully addressed. These include children who experienced 9/11 through the death of family members, adolescents who have been subjected to bullying, soldiers and others with combat trauma, LGBTQIA+ trauma survivors, those who have suffered the trauma of racism and institutional oppression—such as incarcerated and formerly incarcerated African American women—refugees who have experienced trauma, and Native Americans who have experienced intergenerational trauma. Finally, the impact on the clinician and the implications for teaching and supervision will be discussed.

Although there has been much scholarship devoted to the study of trauma, the field has expanded rapidly during the last decade as a result of several significant developments. From an earlier focus on the interpersonal aspects of trauma, including child abuse and domestic violence, traumatic experiences have taken on political and social dimensions, e.g., the events of 9/11, the war on terror, combat associated with recent wars in Afghanistan and Iraq, institutional racism, and the refugee crisis. Finally, the rash of school shootings in American public schools, increasingly linked to the problem of bullying, has also recently entered the public consciousness. These complex social and political phenomena have added to the magnitude of traumatic experiences in everyday life and created a more challenging task for mental health professionals dealing with trauma and its aftermath. Accordingly, this volume will present new developments in the conceptualization of trauma and trauma-related interventions from diverse theoretical and clinical perspectives, with special attention paid to emerging clinical groups and populations.

REFERENCES

American Psychiatric Association. 1980. *Diagnostic and Statistical Manual of Mental Disorders*. 3rd ed. Washington, DC: APA Publishing.
Baer, R., and D. Huss. 2008. "Mindfulness and Acceptance-Based Therapy." In *Twenty-First Century Psychotherapies*, ed. J. Lebow, 123–166. Hoboken, NJ: John Wiley.

Basham, K., and Miehls, D. 2006. *Transforming the Legacy: Couple Therapy with Survivors of Childhood Trauma*. New York: Columbia University Press

Breuer, J., and Freud, S. (1893) 1962. "On the Psychical Mechanisms of Hysterical Phenomena: A Preliminary Communication." In *The Standard Edition of the Complete Psychological Works of Sigmund Freud*, ed. and trans. J. Strachey, vol. 2, 1–181. London: Hogarth Press.

Briere, J., and C. Scott. 2006. *Principles of Trauma Therapy: A Guide to Symptoms, Evaluation and Treatment*. Thousand Oaks, CA: Sage.

Caplan, G. 1961. *An Approach to Community Mental Health*. New York: Grune and Stratton.

Courtois, C. 2004. "Complex Trauma, Complex Reactions: Assessment and Treatment." *Psychotherapy: Theory, Research, Practice, Training* 41 (4): 412–425.

Courtois, C., and J. Ford, eds. 2009. *Treating Complex Traumatic Stress Disorders: An Evidence Based Guide*. New York: Guilford Press.

Diamond, D. 2004. "Attachment Disorganization: The Reunion of Attachment Theory and Psychoanalysis." *Psychoanalytic Psychology* 21 (2): 276–299.

Everly, G., and J. Mitchell. 1999. *Critical Incident Stress Management (CISM): A New Era and Standard of Care in Crisis Intervention*. Ellicott City, MD: Chevron.

Ferenczi, S. (1933) 1955. "The Confusion of Tongues Between the Adult and the Child: The Language of Tenderness and the Language of Passion." In *Final Contributions to the Problems and Methods of Psychoanalysis*, ed. M. Balint, 156–167. New York: Brunner/Mazel.

Figley, C. 1978. *Stress Disorders Among Vietnam Veterans: Theory, Research and Treatment Implications*. New York: Brunner/Mazel.

Fisher, J., and Ogden, P. 2009. "Sensorimotor Psychotherapy." In Courtois and Ford 2009, 312–328.

Foa, E. 2006. "Psychosocial Therapy for Posttraumatic Stress Disorder." *Journal of Clinical Psychiatry* 67:40–45.

Foa, E., E. Hembree, S. Cahill, S. Rauch, D. Riggs, N. Feeny, and E. Yadin. 2005. "Randomized Trial of Prolonged Exposure for Posttraumatic Stress Disorder With and Without Cognitive Restructuring: Outcome at Academic and Community Clinics." *Journal of Consulting and Clinical Psychology* 73 (5): 953–964.

Follette, V., J. Briere, D. Rozelle, J. Hopper, and D. Rome. 2015. *Mindfulness-Oriented Interventions for Trauma: Integrating Contemplative Practices*. New York: Guilford Press.

Ford, J., and C. Courtois. 2009. "Defining and Understanding Complex Trauma and Complex Traumatic Stress Disorders." In Courtois and Ford 2009, 13–30.

Fratteroli, J. 2006. "Experimental Disclosure and Its Moderators: A Meta Analysis." *Psychological Bulletin* 132:823–865.

Freud, S. (1896) 1962. "The Aetiology of Hysteria." In *The Standard Edition of the Complete Psychological Works of Sigmund Freud*, ed. and trans. J. Strachey, vol. 3, 189–221. London: Hogarth Press.

Hayes, S., and K. Strosahl. 2004. *A Practical Guide to Acceptance and Commitment Therapy*. New York: Springer.

Herman, J. 1981. *Father-Daughter Incest*. Cambridge, MA: Harvard University Press.

——. 1992. *Trauma and Recovery*. New York: Basic Books.

Kabat-Zinn, J. 1990. *Full Catastrophe Living: Using the Wisdom of Your Body and Mind to Face Stress, Pain and Illness*. New York: Delacorte.

——. 2003. "Mindfulness Based Intervention in Context: Past, Present, and Future." *Clinical Psychology: Science and Practice* 10:144–156.

——. 2005. *Coming to Our Senses*. New York: Hyperion.

Kardiner, A. 1941. *The Traumatic Neuroses of War*. New York: Hoeber.

Kardiner, A., and H. Spiegel. 1947. *War, Stress, and Neurotic Illness: The Traumatic Neuroses of War*. New York: Hoeber.

Krystal, H., ed. 1968. *Massive Psychic Trauma*. New York: International Universities Press.

——. 1978. "Trauma and Affects." *Psychoanalytic Study of the Child* 33:81–116.

——. 1988. *Integration and Self Healing: Affect, Trauma, and Alexithymia*. Hillsdale, NJ: Analytic Press.

Levine, P. 1997. *Waking the Tiger: Healing Trauma*. Berkeley, CA: North Atlantic Books.

Lifton, R. 1973. *Home from the War: Vietnam Veterans: Neither Victims nor Executioners*. New York: Simon and Schuster.

Lindemann, E. 1944. "Symptomatology and Management of Acute Grief." *American Journal of Psychiatry* 101:141–148.

Linehan, M. 1993a. *Cognitive Behavioral Treatment of Borderline Personality Disorder*. New York: Guilford Press.

——. 1993b. *Skills Training Manual for Treating Borderline Personality Disorder*. New York: Guilford Press.

Litz, B., N. Stein, E. Delaney, L. Lebowitz, W. Nash, C. Silva, S. Maguen. 2009. "Moral Injury and Moral Repair in War Veterans: A Preliminary Model and Intervention Strategy." *Clinical Psychology Review* 29 (8): 695–706.

McDougall, J. 1989. *Theaters of the Body*. New York: Norton.

Mitchell, J. 1983. "When Disaster Strikes: The Critical Incident Stress Debriefing Process." *Journal of Emergency Medical Services* 8:36–39.

Parad, H., and G. Caplan. 1960. "A Framework for Studying Families in Crisis." *Social Work* 5 (3): 3–15.

Russell, D. 1984. *Sexual Exploitation: Rape, Child Sexual Abuse, and Sexual Harassment*. Beverly Hills, CA: Sage.

Schore, A. 2003. "Early Relational Trauma, Disorganized Attachment and the Development of Predisposition to Violence." In *Healing Trauma: Attachment, Mind, Body, and Brain*, ed. M. Solomon and D. Siegel, 107–167. New York: Norton.

——. 2011. "The Right Brain Implicit Self Lies at the Core of Psychoanalysis." *Psychoanalytic Dialogues* 21 (1): 75–100.

Seery, M., R. Silver, A. Holman, W. Ence, and T. Chu. 2008. "Expressing Thoughts and Feelings Following a Collective Trauma: Immediate Responses to 9/11 Predict Negative Outcomes in a National Sample." *Journal of Counseling and Clinical Psychiatry* 76 (4): 657–667.

Segal, Z., J. Williams, and J. Teasdale. 2002. *Mindfulness Based Cognitive Therapy for Depression: A New Approach to Preventing Relapse*. New York: Guilford Press.

Shalev, A., and R. Ursano. 1990. "Group Debriefing Following Exposure to Traumatic Stress." In *War Medical Services*, ed. J. E. Lundeberg, U. Ott, and B. Rybeck, 192–207. Stockholm: Forsvarets Forskningsanstalt.

Shay, J. 1994. *Achilles in Vietnam: Combat Trauma and the Undoing of Character*. New York: Atheneum.

Sherman, M., D. Zanotti, and D. Jones. 2005. "Key Elements in Couples Therapy with Veterans with Combat-Related Posttraumatic Stress Disorder." *Professional Psychology: Research and Practice* 36 (6): 626–633.

Terr, L. 1979. "Children of Chowchilla: A Study of Psychic Trauma." *Psychoanalytic Study of the Child* 34:552–623.

van der Hart, O. 2016. "Pierre Janet, Sigmund Freud, and Dissociation of the Personality: The First Codification of a Psychodynamic Depth Psychology." In *The Dissociative Mind in Psychoanalysis*, ed. E. Howell and S. Itzkowitz, 44–56. New York: Routledge.

van der Kolk, B. 2005. "Developmental Trauma Disorder: Toward a Rational Diagnosis for Children with Complex Trauma Histories." *Psychiatric Annals* 35 (5): 401–408.

——. 2014. *The Body Keeps the Score: Brain, Mind, and Body in the Healing of Trauma*. New York: Penguin.

van der Kolk, B., A. C. McFarlane, and L. Weisaeth, eds. 1996. *Traumatic Stress: The Effects of Overwhelming Experience in Mind, Body, and Society*. New York: Guilford Press.

van der Kolk, B., O. van der Hart, and G. Marmar. 1996. "Dissociation and Information Processing in Posttraumatic Stress Disorder." In van der Kolk, McFarlane, and Weisaeth 1996, 303–327.

van Emmerik, A., J. Kamphuis, A. Hulsbosch, and P. Emmelkamp. 2002. "Single Session Debriefing After Psychological Trauma: A Meta Analysis." *Lancet* 360: 766–771.

2

Cognitive-Behavioral Therapy

▸ A. ANTONIO GONZALEZ-PRENDES, STELLA RESKO,
and CAITLIN M. CASSADY

COGNITIVE-BEHAVIORAL THERAPIES (CBT) have garnered a substantial body of research establishing them as effective interventions to treat trauma in adults, children, and adolescents (Cukor et al. 2009; Cusack et al. 2016; Ehlers et al. 2010; Hofmann et al. 2012; Kar 2011). Cognitive-behavioral approaches are recommended for the treatment of trauma by the Department of Veterans Affairs and Department of Defense's (VA/DoD) Clinical Practice Guidelines (2017) and by the National Institute for Health and Care Excellence (NICE) (2005). This chapter presents an overview of leading cognitive-behavioral therapy models used in the treatment of traumatized individuals. They include cognitive therapy/reframing, or CT (which includes the Ehlers and Clark model and cognitive-processing therapy, or CPT), exposure therapies (which include prolonged exposure, or PE, and virtual-reality exposure, or VRE), trauma-focused cognitive-behavioral therapy (TF-CBT), eye movement desensitization and reprocessing (EMDR), stress-inoculation training (SIT), systematic desensitization (SD), and seeking safety (SS). We include descriptions of the key assumptions that frame each approach, the main strategies associated with it, the treatment process it entails, and a brief overview of the empirical support for it. In the final section of the chapter, we go into more detail about the growing body of research that has evaluated the effectiveness of cognitive-behavioral treatments for PTSD.

COGNITIVE THEORY

Cognitive-behavioral therapies (CBT) encompass a broad range of therapeutic strategies influenced by behavioral and cognitive theories. They all emphasize the centrality of cognitions and their primary influence on the emotional and behavioral responses to life situations. Cognitive-behavioral theory posits that cognitions in the form of attributions, perceptions, judgments, and meanings that a person attaches to an event, rather than the event itself, are the prime determinants of one's emotional and behavioral responses to the event (Beck 1976; Beck et al. 1979).

Although cognitive-behavioral therapies include various approaches encompassing a wide range of strategies, Dobson and Dobson (2017) suggest that all CBT treatment models have three fundamental principles. The first is the *access hypothesis*, which states that the content of our thoughts can be known and is accessible. This does not mean that all our thoughts are in our immediate awareness or available for immediate recall. However, with proper effort and attention, thoughts can be accessed and brought into awareness. The second assumption is the *mediation hypothesis*, which states that our thoughts mediate between situations we face and how we respond to them. It underscores the importance of meaning-making in the interpretation of life events. The meaning we attach to our interpretation of an event influences how we will respond to it. For instance, two individuals faced with the same situation (e.g., a broken relationship) may react differently based on the meaning that each attaches to it. One may interpret the loss of the relationship as "I am unlovable, I will never find anyone else, and I will never be happy again" and consequently feel depressed. The other may think, "I am glad to be out of this oppressive relationship" and feel relief and happiness. The third assumption is the *change hypothesis*, which states that we can intentionally change our emotional and behavioral responses to situations by purposefully targeting and changing our thinking. By focusing our cognitions in a more balanced and realistic direction, we can experience healthier and more functional and adaptive responses to life events.

Another important aspect of CBT has been the attempt to link specific patterns of thinking to specific disorders or to the experience of maladaptive emotional reactions. For instance, persons with post-traumatic stress disorder (PTSD) may experience dysphoric states underscored by anxiety, depression, or both. Aaron Beck's *cognitive triad of depression* model (Beck et al. 1979) helps to explain the thinking of persons experiencing depression. This model holds that depressive states are linked to idiosyncratic, negative appraisals of the self ("I am incompetent"; "I am a failure"), the future ("I will never get out of this mess"), and people ("No one cares"; "People are just out for themselves"). These cognitions are consistent with criterion D of the diagnostic criteria for PTSD as outlined in the fifth edition of the American Psychiatric Association's *Diagnostic and Statistical Manual of Mental Disorders (DSM-V)* (2013). Anxiety reactions are associated with overactive schemas of danger that lead the individual to appraise situations as threatening (either physically or psychologically), even in cases where there is no apparent danger. Persons with anxiety disorders often learn to manage their anxiety, albeit maladaptively, by avoiding the feared stimulus. Avoidance within the context of PTSD is discussed later in this chapter in the Cognitive-Behavioral and Conceptualization of PTSD and Learning Theories sections.

In cognitive therapy two mechanisms are central to the therapeutic process: collaborative empiricism and the Socratic method (Beck 2011; Newman 2013). Collaborative empiricism, or collaborative hypothesis testing (Scott and Freeman 2010), refers to the formation of a therapeutic alliance in which the client and therapist work together to uncover and evaluate evidence that supports or contradicts the targeted belief. This process of identifying and evaluating evidence to reframe negative cognitions takes place within the context of the Socratic method or Socratic questioning. The therapist uses open-ended questions to help clients recover information or knowledge that they already possess and that is relevant to the targeted problem. The objective is a reevaluation of a previously held erroneous conclusion and the construction of a new perspective (Scott and Freeman 2010).

COGNITIVE-BEHAVIORAL CONCEPTUALIZATION OF PTSD

Evidence suggests that the way individuals emotionally and cognitively process a traumatic experience contributes to the development and maintenance of PTSD (Clark and Ehlers 2004; Ehlers and Clark 2000; Foa and Kozak 1986). For instance, a person who makes erroneous inferences or attributions about the causes and consequences of trauma is more likely to experience difficulties processing the memory of the trauma, thereby increasing the risk of PTSD (Kaczkurkin and Foa 2015). It is the individual's interpretation and appraisal of the trauma and the ensuing memory that contribute to persistent PTSD. Therefore, cognitive therapy for PTSD focuses on teaching clients how to identify, evaluate, and reframe the dysfunctional cognitions that contribute to intense negative emotions and behavioral reactions (Ehlers and Clark 2000; Hembree and Foa 2004).

Although it is normal to experience acute reactions following exposure to a traumatic episode, most people will heal properly without developing PTSD (Foa, Stein, and McFarland 2006; Foa, Ehlers, et al. 1999). We must ask what factors differentiate individuals who develop PTSD following exposure to trauma from those who do not. Although a comprehensive discussion of risk factors for or predictors of PTSD is beyond the scope of this chapter, other authors have identified a broad range of them (see Bryant 2017; Ehlers and Clark 2006; Ozer et al. 2003; Tang et al. 2017). We are interested in looking at cognitive factors that may increase the risk of PTSD following exposure to trauma. For instance, Bryant (2017) cites evidence that the tendency to engage in pretrauma catastrophic thinking is a predictor of PTSD in firefighters. Another perspective of cognitive predictors comes from a study of paramedics by Wild et al. (2016), who concluded that rumination about memories of stressful events predicted PTSD following exposure to trauma. The role of rumination as a predictor of PTSD has been supported in other studies, including an investigation of risk factors of PTSD following stillbirth (Horsch, Jacobs, and McKenzie-Harg 2015) and an investigation of adolescent survivors of natural disaster (Zhou et al. 2015). Ozer et al. (2003) found that peritraumatic dissociation during or immediately following the experience of trauma increased the risk of PTSD. The authors suggested that the "in-the-moment appraisal and meaning of the traumatic stressor may have as much to do with explaining who develops PTSD as do more static factors such as adjustment, prior exposure, or concurrent psychopathology" (69). Another cognitive factor, *anxiety-sensitivity*, defined as the propensity to interpret arousal-related sensations as dangerous and harmful, has also been identified has a significant predictor of PTSD (Fedoroff, Asmundson, and Koch 2000).

Foa and Riggs (1993) and Foa and Rothbaum (1998) suggested that persons with PTSD are characterized by two extreme and flawed central beliefs that relate to how they evaluate themselves and the world. The first is that the self is totally incompetent. The second, reflecting the individual's worldview, is that the world is an entirely threatening and dangerous place (Rauch and Foa 2006). This universal perspective of the world fails to discriminate between possibly safe and possibly unsafe aspects of the world. For these individuals, the traumatic event often serves as "confirmation" of their beliefs antedating the trauma. This interpretation is supported by Dunmore, Clark, and Ehlers (1999), who studied cognitive factors that contributed to the onset and maintenance of PTSD in ninety-two assault victims and compared those who had developed PTSD with those who had not. They reported that cognitive factors associated with the onset and persistence of PTSD included beliefs related to devaluation of the personality (e.g., "I am a loser"; "I am disgusting"), the person's safety (e.g., "There is no safe place"; "People have bad intentions"), and the world (e.g., "The world is dark"; "There is no justice in this world"). Individuals who hold these beliefs tend to feel more persistent and intense apprehension and uncertainty and would be more likely to interpret traumatic events as characteristic of a "dangerous" world. Such interpretation may result in fear and avoidance. At the same time, the view of the self as "incompetent" diminishes the person's ability to cope with adversity. An individual who sees the self in this way is less likely to feel capable of coping with the pain of the actual trauma or the unpleasantness of the memory, and instead would feel overwhelmed and crushed by the weight of the trauma memory.

A central theme contributing to the onset and persistence of PTSD is a perception of ongoing threat even when the dangerous situation happened long ago (Dunmore, Clark, and Ehlers 1999). A person with PTSD is likely to have recurrent false alarms brought on by an exaggerated sense of danger. In anxiety-based disorders, overactive schemas of danger or threat activate and maintain disabling anxiety (Beck, Emery, and Greenberger 1985; Ehlers and Clark 2000; Hembree and Foa 2004; Rauch and Foa 2006). Researchers have advanced several explanations of why some individuals experience this persistent, exaggerated sense of threat. One explanation is the process of avoidance and "seeking safety" (Dunmore, Clark, and Ehlers 1999). Avoiding trauma reminders and retreating to a "safe" place represent a less threatening alternative than facing the situations, places, or experiences that activate fears, vulnerabilities, and negative beliefs about oneself and one's environment. However, as Foa, Steketee, and Rothbaum (1989) have argued, this process may work for some anxieties (e.g., phobias) but not so much for PTSD, in which the varying and unstable nature of situations that engender fear makes the attainment of a "safe" place, through the avoidance of feared situations, more difficult. At the same time, such attempts to avoid factors associated with the original trauma do not provide the person with opportunities to evaluate the validity of erroneous beliefs or to gain corrective emotional experiences.

On the other hand, individuals who frame a traumatic experience as a unique and isolated occurrence that does not alter their broader views of the world or self are more likely to process the trauma, emotionally and cognitively, in a way that leads to healing and successful recovery (Clark and Ehlers, 2004). Two approaches that have been used to conceptualize PTSD are learning theories and emotional-processing theory.

LEARNING THEORIES

Learning theories are most often associated with behavioral approaches that focus on modifying behavior by manipulating environmental cues (i.e., antecedents or reinforcers). Learning theories have focused on explaining how the mechanisms of fear and avoidance of the traumatic memory associated with PTSD are conditioned, activated, and reinforced. Although avoidance of a feared or dangerous situation has an adaptive function, pathological avoidance of situations where there is no perceptible or tangible threat or danger can severely limit one's ability to cope, thus reducing quality of life (Barlow 2002; Krypotos et al. 2015). Avoidance of factors directly associated with the trauma, or that serve as reminders of the trauma, reinforces dysfunctional beliefs about the trauma and interferes with recovery (Foa, Stein, and McFarlane 2006). Along these lines, Sheynin et al. (2017) studied 119 male and female participants with and without severe PTSD symptoms to examine differences in the operant acquisition and extinction of avoidance. The results showed that individuals with severe PTSD symptoms acquired avoidance at a faster rate and showed a greater propensity toward avoidance of reminders of the trauma than those without severe PTSD symptoms.

Several behavioral-based perspectives have been offered to explain the acquisition of fear and avoidance. Fears can be acquired through classical conditioning as a result of exposure to a single event or a series of traumatic events (Wolpe 1990), or they can be learned vicariously through the process of observation (Bandura 1977, 1986). That is, a person may learn to react with fear by observing others' fearful reactions to specific objects or events.

Mowrer's (1956, 1960) two-factor theory represents one of the first attempts to provide a behavioral explanation for the acquisition and maintenance of the fear and avoidance associated with anxiety disorders in general and PTSD in particular (Cahill et al. 2009; Hembree and Foa 2004). Mowrer suggested that fear and avoidance are learned through a two-part process that includes both classical and operant conditioning. Anticipatory fear is acquired through the process of classical conditioning, and relief from this fear takes place when the danger signal is terminated through active avoidance of the feared object or situation, thus creating a secondary negative reinforcement of the avoidance behavior (i.e., operant conditioning) (Krypotos et al. 2015). For example, consider the case of a person who was assaulted in an elevator. In the classical conditioning model, unhealthy fear may develop when an otherwise neutral condition (i.e., being in an elevator) is associated with a dangerous outcome (e.g., an assault). Following the assault, the person may find himself or herself reacting to being in elevators with the same level of fear associated with the original dangerous event. Furthermore, it is possible that through the process of generalization the fear will expand to other places or situations (e.g., being in a small, confined space) that remind the individual of the trauma; the person will avoid those situations as well. That is, reminders of the trauma may trigger the same anticipatory fear response and engender the same avoidance behaviors associated with the original stimulus. Moreover, the avoidant behavior becomes operantly conditioned as it is negatively reinforced by providing the person with escape or relief from the unpleasant experience of fear and anxiety. Mowrer's two-factor theory assumes a close relationship between fear and avoidance; that is, fear motivates avoidance, and avoidance reduces fear. Consequently, it is expected that once the fear factor has been eliminated, the avoidance behaviors will stop. However, it has been argued that in some instances avoidance may continue after the elimination of the fear factor or in situations that are essentially nonthreatening (Krypotos et al. 2015; Sheynin et al. 2017).

Although traditional learning theories explain the acquisition of fear and the process of avoidance seen in PTSD, these theories have received some criticism for falling short of explaining the full spectrum of PTSD symptoms (see Foa, Steketee, and Rothbaum 1989; Hembree and Foa 2004). Of note is the inability to account for generalization of fear across dissimilar situations and the failure to include thoughts, appraisals, and meaning concepts (e.g., dangerousness) associated with the traumatic memory.

EMOTIONAL-PROCESSING THEORY

Emotional processing is a central aspect of the experience of trauma. Emotional-processing theory provides an integrated framework to analyze and explain the onset and maintenance of PTSD. This theoretical approach combines insight from the learning, cognitive, and behavioral theories of PTSD and builds on the idea that it is not unusual for emotional experiences to continue to affect one's behaviors long after the event originally associated with the emotion has passed. Emotional processing refers to a mechanism whereby new information is absorbed into an already existing schema (e.g., a fear structure), resulting in either a decrease or increase in emotional reactivity (Foa, Huppert, and Cahill 2006; Foa and Kozak 1986; Rauch and Foa 2006; Rachman 1980). Foa, Huppert, and Cahill (2006) suggest that for many persons exposed to trauma, emotional processing occurs spontaneously as new information that is incompatible with the fear structure modifies said structure and leads to a natural recovery. However, for other individuals exposed to trauma, emotional processing does not occur spontaneously. For these individuals the emotional reexperience of the trauma engenders a pattern of avoidance that prevents the acquisition of new information that could potentially modify the fear structure, thus interfering with a successful recovery and sustaining the presence of PTSD symptoms (Foa, Steketee, and Rothbaum 1989; Foa and Jaycox 1999). In such cases, cognitive-behavioral treatments, particularly exposure-based therapies, can help facilitate the corrective emotional processing of the trauma memory.

Foa and Kozak (1986) suggest that emotions are represented by information structures in memory. In the case of fear, the associated memory includes information specific to the feared stimulus, such as cues (e.g., sensory reminders: smells, sounds, etc.), overt responses (verbal, physiological, and behavioral) to the stimulus, and the meaning that the individual has attached to the stimulus. The overall function of this information structure is to help the individual escape or avoid the perceived threat or danger (Foa and Kozak 1986). The meaning attached to the memory, usually in the form of an attribution of dangerousness or some catastrophic outcome (e.g., "I will die"; "I will lose control"; I will faint"), prevents the individual from confronting the traumatic memory and effectively engaging in the emotional and cognitive processing of the information underlying the memory. Thus, as previously mentioned, the individual reacts to the memory with the same cognitive, affective, and behavioral responses associated with the original trauma. In a sense, the individual fear structure is virtually "stuck" in a moment in time that has passed but has not been processed or "digested" in an effective and healthy manner.

Foa and Kozak (1986) suggest that for effective emotional processing to take place, there must be an activation and modification of the memory structure that underlies the fear. This process includes, first, creating access to the complete memory of the event to reactivate the fear structure through the process of exposure (imaginal, in-vivo, or virtual-reality) and, second, helping the individual access new information incompatible with the existing maladaptive information to modify the fear structure and engender a healthier response to the memory.

COGNITIVE-BEHAVIORAL THERAPIES FOR PTSD

The goal of cognitive-behavioral therapy for PTSD is to teach clients strategies to identify and restructure trauma-related, irrational beliefs that engender unhealthy negative emotions and lead to dysfunctional behaviors (Hembree and Foa 2004). Cognitive-behavioral therapies for PTSD include two key elements: (1) revisiting the trauma memory to activate it and make it accessible to change, and (2) introducing information that is incompatible with the existing fear structure and that helps to modify such structure. The revisiting of the trauma memory can be done through exposure (imaginal, in-vivo, or virtual-reality) (Foa et al. 1991), in the form of written accounts of the trauma (Resick and Schnicke 1992; Resick, Monson, and Chard 2017), or by using Socratic questioning to elicit information about the memory (Ehlers and Clark 2000). Once the trauma memory is activated, new information that is incompatible with the existing fear structure is introduced to help modify the meaning attached to the memory. Through this process, the client learns to discriminate between the traumatic event of the past and the reality of the present (Ehlers as cited in Schnyder et al. 2015) and becomes able to see the traumatic event as a unique and discrete occurrence that is not definitive of the self, the world, or others.

While discussing reactions that typically follow exposure to a traumatic experience, Foa, Huppert, and Cahill (2006) noted three factors associated with recovery from the trauma: (1) emotional engagement with the trauma memory, (2) change in trauma-related cognitions, and (3) organization of the trauma narrative. The authors hypothesized that peritraumatic emotional disengagement (i.e., dissociation during or following the experience of trauma) increases the risk of severe PTSD. They also posited that successful recovery is associated with a change in perspective rooted in a more realistic view of the self and the world and a more discriminating view of the traumatic experience. Foa, Stein, and McFarlane (2006) also suggested that following exposure to trauma, a highly organized and articulated narrative of the trauma is associated with greater recovery. Conversely, individuals with PTSD are more likely to provide fragmented, disengaged, and disorganized accounts of the trauma. This fragmentation and disorganization of the trauma memory coupled with the lack of emotional engagement exhibited by persons with PTSD can be conceptualized as representing the individual's attempt to protect herself or himself from the emotional pain of the trauma. Consequently, CBT-based treatments of trauma include strategies that address these three factors.

Cognitive-behavioral therapy models to treat PTSD share some common characteristics, although their emphasis and presentation may vary depending on the specific model. According to Schnyder et al. (2015), the commonalities include:

- Psychoeducation
- Teaching emotional regulation and coping skills
- Exposure to or revisiting of the trauma memory
- Cognitive processing, restructuring, or meaning-making
- Working with emotions (although fear is often the main target, other emotions such as anger, shame, guilt, sadness, etc., are addressed)
- Development of a cohesive and emotionally engaged trauma narrative

Studies have shown that cognitive therapy alone can be an effective treatment of PTSD (Ehlers et al. 2003; Resick et al. 2008). Here we present an overview of two cognitive-behavioral therapy-based models to treat PTSD: the Ehlers and Clark model, and cognitive-processing therapy (CPT) (Resick and Schnicke 1992; Resick Monson, and Chard 2017).

Ehlers and Clark Model

At the core of the Ehlers and Clark model is the collaborative development of an individualized case formulation that provides the framework for treatment (Ehlers as cited in Schnyder et al. 2015). Clark and Ehlers (2004) and Ehlers and Clark (2000) specify three therapy goals in the treatment of PTSD: (1) to reduce intrusions and the reexperiencing of the traumatic memory, (2) to modify excessive negative appraisals, and (3) to eliminate dysfunctional cognitive and behavioral strategies. According to Ehlers et al. (2013, 745) this model of treatment suggests that

> people with PTSD perceive a serious current threat which has two sources, excessively negative appraisals of the trauma and/or its sequelae and characteristics of trauma memories that lead to re-experiencing symptoms. The problem is maintained by cognitive strategies and behaviors (such as thought suppression, rumination, and safety-seeking behaviors) that are intended to reduce the sense of current threat but maintain the problem by preventing change in the appraisals or trauma memory, and/or by increasing symptoms.

Ehlers and Clark (2000) propose a treatment model that incorporates the following elements:

- *Detailed assessment interview.* The objectives of this process include: to identify possible problematic cognitive themes that need to be addressed in treatment; to specify the worst aspects of the trauma and the most painful moment associated with it; to underscore predominant emotions associated with the event; to illuminate problematic appraisals of trauma sequelae; to identify specifics of the problematic and dysfunctional cognitive and behavioral attempts to cope (i.e., how they have tried to put the trauma behind them; how they deal with intrusions; what they fear will happen if they allow themselves to dwell on the trauma); and to identify the characteristics of the trauma memory and intrusions.
- *Rationale for treatment.* A key aspect of treatment is to ensure that the client understands the rationales behind the therapeutic strategies employed. The discussion should include an explanation of the nature of PTSD and its symptoms; a description of how the client's attempts to cope with the trauma, most likely through avoidance, may produce temporary relief from anxiety but can contribute to maintaining the symptoms of the disorder;

and an explanation that to counteract avoidance and fully process the trauma, the client will need to confront the unpleasant memory.

- *Thought-suppression experiment.* This strategy allows clients to understand how attempts to suppress intrusive memories by pushing them away from consciousness paradoxically reinforces and increases the impact of such memories. Instead, clients are encouraged to use an alternative approach: rather than try to "push" the memory from their consciousness, they should accept it, observe it, and allow it to come and go, as if they were watching a twig floating in a stream of water, bobbing up and down and passing by.

- *Psychoeducation.* The client is educated about the trauma and helped to access informational resources that may assist in rectifying mistaken assumptions about possible physical damage associated with the trauma.

- *Reclaiming one's life.* The client is encouraged to reclaim aspects of his or her life (e.g., activities and other pursuits) that were given up as a result of the trauma. As Ehlers and Clark (2000) suggest, the process helps clients become "unstuck" from the moment in their past when they experienced the trauma. Instead, the client attempts to recover his or her former self by reconnecting with lost interests and social contacts.

- *Reliving with cognitive restructuring.* This step involves reliving or revisiting the trauma. The client receives a detailed explanation of the rationale behind this strategy. The client is then asked to revisit the trauma, recounting the original event in as much detail and as vividly as possible. This helps the client connect with the feelings and cognitions associated with the trauma. Cognitive-reframing strategies help the client identify and discuss dysfunctional cognitions uncovered in the "reliving" and to reframe such beliefs into healthier alternative perspectives, which are then integrated into subsequent relivings.

- *In-vivo exposure.* In-vivo exposure requires revisiting powerful reminders of the original trauma—for example, sites, smells, sounds, and activities—that have been systematically avoided. The process helps the client to discriminate between harmless reminders of the trauma and the danger of the actual trauma, thus challenging patterns of overgeneralization that have led the client to avoid elements unrelated to the original trauma, and confronting the various irrational appraisals attached to the sequelae of the trauma.

- *Identifying triggers of intrusive memories or emotions.* This process aims to enhance the ability to discriminate between past and present stimuli. Clients are encouraged to carefully monitor the context within which the intrusions occur and the triggers (e.g., sensations, feelings, situations, cognitions) associated with them. Therapist and client then engage in a detailed discussion of similarities and differences between the past and present contexts of the triggers, facilitating a higher level of stimulus discrimination.

- *Imagery techniques.* The use of imagery helps clients elaborate on and change the meaning of the trauma memory. It may help clients "tie up loose ends" (e.g., saying good-bye to a friend or relative), bringing closure to aspects of the trauma.

Cognitive-Processing Therapy (CPT)

Although cognitive-processing therapy, or CPT, originally was developed to help sexual assault victims address the symptoms of PTSD (Resick and Schnicke 1992), the model has expanded and been used extensively to help military-related PTSD and other forms of trauma. A significant issue in the development of CPT is the shifting emphasis placed on the formulation of a written account of the trauma. Whereas in the early years the written account was seen as a central aspect of CPT, more recent studies have shown no differences between CPT with and without the written account (Resick et al. 2008; Walter et al. 2014). As a result, cognitive-processing therapy can be provided with the written account (CPT+A) or without (CPT) (Resick, Monson, and Chard 2017). However, the authors suggest using caution before eliminating the written account from all treatment protocols as some clients may need that kind of exposure to access and correct dysfunctional emotions. Below we offer an outline of the CPT+A model (Resick et al. 2008; Resick and Schnicke 1992). For more detailed information about the two models, see Resick, Monson, and Chard (2017).

At the core of CPT's conceptual framework of PTSD is the conflict that may exist between old information stored by the individual in various schemas and new information derived from the trauma. Resick and Schnicke (1992) propose that the symptoms of PTSD indeed result from the conflict between new information (e.g., "I have just been raped") and existing schemas (e.g., "Nice people do not experience rape"). The authors point out that these conflicts may be concerned not only with themes of danger and safety (e.g., "The world is dangerous"; "My home is not a safe place") but also with themes reflecting self-esteem, competence, or intimacy. Thus, the focus of CPT is on helping clients resolve "stuck points" that represent conflicts between prior schemas and new information derived from the traumatic experience.

Typically, CPT is offered over twelve sessions (Resick, Monson, and Chard 2006; Resick et al. 2008) that encompass several components. The sessions are structured as follows:

- Session 1: Psychoeducation about PTSD and rationale for treatment
- Session 2: Understanding the link between thoughts, emotions, and behaviors
- Session 3: Writing a detailed account of the most traumatic event and experiencing full emotional engagement while doing so
- Session 4: Cognitive therapy regarding self-blame and other distortions associated with the event; rewriting the account as homework
- Session 5: Processing the account and writing about a second trauma
- Session 6: Cognitive restructuring of beliefs and meaning of the event and implications of the trauma
- Sessions 7–12: Addressing a particular theme each week (e.g., trust, safety, etc.) to develop and practice alternative and balanced self-statements to correct dysfunctional overgeneralization about the theme
- Session 11: Rewriting the account to incorporate new beliefs
- Session 12: Evaluating the new account to highlight gains made in treatment and areas of attention for the future

Homework and group discussion, along with suggestions for adaptive self-statements that help clients resolve conflict and get past "stuck points," are included in the treatment.

Exposure Therapies (Prolonged and Virtual-Reality)

Even though most cognitive-behavioral approaches to treat trauma include a form of revisiting of (i.e., exposure to) the trauma memory, some, such as prolonged imaginal exposure (PE) and virtual-reality exposure (VRE), make the exposure element the centerpiece of treatment. In these models, exposure is the essential tool used to counteract the avoidant behaviors that maintain the fear structure and prevent new learning from taking place (Kaczkurkin and Foa 2015). However, Dobson and Dobson (2017) suggest that the critical aspect of exposure therapy is the learning that takes place as a result of the client's interpretation of the exposure experience.

Therefore, it is not just the revisiting of the experience that allows for the integration of new information into a more balanced view of the self, the world, and others, but also the emotional and cognitive processing that follows the exposure.

Exposure approaches to treat trauma vary in the type of contact with the feared object and the level of intensity of the exposure. Some approaches use graduated exposure: a series of hierarchical steps starting with the least and advancing to the most anxiety-provoking stressors. Other techniques use a flooding approach: a more abrupt confrontation with the object of avoidance. Exposure therapy can also take the form of imaginal exposure—repeated revisiting of the traumatic experience via visualization—or in-vivo exposure, in which the person confronts the feared object face to face. The length of the exposure exercise may be brief or prolonged. Some exposure approaches, such as systematic desensitization (Wolpe 1990), combine graduated exposure with relaxation strategies, whereas others, such as PE (Foa and Kozak 1986), do not. Other forms of exposure—such as interoceptive exposure, which is used to treat panic disorders, and exposure and response prevention (EX/RP), which is used to treat obsessive-compulsive disorders—are not addressed in this discussion.

PROLONGED EXPOSURE (PE)

PE, also referred to as imaginal exposure, is based on emotional-processing theory, discussed earlier in the chapter. Foa (as cited in Schnyder et al. 2015) has indicated that there are two principal components to prolonged exposure. The first is the repeated imaginal reliving and recounting of the traumatic memory, followed by the processing of the exposure experience, which in turn allows for the corrective processing of emotions associated with the trauma and the assimilation of new and healthier perspectives. The second is the integration of in-vivo exposure exercises to confront trauma-related situations—that is, objects or other environmental cues that trigger pathological anxiety and fear (Hembree and Foa 2004). The imaginal (with processing) and in-vivo exposure elements of PE provide the experiences for the dismantling of the maladaptive fear structure.

Cahill et al. (2009) and Hembree and Foa (2004) discuss several mechanisms by which exposure to the trauma memory (and associated cues) leads to improvement in PTSD. First, habituation to the trauma memory and associated cues is facilitated by repeated imaginal or in-vivo exposure. As clients revisit the memory and retell the story, they begin to feel less anxious. This is akin to repeatedly watching a horror movie and finding out that after several times the movie has lost some of its original impact. However, effective exposure therapy goes beyond habituation to provide a corrective emotional and cognitive experience (i.e., new learning), underscoring the fact that avoidance is not necessary to reduce the level of anxiety (Cusack et al. 2016; Kaczkurkin and Foa 2015). Second, confronting the memory actively blocks the process of avoidance. Third, the process of exposure, facilitated by a supportive and empathic therapist, helps clients discredit the unhealthy notion that thinking about the trauma is as dangerous as the trauma itself. Fourth, through repeated exposure to the trauma memory, clients begin to differentiate aspects associated with the past original trauma from present situations to which they have generalized the fear and anxiety. As a result, the trauma is gradually framed as a unique event rather than as an overgeneralized definition that the world is extremely dangerous or that the client is extremely incompetent. By decreasing generalization, the anxiety and fear projected onto non-trauma-related situations begin to dissipate. Fifth, the processing that follows the exposure exercises allows clients to reevaluate and reframe the negative meanings they attach to self, world, and others. Sixth, as individuals gradually and repeatedly engage in the confrontation of the trauma memory and its associated cues, they begin to feel more in control of their lives, with an increasing sense of competence and mastery. Last, repeated visits to the trauma memory, each one eliciting more detail about and deeper emotional engagement with the experience, together with the ensuing processing of the experience, help to piece together the fragmentation of the memory, allowing the client to develop a more cohesive and coherent narrative of the event (Foa, Huppert, and Cahill 2006).

Exposure therapy generally ranges from nine to twelve sessions, each approximately ninety minutes in length, offered weekly or biweekly (Foa et al. 1991; Foa et al. 2005; Hembree and Foa 2004). The length of exposure has been the subject of debate. Prolonged-exposure sessions were originally ninety minutes, with forty minutes devoted to imaginal exposure. Some studies have shown no difference between the longer sessions and shorter ones (sixty minutes with twenty minutes of imaginal exposure) (Nacasch et al. 2015; van Minnen and Foa 2006).

According to Hembree and Foa (2004), PE treatment encompasses four integral components: education, breathing retraining, imaginal exposure to the trauma memory, and in-vivo exposure between sessions to factors or cues associated with the trauma. The first two sessions are normally devoted to gathering background information, explaining the treatment rationale, educating the client about PTSD and its sequelae, breathing retraining, and planning treatment. In the third session, the process of imaginal exposure begins. The client sits comfortably, closes his or her eyes, and imagines as vividly as possible the actual trauma. Then the client recounts aloud the details of the trauma, describing it in the present tense as if it were happening now, and using the pronoun *I* as he or she retells the story. As the client recounts the trauma, he or she is encouraged to verbalize the emotions, cognitions, and sensations experienced. Throughout a prolonged-exposure session the client will recount the trauma several times. The therapist remains nonintrusive, except for brief interjections to ask for more detail, elicit emotional reactions and cognitions, and assess the level of the client's anxiety. With each retelling of the trauma, the client is encouraged to provide more vivid details about the event while at the same time engaging in a deeper level of emotional connection to it. Exposure sessions are tape-recorded, and the client is given the assignment of listening to the recordings daily between sessions. Additional homework may include in-vivo exposure to environmental cues and to feared and avoided situations that have been deemed safe by the client and therapist (Foa et al. 1991). The rest of the sessions continue in a similar fashion, with repeated imaginal exposures, tape-recording of the session, and homework assignments. In the final session the client is asked to summarize what was learned in treatment and to discuss his or her progress.

VIRTUAL-REALITY EXPOSURE (VRE)

The computer-generated therapy VRE has been found effective for treating PTSD (Botella et al. 2015; Morina et al. 2015; Powers and Emmelkamp 2008; Rizzo and Shilling 2018). VRE follows the principles of prolonged exposure in that it provides an opportunity to activate the client's fear structure and to access new information that will modify said structure. VRE takes the client into a visual, three-dimensional representation of real-world scenarios that simulate traumatic environments faced by the client and artificially stimulates sensory responses to fully immerse the client into a reliving of the traumatic experience (Botella et al. 2017; Parsons and Rizzo 2008; Rothbaum et al. 2003; Rothbaum 2006).

Although the use of VRE as a psychotherapeutic tool is relatively new, the science and technology behind it have been around for years in the form of flight simulators, computer games, and science fiction (Botella et al. 2017; Rizzo and Shilling 2018). In 1999 Rothbaum et al. described one of the first uses of VRE for PTSD in a case study of a Vietnam veteran. A later study with Vietnam veterans (Rothbaum et al. 2001) provided further evidence of the efficacy of the new approach. Since then, VRE programs have been developed to create various trauma-related scenarios. The different systems include programs associated with rural and urban combat (e.g., Virtual Iraq/ Afghanistan, the BRAVEMIND system) (Rizzo et al. 2015; Rizzo and Shilling 2018) and with the World Trade Center attacks of 9/11 (Virtual World Trade Center) (Rizzo et al. 2015). Baños et al. (2009) developed EMMA's World, which has expanded the possibilities of virtual-reality uses by re-creating a large variety of situations. EMMA's World provides a versatile alternative to earlier VR systems that targeted specific populations with very specific traumas. It allows for the creation of individualized environments that can be applied to different problems with different populations, including veterans; victims of sexual assault, childhood abuse, disasters, and automobile accidents; and others (Baños et al. 2009). It allows for a VR environment that can be tailored to evoke emotions and symbols that match individual experiences of trauma. The applications of VRE have expanded significantly in the past twenty years; for more detailed discussions see Botella et al. (2017) and Rizzo and Shilling (2018).

VRE comes in different formats. Rizzo and Shilling (2018) describe two: immersive and nonimmersive. The immersive option, which creates a more vivid illusion of being in the real-life experience, involves the use of head-mounted displays, tracking sensors, three-dimensional graphics, and other computer technologies to create a "simulated world that changes in a natural and intuitive way to head and body motion" (3). The therapist manages the intensity of the virtual environment by providing and controlling visual, auditory, and olfactory cues, thus allowing for a fuller activation of and emotional engagement with the client's fear structure. The less intensive nonimmersive option involves viewing and interacting with images on a computer screen or TV monitor—akin to playing a computer game.

The progression of VRE sessions is similar to that of prolonged imaginal exposure: ninety-minute weekly or biweekly sessions over the course of four to twelve weeks. Generally, the first two sessions involve a detailed assessment of the client and the presenting problem, psychoeducation, and preexposure preparation. By the third session the client engages with VR exposure to the feared situations, followed by a debriefing, or emotional and cognitive processing, of the exposure experience (Alsina-Jurnet, Carvallo-Beciu, and Gutiérrez-Maldonado 2007; Difede and Hoffman 2002; Gerardi et al. 2008; North, North, and Coble 1998; Reger and Gahm 2008; Rothbaum et al. 2003). During pretreatment preparation, it is important to identify the most traumatic memories and include ratings (often self-reported) of the intensity of the distress associated with each. Rothbaum et al. (2003) suggest also including psychometric measures of physiological responses (i.e., heart rate and skin conductance) as they provide a more accurate and objective evaluation of the alleviation of negative emotional arousal than self-reporting. The processing and debriefing that follow each episode of exposure therapy are critical aspects of treatment, without which the chances for therapeutic success are diminished (Cahill et al. 2009; Jaycox, Foa, and Morral 1998).

VRE offers some benefits over traditional imaginal or in-vivo exposure therapies. One is that it can overcome the disadvantages that some clients experience with traditional imaginal exposure. Certain individuals may have difficulties visualizing or evoking the trauma memory with specificity, or may experience reluctance to repeatedly narrate the trauma. This could result in a failure to fully engage emotionally with the memory, thus limiting the effectiveness of the intervention. VRE eliminates the need for intense imaginal skills by facilitating greater immersion in the traumatic event (Botella et al. 2015; Cukor et al. 2009; Rizzo et al. 2006). Similarly, Alsina-Jurnet, Carvallo-Beciu, and Gutiérrez-Maldonado (2007) suggest that VRE offers advantages over in-vivo exposure, for which the logistics of the exposure experience can be complex and limiting.

Nonetheless, despite the significant body of evidence supporting the use of VRE with PTSD and other anxiety disorders, Botella et al. (2015) and Rizzo and Shilling (2018) have identified aspects of VRE that need to be addressed to further disseminate and facilitate its use. A significant concern is the cost of the technology, particularly as it relates to the use of the fully immersive systems, which seem to provide greater benefit. The cost of the equipment and technology may prohibit VRE from being a feasible alternative for community-based mental health agencies that lack the necessary resources to provide the service. Consequently, individuals of low socioeconomic background, who often receive services from community agencies, may not have access to VRE therapy. Other issues that limit the use of VRE are the lack of well-trained providers and a reluctance to use the technology among some clinicians who prefer more traditional methods. Despite these limitations, Botella et al. (2015) and Rizzo and Shilling (2018) call for additional research to expand awareness of the effectiveness of the method across various cultures and populations.

As is true of any form of evolving technology that is used in psychotherapy, practitioners must ensure that services are provided in an ethical manner that safeguards the rights, privacy and confidentiality, and well-being of the client. Ethical issues in computer- and technology-assisted therapies may parallel those of traditional face-to-face approaches, but there are some concerns particular to the use of technology that clinical social workers and other mental health practitioners need to consider. An important one is the level of competency of the therapist in understanding and managing the technology to ensure that clients obtain the maximum benefit from the intervention. Therapists using VRE must have the proper training and supervision to provide the highest quality of service to their clients. Another is the client-therapist collaborative relationship. It is incumbent on the therapist to make sure that computer-assisted therapies are provided within the same collaborative and empathic framework as traditional CBT therapies. Keeping in mind that client empowerment and a collaborative relationship are at the core of the practice of CBT, therapists using VRE must actively seek and elicit the client's participation and input at every step of the process. This includes informing the client of the risks and benefits of the intervention and of the availability of alternatives. A final issue is accessibility. The ethical approach is to ensure that effective treatments are affordable and available to economically disadvantaged individuals who otherwise would be unable to access such services.

Trauma-Focused CBT (TF-CBT)

Among the several CBT-based models to help traumatized children, the one that has been most widely disseminated and has the strongest empirical support is trauma-focused cognitive-behavioral therapy, or TF-CBT (Cohen, Mannarino, and Deblinger 2017). Several studies have established TF-CBT as an effective treatment to address different types of trauma in children and youth (Cary and McMillen 2012; de Arellano et al. 2014; Dorsey et al. 2017; Kowalik et al. 2011).

TF-CBT incorporates developmentally appropriate levels of exposure, processing, and skills building to address the unique and complex ways in which children and youth ages three to eighteen experience trauma. TF-CBT helps children cope with the symptoms and reminders of the trauma; address the meaning of the event; and, when appropriate, process grief associated with the death of a parent or other important figure in their lives. Although TF-CBT is delivered within a structured format in twelve to sixteen sessions, adaptability and flexibility are encouraged to allow the therapist to provide treatment in a way that meets the developmental needs of the child and is respectful of individual, family, community, and cultural values. As such, the treatment may be longer (around twenty-five sessions) for children with complex trauma. As is the case with regular CBT, TF-CBT is a strengths-based approach that aims to provide clients with cognitive, behavioral, and other life skills to enhance their ability to eventually cope and solve problems on their own (Cohen, Mannarino, and Deblinger 2017). Acknowledging the repercussions that a child's trauma has across the family and understanding that children's response to trauma is mediated by the quality of the emotional support they receive, Cohen and colleagues encourage the active participation of nonoffending parents and caregivers. Parents participate both in individual sessions and in joint sessions with the child. As a result, family involvement is seen as an essential aspect of TF-CBT and a predictor of therapeutic success. TF-CBT also recognizes that a child's traumatic experiences often represent a betrayal of the expectation that children will be kept safe by parents, caregivers, and society at large. Therefore, the therapeutic relationship assumes a central role in the child's life, and the therapist strives to establish an atmosphere of safety, trust, acceptance, and empathy toward the client (Cohen, Mannarino, and Deblinger 2017).

Cohen, Mannarino, and Deblinger (2017) represent the key treatment components of TF-CBT in the acronym PRACTICE: (1) psychoeducation about the trauma and common responses to it, and also about parenting skills, (2) relaxation strategies (e.g., diaphragmatic breathing, imagery), (3) affective modulation, (4) cognitive coping to identify and reframe maladaptive meaning attached to the trauma, (5) trauma narration and processing (in which trauma memories are addressed and processed through discussion or writing), (6) in-vivo mastery of trauma reminders to counterbalance avoid-ant tendencies and to promote self-efficacy, (7) joint parent-child sessions, and (8) enhancement of future safety and development. These components are provided over three phases. Phase one is stabilization and skill building (components 1–4), phase two is trauma narration and processing (compo-nent 5), and phase three is consolidation and closure (components 6–8). Each phase corresponds to approximately one-third of the overall treatment epi-sode. However, Cohen, Mannarino, and Deblinger (2017) suggest that children who have experienced complex trauma may need more time in the stabilization phase. Although children and parents receive the various com-ponents of treatment in their individual sessions, joint sessions provide an opportunity to practice skills and to gradually develop more open commu-nication about the trauma.

Eye Movement Desensitization and Reprocessing (EMDR)

EMDR was initially developed by Francine Shapiro (1989a, 1989b) to reduce the distress of traumatic memories. According to Shapiro (2018), most psychopathologies are rooted in early life, and the goal of EMDR is to "rapidly metabolize the dysfunctional residue from the past and trans-form it into something useful" (xii) by incorporating new meaning, in-sights, and affect. The process involves a three-pronged approach that addresses the etiology of a traumatic event (the past), the triggers of the PTSD symptoms (the present), and the development of templates to cope with upsetting events (the future) (Shapiro 2007). The therapist uses directive questioning to desensitize the client through a brief imagined exposure to the traumatic memory (Shapiro 2001). The client is asked to provide a negative or dysfunctional cognition of the trauma and to iden-tify places in the body where the physical sensations are felt. After focus-ing on the traumatic memory and the negative cognition, emotion, and physical sensations, the client receives bilateral stimulation. Most com-monly, it involves therapist-directed saccadic eye movements, with the therapist moving his or her fingers back and forth in front of the client's face after instructing the client to follow the movement with his or her eyes (Shapiro 2001). The sequence is repeated until the accompanying level of disturbance has subsided and the dysfunctional cognitions about the trauma have been ameliorated (Shapiro 2007).

Shapiro (2018) describes eight phases in the process of EMDR treatment: (1) obtaining a detailed history, developing rapport, and planning treatment, (2) preparation by explaining the theory and process of therapy, setting expectations, and developing a therapeutic bond, (3) assessing and defining the specifics of the traumatic experience, (4) reprocessing and desensitizing the trauma memory, (5) installation of healthy beliefs, (6) a body scan to identify and process residual physical sensations and tensions, (7) closure to ensure that each session ends with the client feeling calm and balanced, and (8) reevaluation at the start of each session to monitor the client's progress from session to session.

Although EMDR has been widely adopted, is recommended as an effective treatment for PTSD (Chen et al. 2014; Foa et al. 2009; Spates & Rubin, 2012), and, according to the EMDR Institute (2018), is used by over a hundred thousand clinicians throughout the world, the effectiveness of the eye movement component of EMDR has been questioned. This form of stimulation is a unique albeit controversial aspect of the treatment. For instance, several studies have found that eye movements do not enhance EMDR outcomes (e.g., Cahill, Carrigan, and Frueh 1999; Devilly and Spence 1999; Pitman et al. 1991; Renfrey and Spates 1994). Similarly, the International Society for Traumatic Stress Studies (Foa et al. 2009), although it endorsed EMDR as an effective treatment for PTSD, suggested that no evidence exists to support the use of eye movement or any other form of alternating movement for producing change in EMDR. On the other hand, a meta-analysis on the contributions of eye movement in EMDR by Lee and Cuijpers (2013) found medium to large effect-size advantages for the use of eye movement in processing emotional memories. Shapiro (2018) states that eye movements are only one form of bilateral stimulation. Davidson and Parker (2001) suggest that other dual-attention tasks—such as finger tapping or paying attention to sounds or lights—presented on alternating sides have been found effective in activating the processing of information and achieving treatment effects.

Rather notably, the scientific community has been divided over the absence of an empirically validated model explaining the effectiveness of EMDR (Coubard 2016; Gunter and Bodner 2009; Perkins and Rouanzoin 2002; Rodenburg et al. 2009). Several hypotheses have been proposed to explain the treatment mechanism underlying EMDR (see Coubard 2016). Stickgold (2007), for example, has suggested that EMDR may activate a neurobiological state similar to REM sleep. Others have suggested a working-memory account of EMDR, which posits that unpleasant memories become less vivid and less emotional when eye movements use up the brain's resources for processing visuospatial information (Gunter and Bodner 2009; Kavanagh et al. 2001). Because an understanding of EMDR's treatment mechanism is lacking, additional research is needed.

Stress-Inoculation Therapy (SIT)

Stress-inoculation therapy (also known as stress-inoculation training or SIT) helps clients acquire and practice coping skills to manage their anxiety effectively and increase their level of confidence in using those skills in specific anxiety-provoking situations (Meichenbaum 1993, 1996). SIT has been used as a treatment model both to assist individuals facing the aftermath of trauma and preventively as a means of self-inoculation against future stressors (Meichenbaum 1996). SIT utilizes a three-phase, overlapping approach: (1) conceptualization, (2) development of strategies and rehearsal, and (3) application and follow-through. The approach to implementing these phases varies depending on the nature of the trauma (i.e., acute and time-limited versus prolonged, ongoing, or repetitive) and the resources and coping abilities of the client (Meichenbaum 2007).

During the conceptualization phase the goal is to establish a collaborative relationship with the client while enhancing the client's understanding and awareness of the nature of PTSD and the response to the trauma. After the client has developed an understanding of PTSD and the dynamics behind the symptoms, treatment moves to the skills-acquisition and -rehearsal phase, in which the goal is to provide the client with cognitive and behavioral strategies to manage and reduce the anxiety associated with the trauma. These skills include cognitive restructuring, relaxation and breathing techniques, thought stopping, covert modeling, problem solving, interpersonal communication skills, attention diversion, and self-instructional training. They are tailored to the specific stressors faced by the client and are rehearsed during the therapy session by employing role play, during which the therapist teaches and models the skills. During the application and follow-through phase, the client is expected to apply the learned skills to memories related to the trauma and to increasing levels of stressful cues outside the therapeutic environment. Techniques such as modeling, role play, and graduated in-vivo exposure continue to be used through this phase. The therapist focuses both on reinforcing the client's successful application of the skills learned in therapy to outside events and on troubleshooting problems or setbacks that may arise.

Relapse-prevention strategies and attributional procedures are used throughout SIT to ensure that the client can identify triggers and high-risk situations and also give him- or herself proper credit for gains made and the successful application of coping skills (Meichenbaum 1996). In most cases SIT consists of eight to fifteen one-hour sessions weekly or biweekly, with follow-up "booster" sessions scheduled for three to twelve months after therapy (Meichenbaum 2007).

A study by Hourani et al. (2016) demonstrated the use of teaching SIT as a preventive measure to protect against PTSD in soldiers prior to deployment. The practice guidelines from the International Society of Traumatic Studies (Foa et al. 2009) recommend SIT as a first-line treatment for PTSD among female sexual assault victims. However, the authors note that there is inconclusive evidence supporting the use of SIT for PTSD among veterans. Similarly, a systematic review and meta-analysis of psychological treatments for adults with PTSD (Cusack et al. 2016) concluded that there is insufficient evidence to determine SIT's efficacy for adults with PTSD. Other studies have suggested that adding SIT to PE does not have any discernible enhancement on the effectiveness of PE (Foa, Dancu, et al. 1999; Kehle-Forbes et al. 2013).

Systematic Desensitization (SD)

Systematic desensitization, or SD, is a form of behavior therapy that combines graduated exposure to the fear-inducing object or situation with relaxation strategies (Wolpe 1990). Grounded in classical conditioning theory, SD is based on the principle of counterconditioning or reciprocal inhibition. The notion is that in the face of a feared object, one cannot be anxious and relaxed at the same time. The exposure takes place imaginally, in vivo, or in a combination of the two. SD encompasses three levels: (1) identification of the target stressor and construction of a hierarchy or fear ladder, (2) relaxation training, and (3) systematic pairing of relaxation with exposure to anxiety-provoking stimuli (Sundel and Sundel 2018). In the first level, after identifying the target stressor, client and therapist develop a hierarchy of action steps or scenarios, from lowest to highest intensity, to assist the client in gradually approaching the feared situation. Next, the client is trained in relaxation strategies (e.g., progressive muscle relaxation, diaphragmatic breathing) and in the formation of a relaxing or neutral mental image. In the third phase, once relaxation is induced using the steps previously learned, the client is introduced to the first (lowest-intensity) scene in the hierarchy of scenarios. The process is repeated until the client can experience exposure to a particular scene with minimal or no anxiety. Then scenes from the next level of the hierarchy are introduced. The process continues until the client can progress through the entire hierarchy, facing the most-feared level with no or minimal anxiety.

Although studies have supported the use of SD to treat various types of phobias (see Berman, Miller, and Massman 1985), the evidence behind its use for PTSD is mixed at best. Foa et al. (2009, 553) state that systematic desensitization for PTSD "has not received strong support from well-controlled studies" and cite serious methodological problems with some of the studies.

Seeking Safety (SS)

Seeking safety, or SS (Najavits et al. 1998), was originally developed to help women who were struggling with the comorbidity of PTSD and substance abuse. However, since its original development, SS has expanded its application to a broad range of individuals, including adults and adolescents of both sexes. Treatment addresses twenty-five different cognitive, behavioral, and interpersonal topics—one per session—in fifty- to ninety-minute individual or group sessions. Topics include psychoeducation about trauma and substance use, a wide array of coping and interpersonal skills, self-care, emotion modulation and regulation, meaning-making, and others. The aim is to bring about an effective recovery from the sequelae of PTSD and substance-use disorders (Najavits 2017).

Najavits (2003) outlines five integral principles of the SS model. The first is safety as the priority. The focus here is to teach the client coping skills that will help to stabilize him or her and provide safety from substances, dangerous relationships, and destructive symptoms. The second principle revolves around the integration of treatment for both PTSD and substance use. Given the reciprocal interaction between trauma and substance use, the

integrated aspect of the model provides the opportunity to treat both problems simultaneously. The third principle is a focus on ideals. Persons
struggling with the effects of trauma and substance abuse often feel defeated,
hopeless, and demoralized. Seeking safety aims to restore lost ideals, hope,
self-care, and self-respect. The fourth principle relates to the four content areas that form the core of treatment: cognitive, behavioral, interpersonal,
and case management. This attention paid to a broad range of needs aims
to reestablish balance and safety in the client's life. The fifth principle, which
focuses on the therapist's processes, acknowledges the challenges that therapists face when working with traumatized individuals who have substance-
use histories. The focus for the therapist on developing competency and
attending to self-care is an important aspect of SS. The aim is to provide compassionate and effective services to clients. Seeking safety has garnered a
significant body of empirical support and has been deemed a useful model
to treat co-occurring PTSD and substance abuse (Foa et al 2009).

EMPIRICAL EVALUATIONS OF CBT TREATMENTS FOR PTSD

When evaluated from a broad perspective, several cognitive-behavioral ther-
apies have substantial evidence supporting their efficacy for the treatment
of PTSD. These include PE, EMDR, SIT, and VRE (Benish, Imel, and
Wampold 2008; Bisson et al. 2007; Bisson et al. 2013; Bradley et al. 2005;
Cusack et al. 2016; Foa et al. 1991; Foa, Dancu, et al. 1999; Hien et al. 2010;
Hourani et al. 2016; Ponniah and Holon 2009; Seitz et al. 2014; Serino et al.
2014; Seidler and Wagner 2006). For veterans and military personnel,
PE has been labeled the "gold standard" (Rauch, Eftekhari, and Ruzek
2012, 679).

In a meta-analysis of randomized studies (N = 38), Bisson et al. (2007)
concluded that the first line of effective individual treatment for PTSD
should be trauma-focused cognitive-behavior therapy or EMDR. (We should
point out that Bisson and colleagues use the term *trauma-focused cognitive-
behavior therapy*, or *TFCBT*, generically to mean treatments that include
some form of exposure to memories of the traumatic event. It is not the same
as the TF-CBT model [Cohen, Mannarino, and Deblinger 2017] described
earlier in the chapter to treat trauma in children and adolescents.) At the
same time, the authors indicate limited support for the use of stress management and group CBT to alleviate symptoms of PTSD. The analysis also

indicated that non-trauma-focused therapies did not have clinically significant effects on PTSD. The authors explain that this is a possible result of the limited number of studies available, and not necessarily a sign of the therapies' ineffectiveness. Another study conducted by Bisson et al. (2013) further supported the notion that TFCBT is more effective than no treatment (based on wait-list controls) or treatment as usual to reduce symptoms of PTSD.

Cusack et al. (2016) conducted a systematic review and meta-analysis of psychological treatments for adults with PTSD that included randomized control trials (N = 64). Efficacy was reported based on "strength of evidence" standards established by Owens et al. 2010 (as cited in Cusack et al. 2016). Several of the treatment conditions tested CBT modalities such as cognitive therapy, cognitive restructuring, CPT, SIT, PE, and EMDR. Evidence was insufficient to determine efficacy for SIT. However, for cognitive therapy, including CPT, results showed efficacy in reducing PTSD symptoms, improving depression and anxiety symptoms, reducing disability associated with PTSD, and achieving loss of the PTSD diagnosis. For exposure-therapy studies (mostly PE), the evidence supported efficacy for reducing PTSD symptoms, reducing depression symptoms in adults with PTSD, and loss of diagnosis (134). Analysis of EMDR studies yielded similar results; however, the strength of evidence was lower for EMDR than for PE.

In another meta-analytic study, Ponniah and Hollon (2009) reviewed randomized studies (N = 57) of psychological therapies for PTSD and ASD (acute stress disorder) to determine which therapies are empirically supported, and concluded that trauma-focused CBT is effective in the treatment of PTSD. Exposure, with or without cognitive restructuring, was found to produce greater reductions in PTSD symptoms when compared with no treatment or minimal interventions, relaxation training, and supportive counseling. The study also found that cognitive restructuring alone, without exposure, was more effective than treatment as usual and relaxation training. EMDR was found to be effective in treating PTSD, although the authors temper their support of EMDR, pointing out that fewer studies have been conducted on the use of EMDR to treat PTSD. SIT was found to be "possibly efficacious" for the treatment of PTSD.

In terms of treatment-specific outcomes, several meta-analytic reviews suggest that EMDR is an effective treatment for PTSD (Bisson et al. 2007; Bisson et al. 2013; Bradley et al. 2005; Davidson and Parker 2001; Van Etten and Taylor 1998), possibly as effective as exposure therapies (e.g., Ironson et al. 2002; Lee et al. 2002; Lee, Taylor, and Drummond 2006; Rothbaum, Astin, and Marsteller 2005). In six different studies using clinician-based assessments of PTSD symptoms, EMDR resulted in significantly better outcomes than no treatment (based on wait-list controls) or treatment as usual. Other researchers, however, have critiqued the evidence base for EMDR (e.g., Herbert et al. 2000; McNally 1999). They are concerned by the aggressive marketing and dissemination strategies employed by EMDR's developers and have argued that EMDR may simply be a variant of exposure therapy. Nevertheless, EMDR is one of the "treatments of choice" recommended by the National Institute for Health and Care Excellence (Bisson et al. 2013, 2). Rodenburg et al. (2009) have claimed that there is considerably less evidence for incremental efficacy to indicate that EMDR is a significant improvement over other established PTSD treatments. However, a Cochrane Review from Bisson et al. (2013), noted some evidence that individual EMDR and TFCBT were superior to waitlist/usual care in reducing PTSD symptoms. The authors also indicated that EMDR, TFCBT, and non-TFCBT (i.e., SIT) were equally effective immediately after treatment. Non-TFCBT therapies teach skills to manage the stress and anxiety associated with trauma without the exposure component of TFCBT. However, EMDR and TF-CBT were superior to non-TFCBT at one to four months' follow-up. Further, individual TFCBT, EMDR, and non-TFCBT were more effective than other therapies (e.g., person-centered therapy, hypnotherapy, psychodynamic therapy, and present-centered treatments); however, this finding must be considered within the context of the relatively few empirical studies available that focused on "other therapies." The authors suggested that the "other therapies" may have shown better results with a larger number of studies. Nonetheless, the authors concluded that, at present, TFCBT and EMDR have the best evidence to reduce symptoms of PTSD.

Stress-inoculation training (SIT), prolonged exposure (PE), and the combination of the two have been found to effectively reduce PTSD symptoms, anxiety, and depression in female victims of assault (Foa et al. 1991; Foa, Dancu, et al. 1999). The 1991 study involved forty-five female victims of rape or attempted rape randomly assigned to treatment (PE or SIT), supportive counseling, or wait-list conditions. Both treatment arms showed significant reductions of symptoms when compared to supportive counseling and wait-list conditions. SIT appeared to provide more immediate relief of symptoms because its focus is on anxiety management. PE may produce immediate increases in anxiety as a result of exposure to the traumatic memory. However, the emotional processing of the trauma, a central feature of PE, with cognitive reframing of its theme of dangerousness may result in longer-lasting effects. Another study (Foa, Dancu, et al. 1999) comparing PE and SIT supported the effectiveness of both treatments individually and a combination of the two to treat PTSD in female assault victims. The comparison revealed that all three active treatments were superior to wait-list conditions in reducing symptoms of PTSD and depression, but there were no significant differences among the three.

More recent research has shown promise for SIT as a training mechanism for future soldiers at risk of experiencing stress and trauma in active deployment. Hourani et al. (2016) conducted a study to test the effects of a predeployment stress-inoculation-training intervention (PRESIT). The authors collected predeployment data from 351 active-duty male members of the Marine Corps who were then randomly assigned to either PRESIT or a control intervention. The control group received a current best-practices twenty-minute lecture and slide presentation to help them identify potential stressors, signs and symptoms of stress, recommended self-help behaviors, and resources for seeking professional help. The PRESIT intervention included three modules: (1) education about combat and operational stress control, (2) coping-skills training, including breathing relaxation with biofeedback, and (3) practice of skills and knowledge learned in the first two modules while being exposed to video simulation of potential stressors. Two days after the initial training, both groups received a forty-five-minute refresher session. Following a seven-month deployment to Afghanistan, data were collected from 263 participants. The results of the study suggest that participants receiving PRESIT exhibited lower levels of autonomic arousal than participants in the control group, and those in the control group were seven times more likely to meet criteria for PTSD than the PRESIT group. Although the authors acknowledge several limitations, they suggest that the study provides initial evidence for the use of PRESIT as a preventive measure to reduce the risk of PTSD. Additionally, the study provides another example of the integration of "cyber," "virtual-reality," or "multimedia" interventions into the treatment or prevention of PTSD. Along these lines, a systematic review of the use of cyber interventions in SIT methodology by Serino et al. (2014) suggests that interventions using simulated stress environments for military personnel and others at risk of developing stress disorders like PTSD may be promising as a clinical approach to preventing these disorders. However, future studies should focus on improving methodological rigor in sampling and measurement as well as on identifying the most effective technologies for implementing SIT principles.

Technological advancements such as virtual reality have been used to apply exposure-therapy principles in clinical research. Although virtual-reality exposure (VRE) is still a relatively new implementation of CBT principles, a body of evidence from the last two decades suggests that it is effective for treating PTSD in military personnel (Seitz et al. 2014), in those who experienced terrorist attacks (Rizzo et al. 2015; Difede et al. 2007), and in others who experienced various kinds of trauma (Botella et al. 2010). A 2012 systematic review (Gonçalves et al.) found that VRE was at least as effective as traditional exposure therapies and might be particularly useful in treating PTSD sufferers who are resistant to more traditional exposure therapies.

Difede et al. (2007) evaluated a sample of twenty-two rescue workers, mostly middle-aged males, who met criteria for PTSD following rescue operations after the attacks on the World Trade Center (WTC). The participants were randomly assigned to VRE (N = 13) or a waiting list (N = 9). The results revealed significant decreases across all domains of PTSD symptoms and a large effect size of 1.54 for between-groups post-treatment comparisons. The findings suggest that VRE is an effective tool for enhancing exposure therapy to treat rescue workers involved in civilian disasters such as terrorist attacks, and particularly useful for those who cannot engage in imaginal exposure therapy.

Botella et al. (2010) noted that VRE has chiefly been developed for those who have endured war trauma, combat violence, or similar experiences rather than for those who have experienced other types of traumas, such as rape, domestic violence, or physical abuse. The researchers developed a treatment plan using an adaptive display called EMMA's World, described earlier in the chapter. Researchers tested a traditional prolonged-exposure CBT intervention against the CBT intervention enhanced with EMMA's World for ten participants who had developed PTSD from experiences of robbery, motor vehicle accident, "mobbing at the workplace," assault, or domestic violence (68). Although there were no statistically significant differences between the groups, both showed improvements in several measures: CAPS in both frequency and intensity (CBT = ns, CBT+EMMA = $p < 0.04$), Davidson Trauma Scale in both frequency and intensity (CBT = $p < 0.04$, CBT+EMMA = $p < 0.04$), and Posttraumatic Cognitions Inventory (CBT = $p < 0.04$, CBT+EMMA = $p < 0.04$). Notwithstanding the limitations of the small sample size and nonrandom assignment, these results suggest that a VR-enhanced prolonged-exposure CBT treatment is at least as beneficial as the traditional non-VR treatment for those experiencing PTSD from varied sources and who are less amenable to a "one-size-fits-all" VR experience.

The available research suggests that VRE could be used either as a stand-alone treatment or as part of a comprehensive therapy approach for persons suffering from stress related to either combat or civilian trauma (Difede et al. 2007; Rizzo et al. 2015; Seitz et al. 2014). Although additional study is needed to solidify its benefits and effectiveness, the research by Botella et al. (2010) shows that it may be at least as effective as traditional exposure-therapy models. VRE offers the advantage of allowing victims to re-create a traumatic event under controlled conditions that facilitate habituation and cognitive restructuring (Rothbaum et al. 2001).

Seeking safety (SS) has garnered a significant body of support and has been deemed by the International Society for Traumatic Stress Studies (Foa et al. 2009) as an established and effective treatment for co-occurring PTSD and substance-use disorders (Hien et al. 2010). It shows consistent positive outcomes and is superior to treatment as usual (TAU) with particularly challenging populations (Foa et al. 2009). A systematic meta-analysis by Lenz, Henesy, and Callender (2014) reviewed twelve studies in which SS was tested against no treatment/wait-list conditions or alternative treatments for its effects on PTSD symptoms or substance use. For PTSD symptoms, studies comparing SS with wait-list conditions yielded a medium mean effect size (-0.56, 95% CI [-0.75, -0.37]), and "effect sizes within the distribution of studies were homogenous, indicating that less than 1% of the variability was due to between-studies heterogeneity" (56). This was not the case, however, in the analysis of SS versus alternative treatment models. The mean effect size was also medium (-0.47, 95% CI [-1.27, 0.34]), but the confidence interval was much larger, and thus the null hypothesis regarding treatment effect could not be rejected. Furthermore, Cochran's analysis for homogeneity of effect-size distribution revealed that "98% of the total variability was due to between-studies heterogeneity" (56). Thus, differences in PTSD symptoms were only statistically significant for SS against wait-list conditions or no treatment. Regarding substance use, only two studies that met inclusion criteria for analysis included outcomes on substance use. Therefore, only SS versus treatment as usual was analyzed for effect size. The mean effect size for this comparison was small, the null hypothesis could not be rejected (-0.19, 95% CI [-0.52, 0.14]), and 87% of the total variability was due to between-studies heterogeneity (57). On both PTSD and substance-use outcomes in a comparison of SS with alternative treatments, ethnicity was a moderating variable. White/Caucasian samples yielded higher treatment effects when compared with samples including ethnic-minority participants. This meta-analysis suggests that SS is more effective than no treatment but possibly less effective for members of minority ethnic groups. However, only one of the studies included male participants, limiting its generalizability.

The findings of Lenz, Henesy, and Callender (2014) are in line with a more recent RCT evaluating SS against TAU in a sample of forty incarcerated women (Tripodi et al. 2017). In this study, SS appeared more effective than TAU, but differences were often not statistically significant or persistent at four-month follow-up. For PTSD severity measured on the PTSD Checklist-Civilian (PCL-C) version, both groups of women improved from pretest to post-test and follow-up, and SS improvements yielded greater point differences on the PCL-C across measurement times when compared with the control group. However, the results were not statistically significant. The study also measured between-group differences in depression scores, which were significant for greater improvements in the SS group at post-test, but no longer significant at four-month follow-up. These findings may have been confounded by pretest differences between the SS and TAU groups that persisted despite randomization to groups.

SUMMARY AND CONCLUSIONS

Cognitive-behavioral therapies offer a variety of empirically supported interventions to treat PTSD in adults, children, and adolescents. The available evidence supports the notion that trauma-focused cognitive-behavioral treatments (i.e., those that incorporate either imaginal, virtual-reality, or written-narrative exposure) and EMDR are effective therapies for PTSD. It is also clear that the manner in which exposure is presented and the intensity of the experience varies across treatment models. Because CBT models for PTSD are relatively brief, they can provide efficacious and cost-effective treatment alternatives, as shown by Greer et al. (2014) in a study comparing the annual cost of implementing a TF-CBT program versus treatment as usual for trauma-exposed children.

One fact worth noting: although our review points out that exposure-based CBT models are more effective than nonexposure models, a study by Barrera et al. (2013) found no difference in effect sizes between group cognitive-behavior therapy (GCBT) for PTSD with and without exposure; both treatment conditions were effective. This matter deserves further investigation. Still, the consensus suggests that exposure strategies are helpful for activating the fear structure, thus making it available for modification by the introduction of new information that is incompatible with the original schema.

Despite the documented success of exposure-based therapies for PTSD, our review also highlights existing issues that call for further attention. For instance, some studies have suggested that exposure therapies have high attrition rates (~26%), which implies that some individuals do not respond well to those types of treatment and are more likely to drop out (Barrera et al. 2013; Bisson et al. 2013; Bryant 2011; Cahill et al. 2009; Markowitz et al. 2015). Future research may focus on identifying factors to reduce the attrition rate and thereby increase the therapies' effectiveness and retention. This may entail determining more particularly which type of treatment would provide benefit for which specific type of trauma (e.g., combat, rape, accidents) and for which specific groups—that is, effectively matching treatment to a particular client, problem, or characteristic (Vonk, Bordnick, and Graap 2006).

We also found a scarcity of studies that specifically focused on racial and ethnic minorities. Additional research focused on minority populations may help to identify factors that could make these therapies more culturally responsive to the needs of such populations. Along similar lines, Forneris et al. (2013), in a systematic review of interventions to prevent PTSD, called for additional research focusing on specific subgroups such as victims of terrorism, refugees, first responders, individuals with co-occurring conditions, and racial and ethnic minorities. Finally, it is important to ensure the affordability and wide dissemination of effective treatments such as VRE to make them available to low-income populations and community-based mental health agencies.

Overall, CBT-based models for PTSD provide effective alternatives to treat traumatized individuals. At the same time, they continue to generate abundant research that contributes to their ongoing refinement and effectiveness.

REFERENCES

Alsina-Jurnet, I., C. Carvallo-Beciu, and J. Gutiérrez-Maldonado. 2007. "Validity of Virtual Reality as a Method of Exposure in the Treatment of Test Anxiety." *Behavior Research Methods* 39:844–851.

American Psychiatric Association. 2013. *Diagnostic and Statistical Manual of Mental Disorders.* 5th ed. Arlington, VA: American Psychiatric Association.

Bandura, A. 1977. "Self Efficacy: Toward a Unifying Theory of Behavioral Change." *Psychological Review* 84:191–215.

——. 1986. *Social Foundation of Thought and Action: A Social Cognitive Theory.* Englewood Cliffs, NJ: Prentice-Hall.

Baños, R. M., C. Botella, V. Guillen, A. García-Palacios, S. Quero, J. Breton-López, and M. Alcaniz. 2009. "An Adaptive Display to Treat Stress Related Disorders: EMMA's World." *British Journal of Guidance and Counselling* 37:347–356.

Barlow, D. H. 2002. *Anxiety and Its Disorders: The Nature and Treatment of Anxiety and Panic.* New York: Guilford Press.

Barrera, T. L., J. M. Mott, R. F. Hofstein, and E. J. Teng. 2013. "A Meta-analytic Review of Exposure in Group Cognitive-Behavioral Therapy for Posttraumatic Stress Disorder." *Clinical Psychology Review* 33:24–32. doi:10.1016/j.cpr.2012.09.005.

Beck, A. T. 1976. *Cognitive Therapy of the Emotional Disorders.* New York: Penguin Books.

Beck, A. T., G. Emery, and R. L. Greenberger. 1985. *Anxiety Disorders and Phobias: A Cognitive Perspective.* New York: Basic Books.

Beck, A. T., A. J. Rush, B. F. Shaw, and G. Emery. 1979. *Cognitive Therapy of Depression.* New York: Guilford Press.

Beck, J. S. 2011. *Cognitive Therapy: Basics and Beyond.* 2nd ed. New York: Guilford Press.

Benish, S. G., Z. E. Imel, and B. E. Wampold. 2008. "The Relative Efficacy of Bona Fide Psychotherapies for Treating Post-Traumatic Stress Disorder: A Meta-analysis of Direct Comparisons." *Clinical Psychology* 28:746–758.

Berman, J. S., R. C. Miller, and P. J. Massman. 1985. "Cognitive Therapy Versus Systematic Desensitization: Is One Treatment Superior?" *Psychological Bulletin* 97 (3): 451–461.

Bisson, J. I., A. Ehlers, R. Matthews, S. Pilling, D. Richards, and S. Turners. 2007. "Psychological Treatments for Chronic Posttraumatic Stress Disorders: Systematic Review and Meta-analysis." *British Journal of Psychiatry* 190:97–104.

Bisson, J. I., N. P. Roberts, M. Andrew, R. Cooper, and C. Lewis. 2013. "Psychological Therapies for Chronic Post-Traumatic Stress Disorder (PTSD) in Adults." *Cochrane Library* 2013 (12): CD003388. doi:10.1002/14651858.CD003388 .pub4.

Botella, C., R. M. Baños, A. García-Palacios, and S. Quero. 2017. "Virtual Reality and Other Realities." In *The Science of Cognitive Behavioral Therapy*, ed. S. G. Hofmann and G. J. G. Asmundson, 551–590. London: Academic Press.

Botella, C., A. García-Palacios, V. Guillen, R. M. Baños, S. Quero, and M. Alcaniz. 2010. "An Adaptive Display for the Treatment of Diverse Trauma PTSD Victims." *Cyberpsychology, Behavior, and Social Networking* 13 (1): 67–71.

Botella, C., B. Serrano, R. M. Baños, and A. García-Palacios. 2015. "Virtual Reality Exposure-Based Therapy for the Treatment of Post-Traumatic Stress Disorder: A Review of Its Efficacy, the Adequacy of the Treatment Protocol, and Its Acceptability." *Neuropsychiatric Disease and Treatment* 11:2533–2545. doi:10.2147/NDT.S89542.

Bradley, R., J. Greene, E. Russ, L. Dutra, and D. Westen, D. 2005. "A Multidimensional Meta-analysis of Psychotherapy for PTSD." *American Journal of Psychiatry* 162:214–227.

Bryant, R. A. 2011. "Psychological Interventions for Trauma Exposure and PTSD." In *Post-Traumatic Stress Disorder*, ed. D. J. Stein, M. J. Friedman, and C. Blanco, 171–202. Oxford: Wiley.

Bryant, R. A. 2017. "Posttraumatic Stress Disorder." In *The Science of Cognitive Behavioral Therapy*, ed. S. G. Hofmann and G. J. G. Asmundson, 319–336. London: Academic Press.

Cahill, S. P., M. H. Carrigan, and B. C. Frueh. 1999. "Does EMDR Work? And If So, Why? A Critical Review of Controlled Outcome and Dismantling Research." *Journal of Anxiety Disorders* 13 (1–2): 5–33.

Cahill, S. P., B. O. Rothbaum, P. A. Resick, and V. M. Follette. 2009. "Cognitive-Behavioral Therapy for Adults." In *The Effective Treatment for PTSD: Practice*

Guidelines from the International Society for Traumatic Stress Studies, ed. E. B. Foa, T. M. Keane, M. J. Friedman, and J. A. Cohen, 139–222. New York: Guilford Press.

Cary, C. E., and J. C. McMillen. 2012. "The Data Behind the Dissemination: A Systematic Review of Trauma-Focused Cognitive Behavioral Therapy for Use with Children and Youth." *Children and Youth Services Review* 34:748–757. doi:10.1016/j.childyouth.2012.01.003.

Chen, Y.-R., K.-W. Hung, J.-C. Tsai, H. Chu, M.-H. Chung, S.-R. Chen, . . . K.-R. Chou. 2014. "Efficacy of Eye-Movement Desensitization and Reprocessing for Patients with Posttraumatic Stress Disorder: A Meta-analysis of Randomized Controlled Trials." *PLOS One* 9 (8): e103676.

Clark, D. M., and A. Ehlers. 2004. "Posttraumatic Stress Disorders from Cognitive Theory to Therapy." In *Contemporary Cognitive Therapy: Theory, Research, and Practice*, ed. R. L. Leahy, 141–160. New York: Guilford Press.

Cohen, J. A., A. P. Mannarino, and E. Deblinger. 2017. *Treating Trauma and Traumatic Grief in Children and Adolescents*. New York: Guilford Press.

Coubard, O. 2016. "An Integrative Model for the Neural Mechanism of Eye Movement Desensitization and Reprocessing (EMDR)." *Frontiers in Behavioral Science* 10 (52): 1–17. doi:10.3389/fnbeh.2016.00052.

Cukor, J., J. Spitalnick, J. Difede, A. Rizzo, B. O. Rothbaum. 2009. "Emerging Treatments for PTSD." *Clinical Psychology Review* 29:715–726.

Cusack, K., D. E. Jonas, C. A. Forneris, C. Wines, J. Sonis, J. C. Middleton, . . . B. N. Gaynes. 2016. "Psychological Treatments for Adults with Posttraumatic Stress Disorders: A Systematic Review and Meta-analysis." *Clinical Psychology Review* 43:128–141. doi:10.1016/j.cpr.2015.10.003.

Davidson, P. R., and K. C. H. Parker. 2001. "Eye Movement Desensitization and Reprocessing (EMDR): A Meta-analysis." *Journal of Consulting and Clinical Psychology* 69 (2): 305–316.

de Arellano M. A., D. R. Lyman, L. Jobe-Shields, P. George, R. H. Dougherty, A. S. Daniels, and M. E. Delphin-Rittmon. 2014. "Trauma-Focused Cognitive-Behavioral Therapy for Children and Adolescents: Assessing the Evidence." *Psychiatric Services* 65 (5): 591–602. doi:10.1176/appi.ps.201300255.

Department of Veterans Affair and Department of Defense. 2017. "VA/DOD Clinical Practice Guideline for the Management of Posttraumatic Stress Disorder and Acute Stress Disorder." Retrieved 4/25/18 from https://www.healthquality.va.gov/guidelines/MH/ptsd/VADoDPTSDCPGFinal012418.pdf.

Devilly, G. J., and S. H. Spence. 1999. "The Relative Efficacy and Treatment Distress of EMDR and a Cognitive-Behavior Trauma Treatment Protocol in the Amelioration of Posttraumatic Stress Disorder." *Journal of Anxiety Disorders* 13 (1–2): 131–157.

Difede, J., J. Cukor, N. Jayasinghe, I. Patt, S. Jedel, L. Spielman, . . . H. G. Hoffman 2007. "Virtual Reality Exposure Therapy for the Treatment of Posttraumatic Stress Disorder Following September 11, 2001." *Journal of Clinical Psychiatry* 68:1639–1647.

Difede, J., and H. G. Hoffman. 2002. "Virtual Reality Exposure Therapy for World Trade Center Post-Traumatic Stress Disorder: A Case Report." *Cyber Psychology and Behavior* 5:529–535.

Dobson, D., and K. S. Dobson. 2017. *Evidenced-Based Practice of Cognitive-Behavioral Therapy*. 2nd ed. New York: Guilford Press.

Dorsey, S., K. A. McLaughlin, S. E. U. Kerns, J. P. Harrison, H. K. Lambert, E. C. Briggs, . . . L. Amaya-Jackson. 2017. "Evidence-Based Update for Psychosocial Treatments for Children and Adolescents Exposed to Traumatic Events." *Journal of Clinical Child and Adolescent Psychology* 46 (3): 303–343. doi:10.1080/15374416.2016.1220309.

Dunmore, E., D. M. Clark, and A. Ehlers. 1999. "A Prospective Investigation of the Role of Cognitive Factors in Persistent Posttraumatic Stress Disorder (PTSD) After Physical or Sexual Assault." *Behaviour Research and Therapy* 39:1063–1084.

Ehlers, A., J. Bisson, D. M. Clark, M. Creamer, S. Pilling, D. Richards, . . . W. Yule. 2010. "Do All Psychological Treatments Really Work the Same for Posttraumatic Stress Disorder?" *Clinical Psychology Review* 30:269–276.

Ehlers, A., and D. M. Clark. 2000. "A Cognitive Model of Posttraumatic Stress Disorder." *Behaviour Research and Therapy* 38:319–345.

Ehlers, A., and D. M. Clark. 2006. "Predictors of Chronic Posttraumatic Stress Disorders: Trauma, Memories, and Appraisals." In *Pathological Anxiety: Emotional Processing in Etiology and Treatment*, ed. B. Rothbaum, 3–24. New York: Guilford Press.

Ehlers, A., D. M. Clark, A. Hackmann, F. McManus, M. Fennell, C. Herbert, and R. Mayou. 2003. "A Randomized Controlled Trial of Cognitive Therapy, a Self-Help Booklet, and Repeated Assessments as Early Interventions for Posttraumatic Stress Disorder." *Archives of General Psychiatry* 60:1024–1032. doi:10.1001/archpsyc.60.10.1024.

Ehlers, A., N. Grey, J. Wild, R. Stott, S. Liness, A. Deale, . . . D. Clark. 2013. "Implementation of Cognitive Therapy for PTSD in Routine Clinical Care: Effectiveness of Moderators of Outcome in a Consecutive Sample." *Behaviour Research and Therapy* 51:742–752.

EMDR Institute. 2018. "What Is EMDR?" Accessed April 9, 2019. http://www .emdr.com/frequent-questions/.

Fedoroff, I. C., S. Taylor, G. J. G. Asmundson, and W. J. Koch. 2000. "Cognitive Factors in Traumatic Stress Reactions: Predicting Symptoms from Anxiety Sensitivity and Beliefs About Harmful Events." *Behavioural and Cognitive Psychotherapy* 28 (1): 5–15.

Foa, E. B., C. V. Dancu, E. A. Hembree, L. H. Jaycox, E. A. Meadows, and G. P. Street. 1999. "A Comparison of Exposure Therapy, Stress Inoculation Training, and Their Combination for Reducing Posttraumatic Stress Disorder in Female Assault Victims." *Journal of Consulting and Clinical Psychology* 67:194–200.

Foa, E. B., A. Ehlers, D. M. Clark, D. F. Tolin, and S. M. Orsillo. 1999. "The Posttraumatic Cognitions Inventory (PTCI): Development and Validation." *Psychological Assessment* 11:303–314.

Foa, E. B., E. A. Hembree, S. P. Cahill, S. A. M. Rauch, D. S. Riggs, N. C. Feeny, and E. Yadin. 2005. "A Randomized Trial of Prolonged Exposure for Posttraumatic Stress Disorder With and Without Cognitive Restructuring: Outcome at Academic and Community Clinics." *Journal of Consulting and Clinical Psychology* 73:953–964. doi:10.1037/0022-006X.73.5.953

Foa, E. B., J. D. Huppert, and S. P. Cahill. 2006. "Emotional Processing Theory: An Update." In *Pathological Anxiety: Emotional Processing in Etiology and Treatment*, ed. Barbara Rothbaum, 3–24. New York: Guilford Press.

Foa, E. B., and L. H. Jaycox. 1999. "Cognitive-Behavioral Theory and Treatment of Posttraumatic Stress Disorder." In *Efficacy and Cost-Effectiveness of Psychotherapy*, ed. D. Spiegel, 23–61. Washington, DC: American Psychiatric Press.

Foa, E. B., T. M. Keane, M. J. Friedman, and J. A. Cohen. 2009. *Effective Treatments for PTSD: Practice Guidelines from the International Society for Traumatic Studies*. 2nd ed. New York: Guilford Press.

Foa, E. B., and M. J. Kozak. 1986. "Emotional Processing of Fear: Exposure to Corrective Information." *Psychological Bulletin* 99:20–35.

Foa, E. B., and D. S. Riggs. 1993. "Posttraumatic Stress Disorder in Rape Victims." In *Annual Review of Psychiatry*, ed. J. Oldham, M. B. Riba, and A. Tasman, 2:273–303. Washington, D.C.: American Psychiatric Association.

Foa, E. B., and B. O. Rothbaum. 1998. *Treating the Trauma of Rape: A Cognitive Behavioral Therapy for PTSD*. New York: Guilford Press.

Foa, E. B., B. O. Rothbaum, D. S. Riggs, and T. B. Murdock. 1991. "Treatment of Posttraumatic Stress Disorder in Rape Victims: A Comparison Between Cognitive-Behavioral Procedures and Counseling." *Journal of Counseling and Consulting Psychology* 59:715–723.

Foa, E. B., D. J. Stein, and A. C. McFarlane. 2006. "Symptomatology and Psychopathology of Mental Health Problems After Disaster." *Journal of Clinical Psychiatry* 67 (2): 15–25.

Foa, E. B., G. Steketee, and B. O. Rothbaum. 1989. "Behavioral/Cognitive Conceptualizations of Post-Traumatic Stress Disorder." *Behavior Therapy* 20:155–176.

Forneris, C. A., G. Gertlehner, K. A. Brownley, B. N. Gaynes, J. Sonis, E. Coker-Schwimmer, . . . K. N. Lohr. 2013. "Interventions to Prevent Posttraumatic Stress Disorder: A Systematic Review." *American Journal of Preventive Medicine* 44 (6): 635–650. doi:10.1016/j.amepre.2013.02.013.

Gerardi, M., B. O. Rothbaum, K. Ressler, M. Heekin, and A. Rizzo. 2008. "Virtual Reality Exposure Therapy Using Virtual Iraq: A Case Report." *Journal of Traumatic Disorders* 21:209–213.

Gonçalves, R., A. L. Pedrozo, E. S. F. Coutinho, I. Figueira, and P. Ventura. 2012. "Efficacy of Virtual Reality Exposure Therapy in the Treatment of PTSD: A Systematic Review." *PLOS One* 7 (12): e48469. doi:10.1371/journal.pone .0048469.

Greer, D., D. J. Grasso, A. Cohen, and C. Webb. 2014. "Trauma-Focused Treatment in a State System of Care: Is It Worth the Cost?" *Administration and Policy in Mental Health and Mental Health Services Research* 41 (3): 317–323. doi:10.1007/s10488-013-0468-6.

Gunter, R.W., and G. E. Bodner. 2009. "EMDR Works . . . But How? Recent Progress in the Search for Treatment Mechanisms." *Journal of EMDR Practice and Research* 3 (3): 161–168. doi:10.1891/1933-3196.3.3.161.

Hembree, E. A., and E. B. Foa. 2004. "Promoting Cognitive Change in Posttraumatic Stress Disorder." In *Cognitive Therapy Across the Lifespan: Evidence and Practice*, ed. M. A. Reinecke and D. A. Clark, 231–257. New York: Cambridge University Press.

Herbert, J. D., S. O. Lilienfeld, J. M. Lohr, R. W. Montgomery, W. T. O'Donohue, G. M. Rosen, and D. F. Tolin. 2000. "Science and Pseudoscience in the Development of Eye Movement Desensitization and Reprocessing: Implications for Clinical Psychology." *Clinical Psychology Review* 20 (8): 945–971.

Hien, D. A., A. N. Campbell, L. M. Ruglass, M. C. Hu, and T. Killeen. 2010. "The Role of Alcohol Misuse in PTSD Outcomes for Women in Community Treatment: A Secondary Analysis of NIDA's Women and Trauma Study." *Drug and Alcohol Dependence*, 111 (1): 114–119. doi:10.1016/j.drugalcdep.2010.04.011.

Hofmann, S., A. Asnaani, I. J. J. Vonk, A. T. Sawyer, and A. Fang. 2012. "The Efficacy of Cognitive Behavioral Therapy: A Review of Meta-analyses." *Cognitive Therapy and Research* 36:427–440. doi:10.1007/s10608-012-9476-1.

Horsch, A., I. Jacobs, and K. McKenzie-Harg. 2015. "Cognitive Predictors and Risk Factors of PTSD Following Stillbirth: A Short-Term Longitudinal Study." *Journal of Traumatic Stress* 28 (2): 110–117. doi:10.1002/jts.21997.

Hourani, L., S. Tueller, P. Kizakevich, G. Lewis, L. Strange, B. Weimer, . . . and J. Spira. 2016. "Toward Preventing Post-Traumatic Stress Disorder: Development and Testing of a Pilot Predeployment Stress Inoculation Training Program." *Military Medicine* 181 (9): 1151–1160. doi:10.7205/MILMED-D-15-00192.

Ironson, G., B. Freund, J. Strauss, and J. Williams. 2002. "Comparison of Two Treatments for Traumatic Stress: A Community-Based Study of EMDR and Prolonged Exposure." *Journal of Clinical Psychology* 58 (1): 113–128.

Jaycox, L. H., E. B. Foa, and A. R. Morral. 1998. "Influence of Emotional Engagement and Habituation on Exposure Therapy for PTSD." *Journal of Consulting and Clinical Psychology* 66:185–192.

Kaczkurkin, A. N., and E. B. Foa. 2015. "Cognitive-Behavioral Therapy for Anxiety Disorders: An Update on the Empirical Evidence." *Dialogues in Clinical Neuroscience* 17 (3): 337–346.

Kar, N. 2011. "Cognitive Behavioral Therapy for the Treatment of Post-Traumatic Stress Disorder." *Neuropsychiatric Disease and Treatment* 7:167–181. doi:10.2147/NDT.S10389.

Kavanagh, D. J., S. Freese, J. Andrade, and J. May. (2001). "Effects of Visuospatial Tasks on Desensitization to Emotive Memories." *British Journal of Clinical Psychology* 40 (3): 267–280.

Kehle-Forbes, S. M., M. A. Polusny, R. MacDonald, M. Murdoch, L. A. Meis, and T. J. Wilt. 2013. "A Systematic Review of the Efficacy of Adding Nonexposure Components to Exposure Therapy for Posttraumatic Stress Disorder." *Psychological Trauma: Theory, Practice, and Policy* 5 (4): 317–322. doi:10.1037/a0030040.

Kowalik, J., J. Weller, J. Venter, and D. Drachman. 2011. "Cognitive Behavioral Therapy for the Treatment of Pediatric Posttraumatic Stress Disorder: A

Review and Meta-analysis." *Journal of Behavioral Therapy and Experimental Psychiatry* 42:405–413. doi:10.1016/j.jbtep.2011.02.002.

Krypotos, A-M., M. Effting, M. Kindt, and T. Beckers. 2015. "Avoidance Learning: A Review of Theoretical Models and Recent Developments." *Frontiers in Behavioral Neuroscience* 9 (189). doi:10.3389/fnbeh.2015.00189.

Lee, C. W., H. Gavriel, P. Drummond, J. Richards, and R. Greenwald. 2002. "Treatment of PTSD: Stress Inoculation Training with Prolonged Exposure Compared to EMDR." *Journal of Clinical Psychology* 58:1071–1089.

Lee, C. W., G. Taylor, and P. Drummond. 2006. "The Active Ingredient in EMDR; Is It Traditional Exposure or Dual Focus of Attention?" *Clinical Psychology and Psychotherapy* 13:97–107.

Lee, W. L., and P. Cuijpers. 2013. "A Meta-analysis of the Contribution of Eye Movements in Processing Emotional Memories." *Journal of Behavior Therapy and Experimental Psychiatry* 44:231–239. doi:10.1016/j.jbtep.2012.11.001.

Lenz, A. S., R. Henesy, and K. Callender. 2016. "Effectiveness of Seeking Safety for Co-Occurring Posttraumatic Stress Disorder and Substance Use." *Journal of Counseling and Development* 94 (1): 51–61. doi:10.1002/jcad.12061.

Markowitz, J. C., E. Petkova, Y. Neria, P. E. Van Meter, Y. Zhao, E. Hembree, . . . R. D. Marshall. 2015. "Is Exposure Necessary? A Randomized Clinical Trial of Interpersonal Psychotherapy for PTSD." *American Journal of Psychiatry* 172 (5): 430–440. doi:10.1176/appi.ajp.2014.

McNally, R. J. 1999. "EMDR and Mesmerism: A Comparative Historical Analysis." *Journal of Anxiety Disorders* 13 (1–2): 225–236.

Meichenbaum, D. H. 1993. "Stress Inoculation Training: A 20-Year Update." In *Principles and Practice of Stress Management*, 2nd ed., ed. P. M. Lehrer and R. L. Woolfolk, 373–406. New York: Guilford Press.

Meichenbaum, D. H. 1996. "Stress-Inoculation Training for Coping with Stressors." *Clinical Psychologist* 49:4–7.

Meichenbaum, D. 2007. "Stress Inoculation Training: A Preventative and Treatment Approach." In *Principles and Practice of Stress Management*, 3rd ed., ed. P. M. Lehrer, R. L. Woolfolk, and W. S. Sime, 497–518. New York: Guilford Press.

Morina, N., H. Ijntema, K. Meyerbröker, and P. M. G. Emmelkamp. 2015. "Can Virtual Reality Exposure Therapy Gains Be Generalized to Real-Life? A Meta-analysis of Studies Applying Behavioral Assessments." *Behaviour Research and Therapy* 74:18–24. doi:10.1016/j.brat.2015.08.010.

Mowrer, O. H. 1956. "Two-Factor Learning Theory Reconsidered, with Special Reference to Secondary Reinforcement and the Concept of Habit." *Psychological Review* 63:114–128.

Mowrer, O. H. 1960. *Learning Theory and Behavior*. New York: Wiley.

Nacasch, N., J. D. Huppert, Y. J. Su, Y. Kivity, Y. Dinshtein, R. Yeh, and E. B. Foa. 2015. "Are 60-Minute Prolonged Exposure Sessions with 20-Minute Imaginal Exposure to Traumatic Memories Sufficient to Successfully Treat PTSD? A Randomized Noninferiority Clinical Trial." *Behavior Therapy* 46 (3): 328–341. doi:10.1016/j.beth.2014.12.002.

Najavits, L. M. 2003. "Seeking Safety: A New Psychotherapy for Posttraumatic Stress Disorder and Substance Abuse." In *Trauma and Substance Abuse: Causes, Consequences, and Treatment of Comorbid Disorders*, ed. P. Ouimette and P. Brown, 147–169. Washington, DC: American Psychological Association.

Najavits, L. M. 2017. *Recovery from Trauma, Addiction, or Both*. New York: Guilford Press.

Najavits, L. M., R. D. Weiss, S. R. Shaw, and L. R. Muenz. 1998. "'Seeking Safety': Outcome of a New Cognitive-Behavioral Psychotherapy for Women with Posttraumatic Stress Disorder and Substance Dependence." *Journal of Traumatic Stress* 11:437–456.

National Institute for Health and Care Excellence. 2005. "Posttraumatic Stress Disorder: Management." March. https://www.nice.org.uk/guidance/cg26. (Updated December 2018 to https://www.nice.org.uk/guidance/ng116.)

Newman, C. F. 2013. *Core Competencies in Cognitive-Behavioral Therapy*. New York: Routledge.

North, M. M., S. M. North, and J. R. Coble. 1998. "Virtual Reality Therapy: An Effective Treatment for the Fear of Public Speaking." *International Journal of Virtual Reality* 3:1–6.

Ozer, E. J., S. Best, T. L. Lipzey, and D. S. Weiss. 2003. "Predictors of Posttraumatic Stress Disorder and Symptoms in Adults: A Meta-analysis." *Psychological Bulletin* 129 (1): 52–73.

Parsons, T. D., and A. A. Rizzo. 2008. "Affective Outcomes of Virtual Reality Exposure Therapy for Anxiety and Specific Phobias: A Meta-analysis." *Journal of Behavior Therapy and Experimental Psychiatry* 39:250–261.

Perkins, B. R., and C. C. Rouanzoin. 2002. "A Critical Evaluation of Current Views Regarding Eye Movement Desensitization and Reprocessing (EMDR): Clarifying Points of Confusion." *Journal of Clinical Psychology* 58 (1): 77–97.

Pitman, R. K., B. Altman, E. Greenwald, R. E. Longpre, M. L. Macklin, R. E. Poire, and G. S. Steketee. 1991. "Psychiatric Complications During Flooding Therapy for Posttraumatic Stress Disorder." *Journal of Clinical Psychiatry* 52 (1): 17–20.

Ponniah, K., and S. D. Hollon. 2009. "Empirically Supported Psychological Treatments for Adult Acute Stress Disorder and Posttraumatic Stress Disorder: A Review." *Depression and Anxiety* 26:1086–1109.

Powers, M. B., and P. M. G. Emmelkamp. 2008. "Virtual Reality Exposure Therapy for Anxiety Disorders: A Meta-analysis." *Journal of Anxiety Disorders* 22:561–569.

Rachman, S. 1980. "Emotional Processing." *Behavior Research and Therapy* 18:51–60.

Rauch, M., A. Sheila, A. Eftekhari, and J. I. Ruzek. 2012. "Review of Exposure Therapy: A Gold Standard for PTSD Treatment." *Journal of Rehabilitation Research and Development* 49 (5): 679–687.

Rauch, S., and E. Foa. 2006. "Emotional Processing Theory (EPT) and Exposure Therapy for PTSD." *Journal of Contemporary Psychotherapy* 36:61–65. doi:10.1007/s10879-006-9008-y.

Reger, G. M., and G. A. Gahm. 2008. "Virtual Reality Exposure Therapy for Active Duty Soldiers." *Journal of Clinical Psychology: In Session* 64:940–946.

Renfrey, G., and C. R. Spates. 1994. "Eye Movement Desensitization: A Partial Dismantling Study." *Journal of Behavior Therapy and Experimental Psychiatry* 25 (3): 231–239.

Resick, P. A., T. E. Galovski, M. O. Uhlmansiek, C. D. Scher, G. A. Clum, and Y. Yoing-Xu. 2008. "A Randomized Clinical Trial to Dismantle Components of Cognitive Processing Therapy for Posttraumatic Stress Disorder for Female Victims of Interpersonal Violence." *Journal of Consulting and Clinical Psychology* 76 (2): 243–258. doi:10.1037/0022-006X.76.2.243.

Resick, P. A., C. M. Monson, and K. M. Chard. 2006. *Cognitive Processing Therapy: Veteran/Military Version.* October. http://alrest.org/pdf/CPT_Manual_-_Modified_for_PRRP%282%29.pdf.

Resick, P. A., C. M. Monson, and K. M. Chard. 2017. *Cognitive Processing Therapy for PTSD: A Comprehensive Manual.* New York: Guilford Press.

Resick, P. A., and M. K. Schnicke. 1992. "Cognitive Processing Therapy for Sexual Assault Victims." *Journal of Consulting and Clinical Psychology* 60:748–756.

Rizzo, A., J. Cukor, M. Gerardi, S. Alley, C. Reist, M. Roy, . . . J. Difede. 2015. "Virtual Reality Exposure for PTSD Due to Military Combat and

Terrorist Attacks." *Journal of Contemporary Psychotherapy* 45 (4): 225–264. doi:10.1007/s10879-015-9306-3.

Rizzo, A., J. Pair, K. Graap, B. Manson, P. J. McNerney, B. Wiederhold, . . . and J. Spira. 2006. "A Virtual Reality Exposure Therapy Application for Iraq War Military Personnel with Post-Traumatic Stress Disorder: From Training to Toy to Treatment." In *NATO Advanced Research Workshop on Novel Approaches to the Diagnosis and Treatment of Posttraumatic Stress Disorder*, ed. M. Roy, 235–250. Washington, DC: IOS Press.

Rizzo, A., and R. Shilling. 2018. "Clinical Virtual Reality Tools to Advance the Prevention, Assessment, and Treatment of PTSD." *European Journal of PsychoTraumatology* 8:1–20. doi:10.1080/20008198.2017.1414560.

Rodenburg, R., A. Benjamin, C. de Roos, A. M. Meijer, and G. J. Stams. 2009. "Efficacy of EMDR in Children: A Meta-analysis." *Clinical Psychology Review* 29 (70): 599–606.

Rothbaum, B. O. 2006. "Virtual Reality Exposure Therapy." In *Pathological Anxiety: Emotional Processing in Etiology and Treatment*, ed. Rothbaum, 227–244. New York: Guilford Press.

Rothbaum, B. O., M. C. Astin, and E. Marsteller. 2005. "Prolonged Exposure Versus Eye Movement Desensitization and Reprocessing (EMDR) for PTSD Rape Victims." *Journal of Traumatic Stress* 18:607–616.

Rothbaum, B. O., L. Hodges, R. Alarcon, D. Ready, F. Shahar, K. Graap, . . . D. Baltzell. 1999. "Virtual Reality Exposure Therapy for PTSD Vietnam Veterans: A Case Study." *Journal of Traumatic Stress* 12 (2): 263–271.

Rothbaum, B. O., L. F. Hodges, D. Ready, K. Graap, and R. D. Alarcon. 2001. "Virtual Reality Exposure Therapy for Vietnam Veterans with Posttraumatic Stress Disorder." *Journal of Clinical Psychiatry* 62:617–622.

Rothbaum, B. O., A. M. Ruef, B. T. Litz, H. Han, and L. Hodges. 2003. "Virtual Reality Exposure Therapy of Combat-Related PTSD: A Case Study Using Psychophysiological Indicators of Outcome." *Journal of International Psychotherapy: An International Quarterly* 17:163–178.

Schnyder, U., A. Ehlers, T. Elbert, E. B. Foa, B. P. R. Gersons, P. Resick, . . . and M. Cloitre. 2015. "Psychotherapies for PTSD: What Do They Have in Common?" *European Journal of Psychotraumatology* 6:28186. doi:10.3402/ejpt .v6.28186.

Scott, J., and A. Freeman. 2010. "Beck's Cognitive Therapy." In *Cognitive and Behavioral Theories in Clinical Practice*, ed. N. Kazantzis, M. A. Reinecke, and A. Freeman, 28–75. New York: Guilford Press.

Seidler, G. H., and F. E. Wagner. 2006. "Comparing the Efficacy of EMDR and Trauma-Focused Cognitive-Behavioral Therapy in the Treatment of PTSD: A Meta-analytic Study." *Psychological Medicine* 36:1515–1522.

Seitz, C. A., S. Poyrazli, M. A. Harrisson, T. Flickinger, and M. Turkson. 2014. "Virtual Reality Exposure Therapy for Military Veterans with Posttraumatic Stress Disorder: A Systematic Review." *New School Psychology Bulletin* 11 (1): 15–29.

Serino, S., S. Triberti, D. Villani, P. Cipresso, A. Gaggioli, and G. Riva. 2014. "Toward a Validation of Cyber-Interventions for Stress Disorders Based on Stress Inoculation Training: A Systematic Review." *Virtual Reality* 18 (1): 73–87. doi:10.1007/s10055-013-0237-6.

Shapiro, F. 1989a. "Efficacy of the Eye Movement Desensitization Procedure in the Treatment of Traumatic Memories." *Journal of Traumatic Stress* 2 (2): 199–223.

Shapiro, F. 1989b. "Eye Movement Desensitization: A New Treatment for Post-Traumatic Stress Disorder." *Journal of Behavior Therapy and Experimental Psychiatry* 20:211–217.

Shapiro, F. 2001. *Eye Movement Desensitization and Reprocessing: Basic Principles, Protocols, and Procedures,* 2nd ed. New York: Guilford Press.

Shapiro, F. 2007. "EMDR and Case Conceptualization from an Adaptive Information Processing Perspective." In *Handbook of EMDR and Family Therapy Processes*, ed. F. Shapiro, F. Kaslow, and L. Maxfield, 3–36. New York: Wiley.

Shapiro, F. 2018. *Eye Movement Desensitization and Reprocessing (EMDR) Therapy: Basic Principles, Protocols and Procedures,* 3rd ed. New York: Guilford Press.

Sheynin, J., C. Shind, M. Radell, Y. Ebanks-Williams, M. W. Gilbertson, K. D. Beck, and C. E. Myers. 2017. "Greater Avoidance Behavior in Individuals with Posttraumatic Stress Disorder Symptoms." *Stress: The Journal on the Biology of Stress* 20 (3): 285–293. doi:10.1080/10253890.2017.1309523.

Spates, C. R. and S. Rubin. 2012. "Empirically supported psychological treatments: EMDR". In *The Oxford Handbook of Traumatic Stress Disorders*, ed. J. G. Beck and D. M. Sloan, 449–462. New York: Oxford University Press.

Stickgold, R. 2007. "Of Sleep, Memories and Trauma." *Nature Neuroscience* 10 (5): 540–542.

Sundel, M., and S. S. Sundel. 2018. *Behavior Change in the Human Services.* 6th ed. Thousand Oaks, CA: Sage.

Tang, B., Q. Deng, D. Glik, J. Dong, and L. Zhang. 2017. "A Meta-Analysis of Risk Factors for Post-Traumatic Stress Disorder (PTSD) in Adults and Children

After Earthquakes." *International Journal of Environmental Research and Public Health* 14:1–20. doi:10.3390/ijerph14121537.

Tripodi, S. J., A. M. Mennicke, S. A. McCarter, and K. Ropes. 2017. "Evaluating Seeking Safety for Women in Prison: A Randomized Controlled Trial." *Research on Social Work Practice—Online First.* doi:10.1177/1049731517706550.

Van Etten, M. L., and S. Taylor. 1998. "Comparative Efficacy for Posttraumatic Stress Disorders: A Meta-analysis." *Clinical Psychology and Psychotherapy* 5 (3): 126–144.

van Minnen, A., and E. B. Foa. 2006. "The Effect of Imaginal Exposure Length on Outcome of Treatment for PTSD." *Journal of Traumatic Stress* 19 (4): 427–438.

Vonk, E., P. Bordnick, and K. Graap. 2006. "Cognitive-Behavioral Therapy for Posttraumatic Stress Disorder: An Evidence-Based Approach." In *Foundations of Evidence-Based Social Work Practice*, eds. A. R. Roberts and K. R. Yeager, 323–335. New York: Oxford University Press.

Walter, K. H., B. D. Dickstein, S. M. Barnes, and K. M. Chard. 2014. "Comparing Effectiveness of CPT to CPT-C Among U.S. Veterans in Interdisciplinary Residential PTSD/TBI Treatment Program." *Journal of Traumatic Stress* 27:438–445. doi:10.1002/jts21934.

Wild, J., K. V. Smith, E. Thompson, F. Bear, M. J. J. Lommen, and A. Ehlers. 2016. "A Prospective Study of Pre-Trauma Risk Factors for Post-Traumatic Stress Disorder and Depression." *Psychological Medicine* 46:2571–2582. doi:10.1017/S0033291716000532.

Wolpe, J. 1990. *The Practice of Behavior Therapy.* 4th ed. New York: Pergamon.

Zhou, X., X. Wu, F. Fu, and Y. An. 2015. "Core Belief Challenge and Rumination as Predictors of PTSD and PTG Among Adolescent Survivors of the Wenchuan Earthquake." *Psychological Trauma: Theory, Research, Practice, and Policy* 7 (4): 391–397. doi:10.1037/tra0000031.

3

Psychoanalytic Theory, Part 1

> *JERROLD R. BRANDELL*

BEGINNING WITH THE CLASSICAL formulations of Sigmund Freud, the concept of trauma has gradually attained a superordinate status in the psychoanalytic literature. Indeed, the idea of trauma runs as a common thread across generational and ideological lines in psychoanalysis and has been addressed by every major psychoanalytic school, from Freud and Breuer's earliest forays into the treatment of hysteria to the relational theories of contemporary psychoanalysis. In this chapter, we will begin by exploring Freud's conceptions of trauma, paying close attention to his views on hysteria, the concept of danger situations, and the ego's signal anxiety and defensive functions. This will be followed by a discussion of the trauma in relation to object loss. Next, the chapter will explore in depth the centrality of trauma as a theme in the work of Otto Rank and Sandor Ferenczi, two of Freud's earliest disciples. We will then turn to the literature associated with British object-relations theories, examining the contributions of such writers as W. R. D. Fairbairn, D. W. Winnicott, and Michael Balint. Finally, views of trauma associated with psychoanalytic self psychology and the seminal writings of Heinz Kohut and his followers will be discussed and illustrated through the use of a brief clinical vignette.[1]

TRAUMA DEFINED

Before discussing various psychoanalytic contributions to our understanding of trauma, it may be helpful to define the term. In everyday discourse, the word *trauma* is often used more or less interchangeably with *stress*, which has led to a gradual erosion of meaning and clarity. Difficult writing assignments, excessive workload, anxiety-generating conversations—virtually anything that causes some measure of stress may now be popularly characterized as traumatic. Such generic usage has led to a trivialization of the concept, but it has also led to a blurring of the distinction between traumatic events and traumatic response (Allen 2001). A somewhat more clinically useful definition, which appears in *Webster's New College Dictionary*, defines *trauma* as "an emotional shock that creates substantial and lasting damage to the psychological development of the individual, generally leading to neurosis; something that severely jars the mind or emotions" (1995, 1173). Such a definition is more in keeping with psychoanalytic conceptions of trauma; it establishes that trauma is not an event but a response to an event and, further, that it represents an enduring adverse response to an event (Allen 2001, 6).

In their glossary of psychoanalytic terminology and concepts, Moore and Fine offer a definition that is arguably more compatible with classical and object-relational ideas. They consider trauma to represent

> the disruption or breakdown that occurs when the psychic apparatus is suddenly presented with stimuli, from either within or without, that are too powerful to be dealt with or assimilated in the usual way. A postulated stimulus barrier or protective shield is breached, and the ego is overwhelmed and loses its mediating capacity. A state of helplessness results, ranging from total apathy and withdrawal to an emotional storm accompanied by disorganized behavior bordering on panic. Signs of autonomic dysfunction are frequently present.
>
> (Moore and Fine 1990, 199)

Other psychoanalytic writers have made useful distinctions between "relatively impersonal trauma" (e.g., natural disasters, technological disasters, automobile accidents) and "interpersonal trauma" (e.g., criminal assault, rape, sexual harassment, war, political violence), arguing that traumas associated with the latter group are, generally speaking, far more problematic and likely to culminate in serious mental disorders than those in the former group (Allen 2001). Other chapters of this book discuss some of these topics in substantially greater depth. This chapter's focus is limited to psychoanalytic conceptions of trauma.

FREUDIAN CONCEPTIONS OF TRAUMA

As suggested in chapter 1, foundational psychoanalytic conceptions of trauma are traceable to Sigmund Freud's ideas regarding the treatment of

19th cen.

Time line

Freud

Breuer

hysteria, which are rooted in the seminal *Studies on Hysteria*, a work he coauthored with Josef Breuer more than 125 years ago ([1893–1895] 1961). In the introductory chapter, Freud and Breuer quickly established the importance of "external events" in giving rise to and shaping hysterical symptoms. At times, the connection between a particular precipitating event and the outbreak of hysterical illness was relatively uncomplicated to discern, as the following example illustrates: "We may take as a very commonplace instance a painful emotion arising during a meal but suppressed at the time, and then producing nausea and vomiting which persists for months in the form of hysterical vomiting" ([1893–1895] 1961, 4).

At other times, Freud and Breuer asserted, the connection between the external event and the appearance of symptoms was more symbolic in nature, and therefore somewhat more challenging to deconstruct. Significantly, however, Freud and Breuer made a clear connection between hysteria and the traumatic or "war" neuroses, suggesting that the common element in both is the affect of fright. In fact, they argued that "any experience which calls up distressing affects—such as fright, anxiety, shame, or physical pain—may operate as a trauma" ([1893–1895] 1961, 6).

Freud and Breuer also focused on the importance of "abreaction" or catharsis as a means of discharging such pent-up affects. Relief from hysterical symptoms, they wrote, could be achieved via the "cathartic method," a procedure originally developed by Josef Breuer, the aim of which was to facilitate release of suppressed emotions. Many psychoanalytic historians have observed that the early conceptions of trauma and its treatment via the cathartic method relied heavily on principles of psychological functioning rooted in the physicalistic science of Freud's era, most notably the writings of Gustav Fechner. Accumulating psychic energy or tensions is presumed to require "discharge" in the interest of maintaining the organism's *constancy*, a corollary of which is that humans seek to avoid unpleasure or eliminate it via the most expedient route. In the case of hysterical illness, Freud and Breuer hypothesized, abreaction of the psychic tensions had for various reasons simply not occurred, leading to a "'damming up" of psychic energy. In Freud's early view, such "dammed up energy," or *libido*, a term he later adopted, needed to be released for the patient's symptoms to be ameliorated.

FREUD'S EXPERIMENTATION WITH HYPNOSIS

Although Freud was at first highly enthusiastic about the beneficial effects of hypnotic treatment with his hysterical patients, he soon discovered that the initial symptom relief the patients reported could not be sustained over time. This, however, is but one of several reasons advanced to explain his gradual disillusionment with the technique. It has been suggested that Freud's lack of skill in using hypnotic techniques may have been a factor (Erika Fromm, personal communication, 1997). Ernest Jones has underscored Freud's retrospective claim, made some time after his decision to discontinue hypnotic treatment of his hysterical patients, that hypnosis obscured the patient's resistance. The basic problem with hypnosis was not that it did away with the resistance bur rather that resistance was circumnavigated; thus, such treatment could yield only imperfect data and temporary success (Jones 1955).

Fromm and Nash offer a somewhat different explanation. Modeling his work after that of his mentors, Charcot and Bernheim, Freud relied on what have been termed authoritarian techniques for inducing the hypnotic trance state in his patients. He frequently would place his hand on the patient's forehead, exerting slight pressure, or even hold the patient's head between his palms and give the command to sleep. In his work with Emmy von N, considered a paradigmatic illustration of the dynamic treatment of hysteria, Freud "sternly positioned his index finger in front of the patient's face and called out 'Sleep!'" (Freud and Breuer [1893–1895] 1961, cited in Fromm and Nash 1997, 16). Fromm and Nash observe that although such techniques for trance induction seem peculiar by contemporary standards for hypnotherapeutic practice, they would have been regarded as conventional among physicians in Freud's day (Freud and Breuer [1893–1895] 1961, cited in Fromm and Nash 1997, 16). They maintain that Freud turned away from hypnosis because the technique as he used it "had more to do with coercion than understanding" (Fromm and Nash 1997, 16). The notion of treating a patient coercively to obtain data was at variance with Freud's scientific ideal, that of detached neutrality.

At about the same time that Freud gave up hypnotic treatment in favor of a new clinical approach that emphasized such critical elements as free association, interpretation, and transference, he also reluctantly relinquished what is now commonly referred to as the "seduction hypothesis." According to Freud's original seduction theory, a veritable occurrence of sexual molestation perpetrated on the child by an adult was presumed to have taken place, although Freud finally replaced this theory with a more purely psychological one. He concluded that such reports, in many if not most instances, were functions of unconscious, intrapsychically based desires and conflicts rather than based on veridical, historically based, experienced events. Nevertheless, even years later, Freud continued to believe that "seduction has retained a certain significance for etiology," observing that in the cases of Katharina and Fraulein Rosalia H, the patients had been sexually assaulted by their fathers (Gay 1988).

TRAUMA, DANGER SITUATIONS, AND THE FUNCTION OF THE DEFENSES

Freud's ideas about the nature and mechanism of psychic trauma evolved gradually. Although as I have already suggested Freud's early understanding of trauma depended to a considerable degree on actual, experienced events, he ultimately came to understand and define trauma quite differently. When he wrote about the topic in 1917, he observed, "We apply it to an experience which within a short period of time presents the mind with an increase of stimulus too powerful to be dealt with or worked off in the normal way . . . [thus resulting] . . . in permanent disturbances of the manner in which the energy operates" ([1917] 1961e, 275).

However, less than ten years later, in his seminal *Inhibitions, Symptoms, and Anxiety* ([1926] 1961c), Freud's emphasis had changed. First, he further clarified the difference "between anxiety as a direct and automatic reaction to a trauma and anxiety as a *signal* of the danger of the approach of such a trauma" (80, italics added). With his new emphasis on the "signal anxiety" function of the ego, Freud was able to offer a more satisfying explanation for how traumatic states might be averted or prevented, namely, through the organism's avoidance of the helplessness and incapacitating anxiety associated with traumatic states. This in turn depended on the organism's capacity to give itself a small degree of anxiety to take expedient action (i.e., signal anxiety). Second, Freud seemed less focused on trauma as representing a redistribution of psychic energy and more interested in the ego's role in preventing or mitigating such trauma, a development tied to the expanded and more fully articulated conception of the ego and its functions presented just three years earlier, in *The Ego and the Id* ([1923] 1961b). Finally, Freud elaborated on the traumatic potential of various normative, developmental experiences, which have also been termed "danger situations."

Freud's discovery that childhood wishes were regularly associated with anxiety (i.e., fear) led him to conclude that such fears fall into one of four basic categories, each representing a specific danger situation. The earliest and most basic anxiety involved the loss of the object (mother or primary caretaker); the next, developmentally speaking, arose from the child's fear of losing the object's love; the third involved the fear of punishment, particularly by genital mutilation/castration; and the last developed from the internalized fear of one's own moral precepts or conscience, which depended on the establishment of a functioning superego. According to Freud's classical theory, when a wish comes to be associated with any of these dangers, the impulse toward enactment leads to a dramatic increase in anxiety. Such anxiety may increase to traumatic levels without the supervention of reassuring caregivers or without other, independent measures. In Freud's view, the child gradually learns ways to diminish these anxieties, which are termed *defense operations* or simply *defenses*. Perhaps the most important of these is repression, which is sometimes referred to as the *paradigmatic defense*. Repression involves a shifting of attention away from tempting but dangerous wishes, effectively barring them from consciousness. Freud, his disciples, and several succeeding generations of psychoanalysts eventually identified at least twenty-two major and twenty-six minor defenses (Laughlin 1979). In Freud's estimation, however, no defense is fully effective in warding off anxiety, and this is arguably most true in the instance of anxiety that stems from a traumatic experience. Finally, although any specific defense or constellation of defenses may be employed in the service of protecting an individual from the incapacitating anxiety associated with a traumatic experience, the more "primitive" dissociative defenses (i.e., depersonalization, derealization) are the most frequently encountered in clinical work with traumatized patients.

In *Studies on Hysteria*, Freud wrote of a "splitting of the mind" following a psychic trauma, a term that was eventually replaced by the more familiar *dissociation*. Dissociation is defined as an altered state of consciousness designed to protect a subject from experiences of an overwhelmingly traumatic nature. When the experience involves distortions of the subject's bodily self-experience only, the term *depersonalization* is sometimes used; when the distortions involve apprehension of external stimuli, the term *derealization* may be employed. *Fugue states* and *hysterical conversion reactions* are also dissociative in nature. Early childhood trauma, Freud and Breuer concluded as early as 1893, led to a repeated overuse of dissociation, to the point at which it became the "individual's primary psychological defense, manifesting itself in dramatic alterations in the experience of self and world" (Fromm and Nash 1997, 221).

OBJECT LOSS, GRIEF, AND MOURNING

As suggested in the preceding section, the loss of an object constitutes the most significant form of early anxiety and under certain circumstances may be considered traumatic. At the same time, it is recognized that mourning, the process through which psychic equilibrium is reestablished after an object loss, is incompatible with the experience of trauma; indeed, successful mourning carries with it the great likelihood that a loss will not be experienced as an enduring trauma. Before discussing traumatic loss, however, it may be useful to clarify the difference between traumatic loss and the mourning process associated with normal bereavement.

Mourning is most often initiated by the loss through death of a (real) object but may also occur in connection with other forms of loss, for example, the loss of a limb or other body part, physical abilities, one's belief in an ideal, or one's freedom (Moore and Fine 1990). Aggrieved individuals report a predominant mood of pain and exhibit a loss of interest in the outside world. They are preoccupied with memories of the lost object and are largely incapable of making new emotional investments (Moore and Fine 1990). The capacity of an individual to complete the process of mourning is affected by a range of factors, such as the level of object maturity the individual has achieved, the capacity to tolerate painful affects, how successful the individual is in regulating self-esteem, how dependent he or she has been on the object, and the exact circumstances of the loss (Moore and Fine 1990). Moreover, mourning is believed to occur in stages and, when successful, leads to a healing of the ego and the restoration of psychological well-being. Psychoanalytic authors have suggested that the work of mourning includes three phases, which unfold in an epigenetic fashion:

- Understanding, accepting, and coping with the loss and its circumstances
- The mourning proper, which involves withdrawal of attachments to and identifications with the lost object (decathexis)

- Resumption of an emotional life in harmony with one's level of maturity, which frequently involves establishing new relationships (recathexis)

(Moore and Fine 1990, 122)

But what of traumatic loss? When is a loss traumatic, and which features are likely to culminate in such an experience of loss? Although traumatic loss is certainly possible in adulthood, developmental immaturity and reliance on objects increases the potential for loss of a meaningful object to trigger a traumatic reaction in childhood. Put somewhat differently, children and adolescents who have suffered the loss of a parent or other important caregiver are on that account alone more likely to experience the loss as traumatic, other factors being equal. The circumstances of the loss (e.g., prolonged illness versus sudden death from natural causes or parental suicide) can also have great significance. Nevertheless, there is a certain danger in applying this probability to all losses occurring in childhood or adolescence. Anna Freud observes:

> Whenever I am tempted to call an event in a child's or adult's life "traumatic," I shall ask myself some further questions. Do I mean the event was upsetting, that it was significant for altering the course of further development; that it was pathogenic? Or do I really mean traumatic in the strict sense of the word, i.e., shattering, devastating, causing internal disruption, by putting ego functioning and ego mediation out of action?
>
> (1967, 242)

The general utility of Anna Freud's admonition notwithstanding, there is now general consensus in the field of child psychoanalysis that the death of one's parent in childhood or adolescence is an event of such magnitude that it taxes even the most emotionally resilient child's capacities (Altschul and Pollock 1988). Such a loss may indeed be "shattering" and "devastating," to use Anna Freud's litmus test, despite the fact that the capacity of children to mourn a loss is now generally acknowledged as possible. However, various factors tend to complicate and derail the mourning process in children and adolescents.

As mentioned, the child is naturally dependent on the parent for continuous support and assistance in negotiating the course of development. However, in many instances, the surviving partner, owing to that person's own preoccupation with the loss, may be less available for the child to lean on. Families may also deal quite differently with the death of a family member. In some families, grieving children may be admonished to be strong for the surviving parent, or there may be an expectation that sad affects should be expressed during the period of acute mourning but not later, as though the mourning process were well defined and finite. Less than ideal child-care arrangements may be forced on the child, and so forth. Although none of these variables alone may be responsible for a pathological mourning process, the child's greater vulnerability to disruptions in cognitive, affective, and social development certainly increases that probability. In one psychoanalytic author's opinion, parental "death is almost always traumatic in the disruption it brings to the ongoing life of the family and the flooding of the child's experiencing and integrative capacities" (Samuels 1990, 22).

OTTO RANK AND BIRTH TRAUMA

Otto Rank (1884–1939) was one of Freud's earliest adherents and is remembered by psychoanalytic historians for several important contributions, including his writings on the human will as a creative force (Rank 1945) and on the process of termination, as well as for an early, joint undertaking with Sandor Ferenczi widely regarded as a precursor to later efforts to shorten the duration of psychoanalytic treatment (Ferenczi and Rank 1925). But the work with which Rank's name is almost reflexively identified is his 1924 book, *The Trauma of Birth*.

In this work, Rank hypothesized that the experience of birth involved a physical trauma and called forth a very basic form of anxiety in the human infant. Birth is traumatic, in Rank's view, both because it brings about an abrupt end to the nirvana-like intrauterine state and also because the neonate is flooded by stimuli that cannot be mastered. As such, the trauma of birth is understood to represent primal anxiety. There are two basic outcomes in the effort to master such massive anxiety, according to Rank. The first, a fixation of the infant's desire to return to the safety of the womb, results in neurosis, whereas the second, which is adaptive and progressive, culminates in creative productivity (Menaker 1982).

Freud initially received Rank's work with interest and seemed willing to acknowledge that birth represented the earliest anxiety state. Freud's 1923 footnote to the Little Hans case also reveals a certain acceptance of Rank's thesis. In it, he states, "Rank's view of the effects of the trauma of birth seems to throw special light on the predisposition to anxiety/hysteria which is so strong in childhood" (Freud [1909] 1961a, 116, note 2).

However, the Rankian birth trauma also represented a fundamental challenge to Freud's ideas regarding the primacy of the drives. Rank was aware of this problem and made some effort to reconcile his view and Freud's by suggesting that castration anxiety was in effect a later phase of the anxiety at birth. But Freud and other psychoanalysts of the time may well have interpreted this differently because Rank's theory seemed to privilege and elevate the mother's contribution to psychological development at the expense of the father's (Gay 1988). Detailed consideration of Rank's ultimate rejection of classical psychoanalytic formulations and, more particularly, of his relationship with Freud is beyond the scope of this chapter, although a brief summary of Freud's views on Rank's thesis may nevertheless be useful as we consider the fate of Rank's ideas regarding trauma.

As suggested above, Freud seemed willing to consider the experience of birth to represent a prototype for later experiences of anxiety—the first situation of danger, as it were. He observes that psychoanalysis had already traced the developmental line connecting "the first danger-situation and determinant of anxiety with all the later ones, and . . . that they all retain a common quality in so far as they signify in a certain sense a separation from the mother—at first only in a biological sense, next as a direct loss of the object and later as a loss of the object incurred indirectly" ([1926] 1961c, 151). Moreover, in the years prior to the publication of Rank's book, Freud had himself observed that "the act of birth is the first experience of anxiety and therefore source and model of the affect of anxiety" ([1900] 1961d, 400–401, note 3). However, he was highly critical of Rank's contention that people become neurotic as a direct consequence of their inability to abreact the strength of the trauma experienced in the act of being born and, further, of Rank's view that all subsequent affects of anxiety constitute an effort to abreact the trauma more and more fully. Freud by this time had largely discarded the idea of abreaction as a means of overcoming traumas, based on his earlier failures in treating hysterics hypnotically and via the cathartic method. Although he accepted the idea that powerful affects present at birth serve as a bridge to subsequent danger situations, he rejected the notion that all neuroses are traceable to one original source of trauma.

Although few today accept Rank's thesis as it was originally conceived and formulated, the translation of his ideas regarding the literal, physical

trauma of birth to more metaphorical language regarding the universal experience of separation may offer the theory new meaning. Some writers have
asserted that Rank's birth-trauma theory, to be understood correctly, must
be approached from the vantage point of Rank's other, later contributions.
Rank, Menaker believes, was really writing about the process of separation
and individuation; in effect, his work portrayed the "wish for the oneness
of the womb, with its lack of differentiation, and the driving growth toward
separateness, uniqueness, and individuation of the ego" (Menaker 1982, 64).
In fact, in certain important respects, Rank's ideas adumbrate important
theoretical developments in object-relations theory that occurred many years
after the publication of his book about the birth trauma.

Although Freud and other psychoanalysts of his time rejected Rank's
notion of the birth trauma, his ideas acquired new life in such nondynamic
therapies as Janov's primal therapy and other body-centered psychotherapies.
Janov's primal therapy enjoyed some popularity in the 1970s and 1980s. It is
based on the idea that childhood trauma creates such unbearable pain that
individuals seek escape through neurosis. Through a treatment process that
bears an unmistakable similarity to the cathartic method of Breuer and
Freud, patients are encouraged to undergo "primals." Although Janov has
minimized his ideological debt to Rank, the idea of traumatic birth does
seem to be at the center of Janov's theory, as is the necessity for therapeutic
rebirth via an abreactive process.

SANDOR FERENCZI AND "THE CONFUSION OF TONGUES"

The Hungarian psychoanalyst Sandor Ferenczi (1873–1933) is rightly
regarded as one of Freud's most gifted protégés, and his contributions to the
psychoanalytic movement, particularly in its early years, are arguably second
in importance only to those of Freud himself (Aron and Harris 1993). However, by the early 1930s, Ferenczi had fallen into disfavor with Freud and the
mainstream psychoanalytic movement for several reasons, among them his
experimentation with brief psychoanalytic treatment, the perception that he
promoted dangerous transference regressions in his patients and tried to
cure them through love, his idea of mutual analysis, and, undoubtedly, his
highly ambivalent and tempestuous relationship with Freud and other members of the Freudian inner circle. Another significant area of contention
between Ferenczi and Freud arose in the 1920s and early 1930s, when Ferenczi

rehabilitated Freud's earlier notions about the relationship of trauma to childhood sexual seduction, a theoretical position from which Freud and others in the psychoanalytic movement had taken great pains to distance themselves years earlier.

By the mid-1920s, with the publication of such works as *The Ego and the Id* (Freud [1923] 1961b) and Abraham's paper about libidinal development (Abraham [1924] 1948), psychoanalysis had not only privileged the primacy of the instincts as a determinant of human psychological life but also charted the course of the libido, viewing such development as a phylogenetically determined process, leading inexorably from an early oral stage to mature, adult, genital sexuality. It has been suggested that Freud gave greater acknowledgment to the role of the environment in *The Ego and the Id* than in earlier publications. Nevertheless, even in that work, forces external to the developing infant still pale in comparison to the overriding importance accorded to purely intrapsychic processes. During the same period, Ferenczi began to oppose these ideas as well as others regarding the pathogenesis of neurotic illness, and he actually restored Freud's ideas about sexual seduction and trauma to a central place in his own theory of neurosis (Van Haute and Geyskens 2004).

Ferenczi's own theory of trauma had evolved over a period of years as he paid closer attention to the "child" in his adult patients, or, put somewhat differently, to the role of repetition, regression, and acting out in the treatment situation, as well as to how such phenomena could be used to clinical advantage (Dupont 1993). Ultimately, Ferenczi returned to the idea that actual experiences of trauma played a significant role in the creation of neurotic disturbances (Ferenczi [1930] 1999, 1932). He emphasized that two phases were involved in the production of a trauma: first, there must be a traumatic event, which may or may not be inherently pathogenic, and second, the event must be subject to denial by significant people in the child's life, most notably the child's mother. The denial of the traumatic event, in Ferenczi's estimation, represented the most important pathogenic component (Dupont 1993).

These ideas were further elaborated on in Ferenczi's final published paper, "The Confusion of Tongues Between Adults and the Child" ([1933] 1955). It is this paper, perhaps to a greater degree than any other single contribution of Ferenczi, that is responsible for the renewal of interest in his ideas by the current generation of relational psychoanalysts. In it, Ferenczi asserts that the pathogenicity of trauma, particularly when it is of a sexual nature, cannot be overestimated. It may be useful to comment more specifically on Ferenczi's use of the phrase "confusion of tongues." According to Van Haute and Geyskens (2004):

> Before the trauma, there exists a tie of love between the child and the adult. According to Ferenczi, this intimate relationship is accompanied by all kinds of sexual and oedipal behavior. In play, the child acts out the role of the adult, imitating the adult. In this manner, the relationship between child and adult may assume an erotic form. But Ferenczi emphasizes that for the child, this intimacy remains on the level of *tenderness, imagination and play*. This cannot be said of the adult partner, who interprets as sexual that which the child expresses in the language of tenderness. In that case, the adult considers child's play as sexual desires. . . . In this manner, a confusion of tongues between the child's language of tenderness and the (adult's) language of passion is produced.
>
> (90, emphasis in the original)

The adult responds with sexual passion to the child's desire for tenderness. Insofar as the child has no real capacity to understand or respond to the sexuality of the adult, he or she experiences powerlessness; the child is unable to protest against this misguided interpretation of his or her aim-inhibited, loving feelings. Once confronted with the adult's mature, frankly sexual behavior and the adult's "overpowering force and authority," which are experienced as a violent subjugation of the child's will, children demonstrate physical and moral helplessness. The encounter causes massive anxiety, which at a certain juncture "compels them to subordinate themselves like automata to the will of the aggressor, to divine each one of his desires and to gratify these" (Ferenczi [1933] 1955, 162). The child's identification with the aggressor, including the introjection of the adult's guilt feelings, then occurs, according to Ferenczi.

The trauma is typically compounded by the denial that follows the act. The act is denied not only by the perpetrator but also by others in the child's environment. Adults react with a combination of denial, disavowal, and incomprehension and punish the child for what are believed to be fabrications or distortions of the perpetrator's benevolence. Or even more insidiously, there is no reaction at all, and the child's efforts to describe the trauma are met with silence. Through the process of introjection, the child takes in all these various reactions by the adults around him or her. The child identifies not only with the perpetrator's desire, aggression, and projected guilt but also with the denial and silence of the other adults. Significantly, it is through such identificatory processes that the child strives to maintain a connection to the adults on whom he or she depends (Ferenczi [1933] 1955; Van Haute and Geyskens 2004).

Ferenczi concludes his paper with thoughts about the outcome of such experiences in the child, the clinical consequences of frank sexual abuse. He first speaks of the development of a "precocious maturity," which today might be termed premature sexuality. Ferenczi also explains clinical observations that sexually traumatized patients may have little if any memory of the event as being due in large measure to the disbelief, minimization, and denial exhibited by adults in the child's environment whenever efforts were made to introduce the topic of seduction. In tandem with the child's desire to maintain some sort of loving connection with the parents, such reactions are further reason for the child to disbelieve his or her own veridical recollections and to conclude that the seduction was imagined—simply a fantasy production. However, the memory of the veritable experience of seduction and the attendant trauma do remain, in one sense, alive, although in a fragmented form. Anticipating by several decades the clinical experience of those who work with victims of sexual and other traumas, Ferenczi writes eloquently of a fragmenting of the personality, such that each "split" in the personality behaves as though "it does not know of the existence of the others" (Ferenczi [1933] 1955, 165). What is especially remarkable about this portrayal is how well it resonates with contemporary psychoanalytic understanding of the process and phenomena of dissociation, now universally recognized as a hallmark of the post-traumatic adaptation.

TRAUMA WITHIN THE BRITISH OBJECT-RELATIONS TRADITION: THE WORK OF FAIRBAIRN, WINNICOTT, AND BALINT

There was considerable divisiveness within the British psychoanalytic community by the early 1940s, primarily the result of theoretical differences between Anna Freud and Melanie Klein, which had given rise to an increasingly contentious and acrimonious professional environment. The failure to reconcile the views of those pledging allegiance to Melanie

Klein's object-relations school with the views of those who remained loyal to the more traditional formulations of Anna Freud led to growing disharmony and fracture within the psychoanalytic community.[2] Ultimately, a third group emerged, usually referred to as the middle or independent tradition.

The independent group consisted of a number of seminal thinkers, among them W. R. D. Fairbairn, D. W. Winnicott, Michael Balint, and John Bowlby. Because we discuss Bowlby's ideas regarding trauma in chapter 5, the focus here will be on Fairbairn, Winnicott, and Balint. All these theorists developed object-relations theories based on Klein's basic postulate of an infant who is object seeking from the moment of birth. At the same time, "they also all broke with Klein's premise of constitutional aggression . . . proposing instead an infant wired for harmonious interaction and nontraumatic development but thwarted by inadequate parenting" (Mitchell and Black 1995, 114–115). All have also contributed in significant ways to a vision of trauma sufficiently distinctive from the formulations of Freud and other theorists we have discussed to warrant a separate discussion here.

Fairbairn and the Nature of Libido

Fairbairn believed that libido, the elemental force whose distribution Freud and Abraham had charted in the 1920s, was not pleasure seeking, as they had claimed, but object seeking. In effect, the most fundamental motive in human experience was not for gratification and the discharge of tensions through relationships with others, where the others served simply as the means toward that goal. Rather, in Fairbairn's view, seeking connections with others as an end unto itself was the true aim of libido (Mitchell and Black 1995). When such connections are thwarted in childhood, whether through the frustration of the child's dependency strivings or because the child's efforts to establish healthy and affirming interactions are not met in a reciprocal fashion, the child turns away from external reality. In place of those connections, the child creates a fantasy world of internal objects that contains features of the real-world objects with whom the child cannot establish and maintain meaningful relationships.

Particularly in his work with schizoid individuals, Fairbairn theorized the existence of traumatic experiences in infancy that had caused such individuals to feel unloved as persons in their own right and also to believe that whatever love they felt for their parents was essentially bad or worth-less (Moore and Fine 1990).

Because Fairbairn believed failures in parenting to be essentially univer-sal, differing only in degree or kind, he theorized that all children defend against such traumagenic experiences through a process of ego splitting.

> The child, in Fairbairn's system, becomes like the unresponsive features of the parents: depressed, isolated, masochistic, bullying, and so on. It is through the absorption of these pathological character traits that he feels connected to the parent, who is unavailable in other ways. This internalization of the parents also necessarily creates a split in the ego: part of the self remains directed toward the real parents in the external world, seeking actual responses from them; part of the self is redirected toward the illusory par-ents as internal objects to which it is bound.
>
> (Mitchell and Black 1995, 120)

Fairbairn's theoretical system is, however, a complicated one, for follow-ing this early splitting of the ego, a further split occurs, one "between the alluring, promising features of the parents (the *exciting* object) and the frus-trating, disappointing features (the *rejecting* object)" (Mitchell and Black 1995, 120). Additional splitting culminates into what Fairbairn has termed the "libidinal ego," a part of the self tied to the exciting object in which the subject's sense of longing and hope resides, and the "anti-libidinal ego," an-other part of the self that is identified with the rejecting object and in which "angry and hateful [feelings], despising vulnerability and need" are retained (Mitchell and Black 1995, 120).

It is of considerable interest that Fairbairn appears to have been greatly influenced by his early clinical experiences with abused children. He was par-ticularly impressed by the intensity of the attachment and sense of loyalty they demonstrated toward their abusive parents. Indeed, the absence of plea-sure or gratification that such children experienced with their abusive par-ents did not seem to have much discernible effect on the bond between them. Because primarily painful sequelae followed the object-seeking behavior of these children, Fairbairn eventually understood the painful connections such children later experienced with others as representing a preferred mode of contact, which led to an endless repetition of the same traumatic pattern in all subsequent relationships.

D. W. Winnicott and the False Self

Winnicott was an important middle-tradition developmental theorist who originally trained as a pediatrician and spent more than forty years working with infants and mothers. He is known for a number of contributions that have shaped our contemporary understanding of infancy and of the relations between infants and their caregivers. Many important object-relations concepts, such as primary maternal occupation, good-enough mothering, the holding environment, and true and false selves, are attributable to Winnicott. At least one of his ideas—that of the transitional object, or security blanket—has gradually attained a degree of popularity and general usage equaled only by such Freudian concepts as the unconscious, the ego, or the idea of wish fulfillment.

Perhaps Winnicott's central idea relative to the experience of trauma is his notion of the true and false self. Winnicott wrote that individuals begin life with a true self, an "inherited potential" representing the infant's core self or essence. In a facilitative environment, the true self, which has been equated with the spontaneous expression of the id, continues to develop and becomes firmly established. The false self, on the other hand, is a facade that the child erects to ensure compliance with the mother's inadequate adaptations, whether such maternal failures are in the form of deprivations or impingements on the child's growth (Goldstein 1995). Infants exposed to such repeated deprivations or impingements are able to survive, but in Winnicott's estimation they are able to do so only at the cost of "living falsely" (Winnicott 1960; see also Mishne 1993). Although Winnicott emphasized that the partition or distribution of self-experience into true and false is always present in varying degrees (even in normal infants), the false self has an almost palpable presence in various forms of child and adult psychopathology. Winnicott treated a number of patients with basic pathology of the self, individuals who might have been diagnosed with schizoid or borderline disorders. What impressed him most about such patients was their profound inner alienation. In such patients, "subjectivity itself, the quality of personhood, is somehow disordered" (Mitchell and Black 1995, 124). Winnicott gradually came to understand that these adult patients suffered from "false self disorders," and the bridge he "constructed between the quality and the nuances of adult subjectivity and the subtleties of mother-infant interactions provided a powerful new perspective for viewing both the development of the self" and the process of treatment (Mitchell and Black 1995, 125; see also Brandell 2004).

Thus, although Winnicott's explicit focus was not on the nature of trauma, the idea of developmental trauma remained very central to most of his theoretical and clinical writings.

Michael Balint and the Basic Fault

Michael Balint, like his fellow middle traditionalists, imputed great power to the early relations between infants and mothers, and much like his analyst and mentor, Sandor Ferenczi, he believed that the root of later pathology was frequently established in the faulty or pathological responses of mothers and other caregivers to children's expression of their needs. With the idea of developmental trauma in mind, we may regard Balint's most important contributions to the object-relations literature to reside in his ideas of primary-object love and the basic fault.

Based on his clinical work with very disturbed psychoanalytic patients, Balint came to believe that certain individuals "attempt to remedy their own early deprivations by involving or coercing the analyst into granting them unconditional love which they had been deprived of in childhood" (Greenberg and Mitchell 1983, 182). He termed this the search for "primary object love" and expressed the view that it formed the basis of all subsequent psychological phenomena.

However, the search for primary-object love is closely if not inextricably tied to traumatic breaches in the earliest relationship between infants and caregivers. Such breaches, in Balint's view, give rise to a "basic fault" (Balint 1968), a structural rending of the psyche. According to Fonagy and Target (2003), the basic fault may be legitimately considered to constitute the developmental basis for personality disorders. Phenomenologically speaking, individuals exhibiting basic faults have the "underlying feeling that something is not quite right about" them (138), for which they seek out various environmental remedies. Ultimately, many such patients enter psychoanalysis or other forms of treatment, Balint believed, principally seeking to heal these basic disjunctions in the structure of the self. In his work with such patients, Balint experimented with various clinical approaches that were intended to "recapture missed developmental opportunities" and to reclaim dissociated parts of the self (Mitchell and Black 1995, 136).

A SELF PSYCHOLOGICAL VISION OF TRAUMA: THE WORK OF KOHUT AND HIS FOLLOWERS

Kohut

A relative newcomer among the psychoanalytic theories that constitute contemporary psychoanalysis (classical psychoanalysis, ego psychology, object-relations theories, and relational psychoanalysis, inter alia), self psychology was introduced by American psychoanalyst Heinz Kohut in a series of essays and books published between 1959 and 1984. Although Kohut originally presented the theoretical and technical innovations of his new psychology within the framework of classical drive theory (Greenberg and Mitchell 1983; Kohut 1966, 1971), he later expanded and revised his theory (Kohut 1977, 1984) into a distinctive and fundamentally new psychoanalytic psychology (Brandell 2004).

Kohut introduced an entirely new terminology to psychoanalysis, writing of such phenomena as selfobjects, transmuting internalization, self-cohesiveness, and varieties of selfobject experience (e.g., idealizing, mirroring, and partnering). Although space does not permit a more detailed examination of Kohut's theoretical system, suffice it to say that self psychology encompasses not only a framework for clinical interventions but also a model for understanding certain aspects of normative human development and developmental deviations, as well as a theory of psychopathology.[3]

Kohut's vision of trauma is a distinctive one. Like those of the object-relations theorists discussed in the preceding section, his conception of trauma is fundamentally developmental and intimately tied to the relationship between child and caregiver. Kohut believed that disturbances in self-functioning, which might take any of a variety of forms (e.g., borderline conditions, pathological narcissism, and other personality disorders as well as depression, anxiety disorders, and sexual perversions), are the result of chronically occurring, traumatic breaches in parental empathy. Such breaches might be the result of parental pathology, environmental uncertainties or deficits, or perhaps a combination of the two, but the end result is that the child's need for healthy affirmation, or for soothing and calming, cannot be met. Somewhat paradoxically, Kohut assumed that lapses in parental empathy are inevitable, even necessary for the healthy development of the child's self. However, these breaches are by definition optimally gratifying and optimally frustrating. As such, they serve as a catalyst for the development of healthy self-structures, furnishing the child with just the right amount of frustration to build a cohesive, fully functioning self-system.

Clinical Case Illustration: "Joe"

Joe, an overweight, forty-seven-year-old, upper-middle-class, Italian American Catholic man, originally came for treatment complaining of difficulty in establishing meaningful autonomy from his parents, a "joyless" marriage, and an inability to derive pleasure from his work.[4] Joe managed the family business, a small smelting and refining company founded by his father and uncle some fifty years earlier, which was located in the industrial corridor of a large northeastern city. Joe's father had been an aggressive and highly successful businessman, although in his personal life he was weak, ineffectual, and unable to lend Joe any modicum of real emotional support. Joe had never felt that he could count on his father when the chips were down or in a crisis. At such times, Joe's father was alternately distant or critical and in general seemed largely incapable of any meaningful emotional connection with Joe. He was, moreover, unpredictable; he could "blow" at any moment. Worse yet, Joe believed that his father was contemptuous of him and had been since Joe's childhood.

Relations with his mother were also a source of disappointment and conflict for Joe. From the time he was very young, he found her to be both unreliable and unattuned. She would become very impatient with him when he clung to her at the babysitter's, often leaving him sobbing, and throughout his early and middle childhood she seemed incapable of furnishing him with the emotional safety he required. In fact, he often found himself in the position of placating her or calming her down, generally placing her needs before his in what amounted to a reversal if not a parody of the mother-child relationship. Another significant theme in this relationship was Joe's strong sense that his mother was unable to take delight in his appearance. In fact, she shunned him at times, which caused him to feel small, ashamed, and physically repulsive. His struggle to maintain a normal weight, beginning in early childhood, was in some measure due to hereditary factors but was certainly compounded by the fact that food proved a reliable means of alleviating painful affect states and inner emptiness associated with thwarted selfobject needs in both these relationships.

Although he had never thought of himself as depressed prior to starting treatment, Joe now recognized many of his reactions—both at work and at home—as being depressive in nature. Even when he was successful in cementing a lucrative business deal, for example, it wasn't enough to make him happy. He also acknowledged that raising his kids, which he believed should be a source of genuine gratification, was instead burdensome and draining. After six months of analysis, Joe revealed a recurring fantasy that for him was particularly disturbing and humiliating. In the fantasy, he is traveling alone on a deserted stretch of highway, and he stops at an isolated rest area. He walks into the men's room and is rather surprised to find another man standing near the rear by the toilet stalls. The man cannot be seen clearly because he is in the shadows. Without hesitating, Joe kneels down in front of the man, unzips his fly, and begins to perform fellatio. At first, Joe feels excitement as the man's penis becomes erect, and then, at the moment of orgasm, he feels a sense of both power and primal satisfaction. This is as far as the fantasy goes. Even though Joe had had this fantasy for years, he had spoken of it only once before, during a session with his former therapist. At that time, he had expressed concern that it may mean he is gay. The therapist tried to reassure him that this seemed very unlikely to her, but she didn't encourage him to elaborate the fantasy, and in fact, "moved off the topic pretty quickly." Joe suffered from what has been most aptly characterized in self psychology as a depletion depression: he failed to attain self-cohesiveness owing to the unremitting series of traumatic disappointments that he had suffered in his relationships with both his parents. Indeed, Joe's history was replete with such selfobject failures. Joe's mother, who was chronically overburdened, evinced a marked insensitivity and lack of attunement with her son's emotional needs, further compounded by her own pathological reliance on him as a soothing and calming selfobject. Joe's father, despite his many successes in the business world, had little wisdom to impart to his son and was rarely if ever able to serve as a fount of strength or steadfastness for Joe. Lacking in self-confidence and inner vitality, Joe had gradually come to feel an emptiness that could not be assuaged in his marriage, his interaction with his children, or even his business relationships. He felt devitalized and impotent, was subject to mercurial fluctuations of mood, and was markedly sensitive to narcissistic slights. Joe's capacity for the regulation of his self-esteem was minimal, inasmuch as he was highly reliant on the positive valuation of others.

CONCLUSION

As stated at the beginning of the chapter, conceptions of trauma have been a central focus of the theoretical and clinical literature in psychoanalysis for more than 125 years. Ever since Freud's earliest experiments with hypnosis and the cathartic method in his work with hysterical patients, psychoanalysis has sought to understand the nature and manifestations of trauma and how it may be successfully addressed using psychodynamic treatment approaches. In this century-long odyssey, various ideas have at different times been privileged, only later to be cast aside or supplanted by newer understandings.

Trauma has sometimes been used in a narrower or more limited sense, such that it is carefully differentiated from anxiety and neurotic states (e.g., in the work of Anna Freud and Erna Furman). Other conceptions of trauma, however, place it at the very center of all pathology (e.g., Rank's conception of birth trauma) or emphasize its veridical basis (e.g., Ferenczi) rather than viewing most post-traumatic illness as arising from inner fantasies and the conflicts to which they give rise (e.g., Freud). Some theorists, most notably those whose work is associated with the British or independent tradition in object-relations theory, have tried to understand the relationship of developmental traumas to the ordering of an individual's inner object or representational world. Finally, other psychoanalytic renderings of trauma emphasize the ubiquitous nature of trauma within a parent-child relational milieu in which chronic psychological disappointments occur (e.g., Kohut).

NOTES

1   A separate chapter details the contributions of the newest psychoanalytic psychology, relational psychoanalysis, to our understanding of trauma.

2   For a more detailed description of this epoch in the history of psychoanalysis, the reader is referred to Kohon (1986), Mishne (1993), and Borden (2009).

3   For a more comprehensive overview of psychoanalytic self psychology, the reader is referred to Kohut (1977, 1984) and Perlman and Brandell (2014).
4   This illustration is an adaptation of a psychoanalytic case originally described in J. Brandell (2004, 97–103).

REFERENCES

Abraham, K. (1924) 1948. "A Short Study of the Development of the Libido." In *Selected Papers on Psycho-Analysis*, 418–450. London: Hogarth.

Allen, J. 2001. *Traumatic Relationships and Serious Mental Disorders*. New York: Wiley.

Altschul, S., and G. Pollock. 1988. *Childhood Bereavement and Its Aftermath*. Madison, Conn.: International Universities Press.

Aron, L., and H. Harris, eds. 1993. *The Legacy of Sandor Ferenczi*. Hillsdale, N.J.: Analytic Press.

Aron, L., and H. Harris. 1993. "Sandor Ferenczi: Discovery and Rediscovery." In Aron and Harris 1993, 1–35.

Balint, M. 1968. *The Basic Fault: Therapeutic Aspects of Regression*. London: Tavistock.

Borden, W. 2009. *Contemporary Psychodynamic Theory and Practice*. Chicago: Lyceum.

Brandell, J. 2004. *Psychodynamic Social Work*. New York: Columbia University Press.

Dupont, J. 1993. "Michael Balint: Analysand, Pupil, Friend, and Successor to Sandor Ferenczi." In Aron and Harris, eds., 1993, 145–157.

Ferenczi, S. 1932. *The Clinical Diary of Sandor Ferenczi*, ed. J. Dupont, trans. M. Balint and N. Jackson. Cambridge, Mass.: Harvard University Press.

Ferenczi, S. (1933) 1955. "The Confusion of Tongues Between Adults and the Child." In *The Selected Papers of Sandor Ferenczi. Final Contributions to the Problems and Methods of Psychoanalysis*, ed. and trans. M. Balint, vol. 3, 156–167. New York: Basic Books.

Ferenczi, S. (1930) 1999. "The Principle of Relaxation and Neo-catharsis." In *Selected Writings of Sandor Ferenczi*, ed. J. Borossa, 275–292. London: Penguin.

Ferenczi, S., and O. Rank. 1925. *The Development of Psychoanalysis*. New York: Nervous and Mental Diseases.

Fonagy, P., and I. Target. 2003. *Psychoanalytic Theories: Perspectives from Developmental Psychopathology*. New York: Brunner-Routledge.

Freud, A. 1967. "Comments on Trauma." In *Psychic Trauma*, ed. S. Furst, 233–245. New York: Basic Books.

Freud, S. (1909) 1961a. "Analysis of a Phobia in a Five-Year-Old Boy." In Strachey 1961, vol. 10, 1–149.

Freud, S. (1923) 1961b. "The Ego and the Id." In Strachey 1961, vol. 19, 1–66.

Freud, S. (1926) 1961c. "Inhibitions, Symptoms, and Anxiety." In Strachey 1961, vol. 20, 75–175.

Freud, S. (1900) 1961d. "The Interpretation of Dreams." In Strachey 1961, vols. 4–5, 1–751. London: Hogarth Press.

Freud, S. (1917) 1961e. "Introductory Lectures on Psychoanalysis." In Strachey 1961, vol. 17, part 3, 243–496.

Freud, S., and J. Breuer. (1893–1895) 1961. "Studies on Hysteria." In Strachey 1961, vol. 2, 1–321. London: Hogarth Press.

Fromm, E., and M. Nash. 1997. *Psychoanalysis and Hypnosis*. Madison, Conn.: International Universities Press.

Gay, P. 1988. *Freud: A Life for Our Time*. New York: Norton.

Goldstein, E. 1995. *Ego Psychology and Social Work Practice*. New York: Free Press.

Greenberg, J., and S. Mitchell. 1983. *Object Relations in Psychoanalytic Theory*. Cambridge, Mass.: Harvard University Press.

Jones, E. 1955. *The Life and Work of Sigmund Freud*. Vol. 2, *1901–1919, Years of Maturity*. New York: Basic Books.

Kohon, G., ed. 1986. *The British School of Psychoanalysis: The Independent Tradition*. London: Free Association Books.

Kohut, H. 1966. "Forms and Transformations of Narcissism." *Journal of the American Psychoanalytic Association* 14:243–272.

Kohut, H. 1971. *The Analysis of the Self*. New York: International Universities Press.

Kohut, H. 1977. *The Restoration of the Self*. New York: International Universities Press.

Kohut, H. 1984. *How Does Analysis Cure?* Chicago: University of Chicago Press.

Laughlin, H. 1979. *The Ego and Its Defenses*. Northvale, N.J.: Jason Aronson.

Menaker, E. 1982. *Otto Rank: A Rediscovered Legacy*. New York: Columbia University Press.

Mishne, J. 1993. *The Evolution and Application of Clinical Theory*. New York: Free Press.

Mitchell, S., and M. Black. 1995. *Freud and Beyond: A History of Modern Psychoanalytic Thought*. New York: Basic Books.

Moore, B., and B. Fine. 1990. *Psychoanalytic Terms and Concepts*. New Haven, Conn.: Yale University Press.

Perlman, F., and J. Brandell. 2014. "Psychoanalytic Theory." In *Essentials of Clinical Social Work*, ed. J. Brandell, 42–83. Los Angeles: Sage.

Rank, O. 1945. *Will Therapy and Truth and Reality*. New York: Knopf.

Rank, O. (1924) 1973. *The Trauma of Birth*. New York: Harper and Row.

Samuels, A. 1988. "Parental Death in Childhood." In *Childhood Bereavement and its Aftermath,* ed. S. Altschul and G. Pollock, 19–36. Madison, Conn.: International Universities Press.

Strachey, J., ed and trans. 1961. *The Standard Edition of the Complete Psychological Works of Sigmund Freud*. London: Hogarth Press.

Van Haute, P., and T. Geyskens. 2004. *Confusion of Tongues: The Primacy of Sexuality in Freud, Ferenczi, and Laplanche*. New York: Other Press.

Webster's New College Dictionary II. 1995. Boston: Houghton Mifflin.

Winnicott, D. W. 1960. "The Theory of the Parent-Child Relationship." *International Journal of Psychoanalysis* 41:585–595.

4

Psychoanalytic Theory, Part 2

▸ SHOSHANA RINGEL

RELATIONAL AND INTERSUBJECTIVE PERSPECTIVES

With the emergence of relational and intersubjective perspectives in psycho-analytic treatment, the view of developmental trauma and its implications for psychodynamic treatment have significantly evolved. As stated in the previous chapter, Ferenczi's work ([1933] 1999), which was an important precursor to current psychodynamic trauma theory, departed from Freud's conceptualization of trauma as primarily an intrapsychic phenomenon. Ferenczi viewed his adult patients' symptoms as directly related to external traumas in their childhoods, typically sexual abuse by parents and significant others, and believed their accounts of seduction by parents and other family members. He focused on the interpersonal nature of the traumas rather than viewing the symptoms as signifying internal conflicts related to the patients' unacceptable fantasies, wishes, and desires, which Freud attributed to oedipal longings. Ferenczi's emphasis on external trauma, rather than internal conflict, provided the basis for later understanding of child sexual abuse and its impact on the survivors' internal experience and their patterns of bonding with others.

This chapter will examine the meanings of trauma and its aftermath from the perspective of contemporary relational and intersubjective theories, which are influenced by Ferenczi's work, attachment research, and infant studies. Important contributions from a range of psychoanalytic authors, representing various relational, intersubjective, and contemporary self-psychological perspectives, will be highlighted, including Stern and Bromberg's view of dissociation and multiplicity; Davies and Frawley's idea of role enactments between adult survivors of sexual abuse and their therapists; Bach, Benjamin, Ghent, and Pizer's formulation of binary positions, paradox, and mastery, submission, and surrender; and intersubjective and contemporary self-psychological contributions to the trauma literature by Shane, Shane, and Gales, 1997 and by Stolorow, Lichtenberg, Lachmann, and Fosshage. These writers have been strongly influenced by attachment and infant research with its contributions to the understanding of early attachment trauma and attachment disorganization (see chapter 5).

FERENCZI'S MUTUAL ANALYSIS
AND THE RELATIONAL VIEW OF TRAUMA

In the 1920s, believing that the hierarchical relationship between analyst and patient represented an obstacle to the curative potential of psychoanalysis, Ferenczi briefly experimented with a technique he termed "mutual analysis," which required that the analyst and patient take turns analyzing each other's free associations. However, mutual analysis was misguided in the sense that the therapist-patient relationship is not a symmetrical relationship between two equals but an inherently asymmetrical one, with the focus on the patient rather than the therapist. Professional boundaries and the therapist's expertise play an important role in the treatment, particularly in cases in which patients' boundaries have been severely damaged and their trust violated by those closest to them. Still, Ferenczi was ahead of his time in his efforts to achieve greater flexibility and mutuality between patient and therapist, and his work is regarded as an important influence in contemporary relational conceptions of mutuality and the therapist's self-disclosure (Aron and Harris, 1993). Ferenczi contributed to greater interest in the mutual impact that patient and therapist have on one another and also emphasized the therapist's openness and authenticity. This trend can be discerned in the evolution of the concept of transference and countertransference, from Racker's (1968) construct of complementary and concordant countertransference, to Sandler's (1976) formulation of role responsiveness, to Davies and Frawley's (1994) contemporary idea of patient-therapist role enactments. Davies and Frawley believe that the therapeutic dyad enacts complementary roles based on a patient's history of sexual abuse. These include the victim-perpetrator, the dismissive parent–rejected child, and the victim-rescuer, scenarios in which the therapist may unconsciously assume, for example, the alternating roles of rescuer, perpetrator, and victim. It is easy for a clinician to get pulled into such compelling scenarios and to experience difficulty extricating him- or herself from them, especially if the therapist has a history of trauma. From the relational view, the therapist is increasingly implicated in the enactment and can no longer play the role of the objective outsider who is neutral and anonymous, as formulated in earlier classical conceptions of treatment. Later relational writers (Aron 2006) suggest that enactments are unavoidable phenomena that help patients and therapists process and work through previously unconscious and dissociated relational patterns and affects.

ADULT SURVIVORS OF SEXUAL ABUSE: THE WORK OF DAVIES AND FRAWLEY

Davies

Frawley

In their book about practice with adult survivors of sexual abuse, Davies and Frawley (1994) note that overwhelming experiences of abuse are associated with a greater degree of personality disorganization in patients. The result is that the ego's capacity for organization, synthesis, and symbolization is overstimulated and flooded, such that the abuse experience becomes one of "unformulated experiential chaos." Davies and Frawley observe that "with no self-reflective observing ego to provide even the rudiments of containment, meaning, and structure to the traumatic events, the child exists in a timeless, objectless, and selfless nightmare of unending pain, isolation, and ultimately, psychic dissolution" (1994, 45). In consequence, the usual process of insight work, which privileges introspection and self-reflection, must be substantially modified to reflect these psychic realities.

Dissociated Systems of Self and Object Representation

According to Davies and Frawley, it is not only the memories of specific traumatic experiences that become dissociated from other experiences but also "the organization of mutually exclusive systems of self and object representations" formed in relation to traumatic experiences (1994, 45). The therapeutic process, as a result, must achieve integration not only of the memories themselves but also of patients' varying experiences of self in relation to their fragmented worlds of internal objects.

Sudden Regressions and Experiences of Disorganization

Linking their own clinical experiences in treating sexual abuse trauma survivors to both the trauma literature and the concept of insecure attachment, Davies and Frawley assert that the traumatized child's loss of a secure
base may constitute the most pernicious and damaging psychological
trauma (Davies and Frawley 1994). Because clients' inner object worlds
contain no representations of loving, protective objects, they never develop
the capacity for self-calming and self-soothing at times of stress or for containment of the panic-like states, disorganization, and physiologically mediated states of intense hyperarousal. Accordingly, the authors emphasize
the importance of the clinician's developing familiarity and relative comfort with the patient's abrupt shifts in mood and disorganizing regressive
episodes.

Hyperreactivity and Trauma Response to Arbitrary Stimuli

The clinician's understanding and success in working with such trauma patients may also be enhanced through recognition of the relationship between
seemingly neutral stimuli that co-occur or are temporally associated with
the original trauma. Through what is most easily explained as classical conditioning, such neutral stimuli eventually serve as triggers for the traumatic
response. Davies and Frawley (1994) also believe such reactions to be consistent with ideas advanced by earlier psychoanalytic authors regarding the
foreclosure of symbolic representation (McDougall 1989) and alexithymia
(Krystal 1988).

Perhaps the most important contribution made by Davies and Frawley
(1994), however, inheres in their strong endorsement of the treatment relationship as the vehicle through which "soothing, undoing, and redoing" of
the traumatized patient's life must finally occur. They assert that such
processes are possible only insofar as the patient is able to form a significant
object relationship with the therapist. Although the abreaction of traumatic memories constitutes one aspect of this treatment process, the focus
on the abusive relationship in the context of a new, therapeutic relationship
is essential. As stated above, Davies and Frawley devote considerable attention to the transference-countertransference matrix and the therapist's
"willingness to know" the patient fully (Davies and Frawley 1994).

The relational view emphasizes the intersubjective dynamics between therapist and patient around enactments stemming from the trauma the patient has experienced. Enactments are seen as unavoidable but also as instrumental in helping patients process and understand the previously unconscious relational patterns they find themselves in, their effect on others, and their perception and interpretation of others' words and behaviors.

FLUIDITY, MULTIPLICITY, SHAME, AND DISSOCIATED STATES

Relational psychoanalysis has shifted from an emphasis on a single cohesive self (see the discussion of Kohut in the previous chapter) to a view of internal experience as constructed from multiple self-states that are linked to one another through self-awareness, a sense of continuity, and an overarching coherence (Bromberg 2003b). As described above, the goal of treatment with traumatized patients is to help them become conscious of previously unconscious, dissociated self-states (which include unintegrated emotions, memories, and behaviors related to the patient's traumatic experiences), rather than achieving a state of self-cohesion (Bromberg 1998, 2003a, 2003b). Bromberg suggests that traumatized patients create a mental structure of separate, incompatible self states "so that each can continue to play its own role, unimpeded by awareness of the others" (2003b, 560). Bromberg asserts that dissociative states protect the self from the possibility of potentially traumatic interactions with others whom the patient is fearful of depending on and being disappointed by. These interactions could trigger "affective hyperarousal, including shame, without hope of regulating the affect through the relationship itself" (2003b, 560). Bromberg notes that the dilemma for both therapist and patient is that by developing the capacity for self-reflection during the therapy process, the patient concurrently experiences a threat to the inevitable dismantling of their dissociative structures, thereby creating the possibility or the fear of further traumatization by others, including the therapist.

Bromberg notes that contemporary psychodynamic theory has shifted from a focus on resolving intrapsychic conflicts and strengthening the ego to acceptance and awareness of multiple and fluid self-states in oneself and in others. This shift started with Sullivan (1953) and his notion of the "not me" states, and Donnell Stern's (1997) work on disowned and disavowed self-states in traumatized patients, Bromberg believes in helping patients identify and express their dissociated affective states. He suggests that patients cannot recognize internal conflict unless they first work through the trauma and "own" their dissociated states. Once this integration process has occurred, patients are able to tolerate conflict without feeling compelled to dissociate, a familiar response to intolerable experiences (Bromberg 2003a, 2003b). Donnell Stern addresses the dilemma of the "not me" states, which are disowned and disavowed by the patient. These states need to become better integrated into awareness. Bromberg suggests that therapists' own reflection concerning their dissociative process with the patient is one of the primary tools in the treatment. In other words, therapists need to become aware of moments in the treatment when they, too, may dissociate, and how those moments relate to their own history or to what gets enacted in the here and how between the patient and themselves. For example, does the patient's disappointment or anger toward the therapist result in the therapist's affective withdrawal or other dissociative response? In summary, the relational perspective views the goal of trauma treatment as more fluid communication between the patient's dissociated self states, the therapist's dissociative processes, and the interplay between them, so that more flexible choices and relationships may become available to the patient.

Other authors conceptualize dissociation as a strategy of protecting the self from fragmentation and breakdown through a system of disconnected self-states (van der Hart, Nijenhuis, and Steele, 2006). Dissociation disrupts self-identity and organization, causes unstable relational patterns, and is often associated with isolation and avoidance (Schimmenti and Caretti 2016). Although dissociative processes are typically associated with child abuse and trauma, dissociation has also been linked to parental lack of emotional responsiveness and recognition (Beebe and Lachmann 2014; Slade 2014). When the parent chronically ignores, rejects, or is misattuned to the child's emotional needs, the child becomes susceptible to dissociative strategies, learning to compartmentalize and hide their authentic subjectivity and unacceptable affects and states of mind (Bromberg 2006; Shengold 1989). This dissociative response disrupts the developmental process of coherence and integration between physiological, psychological, and behavioral functions (Putnam 1997; Schimmenti and Caretti 2016). Compartmentalization and detachment have been identified as expectable responses to early developmental trauma, with fear and shame as core affects in maintaining the dissociative system (Lyons, Ruth, et al. 2006). Brandschaft and others describe the concept of pathological accommodation, which happens when the child is faced with the dilemma of mirroring and containing the parent's frightening affective states in order to maintain parental love and validation, but at the cost of sacrificing their own emerging sense of self (Brandschaft, Doctors, and Sorter 2010; Davies 2016).

Psychodynamic authors explore the state of toxic shame, an affect associated with traumatic experience that typically develops in the context of self and other, when feelings of "humiliation, degradation and shame are central to the victim's experience" (Herman 2012, 261). Shame often arises as a response to another's scorn and condemnation (Lewis 1987), and through the violations of one's boundaries, within a context of relationships based on dominance, subordination, and coercion (Herman 2012). Shame has also been described as the experience of disintegration in the presence of a dysregulating other; it thus arises in an intersubjective context with another (De Young 2015) and is often dissociated. Shame arises in the context of helplessness, despair, and collapse when no other options seem possible (van der Hart, Nijenhuis, and Steele 2006). In similarity to other dissociated affects and self-states, shame may be transmitted from parent to child as the parentally disowned shame states are internalized by the child via shaming verbal exchanges or implicit interactions.

In the following vignette, I will describe my work with a dissociative patient who was a survivor of ongoing childhood sexual abuse and who suffered the aftermath of dissociated shame.

Clinical Example 1

Jane is a woman in her sixties who experienced severe sexual abuse that began at an early age and continued through her adolescence. Whenever she mentioned to her parents behaviors of theirs that did not make sense to her, or asked them for confirmation of her memories and observations, they told her that she was crazy and simply imagining things. Jane grew up believing that she had a wonderful family, and that what happened in her room at night was a monstrous dream that had no bearing on her everyday reality. The memories related to the abuse surfaced very gradually when she was an adult, emerging as fragmented visual scenes and bodily experiences. To protect against the horror of the abuse and the emotional rejection she experienced from both parents, Jane dissociated her abuse memories until her father's death, at which time she was an adult with her own family. Jane reported experiencing dissociation and an inability to remember everyday interactions. We later understood that she experienced these encounters, especially with her husband, who was prone to inattentiveness and distractibility, as potential threats to her autonomy, and she was highly sensitive to feeling rejected and ignored. She experienced memory gaps and dissociation and found herself in places without knowing how she got there or what precipitating event had caused her dissociative response. We explored her fragmented memories and her self-states as a baby, a child, an adolescent, and an adult. Jane, who initially believed her family to be as normal as any other, described family dinners in which religious and political subjects were discussed. However, these memories alternated with others, of nights during which the "monster" entered her room and she lived a nightmarish reality that made no sense. When she had tried to communicate her observations of these bizarre events to her family, she was told that she was crazy, which contributed to her self-doubt and sense of unreality and depersonalization. Jane's ability to compartmentalize her experiences and live in separate self-states permitted her to ward off painful memories but also caused unexplained depression and difficulty trusting her own perceptions.

Together, we tried to identify moments when Jane felt ignored and misunderstood or when she felt that I, as her therapist, was taking over her train of thought and shifting the direction in which she was going. When that happened, she felt an overwhelming need to withdraw and disappear. We also devoted much of the treatment to looking at her fragmented memories and finding ways to link them to emotional states and to gain understanding of the splits in her experience of her family and history. As Jane reported her horrific memories with a matter-of-fact tone, completely devoid of feelings, I could experience my own horror, sadness at her terror and isolation as a child, and numbing at some of the unimaginable events she described. By watching my expression and hearing my reactions, Jane, too, started to feel her disowned feelings of overwhelming fear, sadness, and despair, emotions that she had dissociated and disavowed. She became able to make links between previously fragmented memories and to identify her desire to dissociate when remembering the horror or experiencing the slightest rejection and lack of attunement. Jane started to articulate her experience so that we could repair the disruption and continue. She now had greater choice and flexibility in her interactions with others. She could make her need for understanding, recognition, and validation heard and could stay present despite her fear of annihilation.

FROM SADOMASOCHISM, MASTERY, AND SUBMISSION TO SURRENDER AND "THE THIRD"

Sexual accommodation through relationships based on mastery and submission represents an adjustment to early developmental trauma. The inquiry into the dynamics of mastery and submission (or *sadomasochism* in an earlier classical formulation) is actually a time-honored psychoanalytic tradition. Freud viewed sadomasochism as an oedipal accommodation stemming from the original desire for the opposite-sex parent as well as from the guilt triggered in consequence of this unacceptable wish that culminated in the fantasy of being punished, which is both painful and exciting. Freud called this fantasy, which he saw in some of his patients, the "beating fantasy."[1] Freud concluded that the wish to be beaten by the father is "not only the punishment for the forbidden genital relation, but also the regressive substitute for that relation" (Freud [1919] 1955, 189). Bach (1994, 2002, 2006) notes that rather than being an oedipal phenomenon, sadomasochism represents the expression of an earlier developmental trauma and is aimed toward "maintaining the dependent tie to the father or mother or analyst" (Bach 2002, 229). From an attachment perspective, a disruption in early attachment bonds due to parental abuse, lack of nurturing, or loss may culminate in a distortion of love and sexual needs. Bach notes that sexual perversions are a way to seek affect regulation that the parent failed to provide, or alternatively that they may represent a desire to "compensate for hidden feelings of deviance and defectiveness" (Bach 2002, 230). He notes that some parents are unable to take pleasure in the child and are either distant and affectless or labile and unpredictable. With these parents, children are deprived of a sense of their own agency. They feel abandoned and enraged but cannot express their rage toward their parents for fear of losing an essential bond on which they depend, and they typically direct their anger toward themselves. These children will do whatever is necessary to maintain the tie to the parent, and as a consequence the sadomasochistic dyad is created. Bach observes that "these sadomasochistic dyads are a closely coupled system without autonomy for either caretaker or child," who in effect have "become each other's slaves" (Bach 2002, 231). The child's rage is thereby directed either toward the self or toward others through sexualized relationships. Sadists and masochists are both dependent on one another to feel real and complete. Bach views the sadomasochistic relationship as a disorder in sexual regulation based on lack of regulation in the earlier child-caregiver relationship.

In her book *The Bonds of Love*, Benjamin (1988) reflects on the dynamic of mastery and submission from a feminist perspective as she uses the story of O. to discuss the nature of sadomasochism in male-female relationships. According to Benjamin, mastery and submission occur when women subjugate themselves sexually and emotionally to men to help the men feel powerful and in control and to experience a sense of connection, belonging, and being desirable. In these relationships there is no place for autonomy or mutuality, as each member of the dyad provides disowned and disavowed aspects of the other's self, and each needs the other in order to experience a sense of agency and aliveness. Benjamin suggests that patients with a history of trauma develop a rigid self-structure that permits only inflexible binary roles of mastery and submission as well as victim and perpetrator, which she calls the "doer and done to" (Benjamin 2004, 2018). Every subsequent interaction is viewed by the patient from this polarized perspective, and enactments between patient and therapist originate from both finding themselves playing these polarized roles from the patient's history. Benjamin notes that another possibility outside the doer-and-done-to paradigm is for patient and therapist to create a third position from which there is an opportunity for a new understanding to arise, one that is not contingent on the old, dysfunctional roles but offers new options for relational bonding.

Benjamin (2004, 2018) develops the idea of "the third" in more recent papers and books, wherein she delineates the idea of moving from the dynamic of the doer and done to—the two binary poles that maintain a rigid split between victim and perpetrator—to the development of a third position. She characterizes the third in the following way:

> The third is that to which we surrender, and thirdness is the intersubjective mental space that facilitates or results from surrender. . . . The term surrender refers to a certain letting go of the self, and thus also implies the ability to take in the other's point of view or reality. Thus, surrender refers us to recognition, being able to sustain connectedness to the other's mind while

accepting his separateness and difference. Surrender implies freedom from
any intent to control or coerce.

(Benjamin 2004, 6)

In a relationship in which the child experiences the adult's manipulation
of the child to meet the needs of the adult, the child adapts a view of a world
in which polarized roles are the norm, where the roles of the powerful perpetrator who is in control and the victim who is dependent and submissive
are the only options. These roles then structure future relationships, and similar dynamics become enacted between patient and therapist.

Several authors have discussed the notion of a third from different perspectives, including Ogden (1994) and Aron (2006). From Benjamin's point
of view, the third is a position outside such polarized patient-therapist com-
plementarities. Representing the new meaning that emerges between therapist and patient, the third is arrived at through an intersubjective relational
process outside the doer-and-done-to paradigm. The third offers a different
option that allows mutual surrender to each other's experience. Domination
and subjugation are then transformed into mutual collaboration and the discovery of alternative options. The third, therefore, offers the analytic dyad
a way out of old, rigidly held positions based on the patient's familiar traumatic patterns. Possibilities for mutual negotiation and recognition emerge,
and greater flexibility and space become available, thus establishing a new
perspective that both patient and therapist can share. In her formulation of
the third, Benjamin draws on Winnicott's (1971) idea of the transitional
space and Ghent's (1990) reflections on masochism, submission, and surrender. Ghent notes that unlike masochism, with its connotation of distortion
and corruption, submission carries the meaning of "a quality of liberation and
expansion of the self as a corollary to the letting down of defensive barriers"
(108). He adds that unlike in submission, in surrender there is no domination
and control by another person. Surrender emerges as a consequence of free
choice; one surrenders not to a person but to something bigger than oneself,
and the decision to surrender entails greater freedom and clarity, such as what
one experiences, for example, during intense spiritual practice or meditation.
Pizer (1992) addressed the issue of a binary dilemma between patient and therapist, with each holding on to an inflexible position, from the perspective of
the negotiation of paradox. He notes that eventually both members of the
therapeutic dyad find a place of validation and inclusion. This differs mark-

edly from the patient's earlier experience of coercion, exploitation, and manipulation by caregivers and the inevitable choice such situations demanded: submission and loss of self or the risk of losing essential emotional bonds.

Ringstrom (2007) contributes to this discussion by offering the idea of playfulness and improvisation between patient and therapist as a way to process unconscious enactments and transform otherwise potentially traumatic interactions based on the traumatized patient's old internal structures. The relational view places the therapist-patient interaction at the center of enacting, processing, and resolving traumatic self-states through improvisation and attending to dissociated states in both patient and therapist.

Clinical Example 2

Peter is a gay man in his forties who grew up with a domineering, manipulative father and a passive and depressed mother. In addition to an isolated and lonely childhood, Peter experienced rejection and occasional violence from peers during his childhood and adolescence because of his sexual orientation and androgynous appearance. He became highly sensitive to perceived criticism and derogation, protecting himself through social withdrawal and ending several relationships because of real or perceived hurts. Peter learned to use his considerable intellect to shore up his self-esteem by viewing others as inferior. Peter and I enacted these familiar patterns of interaction, which caused frequent impasses and disruptions between us. Peter often perceived me as rejecting and critical, as his peers and colleagues were, unable to understand or empathize with him. In response, I felt greatly constrained in my expression with Peter, restricted to the role of cheerleader and empathic listener or to that of the disappointing, critical, and clueless Other who mistreated him. The only way we seemed able to overcome the impasse was for me to view everything from Peter's point of view and to abandon my own authentic expression and autonomy.

After several years of establishing trust and talking through endless ruptures and disappointments, I learned to admit my shortcomings and mistakes but also helped Peter accept that despite my limitations I was willing to be honest and open with him, remain committed to our work together, and do my best to understand him. As our therapeutic space started to open up, Peter brought in wordplay riddles, enjoying my initial clumsiness in figuring out their meaning but appreciating my willingness to be playful and laugh at his considerable wit. Eventually I became more adept, sometimes even discovering new meanings that he hadn't considered and making him laugh with enjoyment. We found a way to transform our either-or experience into greater mutual play and collaboration. Peter also began to discuss his dreams, and we collaborated in figuring out their meaning, inspired by one another's metaphors and adding layers of interpretation. Peter recounted a dream in which he was walking in his mother's house and explained to me that the house represented his mind, with its complex structure and multiple levels and rooms. In the dream, he finds himself in a low, dark attic, from which he enters an office he hadn't known existed. Then he exits to a lush, green, and well-tended garden. I added that since the house was a metaphor for his inner self, the attic may have represented his current feelings of darkness and hopelessness; the dream suggested that there was a way out to a well-appointed room and to a lovely garden that he hadn't known about, a new solution to the old, habitual way he had experienced his situation.

INTERSUBJECTIVE AND CONTEMPORARY SELF PSYCHOLOGY VIEW OF TRAUMA

Contemporary psychoanalytic theorists who include in their work principles of self psychology along with findings from attachment theory and infant research include Joe Lichtenberg, Frank Lachmann, and James Fosshage (1996, 2002; Lichtenberg 2005). They use Kohut's ideas of empathic resonance as the therapist's primary mode of listening and attunement, and a focus on affect as an essential component of internal experience. They suggest that as a result of early sexual abuse, restricted affect and inability to regulate overwhelming affect are common symptoms in patients and require therapists to provide affect regulation, empathic listening, and attention to all aspects of safety and security in the therapeutic milieu so as not to create a retraumatizing environment. Lichtenberg, Lachmann, and Fosshage developed a theory of motivational systems that expands on Freud's ideas of sexual and aggressive drives as the primary human motivations. They note that when working with patients with a history of sexual abuse, therapists should keep in mind disruptions in the sexual/sensual motivational system and suggest that in the absence of empathic, attuned, and regulating others, children are unable to learn to manage their intense affect states, specifically states of disruption and distress. Dissociation, disorganized attachment patterns, and controlling behaviors through aggression or caretaking of significant others may be the consequence of these early deficits. Contemporary self psychology continues to focus on affect and affect regulation in the treatment of trauma, with the therapist utilizing empathic resonance to access the patient's internal experience and dissociated states. Affect regulation occurs intersubjectively and is based on current infant research (e.g., Beebe, Lachmann, and Tronick, as noted in chapter 5, "Attachment Theory"). Based on this research, we now recognize the dyadic, bidirectional nature of infant-caregiver interactions as well as their corollary, the bidirectional nature of interactions between patient and therapist.

Stolorow (2007) offers a theory of trauma based on his experience with his wife's traumatic loss, which is contextualized within intersubjectivity theory and self psychology and also draws from the philosophical ideas of Heidegger, Husserl, and Gadamer. As the authors mentioned earlier in this chapter do, Stolorow notes the primacy of affect in human experience and the essential role of the caregiver's regulation of the child's affect state through mirroring and idealization. In the absence of others who mirror and regulate, the child's affect remains painful and overwhelming, and the phenomena of dissociation and disavowal of affect and memory prevail. The therapist's attuned, empathic, and regulating functions provide the possibility of a new intersubjective context that can help change what Stolorow calls the patient's "organizing principles," bringing about greater affective flexibility and opening new intersubjective possibilities. Stolorow posits a theory of trauma based on contextuality, absolutisms, temporality, and what he terms the "ontological unconscious." The focus on contextuality in the writings of Stolorow and Atwood (1992) essentially reflects their view that there is no such thing as the Cartesian notion of an "isolated mind." There is continuous bidirectional influence between inner state and outer environmental factors, between the inner reality of the child and the relational bonds with caregivers, and between patient and therapist. Thus, trauma is always the result of confluence between internal and external factors.

Based on his personal experience of loss, Stolorow suggests that the absolutisms that people take for granted in their everyday life, such as a sense of trust, optimism, and objective reality, have no meaning for those who have experienced trauma, who cannot trust in the reliability of everyday events and the security and predictability of everyday life. For trauma survivors, everything seems precarious and subject to sudden destruction and chaos. They feel isolated and alienated from others who have not experienced their loss and trauma. Stolorow notes, "It is in the essence of emotional trauma that it shatters these absolutisms, a catastrophic loss of innocence that permanently alters one's sense of being in the world. Massive deconstruction of the absolutisms of everyday life exposes the inescapable contingency of existence on a universe that is random and unpredictable and in which no safety or continuity of being can be assured" (Stolorow 2007, 16).

Similarly, time or temporality has no meaning after the experience of a traumatic event, and the sense of one's self in the context of time becomes meaningless. For many patients who have experienced trauma, the traumatic past seems to exist in the present time, and there is no sense of present or future apart from the traumatic event. Stolorow suggests that "it is the ecstatical unity of temporality, the sense of stretching along between past and future, that is devastatingly disturbed by the experience of emotional trauma. Experiences of trauma become freeze framed into an internal present in which one remains forever trapped, or to which one is condemned to be perpetually returned through the port keys supplied by life's slings and arrows" (2007, 20).

What Stolorow calls the "ontological unconscious" is the loss of the sense of being through affectivity and through language. Experiences with early lack of attunement, especially linguistic attunement, foreclose one's ability to develop a sense of self that includes affect and language, leaving individuals with a body-based emotional experience that is not subject to understanding and articulation. Stolorow suggests that it is through intersubjective bonds that the sense of being develops and is sustained and that only through intersubjective experiences can one heal from the impact of developmental and other types of trauma. Although much of what Stolorow suggests is not new, his interweaving of his own experience with loss gives his writing a unique sense of poignancy.

CONCLUSION

In this chapter I have summarized important contributions to contemporary psychodynamic theories of trauma emerging from relational theory, intersubjectivity, and contemporary self psychology and influenced by attachment findings and infant research. These contemporary conceptions include enactments between patient and therapist in which the roles of "doer" and "done to" are co-created; the third as a mutual position that helps patient and therapist enter a new and more fluid relational paradigm outside the constrictions of doer–done to dynamics; dissociation and a view of multiple, rather than a single, self-states; and the intersubjective space between the clinician's personal experience of emotional trauma and the patient's experience of absolutisms, temporality, and ontological unconscious. These contemporary trends point to a greater personal engagement of the therapist in the narrative and self-states of the patient; the need for the therapist to draw on his or her personal experiences of relational disruptions, loss, and trauma; and the capacity to engage with the patient more openly and authentically.

Most trauma-focused therapies are based on a structured, phase-based process that includes stabilization, affect regulation, processing of the traumatic experience, and integration of narrative, affect, and somatic states. The psychodynamic approach as presented here is based on the inquiry into implicit, unconscious processes of engagement between patient and therapist, including traumatic enactments, doer and done to, and the integration of dissociative processes between patient and therapist. The inquiry into traumatic affects such as fear, anger, guilt, and shame and how they affect the patient's sense of self and relational structure are also important focuses of treatment. The integration of this relational focus in trauma work has been described by authors of several trauma-focused models (van der Hart, Ninjenhuis, and Steele 2006; Herman 1993; Ogden, Kekuni, and Pain 2006; van der Kolk 2014) and in this writer's opinion may offer a richer, more inclusive, and more flexible dimension to the treatment of trauma. The focus on implicit communication (Beebe and Lachmann 2014) and the relational processes between client and therapist may help revise traumatogenic attachment patterns and help foster integration and the creation of new meaning (van der Hart Nijenhuis, and Steele 2006). These interactions between client and therapist may also facilitate the capacity for mutual recognition and empathy (Benjamin 2004; Bromberg 2006, 2011). A trauma-focused treatment model along with a relational approach would therefore provide a greater range of therapeutic options for trauma survivors.

NOTE

1   It is possible that his paper on the subject was based on his work with his daughter Anna, who was in analysis with him (Bach 2002).

REFERENCES

Aron, L. 2006. "Analytic Impasse and the Third: Clinical Implications of Intersubjectivity Theory." *International Journal of Psychoanalysis* 87:349–368.

Aron, L., and A. Harris. 1993. "Sandor Ferenczi: Discovery and Rediscovery." In *The Legacy of Sandor Ferenczi*, ed. L. Aron and A. Harris, 1–36. Northvale, N.J.: Analytic Press.

Bach, S. 1994. *The Language of Perversion and the Language of Love*. Northvale, N.J.: Jason Aronson.

Bach, S. 2002. "Sadomasochism in Clinical Practice and Everyday Life." *Journal of Clinical Psychoanalysis* 11:225–235.

Bach, S. 2006. *Getting from Here to There: Analytic Love, Analytic Process*. Hillsdale, N.J.: Analytic Press.

Beebe, B. and F. Lachmann. 2014. *The Origins of Attachment: Infant Research and Adult Treatment*. New York: Routledge.

Benjamin, J. 1988. *The Bonds of Love: Psychoanalysis, Feminism and the Problem of Domination*. New York: Pantheon.

Benjamin, J. 2004. "Beyond Doer and Done To: An Intersubjective View of Thirdness." *Psychoanalytic Quarterly* 73:5–46.

Benjamin, J. 2018. *Beyond Doer and Done To: Recognition Theory, Intersubjectivity and the Third*. New York: Routledge.

Brandschaft, B., S. Doctors, and D. Sorter. 2010. *Toward an Emancipatory Psychoanalysis: Brandchaft's Intersubjective Vision*. New York: Routledge.

Bromberg, P. 1998. *Standing in the Spaces: Essays on Clinical Process, Trauma, and Dissociation*. Hillsdale, N.J.: Analytic Press.

Bromberg, P. 2003a. "One Need Not Be a House to Be Haunted: On Enactment, Dissociation and the Dread of 'Not Me': A Case Study." *Psychoanalytic Dialogues* 13:689–709.

Bromberg, P. 2003b. "Something Wicked This Way Comes: Trauma Dissociation and Conflict: The Space Where Psychoanalysis, Cognitive Science and Neuroscience Overlap." *Psychoanalytic Psychology* 20:558–574.

Bromberg, P. 2006. *Standing in the Spaces*. New York: Analytic Press.

Bromberg, P. 2011. *Awakening the Dreamer: Clinical Journeys.* New York: Analytic Press.

Davies, J., and M. Frawley. 1994. *Treating the Adult Survivor of Childhood Sexual Abuse: A Psychoanalytic Perspective.* New York: Basic Books.

Davies, M. J. 2016. "To Dream, Perchance to Think: Discussion of Papers by Noelle Burton and Christopher Bonovitz." *Psychoanalytic Dialogues* 26 (3): 322–330.

DeYoung, P. 2015. *Chronic Shame.* New York: Routledge.

Ferenczi, S. (1933) 1999. "The Confusion of Tongues Between Adults and the Child." In *Selected Writings,* 293–303. London: Penguin.

Freud, S. (1919) 1955. "A Child Is Being Beaten: A Contribution to the Study of the Origin of Sexual Perversions." In *The Standard Edition of the Complete Psychological Works of Sigmund Freud,* ed. and trans. J. Strachey, vol. 17, 175–204. London: Hogarth Press.

Ghent, E. 1990. "Masochism, Submission, Surrender: Masochism as a Perversion of Surrender." *Contemporary Psychoanalysis* 26:108–136.

Herman, J. 1992. *Trauma and Recovery.* New York: Basic Books.

Herman, J. 2012. "Post-traumatic Stress Disorder as a Shame Disorder." In *Shame in the Therapy Hour,* ed. R. Dearing and J. P. Tangney, 261–276. Washington D.C.: APA.

Krystal, H. 1988. *Integration and Self Healing: Affect, Trauma, and Alexithymia.* Hillsdale, N.J.: Analytic Press.

Lewis, H. 1987 "Introduction: Shame the 'Sleeper' in Psychopathology." In *The Role of Shame in Symptom Formation,* ed. H. Lewis, 1–28. Hillsdale, N.J.: Erlbaum.

Lichtenberg, J. 2005. *Craft and Spirit: A Guide to the Exploratory Psychotherapies.* Hillsdale, N.J.: Analytic Press.

Lichtenberg, J., F. Lachmann, and J. Fosshage. 1996. *The Clinical Exchange.* Hillsdale, N.J.: Analytic Press.

Lichtenberg, J., F. Lachmann, and J. Fosshage. 2002. *The Spirit of Inquiry.* Hillsdale, N.J.: Analytic Press.

Lyons-Ruth, K., L. Dutra, M. Schuder, and I. Bianchi. 2006. "From Infant Attachment Disorganization to Adult Dissociation: Relational Adaptations or Traumatic Experiences?" *Psychiatric Clinics of North America* 29:63–86.

McDougall, J. 1989. *Theaters of the Body.* New York: Norton.

Ogden, P., M. Kekuni, and C. Pain. *Trauma and the Body: Sensorimotor Approach to Psychotherapy.* New York: Norton.

Ogden, T. 1994. *Subjects of Analysis.* Northvale, N.J.: Analytic Press.

Pizer, S. 1992. "The Negotiation of Paradox in the Analytic Process." *Psychoanalytic Dialogues* 2:215–240.

Putnam, F. 1997. *Dissociation in Children and Adolescents: A Developmental Perspective.* New York: Guilford Press.

Racker, H. 1968. *Transference and Countertransference.* New York: International University Press.

Ringstrom, P. 2007. "Scenes That Write Themselves: Improvisational Moments in Relational Psychoanalysis." *Psychoanalytic Dialogues* 17 (1): 69–99.

Sandler, J. 1976. "Countertransference and Role Responsiveness." *International Review of Psychoanalysis* 3:43–47.

Schimmenti, A., and V. Caretti. 2016. "Linking the Overwhelming with the Unbearable: Developmental Trauma, Dissociation, and the Disconnected Self." *Psychoanalytic Psychology* 33 (1): 106–128.

Shane, M., E. Shane, and M. Gales. 1997. *Intimate Attachments: Toward a New Self Psychology.* New York: Guilford Press.

Shengold, L. 1989. *Soul Murder: The Effects of Childhood Abuse and Deprivation.* New Haven, Conn.: Yale University Press.

Slade, H. 2014. "Imagining Fear: Attachment, Threat, and Psychic Experience." *Psychoanalytic Dialogues* 24 (3): 253–266.

Stern, D. 1997. *Unformulated Experience: From Dissociation to Imagination in Psychoanalysis.* Hillsdale, N.J.: Analytic Press.

Stolorow, R. 2007. *Trauma and Human Existence: Autobiographical, Psychoanalytic, and Philosophical Reflections.* New York: Analytic Press.

Stolorow, R., and G. Atwood. 1992. *The Context of Being.* Northvale, N.J.: Analytic Press.

Sullivan, H. S. 1953. *The Interpersonal Theory of Psychiatry.* New York: Norton.

van der Hart, O., E. Nijenhuis, and K. Steele. 2006. *The Haunted Self: Structural Dissociation and the Treatment of Chronic Traumatization.* New York: Norton

van der Kolk, B. 2014. *The Body Keeps the Score: Brain, Mind, and Body in the Healing of Trauma.* New York: Penguin.

Winnicott, D. W. 1971. *Playing and Reality.* New York: Routledge.

5

Attachment Theory

▸ SHOSHANA RINGEL

FROM ITS INCEPTION, attachment research has focused on traumatic events in the lives of young children. Attachment theory developed in the context of children's need for attachment and their consequent response to separation and loss. Indeed, John Bowlby conducted his observations in orphanages and hospitals with children who had lost their parents or were separated from them for long periods of time. More recently, infant researchers—including Beebe and her collaborators (Beebe 2005; Beebe et al. 2000), Tronick (1977, 1998, 2002), Lyons-Ruth (Lyons-Ruth et al. 2006; Lyons-Ruth and Jacobvitz 2009), and others—have focused their investigations on children's disorganized attachment in the wake of such traumas as parental misattunement, abuse, or neglect. Children's disorganized attachment is also linked to caregivers' own unresolved loss and trauma, communicated to the child via verbal or nonverbal signals and thereby transmitted from one generation to the next. Neuroscientific findings show that brain development is closely linked to attachment relationships and that attachment disruptions can interfere with normative development of brain structures.

In this chapter, I will elaborate on Bowlby's theory of children's attachment, separation, and loss; Ainsworth's Strange Situation experiment and her identification of early attachment patterns; and Main and Solomon's (1990) criteria of disorganized attachment. I will also examine the Adult Attachment Interview (AAI) and adult attachment categories; infant research with an emphasis on neuroscience, trauma, mentalization, and disorganized attachment. The chapter concludes with several clinical applications of attachment theory and research.

BOWLBY AND AINSWORTH:
SEPARATION AND LOSS, THE STRANGE SITUATION

Bowlby's attachment theory was influenced by Spitz's observations of abandoned babies in hospitals, babies who failed to thrive despite the provision of basic needs such as food and shelter. Bowlby was also influenced by Darwin's evolutionary theory, from which he learned the principle of adaptation to a changing environment and the necessity of caregivers' proximity to and nurturing of their offspring to ensure survival. He learned of Harlow's experiments with baby monkeys who were separated from their mothers and preferred the warmth and softness of a wire-mesh "mother" covered in terry cloth to the metal wire-mesh mother that held milk bottles (Harlow 1958). From Harlow, Bowlby recognized that babies need not only food and shelter but also love and nurturing to survive and thrive. Bowlby applied these findings to human babies and realized that physiological provisions alone were insufficient for optimal development and that emotional nurturing and attentiveness were also required. Through his work with children in orphanages and hospitals, Bowlby recognized the impact of separation and loss on children's development; consequently, traumatic experiences were the context in which his attachment theory took hold (Bowlby 1973). Ahead of the psychoanalytic community of his time, Bowlby recognized that young children had a profound emotional need for their mothers (or other caregivers) and that separation and loss bore a profound impact on their developmental experiences. With his collaborator, James Robertson, who filmed hospitalized children separated from their mothers, Bowlby observed that children responded to separation in three distinct stages: protest, when the children cried inconsolably; despair, when they became listless, depressed, and uninterested in food or play; and detachment, when attachment needs were readjusted and the children became engaged with the hospital environment, nurses, and other children but ignored their mothers when they came to visit (Bowlby 1973). Robertson and Bowlby observed that it took these children some time to trust their mothers again and reach out to them. Bowlby's work also encompassed children's grief and mourning process. He observed that children mourned the death of a parent deeply and that, at times, such grief remained unresolved for many years, either as prolonged mourning or as failed mourning when a secure environment in which to grieve the loss was unavailable to the child (Bowlby 1960,

1963). Bowlby's observations were revolutionary at a time when child psychology was in its infancy. Indeed, much clinical work with children was based on Freud's drive theory, in which the real relationship with caregivers was seen as having far less importance than the child's intrapsychic conflicts. At the time, children were treated by mental health professionals without much attention paid to their relationships with their mothers.

Building on Bowlby's work, Mary Ainsworth, who was initially Bowlby's collaborator (and later an accomplished researcher in her own right), developed the Strange Situation experiment, which led to the identification of three distinct attachment styles in children (Ainsworth et al. 1978). In the experiment, Ainsworth exposed young children ages one and a half to two years of age to experiences of separation and reunion with their mothers. In a laboratory room outfitted with toys, the child spent a few minutes with his or her mother; a stranger entered the room and the mother left; the mother came back; after a while both the stranger and the mother left, and the child remained alone. Finally, the mother returned a second time. Ainsworth observed that children's behavior varied during separation and reunion but was particularly distinct during their reunion with their mothers. Securely attached children would demonstrate attachment behaviors, looking at the mother and seeking contact, but these children were also quite comfortable engaging in exploratory behaviors, playing with toys, and, in general, conveying curiosity about their laboratory-room environment. Although the secure children were distressed when their mothers left, they were easily soothed when the mothers returned, reaching out to be held and soon returning to their play. The "avoidantly attached" children showed apparent independence and autonomy, playing with toys and exploring the room, but lacked interest in their mothers' comings and goings and ignored their return. Observations of interactions between mothers and avoidant children revealed that these mothers were rejecting and discouraging of their children's attachment needs, especially when the children expressed distress or were overly controlling and intrusive. The avoidant style seemed to be a strategy of the children for protecting themselves against painful feelings of rejection and intrusive behaviors by their caregivers. Avoidant children showed consistent interest in exploratory behaviors, but attachment behaviors were minimal. However, studies examining cortisol production (obtained through children's saliva) revealed an interesting discrepancy. Although the avoidant children did not show obvious interest in the mothers' comings and goings, their cortisol levels increased when the mothers left the room or returned, indicating that emotional needs were present but camouflaged. Ainsworth and her collaborators concluded that avoidant children have learned to hide their longing for attachment and bonding because of their frustrating experiences with their mothers (Ainsworth et al. 1978).

Unlike avoidant children, those with an "anxious-ambivalent" style demonstrate a heightened attachment system but little interest in exploratory activities. These children attend to their mothers' every move, becoming very distressed when they leave the room. Such children are not easily soothed when their mothers return, responding to the reunion with ambivalent behaviors that include both reaching out to their mothers to be held and pushing their mothers away. Ambivalent children do not show interest in exploratory behaviors away from the mother and display clinginess and hypervigilance over their mothers' every move. Observations of these children's interactions with their mothers revealed mothers who were inconsistently attentive to their children; at times they were emotionally available and attentive, but at other times they were absent and distracted. Such children have developed a strategy to gain their mothers' attention in any way possible. They are intently focused on their mothers' moods and behavior, at the cost of their developmental need for exploration and autonomy.

Through the Strange Situation experiment, Ainsworth et al. (1978) demonstrated the singular importance of the infant's efforts to maintain proximity with a primary caregiver. The child uses the caregiver as a secure base for exploration of unfamiliar environments and flees to the attachment figure as a safe haven during stressful times (Main, Goldwyn, and Hesse 2002).

ATTACHMENT DISORGANIZATION AND INFANT RESEARCH

Following Ainsworth, Mary Main and Judith Solomon identified an additional attachment style, characterized by the child's contradictory behavior patterns, which they called "disorganized" (Main and Solomon 1990). It included attachment behaviors that alternated with avoidance, freezing, or dazed behaviors, and interrupted movements and expressions. Main and Solomon also identified indications of apprehension in the parent, including the parent's turning or running away and hiding, and disorganization or disorientation in the child, such as the child's wandering, seeming confusion, dazed expression, or rapid changes in affect (Hesse et al. 2003; Lyons-Ruth and Jacobvitz 2009). It was found that disorganized behavior in an infant was rooted in fear—either fear of the caregiver or the infant's perception that the caregiver was fearful of the child. Main, Goldwyn, and Hesse (2002) observed that certain caregivers' behaviors stimulated disorganized behavior in the child. These included threatening posture, facial expression, and movements; frightened behavior, such as retreat and backing away from the infant; dissociative behaviors, such as freezing; timid or deferential behaviors; and intimate or sexualized touching and disorganized behaviors, which match the disorganized behaviors observed in the child (Lyons-Ruth and Jacobvitz 2009). It is important to emphasize that these behaviors were frequently unconscious and are believed to have their origins in unresolved trauma or loss in the parent's own childhood.

Lyons-Ruth and Jacobvitz (2009) further observed that a significant number of disorganized children suffered abuse and neglect, or that the mothers of these children had themselves suffered unresolved loss or trauma. As suggested above, fear plays a major role in the child's response. The child's fear of the caregiver might stem from such behavior as bizarre expressions and movements, hovering too close to the child, or frowning. However, the disorganized child might also perceive the caregiver as being frightened of the child—for instance, when the caregiver backs away or seems timid and anxious around the child, or when the caregiver fails to provide a safe haven for the child (Liotti 2004). Based on their observation of children's and mothers' interactions, Main, Goldwyn, and Hesse (2002) developed scales to identify frightened or frightening parental behaviors. These scales include threatening, frightened, dissociative, timid or deferential, sexualized or romanticized, and disorganized behaviors (Hesse 2009).

In their infant studies, Lyons-Ruth et al. (2006) identified two subgroups of disorganized mother-infant dyads: the helpless-fearful dyad (mothers who project anxiety and fear), and the hostile-intrusive dyad (mothers who demonstrate overly intrusive and role-reversing behaviors, such as mocking and teasing, that lead to an unregulated increase in attachment behaviors) (Diamond 2004). Longitudinal studies with disorganized children show that they express more anger and aggression than secure, avoidant, or ambivalent children (Lyons-Ruth and Jacobvitz 2009). In disorganized children at six years of age, two behavioral patterns were observed: controlling/caregiving behaviors and controlling/punitive behaviors (Moss et al. 2004, cited in Lyons-Ruth and Jacobvitz 2009). "Disorganized controlling" children exhibit punitive, hostile behaviors toward the parents, ordering them around and humiliating them. "Disorganized caregiving" children demonstrate caring behavior to show that they are preoccupied with the parents' well-being (Hesse 1999). The latter group has been identified as disorganized in infancy (Diamond 2004). Although mothers of disorganized caregiving children portray a merger-like relationship with their children, mothers of disorganized controlling children describe themselves as helpless. One mother stated, "I feel him in my space . . . and I think he does too. . . . I might just put out my hand and suddenly he's holding my hand . . . without looking" (Solomon and George 1999, 19).

These infant observations show that the mother's unresolved trauma directly affects the child's disorganized response and contributes more generally to a disorganized attachment pattern in the child. When Main, Goldwyn, and Hesse (2002) and Hesse (1999, 2009) correlated adult attachment patterns from the AAI with children's attachment styles in the Strange Situation, they found that the majority of disorganized children (84 percent) had a parent with an unresolved/disorganized style, suggesting that attachment trauma is transmitted from parents to children.

Attachment-based trauma is linked to several relational disruptions in childhood. Separation is especially traumatic for young children who do not understand the concept of time and temporary separation and experience the separation from their primary caregiver as an abandonment. Threatened abandonment, therefore, can cause deep anxiety in young children who do not understand the concept of temporary separation or literal truth versus threats. A caregiver's death is universally experienced as an abandonment by infants and young children and may lead to the loss of both physical and emotional security. Finally, the experience of abuse and neglect confronts children with an impossible relational dilemma: the caregiver on whom they are physically and emotionally dependent and who is supposed to love and protect them is also the source of pain and threat.

Beebe (2005; Beebe and Lachmann 2014) and Tronick (1977, 1998, 2002) showed that nonverbal signals from caregivers can easily become overstimulating. Based on her split-screen, moment-to-moment observations, Beebe (2005; Beebe and Lachmann 2014) demonstrated how caregivers' facial expressions and movements, such as finger pointing, tickling, and intense gazing, can be frightening and distressing to very young infants. In such situations, infants typically respond by avoiding direct eye contact, turning their heads, and finally crying. These nonverbal communication patterns may lead to coping strategies of withdrawal, dissociation, or disingenuous responses designed to please the caregivers. Slade (2008 demonstrated in a video how children learn to present a "false self." In the clip, a baby attempts to smile when his adolescent mother hovers too close to his crib and makes frightening faces. Although the mother's intent is to make her baby smile, the baby appears quite terrified though fearful of revealing how scared he really is for fear that the mother will retaliate. When the video was later shown to the mother, she was surprised at how frightening her expressions appeared and was able to verbalize the child's inner experience and recognize her lack of attunement. Through such observational experiments, Slade trained teen mothers to improve their maternal skills and become more attuned to their babies' internal states of mind.

In his observational experiments with the "still face," Tronick (1977) demonstrates how infants become highly upset when their caregivers show a lack of responsiveness to their cues. During the experiment, the caregiver is required to maintain a flat expression regardless of whether the infant smiles or is distressed. Consequently the infant becomes increasingly more upset as attempts to receive an empathic and mirroring response from the parent are frustrated. These observations show that from an early age, the reciprocal attunement between a child and the caregiver is instrumental in the child's development of self-regulation and self-soothing capacities. Attunement and mirroring also enable the child to recognize his or her affective experiences as well as others' states of mind. (Tronick's experiments are described in more detail in the next section.)

AFFECT REGULATION AND THE IMPACT OF EARLY TRAUMA

Studies with infants show that they develop some capacity for self-regulation early on. This capacity is enhanced through mutual interactions with caregivers, who provide affect regulation to children through verbal and non-verbal behaviors such as cooing, smiling, holding, and other soothing behaviors. Caregivers can either enhance and amplify children's affect or contain and help diminish infants' distress. Adults' soothing and regulating functions are eventually adopted and internalized by children, who learn to sooth and regulate their emotional reactions. However, children whose caregivers are themselves misattuned and unregulated lack appropriate models and, in consequence, will not learn to regulate their affects. They may learn to regulate via withdrawal and dissociation or through punitive or aggressive behavior toward others. Such behaviors may include hitting, biting, head banging, and, later, self-harming behaviors or interpersonal violence. As stated above, disorganized children were found to be more aggressive than secure, avoidant, or anxious ones.

Based on his research with infants and their mothers, Tronick (1977, 1998, 2002) elaborated on the dyadic nature of mutual regulation within the child-parent relationship. Tronick's understanding of mutual regulation was influenced by Sander's theory of dynamic systems and the self-regulatory developmental model (Nahum 2000). Dynamic systems theory helps us to organize observations of stages of interactions between infants and their mothers, starting from concrete behavioral responses and evolving to the infants' efforts to exercise greater initiative and agency and to move from behavioral interchange to affective regulation and more complex inner experiences. In their observational research, Beebe and colleagues (2000, 2014) found that secure mutual interactions between mothers and infants are characterized by novelty and flexibility in the process of change and development. However, they note that at one end of the developmental spectrum are rigid infant-mother dyads that evince high mutual dependence and attachment, and at the other are loosely attached dyads in which infants and mothers appear unresponsive to one another (Beebe et al. 2000; Beebe and Lachmann 2014). These infant-mother dyads correspond to the ambivalent-preoccupied and the avoidant-dismissive attachment categories in the AAI.

As mentioned earlier, to examine the mutuality in mother-infant (children between the ages of one and two) interactions, Tronick and his collaborators developed a "still face" experiment (Tronick 1977) wherein they observed how infants respond to their mothers' lack of facial responsiveness. Tronick's infant participants are seen to be trying hard to elicit their mothers' responses, then turning away, again looking back, and finally withdrawing. Tronick hypothesizes that infants will try everything in their power to restore a homeostatic affective balance by eliciting their mothers' responsiveness and that this balance represents a dyadic collaboration between infants and mothers. Such interpersonal dyadic regulation is as important as internal regulation, and the two correspond with one another. Tronick (1998) describes an interactive sequence in which the infant pulls the mother's hair, the mother then frowns, and the infant responds by releasing her. Eventually, the mother approaches again with a playful smile, and the infant smiles as well. This interaction suggests that the infant is able to intuit the mother's affective response and react to it with an affective response of his or her own rather than just imitating the mother. Further, it demonstrates mother-infant attunement and mutual regulation. In effect, infants seem to adjust their behavior to repair a state of misattunement.

The cycle of disruption and repair has enormous importance in infant development. Parents' abilities to recognize their own misattuned behaviors and to adjust them or acknowledge the dysjunctions are critical in repairing attachment ruptures. Such efforts also serve to enhance children's sense of agency and security. Through incremental disruption-repair cycles, children learn to deal with frustrations and to recognize difference. Ongoing interactions of this kind between mothers and children contribute to the deepening complexity and sophistication of infants' regulatory systems.

In a related study using video microanalysis, Beebe and her colleagues (Beebe 2005; Beebe and Lachmann 2014) describe how infant self-regulation develops in the context of bidirectional regulation with mothers. From birth, infants show a remarkable capacity to self-regulate through alternating cycles of connection and withdrawal. Beebe notes that gazing is an important nonverbal signal and that infants alternate between face-to-face play with their mothers and looking away to regulate their arousal. They learn to turn their heads in a chase-and-dodge sequence, an action that is also designed to reduce arousal,[1] and they engage in facial matching and vocalizing with their mothers, who, if they are well attuned, can help build positive affects and decrease infants' distress. Beebe (2005; Beebe and Lachmann 2014) found that interactive regulation occurs on a continuum, with one extreme characterized by excessive mutual monitoring and the other by withdrawal. The two extremes appear to parallel anxious-ambivalent and avoidant attachment styles. Such interactions between infants and mothers are designed to regulate emotional arousal and overstimulation through autonomous and dyadic interactions.

Although avoidant and anxious adults may not have experienced the level of trauma linked to the disorganized pattern, they have not developed a sense of felt security based on ongoing affective experiences with their caregivers. Instead, their internal working models are based on a lack of security at times of threat, separation, or loss, or are based on recurrent experiences that reflect misattunement, rejection, and intrusiveness by caregivers. Two main self-regulation strategies were found in insecurely attached people: hyperactivating and deactivating responses. Hyperactivating patterns were found in individuals whose caregivers were preoccupied, inattentive, or anxious and who failed to respond to normal signals from the child. In consequence, the child coped by adopting an anxious-ambivalent pattern. Deactivating responses were found in people whose caregivers engaged in distancing, rejecting, or hostile responses. The child learned to suppress the need for attention and bonding, ultimately developing an avoidant pattern (Mikulincer and Shaver 2009).

Studies with secure, avoidant, and anxiously attached adults show that avoidant people attempt to regulate themselves by deactivating their attachment system. They learn to minimize and defend against experiences of threat, separation, and loss in order to avoid appearing needy and vulnerable. Their self-esteem depends on their ability to overappraise themselves to mask their insecurity and vulnerability. Anxious people tend to exaggerate experiences related to threat, separation, and loss and to heighten their affective responses in consequence. They tend to exaggerate their sense of helplessness and vulnerability and to undervalue themselves. Secure people appraise themselves, events, and experiences realistically. Their self-esteem is stable and based on the capacity to admit vulnerabilities, and they reveal a capacity to adapt to and manage difficult situations (Mikulincer and Shaver 2009).

MENTALIZATION AND THE IMPACT OF EARLY TRAUMA

Fonagy and his collaborators (Fonagy and Bateman 2006, 2008; Fonagy and Target 2008) adopted the concept of mentalization from French psychoanalysts, who had observed a lack of ability to symbolize mental states in some of their patients. In their studies of young children, Fonagy et al. (2002) found that mentalization was not an innate capacity but rather a learned skill based on interactions between children and caregivers, findings that have now been validated by neuroscience and infant research (Beebe and Lachmann 2002; Coan 2008; A. Schore 2011). Mentalization, therefore, is based on mutual interactions between children and parents. Mentalization occurs when parents model to their children how to identify and articulate their affects and cognitions so that the children can learn to identify them and communicate them to others. It also includes children's capacity to read others' states of mind and emotional cues and respond to them empathically. Fonagy suggests that the capacity for mentalization is compromised in many people who have experienced early trauma. Problems with mentalization in young children who have suffered maltreatment manifest in their preference for less symbolic and dyadic play, their lack of empathy for others, poor affect regulation, difficulty in referring to internal mental states, and difficulty understanding emotional (facial) expressions (Fonagy and Target 2008, 19).

The process of mentalization develops gradually. Fonagy and Bateman (2008) termed the initial stage "psychic equivalence," in which children mistake their internal states of mind and fantasies for objective reality. For example, a fear of monsters may translate into the child's belief that a real monster is lurking beneath the bed. In this state of mind, children, as well as adults who have difficulty mentalizing, fail to differentiate between internal and external reality and have difficulty accepting the validity of opposing perspectives and alternate points of view. In the second stage, termed "pretend play," children exclude external reality, and their play, both solitary and collaborative, becomes their reality. This state of mind entails dissociation and the fragmentation of inner reality from an external context. Although pretend play is important in developing social skills, creativity, and fantasy life, it may also result in pathological dissociation and the avoidance of external reality (Fonagy and Bateman 2008; Fonagy et al. 2002).

A parent can help a child move from psychic equivalence and pretend play to the mature stage of mentalization by participating in and mirroring the child's play and fantasy while at the same time providing a relationship rooted in external reality. This promotes the child's capacity to differentiate between self and other and to link pretend activities with external reality (Slade 2008). Based on their own research and that of others (Sroufe, Egeland, and Kreutzer 1990), Fonagy and his associates (2002) found that a child with a secure attachment also shows good mentalization capacities. Fonagy et al. (2002) note that "pretending requires a mental stance involving the symbolic transformation of reality in the presence of and with a view to the mind of others" (48). The caregiver represents external reality but also mirrors the child's internal states without burdening him or her with the caregiver's own subjective needs and affects. Fonagy and colleagues (2002) also note that verbal communication from parent to child and the parent's ability to discuss his or her own mental states and to verbalize the child's mental states facilitates reflective functioning in the child.

Children who experience abuse or neglect may develop internal representations of being bad, incompetent, and unworthy or beliefs in a threatening world and dangerous others. They may develop psychic equivalences of a frightening, unsafe world in which they are constantly threatened, which mirrors their internal reality, or they may withdraw to a dissociated internal world cut off from external reality, the pretend mode, to create a protected space. Such children have difficulty interpreting social cues and communication signals from others. They have trouble interpreting others' emotional states and the impact of their behavior and communication on others. Their ability to form accurate, empathic responses is therefore compromised, and they typically project and displace their own affect states onto others. This creates a distorted view of others and of the nature of interactions with them. For example, they may perceive others to be threatening or themselves to be unworthy, damaged, and unlovable. Fonagy and Bateman (2008) suggest that secure attachment provides a "practice space" for children to develop mentalization skills because they feel safe in the context of a relationship with a trustworthy caregiver. Secure attachment between children and parents is therefore important for the development of mentalization. Children who experience a traumatic attachment relationship lack the safety to develop more integrated and symbolic mentalization skills or to build neurobiological structures that form the basis for cognitive and emotional development. According to Fonagy, the lack of availability of a secure attachment in the very early years may therefore lead to long-term vulnerability from which the individual may find it difficult to recover (Fonagy and Bateman 2008).

Abused children find themselves in the dilemma of having to depend on the threatening parent or on the parent who cannot validate or protect them. They lack a mirroring, safely attuned other to help them experience and identify their thoughts and affects or to help them differentiate between their state of mind and those of others. Instead, they may have to develop dissociative functions to protect themselves, or they may internalize the abusive or nonvalidating parent as a part of their self-representation to create some sense of self in the absence of an empathic, mirroring caregiver (Fonagy and Bateman 2008).

Fonagy and Bateman (2008) suggested that borderline personality disorder (BPD) develops as a result of deficits in the mirroring and validating responses of others. Most individuals with BPD have experienced early childhood abuse, which, in turn, has led to distortions in their perceptions of their own mental states and those of others, particularly when they are angry and distressed. As their relationships become more intimate and intense, their accuracy in perceiving their own experience and the experiences of their partners diminishes. Based on a number of studies (Levy 2005), some using the AAI as a measurement scale, BPD has been strongly linked to insecure attachment and is also associated with disorganized attachment (Fonagy and Bateman 2008). Individuals with BPD have seriously compromised mentalization functions, ultimately leading to "diffused identity, experience of inauthenticity, incoherence and emptiness, an inability to make commitments, disturbances of body image and gender dysphoria" (Fonagy and Bateman 2008, 141). When emotionally aroused, people with BPD tend to misread their own states of mind and the internal states of others. Children who lack sufficient mirroring by early caregivers would tend to see caregivers "as part of [their] self representation" (Fonagy and Bateman 2008, 142). Such individuals present with psychic equivalence, or a concrete thought process and the inability to consider perspectives other than their own.

Marsha Linehan developed a model she termed "dialectical behavioral therapy" to work with individuals suffering from BPD. Her model is based on cognitive-behavioral therapy and a mindfulness-based approach to treatment, includes a team approach with individual and group modalities, and aims to teach patients affect regulation, self-acceptance, and effective social skills (Linehan 1993a, 1993b). Dialectical behavioral therapy has demonstrated positive outcomes in treating such patients. More recently, Fonagy and Bateman (2008) developed a mentalization-based, psychodynamic approach for BPD. Their treatment model emphasizes the clinician's attunement and mirroring as well as the gradual building up of a secure base with BPD patients to allow for the introduction of alternative points of view. The model deemphasizes interpretation inasmuch as this psychodynamic technique is deemed inappropriate for patients with severe personality disorders, who may perceive such therapeutic communications as critical and controlling. The clinician's job is to help patients transition from a rigidified, brittle internal structure, in which self and others are experienced as being all good or all bad and where alternative views do not exist, to a more flexible mode of perception of self and others, in which limitations and failures are an acceptable part of ongoing relationships. This development allows for a more flexible and adaptive response to interpersonal conflicts and other stressful events.

The mentalization-based treatment model considers trauma as well as other contextual sources of personality disorder, such as lack of validation, family chaos, loss and separation, multiple caregivers, neglect, and substance abuse. Fonagy and Bateman (2008) emphasize that "it is less the fact of maltreatment than a family environment that discourages coherent discourse concerning mental states that is likely to predispose the child to BPD" (145). They suggest that such individuals, who possess rigid cognitive structures, cannot benefit from traditional insight-oriented therapy, because they have problems with behavioral and affective dysregulation that requires a more structured approach at times (similar to Linehan's [1993a, 1993b] model of dialectical behavioral therapy). They note that clinicians must strive for a balance between stimulating the attachment system to assist clients in negotiating intimate relationships and not overstimulating clients to the point of disorganization. In addition, clinicians must promote patients' capacity for mentalization. Common features of the treatment include clinicians' providing patients with a clear treatment structure, enhancing patients' compliance, providing a clear focus for the treatment, encouraging attachment between therapist and patient, and finally integrating individual treatment with other treatment modalities and services.

THE IMPACT OF TRAUMA ON ADULT ATTACHMENT

Following Ainsworth et al.'s (1978) development of the Strange Situation, Main, Goldwyn, and Hesse (2002) developed the Adult Attachment Interview (AAI), a questionnaire designed to analyze an adult's state of mind in relation to attachment, separation, loss, and trauma. It includes questions about the responder's early relationships related to these attachment experiences and his or her reflections on and perceptions of the experiences. Two indicators Main and colleagues used to analyze a respondent's transcript were (a) the nature of early relationships described by the respondent, and (b) the states of mind related to the early experiences. Qualities seen to represent an autonomous-secure attachment style include coherence, collaboration (with the interviewer), truthfulness, and focus. The AAI is a research instrument rather than a clinical tool, and it relies on the analysis of written transcripts alone rather than on behavioral and nonverbal cues, which are commonly assessed in clinical practice.

Metacognition, or reflective functioning, is one of the hallmarks of a secure-autonomous attachment style, and it demonstrates the capacity for insight, reflection, and empathy. Main, Goldwyn, and Hesse (2002) suggest that there are three aspects of metacognition: (a) the ability to see beyond surface appearances, (b) the ability to recognize changes in the self over time, and (c) the ability to recognize and accept differences between self and others. Metacognition involves the capacity to think about and reflect on one's mental processes in relation to self and others.

In addition to metacognitive skills (as revealed through the AAI interviews), the attributes of the secure-autonomous personality are the capacity (1) to maintain a coherent view of one's life and history, (2) to accept limitations and imperfections in the self, and (3) to empathize with and forgive others despite difficult life experiences. Put differently, these attributes are the ability to be self-reflective, empathic, flexible, yet integrated. Main and colleagues (2002) observe that a secure attachment style can be "earned" through positive relational experiences later in life, including the therapeutic process. That is, insecure attachment patterns, including the dismissive and preoccupied patterns (discussed in the next paragraph), are not necessarily fixed but can change over time in response to environmental factors—for example, a loving marital relationship, mentoring, a good therapeutic experience. Difficult childhood experiences, therefore, are not the sole determinant of personality style.

In addition to the secure-autonomous category, Main, Goldwyn, and Hesse (2002) identified two attachment categories, the "dismissive" and the "preoccupied." The dismissive style is characterized by the respondent's superficial narrative and poor or stereotypical description of childhood experiences and caregivers, such as "I had a wonderful childhood," or "My mother was like all mothers." These adults seem uncomfortable discussing attachment-based and emotional experiences, have poor insight, and seem to be detached from their feelings. They lack early memories and are either dismissive of their caregivers and attachment experiences or show superficial idealization of them. Dismissive people have been found to have rejecting, emotionally constricted, or intrusive caregivers. Consequently, they have learned to mask their unmet needs and avoid potential disappointments through emotional distancing and pseudoautonomy. They are wary of intimate relationships and tend to have concrete ways of perceiving and communicating their experiences.

Preoccupied adults tend to present with discursive and tangential narratives. They show intense emotional engagement with childhood experiences and caregivers, usually by expressing anger or providing vague, confusing memories on the AAI. They seem not to have developed a sense of self sufficiently individuated from their parents and family of origin. The early experiences of preoccupied people are fragmented and unresolved, and typically they present as needy, dependent, and emotionally labile. Whereas the dismissive style correlates with narcissistic and schizoid personality disorders, the preoccupied attachment pattern correlates with BPD (Blatt and Levy 2003).

Main, Goldwyn, and Hesse (2002) found that the unresolved/disorganized attachment style, when arising from a loss or trauma, can accompany any of the above three primary attachment patterns. Although individuals can show autonomy and security overall, they may demonstrate disorganization and lack of resolution in relation to a specific experience of loss or trauma. Unresolved attachment is characterized by sudden changes in speech patterns, disbelief in the death or abuse, and identification with the dead person or with the perpetrator (e.g., respondents may believe that the dead or abusive person is living inside them). Unresolved/disorganized individuals may also express a sense of responsibility for the loss or trauma that is clearly irrational, and they may hold other irrational beliefs associated with the event. They may provide an extraordinary amount of detail in regard to the event, as though it were intercurrent, even if it occurred many years ago (Hesse et al. 2003; Main, Goldwyn, and Hesse 2002). As stated previously, individuals with an unresolved attachment style may be secure in other areas of their lives, and they typically present with another primary attachment category such as dismissive or preoccupied. It is useful to remember that such individuals are unresolved only in regard to a particular experience of loss or trauma. The personality may not be affected more generally. Symptoms of unresolved patients are similar to symptoms of post-traumatic stress disorder (PTSD) patients, except that the unresolved style is in relation to attachment disruption whereas PTSD concerns other kinds of traumatic events or experiences.

The adult attachment patterns identified by the AAI correlate with children's attachment styles as revealed in the Strange Situation experiment. For example, the autonomous style correlates with the secure attachment style in children, the preoccupied category correlates with the ambivalent-resistant style, and the dismissive pattern correlates with the avoidant style. Whereas the Strange Situation attachment styles are based on behavioral observations, the AAI relies on subjective memories and on the participants' reflections and interpretations. As such, the AAI offers considerable clinical utility, especially with psychodynamically based treatment that focuses on childhood experiences, on the acquisition of insight, and on internal, subjective, and often unconscious processes.

UNRESOLVED GRIEF AND MOURNING
IN CHILDREN AND ADULTS

Based on his observations of orphaned children, Bowlby developed a theory of normal versus pathological mourning. He observed that there are four stages in a normal grief response: numbing; yearning and searching for the deceased; disorganization and disorientation; and finally integration and reorganization (Bowlby 1960, 1963, 1980). Children who show unresolved grief may remain at Bowlby's stage of yearning for the deceased, unable to reach the stage of integration and reorganization. Or they may present with disorganization/disorientation, a pattern that seems to characterize individuals who suffer from prolonged mourning, wherein subsequent losses tend to trigger earlier parental loss. If the relationship with the parent had been ambivalent and difficult, prolonged grief may be accompanied by an array of conflicting feelings toward the deceased. As is discussed later in the chapter, some AAI narratives show unresolved/disorganized (UD) loss, which is characterized by vivid memories of the death or funeral even if it occurred a long time ago; feelings of guilt for the death; disorientation in regard to time, place, and circumstances of the death; and other characteristics that suggest the presence of an unresolved traumatic experience. Some studies have found a correlation between prolonged grief disorder (PGD) and later dissociative symptoms (Boelen, Keijsers, and van den Hout 2012; Bui et al. 2013). Dissociative responses have also been associated with losses related to violence and unpredictable death (Boelen 2015). According to Bowlby (1980), during prolonged mourning subsequent experiences of separation and loss often reignite an earlier grief associated with the loss of loved ones. The mourner remains preoccupied with the loss and the deceased, and the earlier grief response is triggered during subsequent relational disruptions such as breakups, divorce, separation, or other losses. In both cases, the grief remains unresolved and the mourner fails to achieve reorganization and the capacity to return to everyday life.

Failed mourning has been associated with a dismissive attachment category in postdeath studies (Wayment and Vierthaler 2002). Although the mourner's ability to overcome the grief may initially seem to signify resilience, this study suggests that long-term consequences may manifest in somatic and affective symptoms. Attachment researchers continue to investigate how early attachment encounters shape one's experience of loss (Field and Sundin 2001; Fraley and Bonnano 2004). Some findings indicate that the response to loss correlates with attachment patterns based on the Strange Situation (Ainsworth et al. 1978; Ainsworth and Bell 1970). These researchers note that adults' bereavement patterns are partly a function of their attachment history and whether or not they are secure, anxious-ambivalent, or avoidant (Field and Sundin 2001; Hazan and Shaver 1992; Shaver and Tancredy 2001; Wayment and Vierthaler 2002).

Based on their findings, the researchers propose that secure individuals are distressed following the loss of a loved one but are eventually able to adapt and reengage in the world; anxious-ambivalent types show a pattern of chronic (or prolonged) grief that remains unresolved throughout their lives; and avoidant individuals show an apparent absence of grief response but may encounter later difficulties related to their unresolved loss (Fraley and Bonnano 2004; Shaver and Tancredy, 2001).

Based on AAI analyses, secure respondents, unlike dismissive or preoccupied respondents, show the capacity to tolerate an array of complex feelings during the grief process. They demonstrate the facility to sustain uncertainty and ambiguity rather than seek quick solutions (Shaver and Fraley 2008, 56).

DEVELOPMENTAL TRAUMA AND DISSOCIATION

The investigation of attachment disorganization due to misattuned parenting, child maltreatment, or parental loss continues to be an important focus of investigation among infant researchers. They have found that the incidence of dissociation is higher among adolescents with a history of disorganized attachment (Lyons-Ruth et al. 2006; Beebe and Lachmann 2014). Starting with infants' response of fear and dissociative behavior during the Strange Situation, subsequent infant studies (Lyons-Ruth et al. 2006; Beebe et al. 2012) tracked the dynamics of disorganized dyads, in which a lack of early responsiveness to the child's affective needs—in the form of misattunement, dismissal, shaming, or aggression—were shown to be early indications of adolescent dissociation. These studies show that in addition to trauma and abuse, other dynamics in the child/mother dyad—such as a lack of recognition, attunement, and affect regulation—could determine the child's attachment pattern and disorganized response starting as early as four months of age (Beebe and Lachmann 2014). AAI studies with Holocaust survivors who witnessed the murder of family members as young children reveal that those events continued to affect the adult respondents' capacity for empathy, intimacy, and affective experiences, and that the survivors showed disconnection from affective and somatic experience as well as an inability to reflect on or mentalize their overwhelming experience of traumatic loss (Sagi-Schwartz, Koren-Karie, and Joels 2003).

Beebe et al. (2012) suggest that the mother's attuned recognition of the child's mental states is a fundamental factor in the experience of feeling known by another and in the development of the child's capacity to know themselves. Early disrupted communications between infant and parent were found to predict later dissociation (Lyons-Ruth, Bronfman, and Parsons 1999; Slade 2014). Beebe and Lachmann (2014) assert that when the infant is impinged upon, untouched, or ignored when distressed, the infant's affective and cognitive development is disturbed, and processes of coherence and internal integration fail to take place. Other findings have shown that early traumatic loss or childhood traumatic experiences are risk factors for later complicated grief response (Lobb et al. 2010), and that the development of PTSD may be associated with childhood exposure to abuse (van der Kolk 2014).

In a five-year study that included thirty-two Adult Attachment Interviews characterized by unresolved/disorganized (UD) loss, I found that subjects who described early attachment disruptions, conflicts and lack of intimacy with their parents, or other traumatic events in their childhood were likely to exhibit unresolved mourning and dissociative states of mind in response to the loss (Ringel, in press). The study highlights the link between adverse childhood attachment experiences and unresolved grief later in life. Based on these findings, UD grief may be correlated with traumatic factors in the subject's history, such as abusive relationships with caregivers, parental divorce, parental mental illness or PTSD, lack of safety and security during essential developmental periods, or a traumatic manner of death of the deceased from an accident, suicide, or other unexpected cause. These factors contribute to prolonged and complicated grief as well as to dissociative states, and they may lead to an ongoing vulnerability to subsequent losses or relational disruptions. It is significant that dissociative states of mind as defined by Main, Goldwyn, and Hesse (2002) can coexist with a secure/autonomous classification, so that subjects may demonstrate a secure attachment style while at the same time exhibiting dissociative behaviors in regard to loss or trauma in their history. These findings can be useful in identifying and applying clinical interventions with the bereaved. In addition, they show that one's vulnerability to UD loss, and the difficulty in integrating and resolving loss, may be rooted in early attachment experiences. Therefore, processing these early experiences may be essential to gaining new meaning and creating new relational bonds. In my view, it is imperative to work through early traumatic experiences and relational antecedents to help facilitate the integration of UD states of mind in regard to loss.

Clinical studies of mourning and bereavement suggest that finding new meaning following the loss often contributes to integration and resolution (Kosminsky and Jordan 2016; Hasson-Ohayon et al. 2017; Malkinson, Rubin, and Witztum 2006). However, in the case of prolonged and traumatic loss, trauma-focused interventions may be required to help process and integrate dissociated memories and affects related to the loss. Phase-based, trauma-focused treatment includes stabilization, affect regulation, processing of the traumatic experience, and integration of narrative, affective, and somatic states. Moreover, a relational reorientation has been described in several trauma-focused models (van der Hart, Nijenhuis, and Steele 2006; Herman 1993; Ogden, Kekuni, and Pain 2006; van der Kolk 2014). The relational approach emphasizes implicit communication (Beebe and Lachmann 2002) and relational processes between client and therapist that may help revise traumatogenic attachment patterns and facilitate the creation of new meanings (van der Hart, Nijenhuis, and Steele 2006).

Finally, it is unclear whether the AAI has been used with minority populations or with participants from lower socioeconomic strata. To date, it appears that a majority of research respondents are college students and that most come from middle-class households. In some poor or minority communities, including African American, Latino, and Native American, it may not be the norm to discuss childhood experiences, disclose one's negative perceptions of parents, or discuss experiences of loss and trauma. In such client communities, it may take a long time to develop trust, especially with outsiders from a different class, race, or ethnicity (such as the AAI researchers). It is possible, therefore, that the AAI is culturally biased in favor of middle-class, educated respondents, who may be more familiar with a process of self-reflection and may tend to be more trusting of strangers.

CONTRIBUTIONS OF NEUROSCIENCE
TO THE UNDERSTANDING OF TRAUMA

Neuroscience has made important contributions to our understanding of the impact of early attachment disruptions on brain development and of the cognitive, emotional, and behavioral sequelae of such disruptions. Studies show that the effect of trauma on brain structure is quite significant. The brain is composed of three interdependent sections: the brain stem and hypothalamus, primarily associated with the regulation of internal homeostasis; the limbic system, which helps maintain the balance between the internal world and external reality; and the neocortex, which is responsible for analyzing and interacting with the external world. The brain's right hemisphere is involved in nonverbal emotional apprehension and expression, such as tone of voice, facial expression, and visual spatial communication, and is linked to the amygdala, which regulates autonomic and hormonal responses to incoming information. The left hemisphere mediates verbal communication and organizes problem-solving tasks. Failure of left-hemisphere functions may occur during states of extreme arousal (e.g., during traumatic experiences) and is believed to be responsible for experiences of derealization and depersonalization, mental states of mind associated with acute post-traumatic stress (van der Kolk 2003).

Studies with people who suffer chronic PTSD have shown that the structure of the brain changes as a consequence of traumatic experience. For example, the hippocampus decreases in volume, which suggests problems in the absorption and processing of information that originates in the traumatic experience (van der Kolk 2003). This may signify an ongoing dissociation and a misinterpretation of information, resulting in aggressive reactions, withdrawal, and perceptions of events as threats—which are common symptoms of PTSD.

A study in which participants were exposed to the narrative of a traumatic experience demonstrated increased activity only in the right hemisphere, especially in the amygdala, where emotional arousal takes place, but there was a significant *decrease* in activity in the left hemisphere, where interpretation and verbal communication of experiences occur (Rauch et al. 1996, cited in van der Kolk 2003). High levels of activity in the amygdala may indicate an interference with the hippocampus functions of evaluation and categorization of information. The consequence of such failures is that the traumatic experiences fail to become unified and integrated.

One of the major functions of the prefrontal cortex is the regulation of emotions. The right hemisphere is responsible for absorption and processing of emotions through the limbic system, particularly the amygdala, and attends to nonverbal aspects of experience. The left hemisphere processes emotional arousal, categorizes it, and eventually incorporates it into narrative and language (Coan 2008). The process of affect regulation occurs both through interaction with the caregiver, who helps sooth and provide safety and security to the child, and through the internalization of what Bowlby (1973) called "internal working models." The child uses internal representations of the caregiver to help soothe and regulate arousal. These mental representations exist in both procedural (unconscious) and declarative (conscious) memories. Siegel suggests that "the human mind is a process that regulates patterns in the flow of two elements, energy and information. This flow can occur within one brain or two or more brains, so that mind is created in the interaction between neurophysiological processes and interpersonal relationships" (2003, 9).

Procedural memory, which includes emotions, intuition, and fantasy, resides in the right hemisphere and develops through nonverbal interactions between infants and their caregivers. Schore and Schore (2008) suggest that "the mutual regulations between infant and caregiver promote the development and maintenance of synaptic connections during the establishment of functional circuits of the right brain" (11). The left hemisphere, in which explicit (or declarative), linear (logical), semantic (factual), and autobiographical (episodic) memory resides, develops later through verbal interactions between children and caregivers (Schore and Schore 2008). Schore and

Schore note that development of the right brain, which occurs earlier than development of the left brain, "contributes to the development of the emotional self embedded in implicit intersubjective affective transactions" between infant and caregiver (12). These interactions are primarily visual.

Siegel (2003) applies complexity theory to brain development, noting that the developing brain moves toward increasingly complex states, as well as to the regulation of states of activation through both internal and external constraints. The minds of two individuals become linked as a single adaptive and flexible system that is both highly integrated and highly differentiated to create maximal complexity. In a disorganized attachment, the child shows poor differentiation from caregiver interactions, and the parent is unable to perceive distress or provide regulatory functions to the child. Avoidant-dismissive child-parent dyads are characterized by loose linking and a high level of differentiation but little integration. In contrast, flexibility and integration are characteristics of securely attached child-parent dyads. Such dyads can facilitate, absorb, and survive a wide range of stressful situations and traumatic experiences. Brain structure, affect regulation, personality style, and interpersonal skills are all greatly influenced by early traumatic experiences and attachment disorganization.

SUMMARY AND IMPLICATIONS FOR TREATMENT

Attachment theory has principally been used in research protocols until recently. Within the past decade, attachment principles have been applied to interventions with maltreated children (Marvin et al. 2002; Slade 2008) as well as to the improvement of parent-child interactions that may otherwise lead to insecure and disorganized attachment styles. As mentioned previously, Slade (2008) works with young unwed mothers who are unaware that their intrusive behavior may be interpreted as frightening to their children. After the mothers view videos of their interactions with their babies, they are able to recognize the effects of their behaviors on their children and can begin to understand and empathize with the children's inner experience. Other attachment concepts, including affect regulation, the development of a secure base, and the effect of attachment security or insecurity on later development, are the basis for contemporary psychodynamic models. These models include contemporary self psychology, intersubjectivity, and relational theories. Lessons from attachment theory and infant observation also have contributed to the treatment of trauma. It is now recognized that an important aspect of the clinical process with traumatized patients is stabilization and affect regulation. In effect, clinicians must help clients develop strategies for self-soothing and self-regulation en route to the development of more stable and securely based interpersonal relationships. The treatment of complex trauma, in particular, requires that patients and clinicians understand the nature of childhood traumas and their effects on patients' cognitive, affective, and behavioral symptoms as well as on their interpersonal relationships. With the return of combat veterans from two intercurrent wars in Iraq and Afghanistan, PTSD has become a national problem in the United States. Its problems are frequently complicated by the soldiers' earlier traumatic experiences. Such preexisting traumas may exacerbate combat-related symptoms and require both longer psychosocial treatment and short-term exposure techniques, which are not intended to address developmental and contextual factors.

Another attachment-based model is emotion-focused therapy (EFT), a treatment approach that has been used with combat veterans and their spouses as well as with couples in which one or both members struggled with traumatic histories (Johnson 2002; Johnson and Courtois 2009). The principles on which EFT is based include a recognition that attachment needs constitute the primary motivation for couples and that attachment bonds provide a natural regulatory system essential for human emotional survival. Johnson (2002) postulates that dependency needs should not be viewed as pathologically based (i.e., through the lens of Western cultural norms); rather, they are universal and normal. Another EFT principle is that secure attachment allows the child, and later the adult, to look to the primary attachment figure for help in regulating overwhelming affects and for the provision of love and support during times of distress. Having a secure attachment history helps people to achieve greater success in intimate relationships; individuals with secure attachment histories are also more flexible, open, and likely to seek closeness at times of crisis. In contrast, insecure and disorganized attachment histories may lead to "demanding, controlling and pursuing roles in adult relationships" (Johnson and Courtois 2009, 375), and those with avoidant histories may become dismissive adults who employ strategies of withdrawal and distancing from their partners.

Critical elements of the EFT model include assessment of potential violence in the relationship, investigation of the effects of PTSD on each partner's behavior (e.g., self-harm, substance abuse, and other individual safety issues), and education regarding the nature of traumatic stress and its effects on the individual and the couple. The therapeutic bond is of primary significance in the treatment. Interventions include a focus on partners' emotional experiences and their expression (especially marginalized emotions such as sadness and fear rather than anger) and on increasing the capacity for openness and vulnerability between partners. The EFT clinician helps partners reach out to one another for emotional support and encourages them to respond sensitively and empathically to one another's distress and intimacy needs.

These clinical models use attachment principles to provide treatment for traumatized individuals and families. They also provide a link between (a) empirical findings of attachment theory and infant studies and (b) clinical practice. For attachment-based clinicians, it is important to keep in mind that insecure attachment patterns, such as children's avoidant, anxious-resistant, and disorganized styles, and adults' dismissive, preoccupied, and unresolved patterns, intensify when attachment disruptions occur. During times of distress, habitual attachment strategies that are designed to protect against separation, abandonment, and rejection become more strongly manifested. Attachment-based practice benefits patients by providing a secure foundation with their therapists, and also by helping patients process their fear and anger related to past relational disruptions and to empathic disruptions with their therapists. The hope is that patients will learn that other, more flexible strategies are available for them to resolve these disruptions and to maintain and deepen important relational bonds.

NOTE

1   *Chase and dodge* refers to a mother's efforts to establish eye contact with her infant; the infant, who experiences this as intrusive, either averts her or his gaze or turns her or his head away from the mother.

REFERENCES

Ainsworth, M., and S. Bell. 1970. "Attachment, Exploration, and Separation: Illustrated by the Behavior of One Year Olds In Strange Situation." *Child Development* 41:49–67.

Ainsworth, M., M. Blehar, E. Water, and S. Wall. 1978. *Patterns of Attachment.* Hillsdale, N.J.: Lawrence Erlbaum.

Beebe, B. 2005. "Mother-Infant Research Informs Mother-Infant Treatment." *Psychoanalytic Study of the Child* 60:7–46.

Beebe, B., J. Jaffe, F. Lachmann, S. Feldstein, C. Crown, and M. Jasnow. 2000. "Systems Models in Development and Psychoanalysis: The Case of Vocal Rhythm Coordination and Attachment." *Infant Mental Health Journal* 21 (1/2): 99–122.

Beebe, B., and F. Lachmann. 2002. *Infant Research and Adult Treatment: Co-Constructing Interactions.* Hillsdale, N.J.: Analytic Press.

Beebe, B., and F. Lachmann. 2014. *The Origins of Attachment: Infant Research and Adult Treatment.* New York: Routledge.

Beebe, B., F, Lachmann, S. Markese, and L. Bahrick. 2012. "On the Origins of Disorganized Attachment and Internal Working Models: Paper I. A Dyadic Systems Approach." *Psychoanalytic Dialogues* 22 (2): 253–272.

Blatt, S., and K. N. Levy. 2003. "Attachment Theory, Psychoanalysis, Personality Development, and Psychopathology." *Psychoanalytic Inquiry* 23 (1): 102–150.

Boelen, P. A. 2015. "Peritraumatic Distress and Dissociation in Prolonged Grief and Posttraumatic Stress Following Violent and Unexpected Deaths." *Journal of Trauma and Dissociation* 16 (5): 541–550.

Boelen, P. A., L. Keijsers, and M. A. van den Hout. 2012. "Peritraumatic Dissociation After Loss: Latent Structure and Associations with Psychopathology." *Journal of Nervous and Mental Disease* 200 (4): 362–364.

Bowlby, J. 1960. "Grief and Mourning in Infancy and Early Childhood." *Psychoanalytic Study of the Child* 15:3–39.

Bowlby, J. 1963. "Pathological Mourning and Childhood Mourning." *Journal of the American Psychoanalytic Association* 11:500–541.

Bowlby, J. 1973. *Attachment and Loss.* Vol. 2, *Separation.* New York: Basic Books.

Bowlby, J. 1980. *Loss.* London: Hogarth Press.

Bui, E., N. M. Simon, D. J. Robinaugh, N. J. LeBlanc, Y. Wang, N. A. Skritskaya, and M. K. Shear. 2013. "Periloss Dissociation, Symptom Severity, and Treatment Response in Complicated Grief." *Depression and Anxiety* 30 (2): 123–128.

Coan, J. 2008. "Towards a Neuroscience of Attachment." In *Handbook of Attachment: Theory, Research, and Clinical Applications,* ed. J. Cassidy and P. Shaver, 249–268. New York: Guilford Press.

Diamond, D. 2004. "Attachment Disorganization: The Reunion of Attachment Theory and Psychoanalysis." *Psychoanalytic Psychology* 21 (2): 276–299.

Field, N., and E. Sundin. 2001. "Attachment Style in Adjustment to Conjugal Bereavement." *Journal of Social and Personal Relationships* 18 (3): 347–361.

Fonagy, P., G. Gergfely, E. Jurist, and M. Target. 2002. *Affect Regulation: Mentalization and the Development of the Self.* New York: Other Press.

Fonagy, P., and A. Bateman. 2006. "Mechanisms of Change in Mentalization-Based Treatment of BPD." *Journal of Clinical Psychology* 62 (4): 411–430.

Fonagy, P., and A. Bateman. 2008. "Mentalization Based Treatment of Borderline Personality Disorder." In Jurist, Slade, and Bergner, 139–166.

Fonagy, P., and M. Target. 2008. "Attachment, Trauma, and Psychoanalysis." In Jurist, Slade, and Bergner, 15–49.

Fraley, C., and G. Bonanno. 2004. "Attachment and Loss: A Test of Three Competing Models on the Association Between Attachment Related Avoidance and Adaptation to Bereavement." *Personality and Social Psychology Bulletin* 30:878–890.

Harlow, H. 1958. "The Nature of Love." *American Psychologist* 3:673–685.

Hasson-Ohayon, I., T. Peri, I. Rotschild, and R. Tuval-Mashiach. 2017. "The Mediating Role of Integration of Loss in the Relationship Between Dissociation and Prolonged Grief Disorder." *Journal of Clinical Psychology*, (12): 1717–1728.

Hazan, C., and P. R. Shaver. 1992. "Broken Attachments: Relationship Loss from the Perspective of Attachment Theory." In *Close Relationship Loss: Theoretical Approaches*, T. L. Orbuch, 90–107. New York: Springer-Verlag.

Herman, J. 1993. *Trauma and Recovery.* New York: Basic Books.

Hesse, E. 1999. "The Adult Attachment Interview: Historical and Current Perspectives." In *Handbook of Attachment: Theory, Research and Clinical Applications*, eds. J. Cassidy and P. Shaver, 395–433. New York: Guilford Press.

Hesse, E. 2009. "The Adult Attachment Interview: Protocol, Method of Analysis and Empirical Studies." In *Handbook of Attachment: Theory, Research and Clinical Applications.* 2nd ed., ed. J. Cassidy and P. Shaver, 552–598. New York: Guilford Press.

Hesse, E., M. Main, K. Abrams, and A. Rifkin. 2003. "Unresolved States Regarding Loss or Abuse Can Have 'Second Generation' Effects: Disorganization, Role Inversion, and Frightening Ideation in the Offspring and Traumatized Nonmaltreating Parents." In *Healing Trauma: Attachment, Mind, Body and Brain*, ed. M. Solomon and D. Siegel, 57–106. New York: Norton.

Johnson, S. 2002. *Emotionally Focused Couple Therapy with Trauma Survivors: Strengthening Attachment Bonds.* New York: Guilford Press.

Johnson, S., and C. Courtois. 2009. "Couple Therapy." In *Treating Complex Traumatic Stress Disorders: An Evidence-Based Guide*, ed. C. Courtois and J. Ford, 371–390. New York: Guilford Press.

Jurist, E., A. Slade, and S. Bergner, eds. 2008. *Mind to Mind: Infant Research, Neuroscience, and Psychoanalysis*. New York: Other Press.

Kosminsky, P., and J. Jordan. 2016. *Attachment Informed Grief Therapy: The Clinician's Guide to Foundations and Applications*. New York: Routledge.

Levy, K. 2005. "The Implications of Attachment Theory and Research for Understanding Borderline Personality Disorder." *Development and Psychopathology* 17 (4): 959–986.

Linehan, M. 1993a. *Cognitive Behavioral Treatment of Borderline Personality Disorder*. New York: Guilford Press.

Linehan, M. 1993b. *Skills Training Manual for Treating Borderline Personality Disorder*. New York: Guilford Press.

Liotti, G. 2004. "Trauma, Dissociation, and Disorganized Attachment: Three Strands of a Single Braid." *Psychotherapy: Theory, Research, Practice, Training* 41 (4): 472–486.

Lobb, E. A., L. J. Kristjanson, S. M. Aoun, L. Monterosso, G. K. Haikert, and A. Davies. 2010. "Predictors of Complicated Grief: A Systematic Review of Empirical Studies." *Death Studies* 34 (8): 673–698.

Lyons-Ruth, K., E. Bronfman, and E. Parsons. 1999. "Maternal Disrupted Affective Communications, Maternal Frightened or Frightening Behavior, and Disorganized Infant Attachment Strategies." *Monographs of the Society for Research in Child Development* 64 (3): serial no. 258.

Lyons-Ruth, K., L. Dutra, M. Schuder, and I. Bianchi. 2006. "From Infant Attachment Disorganization to Adult Dissociation: Relational Adaptations or Traumatic Experiences?" *Psychiatric Clinical North America* 29:63–86.

Lyons-Ruth, K., and D. Jacobvitz. 2009. "Attachment Disorganization: Genetic Factors, Parenting Contexts, and Developmental Transformation from Infancy to Adulthood." In *Handbook of Attachment: Theory, Research and Clinical Applications*, ed. J. Cassidy and P. Shaver, 666–697. New York: Guilford Press.

Main, M., R. Goldwyn, and E. Hesse. 2002. "Adult Attachment Scoring and Classification Systems." Unpublished manuscript, Regents of the University of California.

Main, M., and J. Solomon. 1990. "Procedures for Identifying Infants as Disorganized/Disoriented During the Strange Situation." In *Attachment in the Pre-*

school Years: Theory, Research, and Intervention, ed. M. Greenberg, D. Cicchetti, and E. M. Cummings, 121–160. Chicago: University of Chicago Press.

Malkinson, R., S. Rubin, and E. Witztum. 2006. "Therapeutic Issues and the Relationship to the Deceased: Working Clinically with the Two-Track Model of Bereavement." *Death Studies* 30:797–815.

Marvin, R., G. Cooper, K. Hoffman, and B. Powell. 2002. "The Circle of Security Project: Attachment Based Intervention with Caregiver Pre-School Child Dyads." *Attachment and Human Development* 4 (1): 107–124.

Mikulincer, M., and P. Shaver. 2009. "Adult Attachment and Affect Regulation." In *Handbook of Attachment: Theory, Research, and Clinical Applications*, ed. J. Cassidy and P. Shaver, 503–531. New York: Guilford Press.

Nahum, J. 2000. "An Overview of Louis Sander's Contribution to the Field of Mental Health." *Infant Mental Health Journal* 21 (1/2): 29–41.

Ogden, P., M. Kekuni, and C. Pain. 2006. *Trauma and the Body: A Sensorimotor Approach to Psychotherapy*. New York: Norton.

Ringel, S. (In Press). "Traumatic Factors and Dissociative Narratives of Unresolved Loss in the Adult Attachment Interview." *New Directions in Psychotherapy and Relational Psychoanalysis*.

Sagi-Schwartz, A., N. Koren-Karie, and T. Joels. 2003. "Failed Mourning in the AAI: The Case of Holocaust Child Survivors." *Attachment and Human Development* 5:398–408.

Schore, A. 2011. "The Right Brain Implicit Self Lies at the Core of Psychoanalysis." *Psychoanalytic Dialogues* 21 (1): 75–100.

Schore, J., and A. Schore. 2008. "Modern Attachment Theory: The Central Role of Affect Regulation in Development and Treatment." *Clinical Social Work Journal* 36 (1): 9–20.

Shaver, P., and C. Fraley. 2008. "Attachment, Loss, and Grief: Bowlby's Views and Current Controversies." In *Handbook of Attachment*, ed. M. Cassidy and P. Shavier (48–77). New York: Guilford.

Shaver, P. R., and C. M. Tancredy. 2001. "Emotion, Attachment, and Bereavement: A Conceptual Commentary." In *Handbook of Bereavement: Consequences, Coping, and Care*, ed. M. S. Stroebe, W. Stroebe, R. O. Hansson, and H. Schut, 63–88. Washington, D.C.: American Psychological Association.

Siegel, D. 2003. "An Interpersonal Neurobiology of Psychotherapy: The Developing Mind and the Resolution of Trauma." In *Healing Trauma: Attachment, Mind, Body, and Brain*, ed. M. Solomon and D. Siegel, 1–56. New York: Norton.

Slade, A. 2008. "The Implications of Attachment Theory and Research for Adult Psychotherapy." In *Handbook of Attachment*, ed. J. Cassidy and P. Shaver, 762–782. New York: Guilford.

Slade, H. 2014. "Imagining Fear: Attachment, Threat, and Psychic Experience." *Psychoanalytic Dialogues* 24 (3): 253–266.

Solomon, J., and C. George. 1999. "The Place of Disorganization in Attachment Theory: Linking Classic Observations with Contemporary Findings." In *Attachment Disorganization*, eds. J. Solomon and C. George, 3–32. New York: Guilford Press.

Sroufe, A., B. Egeland, and T. Kreutzer. 1990. "The Fate of Early Experience Following Developmental Change: Longitudinal Approaches to Individual Adaptation in Childhood." *Child Development* 61:1363–1373.

Tronick, E. 1977. "The Infant's Capacity to Regulate Mutuality in Face to Face Interaction." *Journal of Communication* 27:74–80.

Tronick, E. 1998. "Dyadically Expanded States of Consciousness and the Process of Therapeutic Change." *Infant Mental Health Journal* 19 (3): 290–299.

Tronick, E. 2002. "A Model of Infant Mood States and Sandarian Affective Waves." *Psychoanalytic Dialogues* 12 (11):73–99.

van der Hart, O., E. Nijenhuis, and K. Steele. 2006. *The Haunted Self.* New York: Norton.

van der Kolk, B. 2003. "Posttraumatic Stress Disorder and the Nature of Trauma." In *Healing Trauma*, ed. M. Solomon and D. Siegel, 168–195. New York: Norton.

van der Kolk, B. 2014. *The Body Keeps the Score: Brain, Mind, and Body in the Healing of Trauma.* New York: Penguin.

Wayment, H. A., and J. Vierthaler. 2002. "Attachment Style and Bereavement Reactions." *Journal of Loss and Trauma* 7:129–149.

6

Mindfulness-Oriented Approaches to Trauma Treatment

▸ SHOSHANA RINGEL

THIS CHAPTER PROVIDES a general introduction to mindfulness practice and describes three mindfulness-based, trauma-focused treatment models: acceptance and commitment therapy (ACT), sensorimotor psychotherapy, and internal family systems (IFS) therapy. The chapter addresses the principles of mindfulness-oriented perspectives, such as present-moment awareness, nonidentification, and the acceptance of all arising mental states. The discussion of each of the models includes a clinical vignette, broad principles of practice, and the role of the therapist in the treatment process and research outcomes.

MINDFULNESS PRACTICE AND BUDDHIST PSYCHOLOGY

The practice of mindfulness is based on Buddhism, a spiritual and psychological system taught by the Buddha, who lived and practiced approximately three thousand years ago. According to historical narratives, the Buddha left his protected mansion as a young man to take a walk in the city. He saw an old woman by the side of the road, then a sick man, and finally a corpse, and recognized that suffering, whether due to old age, sickness, or death, was endemic to human existence and therefore inevitable. The Buddha chose to leave his privileged life to seek answers about the nature of suffering and to find the way to liberation from suffering through stringent spiritual practice. After six years of wandering and spiritual seeking, he decided to follow a path of moderation and reflection and eventually attained spiritual realization, or enlightenment. The Buddha realized four noble truths: (1) life is suffering, (2) the cause of suffering is grasping or aversion, (3) there is an end to suffering, and (4) in order to end suffering one must follow the eightfold path. He taught these principles to his disciples, and they became the foundations of Buddhist thought. The four noble truths are based on the Buddha's understanding that attachment to transitory conditions and objects, such as youth, beauty, money, or fame, will lead not to lasting happiness but rather to chronic stress and frustration, for permanent fulfillment based on external and temporary conditions is impossible and therefore always out of reach. Moreover, turning away from and avoiding life's inevitable unpleasant experiences, such as pain, illness, or distressing emotional states, also leads to suffering. The fourth noble truth, the eightfold path, is based on the Buddha's recognition that meditation and insight must be grounded in a moral and ethical life that facilitates equanimity, harmony, and the balance necessary for the attainment of wisdom and insight through a mindfulness meditation practice (Goldstein 2013).

During the 1970s and 1980s, the practice of mindfulness in the United States took place in the context of intensive meditation retreats taught by experienced teachers who had returned from India, Tibet, Thailand, and other Far Eastern countries after having trained for several years. Eventually, the principles of mindfulness practice were integrated into several clinical models of individual and group therapy. Best-known among them are dialectical behavior therapy (DBT), mindfulness-based cognitive-behavior therapy (MBCBT), and acceptance and commitment therapy (ACT). In addition, several other clinical models, which I will describe later in the chapter, integrate mindfulness principles into their theoretical and clinical paradigms, including psychodynamic therapy (Ringel, 2018; Epstein 2007), sensorimotor therapy (Ogden and Minton 2000), and internal family systems therapy (Schwartz 1995, 2013). Mindfulness practice has been used as a method of intervention in trauma and PTSD, and ACT has been employed successfully with veterans suffering from PTSD (Williams et. al, 2007) and with individual survivors of trauma (Orsillo and Batten 2005; Twohig 2009). As suggested by Briere (2015), mindfulness-focused therapy is based on personal insights attained through the direct practice of mindfulness meditation. For this reason, clinicians who practice the approach should have a genuine meditation practice so that they can embody and model personal insights and a lived code of ethics for their clients. As described in the first clinical vignette, an intensive meditation practice or sustained inquiry into traumatic experience that has generally been conducted in solitude may become overwhelming and destabilizing for some clients, and therefore the process of inquiry should be modified based on each client's level of tolerance and psychic organization. Although mindfulness-based clinical inquiry is rooted in the principles of nonidentification and a detached observation of arising mental states, memories, and affects, many survivors of trauma may not be immediately ready to practice detachment from their traumatic experiences and sensory triggers. The therapist must establish a foundation of grounding and stabilization as an initial treatment phase, prior to processing the trauma itself.

BUDDHISM AND THE SELF

The Buddhist tradition asserts that there is no solid, unified self, and it views sensory, affective, and cognitive experiences as fluid and transitory. According to Epstein (2007), a mindfulness meditation practice alters one's relationship to self-fragmentation in that it helps deepen one's awareness and the subsequent realization that affects and mental states are constantly changing and ultimately transitory and unstable, although there is clearly a distinction between a dissociative process that occurs in the natural course of life and pathological dissociation rooted in traumatic experiences (Bromberg 2011; Schimmenti 2016). In Buddhism, the self is seen as an essentially fluid structure that is in a constant process of change and transition; it is fundamentally illusory because it is based on self-constructed identifications and conditioned mental states. Mindful meditation practice intends to lead to an eventual recognition of the emptiness of the self and the impermanence of human experience. From a Buddhist perspective, one's attachment to self-concepts is viewed as a significant cause of pain and suffering (Jennings 2003; Epstein 2007; Safran 2003). Paradoxically, Buddhist thought also suggests that concepts of self and identity are necessary in order to function in everyday life (Goldstein 2013). A well-known Zen story illustrates this conundrum: A seeker sees a monk climbing a mountain with a heavy bag thrown over his shoulder. The seeker asks the monk what enlightenment is, and the monk puts the bag down. The seeker asks, "So, what now?" And the monk picks up the bag and continues walking up the mountain.

In the clinical situation, empathic awareness is embedded in the self/other matrix between client and therapist (Orange 2011). In Buddhist practice, empathy arises out of meditative contemplation as one recognizes the inherent bond of interconnectedness between all living beings (Kulka 2012). A contemplative practice is typically a solitary endeavor, providing a reflective vantage point within oneself, an internal space within which to experience the transitory nature of thoughts, affects, and bodily phenomena. This reflective space includes an inquiry into present experience as the practitioner tracks subtle shifts in the sequence of sensory and affective patterns and gradually becomes aware of mental constructions and self-narratives that are based on conditioned patterns of thought and feelings and often reified into misleading identifications and compartmentalized self-states (Smith 2014). The practice of compassion and empathy holds a special place in mindfulness meditation practice through a focused visualization process called "metta," or loving-kindness meditation, which includes the visualization of loving thoughts toward oneself and others. Metta is one of the few forms of guided meditation procedures in the mindfulness tradition.

PRINCIPLES OF MINDFULNESS PRACTICE

The principles of mindfulness practice include a moment-to-moment attention to and awareness of somatic, affective, and cognitive processes; a perspective of observation, inquiry, and nonidentification with somatic and mental states; and the acceptance of all phenomena as they arise through sensory, affective, and cognitive channels. This approach helps create a reflective vantage point in which client and therapist can hold and regulate traumatic experience.

A meditative, mindful investigation can deepen the therapeutic process through attention to the sensory aspects of experience, which the therapist can facilitate through sustained inquiry that often shifts the focus from narrative and interpretation to somatic experiences and insights embedded in the client's present experience (Safran 2003; Engler 2003; Epstein 1995, 2007; Jennings 2003). Mindful inquiry may therefore help interrupt the client's habitual patterns of negative self-judgments, shame, and conditioned cognitive loops rooted in traumatic experiences, as well as paralyzing fear and avoidance (van der Hart, Nijenhuis, and Steele 2006).

ACCEPTANCE AND COMMITMENT THERAPY (ACT)

ACT is a mindfulness-based approach that has been successful with veterans suffering from PTSD (Williams et al. 2007; Hiraoka et al. 2016; Orsillo and Batten 2005) and other traumatized clients, including survivors of sexual assault (Woidneck, Morrison, and Twohig 2014; Twohig 2009). ACT is a form of CBT that employs mindfulness skills to facilitate functional behavioral change. It uses grounding techniques, visual metaphors, and mindfulness exercises (Hayes, Strosahl, and Wilson 2012). Rather than focusing on symptom reduction and diagnosis, which can lead to pathologizing clients, the approach uses mindfulness procedures and specific behavioral changes to target the functional effect of inner experience on behaviors and to track how thoughts, feelings, and sensory experience affect behaviors (Twohig 2009). ACT is a client-centered approach in that it is a collaborative effort by client and therapist to examine and understand the function of behavior in the context of family, history, and culture (Stoddard, Afari, and Hayes 2014). In addition to teaching mindfulness-based grounding and awareness skills, ACT also follows the Buddhist principle that suffering is due in part to aversion and avoidance; it emphasizes that survivors must face their traumatic memories and experiences from a fresh vantage point of nonidentification and acceptance. Survivors of trauma often use avoidance as a protective strategy, thereby preventing healing that is typically achieved through the processing of traumatic memories and experiences. ACT helps survivors understand the function of avoidance—its benefits and challenges—without pathologizing or judging. ACT also helps facilitate greater flexibility, replacing the rigid dichotomies of self/others, good/bad. It enhances clients' capacity to be in the here and now, encouraging them to observe their traumatic memories and feelings through a present-moment lens that facilitates greater tolerance and the capacity to regulate emotions. ACT shifts the emphasis from pathology and symptoms to functionality and targeted behavioral change (Hayes, Strosahl, and Wilson 2012; McLean and Follette 2016).

Principles of Practice

The six principles of ACT, based on Buddhist psychology, include (a) *acceptance*: the willingness to be with uncomfortable memories, thoughts, sensation, and emotions without judgment or identification, (b) *defusion*:

developing a new relationship to one's thoughts from a stance of nonidentification with (or decentering from) the thoughts, emotions, and other experiences that arise, (c) *self as context*: observing life events without identifying with them (as opposed to self as concept, wherein the self is understood through one's roles, behaviors, and emotions), as well as viewing the self as observer and outside the experience, (d) *values*: identifying one's moral and ethical path based on the eightfold path, and (e) *commitment*: engaging in actions consistent with one's values and the pursuit of justice (Engle and Follette 2015).

The following clinical vignette illustrates principles of mindfulness-based therapy, including observation of embodied experience, nonidentifying, and acceptance of emergent states of mind. The case described integrates mindfulness within a relational framework in which the intersubjective dynamics between client and therapist, and the mutual processing of enactments, are described.

Clinical Example

Kyle grew up with the implicit message that without his mother he could not survive, and so any physical separation from her became painful and frightening. His mother seemed to have undermined any attempt on Kyle's part at separation and autonomy and clearly relied on him for emotional intimacy and soothing. Kyle poignantly recalled being held by his mother as an infant, experiencing safety and security, but also a sense of suffocation and despair. Whenever he lost sight of his mother or had to go to school on his own as a young child, Kyle became frantically anxious and fearful. Though he was now a full-grown adult, Kyle and his mother still texted and called each other several times a day. As he matured, Kyle became aware that his mother needed him to shore up her emotionally distant and unsatisfying marriage and looked to him for the intense intimacy that his father was unable to provide.

Since early childhood, Kyle had felt an overwhelming anxiety that typically manifested in somatic symptoms, including shaking, stammering, and crying uncontrollably, symptoms that caused him deep shame and embarrassment. Kyle also experienced states of dissociation and depersonalization, when he would feel disconnected from his body and would lose the sense of where he was. This typically occurred in situations of severe stress. Though

Kyle tried a variety of treatments, a range of drug regimens, and periodic hospitalization, nothing seemed to have a lasting impact. Because of his debilitating anxiety, Kyle was unable to live his life to the fullest, develop lasting romantic relationships, or even move away from his home town and his parents. Even though most of his friends were pursuing professional careers and marriage, Kyle, approaching middle age, was still single and living a few minutes away from his parents. Though he craved travel and adventure, Kyle would become paralyzed by fear and obsessive ruminations and was unable to follow through on his plans. Though he did not suffer an obvious trauma, his developmental history, as well as hereditary factors, contributed to depression, anxiety, and dissociative symptoms that prevented him from fully functioning in the world.

During our sessions, Kyle was frequently lost in "thought storms"—harsh judgments and self-doubts that frustrated and exhausted him—and he hated himself for being "weak," frightened, and vulnerable. We eventually realized that verbalizing his experience and developing useful insights did not seem to help. We decided to try a mindfulness-based approach that might shift Kyle's focus away from obsessive thought loops and debilitating anxiety, thus allowing us to process his paralyzing conflicts and aversive affects from an embodied vantage point. We hoped that a more somatically based investigation would help Kyle stabilize when he felt flooded by fear, anxiety, and self-doubts and that such an approach would help him regulate his affective states.

Kyle had become involved in meditation practice in an effort to manage his fears and obsessions, and he went on several meditation retreats prior to starting treatment with me. Although he valued the experience of solitary meditation practice during these retreats, he found himself unable to tolerate the intensity of his emotions in the midst of silence and solitude, and he realized that he needed to work with a therapist who could help him tolerate and regulate his intense affective states. For people who have a traumatic history, intensive retreats can trigger somatic states and affects that, without a trained therapist, can become quite overwhelming and destabilizing, and this seems to have happened to Kyle. Kyle knew that mindfulness meditation was a strong interest of mine, and so our decision to pursue a mindfulness-based treatment was mutual. The clinical material described below took place following his month-long hospitalization due to a severe episode of anxiety and depression. Whereas meditation is usually solitary and contemplative in nature, we followed a collaborative meditative process that utilized mutual contemplation and a focus on a present-moment awareness of somatic and affective states (Brach 2013, 2015) along with a relational focus on our intersubjective communication. The sustained inquiry into somatic states allowed for a more embodied and direct experience of Kyle's developmental history and its subsequent implications for his present difficulties. As I encouraged Kyle to follow his somatic and affective experience, I also focused on my own subjective sensory response. The following is a description of several sequential sessions, initially focused on tracking Kyle's moment-to-moment sensory and affective experience, and later elaborating on a disruption that subsequently occurred between us.

CLINICAL PROCESS

As usual, Kyle sat on the couch and carefully arranged his notebooks, pens, a box of tissues, and two pillows, as if creating a protective shell around himself. We started the session with a few moments of silence, following our breath, letting our mind settle, and allowing ourselves to be more present with one another. This process seemed to help assuage some of Kyle's anxiety and alleviate the pressure he experienced to come prepared with an agenda (he was in the habit of bringing in detailed notes and lists on slips of paper or inked on his hand). As we sat in silence, I became aware of my breathing, the silence in the room, and some sense of unease and uncertainty as to what was about to take place. I noticed that Kyle seemed tentative and unsure, and I wondered whether he felt embarrassed as I watched his familiar rituals, perhaps hesitant to reveal his pain and vulnerability.

After a few minutes, Kyle reported that he became aware of overwhelming fear and anxiety associated with his desire to quit his job, which he found stultifying and unbearable. Kyle had tried to change his life several times in the past, but had always failed. We knew that this fear, present very early in his life, had accompanied him for a long time. Continuing to attend to his sensory experience, Kyle reported a frightening sense of the loss of physical boundaries as a memory emerged of his feeling lost as a young child and frantically looking for his mother. By tracking the sequence of sensory and affective states, Kyle saw that he had lived his life in a way that kept him frozen and paralyzed. He described that whenever he imagined a state of solitude and greater autonomy, he experienced an initial sense of excitement and exuberance. He felt energized, vital, and free, and he started to fantasize about going on adventures and living a life in which he might take physical and emotional risks, exploring parts of the world he had only dreamed about. But after a while, he started to be overcome by doubts and uncertainty and to experience terror, panic, and dissociation. Kyle noticed that his body and his surroundings felt disconnected and unreal as he imagined leaving his safe though confining life behind. I asked Kyle to imagine staying in his familiar life and continuing his romantic relationship, and he reported that he started to feel trapped and suffocated, unsure of his identity, and an intense desire to escape. It became clear to us that both of these positions were untenable, either going on his own to experience new adventures or continuing in his familiar milieu. I asked Kyle to describe what he was experiencing at that moment, and he responded that he felt a sense of numbing and disorientation, as if enveloped by a "grey fog." He reported feeling anxious and ungrounded, as if floating in space, and he had a powerful urge to run away. I continued to encourage Kyle to focus on his sensations and feelings, and he became aware of anger at himself for being weak, fearful, and dependent. Then he became angry at his mother, who, because of her insecurities, encouraged him to remain dependent on her and thwarted his halting attempts at autonomy and independence.

Kyle continued to notice the flow of thoughts and sensations, and reported a memory fragment that had surfaced of lying on his mother's belly as a very young child. He was aware of feeling comforted by a sense of warmth and security. His body felt connected to hers, as if he and his mother were one, as if he had no existence apart from her. In the midst of this soothing memory of apparent comfort and security, Kyle noticed a sense of constriction in his throat and suddenly had difficulty breathing. As I encouraged him to continue his somatic tracking, Kyle realized how terrified he was to leave his parents and live on his own. His fear of differentiation conflicted with his desire for independence and autonomy. Though he felt smothered and diminished around his mother, he was unable to separate from the maternal bond and rely on his own resources (Brandchaft, Doctors, and Sorter 2010).

Kyle recognized how pervasive and paralyzing his fear was, but he also observed that his fear was only one in a sequence of other feelings, sensations, and memories. As he realized that his fear was a transitory state, it no longer overwhelmed him. This was an important insight into how his fear was keeping him imprisoned and preventing him from becoming an agent in his own life. During this session and several subsequent sessions, I helped Kyle create a space for a sequence of feelings and sensations associated with early memories and habitual patterns without getting lost in obsessive ruminations and negative self-judgments.

Fear and paralysis became the subject during the following sessions, and although these states of mind were initially important experiences that contributed to significant insights, as Kyle continued to feel imprisoned in those emotions I started to notice my own frustration and impatience. We had been over this ground so many times before, and I became aware that I felt much more drawn to Kyle's excitement and exuberance. Though I did not disclose my sense of impatience to Kyle, my subjective feelings were communicated implicitly one day, and I noticed that Kyle became silent and withdrawn. When I asked him what had happened, he admitted that he suddenly had started to feel ashamed and embarrassed. He realized that he had revealed to me his fear and vulnerability, a part of himself that he had tried to disguise and hide from others and from me, and he was afraid that I was judging him as harshly as he so often judged himself.

I became aware of a complex range of feelings and sensations. I experienced empathy and felt protective of Kyle, and at the same time I recognized a sense of irritation and boredom. I much preferred Kyle's moments of exhilaration, which energized the room and promised new experiences and adventure, rather than the stultifying, paralyzing fear and anxiety that seemed to circle us without the possibility of movement and change. I asked Kyle what he saw in me that had led to his observations. Kyle admitted that at times he sensed that I was somewhat abrupt with him when he became anxious. I wanted to know more about what Kyle had noticed, and he responded that there was something in my expression that intensified his sense of shame and made it difficult for him to share with me his fear and ambivalence. I admitted that at times I did get impatient, and that I also appreciated his insights. He had helped me to become more aware of my own unconscious response, though I wasn't necessarily proud of it. I suggested that we both felt some impatience with his fear and anxiety and perhaps needed to help each other allow this vulnerable part of him to emerge with more patience and empathy, but also without being paralyzed by it. This moment of rupture between us shows how implicit communication, the therapist's self-disclosure and acknowledgement of her own vulnerability, and mutual affective holding led to a transformative moment in the treatment, which allowed Kyle to transcend his fears and a new experience to emerge. I also believe that Kyle's new experience of voicing his doubts in me and in turn receiving validation and acknowledgement encouraged him to trust his perceptions and to shift from a habitual response of dissociation and accommodation to a more authentic self-expression.

At the end of the session, Kyle reported an image that came to him of swimming in a river and arriving at a waterfall. His adult self held his fearful and anxious child self as both jumped into the waterfall and emerged unharmed. As this image suggests, Kyle had found a place of safety in the midst of powerful currents and overwhelming emotions, allowing them to wash over him while transcending his habitual fear, anxiety, and self-imposed limitations.

We discovered, too, that Kyle's anxiety played an important function in protecting him from potential danger and alerting him to consider the future consequences of risky and impulsive actions. We learned to hold his states of fear and doubt so that greater freedom and flexibility could emerge, and eventually we found a way to allow Kyle's fear, along with his sense of adventure and excitement, to be held between us while not overwhelming either of us. Ultimately, we discovered that these two self-states could coexist so that Kyle could live a fuller, more expressive life. Subsequent to this session, whenever Kyle expressed critical feelings toward himself, I would remind him that we both needed to honor and hold his fear and vulnerability and be curious as to what it could tell us. Kyle gradually became more aware of deeply embedded cognitive patterns that exacerbated his anxieties, and he was eventually able to make some significant changes in his life. He moved away from his parents and found more fulfilling employment. Though he is still subject to periods of depression and anxiety, Kyle has established greater autonomy and emotional independence.

SUMMARY

This vignette illustrates the principles of mindfulness-based treatment, which include the moment-to-moment awareness of somatic, affective, and cognitive states as a mutual process between client and therapist. The use of a decentered observation allows for nonidentification to facilitate affect regulation and greater tolerance of discomfort and distress. In addition, it assists in the acceptance of conflicting, and at times painful, affect states that emerge in the present moment. Although history and narrative are still an important focal point in the treatment, they are contextualized within present-moment sensory and affective experience. As this case suggests, mindfulness principles can be integrated quite successfully with a psychodynamic process that also investigates the intersubjective dynamics between client and therapist in the here and now.

SENSORIMOTOR THERAPY

Somatically based models focus on working with the body and sensory experience and utilizing the body to establish safety and to facilitate somatic and affective regulation (Ogden and Goldstein 2017). Ogden and Minton (2000) suggest that working with the subcortical level of body and sensory experience helps facilitate cognitive and affective processing, insofar as the somatic dysregulation experienced by many trauma survivors frequently culminates in distorted perceptions of social and emotional cues. Moreover, dissociated affects and self-states are often more accessible through sensory processing (Haven 2009; van der Kolk 2014). Ogden suggests that a mindfulness-based sensorimotor approach grounds an embodied awareness of oneself in a present-moment relational engagement between client and therapist, a description that contextualizes a solitary contemplative method of sensory observation within a relational matrix of self and other (Ogden and Goldstein 2017).

Ogden integrates attachment research, neuroscience, and mindfulness practice in her sensorimotor intervention model (Ogden, Pain, and Fisher 2006). Levine (1986) has also emphasized the significance of body memory in dissociated traumatic states. Both argue that the body, rather than the traumatic narrative, should be the primary focus of investigation in the processing of trauma and dissociation, especially with adolescents and clients who may struggle with verbal communication and language due to developmental trauma (Warner et al. 2014). Several studies of traumatized adolescents in residential settings have shown significant results with sensorimotor interventions, including diminishing of dissociative, behavioral, and affective symptoms such as anxiety and depression (Warner et al. 2014; Langmuir, Kirsh, and Classen 2012; Haven 2009). Furthermore, current research in neuroscience suggests that somatic experience holds the key to treating early developmental trauma when the capacity for cognitive processing and symbolization is limited (van der Kolk 2014). In addition, van der Kolk asserts that patients develop conditional responses to trauma through fight, flight, and numbing, and that during dissociative episodes the brain's frontal lobes, which process analytic, rational, and verbal functions, are deactivated (2002, 384) and the patient's traumatic memories are not readily available for narrative and cognitive integration. When dissociation occurs between the symbolic (cognitive) and subsymbolic (somatic) levels, individuals may experience affective as well as bodily states that are inaccessible to cognitive processing (Bucci 1997); therefore, early developmental trauma may remain unavailable to verbal memory and communication. Thus, insight alone may be insufficient to achieve the integration of traumatic memories and experiences, although it may have the effect of temporarily overriding the memories.

Neuroscience and the Polyvagal Theory

Sensorimotor therapy integrates mindfulness principles, attachment theory, and neuroscience. The model utilizes the polyvagal theory developed by Porges to explain the "bottom up" approach based on neuroperceptive processes (2001, 2003). The vagus nerve links the brain to key organs, including heart, brain, lungs, throat, and digestive system, and is therefore a key link between somatic, sensory, affective, and cognitive systems. It is highly involved in the system's response to physical and psychological threat through regulating the functions of the sympathetic nervous system (SNS) and the parasympathetic nervous system (PNS). The SNS becomes activated during threat and trauma, resulting in a fight/flight response and hyperarousal. The PNS, active during times of rest and relaxation, affects states of immobilization, numbness, and hypoarousal.

The polyvagal (meaning the vagus nerve with its multiple branches connected to several internal systems) regulatory function may allow for a different approach to deactivation (or downregulation) of the SNS. For example, the vagus nerve can produce calm but alert states, allowing us to stay present when threatened without attacking (fighting) or shutting down (numbing), which is essential for continued social engagement. By balancing sympathetic and parasympathetic activation, one is able to make a realistic appraisal of threat by perceiving nonverbal cues from others, such as behavior, facial expressions, and tone of voice, and to consequently respond with more nuance. The capacity to make accurate interpretations of nonverbal social cues is linked to early attachment experiences, which serve as a relational foundation for learned response. Trauma survivors are typically hypervigilant and reactive, seeing danger in every social situation because of their early relational trauma. Too much stimulation (hyperarousal) or too much inhibition (hypoarousal or dissociation) resulting from past abuse or neglect sets the vagal tone and compromises the brain-body communication system, which in turn has a negative effect on social and emotional functioning in later life. Consequently, if a state of imbalance exists between hyper- and hypoarousal—that is, between the SNS and the PNS—due to early relational trauma, the functional capacity of these two branches of the nervous system may be compromised (Porges 2007). Porges suggests that there are three stages of ANS activation: immobilization, fight/flight, and social engagement. Therapeutic interventions should enhance social engagement (2001). When safety is communicated via social-engagement signals, the clients' defenses are relaxed, and both client and therapist can develop a context of safety based on more accurate neuroperceptive processes (Geller and Porges 2014).

Schore (2011) emphasizes that it is the implicit, unconscious, and emotion-processing mode of communication via right-brain functions (rather than left-brain language functions) that is truly dominant in human experience, and that it is the implicit, nonverbal, "psychobiological" communication processes in early child/parent interactions, and between client and therapist, that ultimately bring about deep and abiding change. These right-brain to right-brain processes include facial, auditory, tactile, and "emotionally charged attachment communications" (Schore 2011, 79). These authors suggest, therefore, that verbal interactions and an emphasis on language alone do not reach the level of implicit communication between client and therapist.

Sensorimotor psychotherapy focuses on the nonverbal affective and bodily based "implicit self." According to Ogden (2015) and others (van der Kolk 2014; Fisher 2011), during trauma, the executive brain (i.e., the prefrontal cortex's capacity to manage conceptual processes) is impaired, while the capacity to enhance emotional processes and their encoding is increased (Arnsten 2009; Schwabe et al. 2012). The processing of traumatic experience thus lies in the implicit and changing sensory, bodily, and affective experience rather than in narrative and explicit verbal communication. In sensorimotor therapy, mindfulness practice is embedded within the moment-to-moment interactions between client and therapist. Rather than being approached in an open-ended way, as in mindfulness meditation practice, it is facilitated through directive inquiry or "directed mindfulness" (Ogden 2015).

PRINCIPLES OF PRACTICE

Ogden suggests that the therapist should hold a dual focus: following the client's narrative while simultaneously attending and tracking the "five building blocks" of present-moment internal experience. The five building blocks are: emotions, thoughts, five-sense perception, movements, and bodily sensations. While the therapist looks to identify unresolved traumas that require processing, she or he also emphasizes self-regulatory resources, positive affect, competency, and mastery (2015, 229). Ogden also suggests that there should be a balance between safety/stabilization and danger, thus allowing traumatic material to be processed within a "window of tolerance" (Siegel 2007) that does not exceed the client's capacities. In addition, the therapist should foster awareness of bodily experience, teach somatic skills to manage hyperactivation, foster affective and somatic regulation skills, and help stabilize and reorganize the autonomic nervous response (Fisher 2011).

As are other trauma-focused models, the sensorimotor approach is a phase-based model, which includes an initial phase of symptom reduction and stabilization, typically through body-centered interventions; a second phase of processing traumatic memory; and a final stage of integration and rehabilitation (Ogden 2015, 234). Several research studies show promise in the use of sensorimotor therapy with trauma survivors, both with groups (Gene-Cos et al. 2016; Langmuir, Kirsh, and Classen 2012; Warner et al. 2013) and with individuals (Ogden and Minton 2000; Ogden, Pain, and Fisher 2006).

CLINICAL VIGNETTE

Ellen was a woman in her fifties who described an abusive childhood with a father who was often critical and frightening. One particular memory stayed with her. At age seven or eight, her father asked her to clean the stove. Apparently unhappy with the outcome, he decided to punish her to "teach her a lesson." He turned the stove burners on and ordered Ellen to hold her palms close to the flame and to keep them there until he gave her permission to stop. Ellen described feeling frozen and terrified, unable to move or speak. I noticed that as Ellen shared this experience with me, her voice grew soft and inaudible, and she seemed numb and frightened.

I asked Ellen to stay grounded in the here and now: to notice her feet on the floor and to take some deep breaths. When Ellen became more relaxed, I asked her to describe the experience with her father and notice what happened in her body. As she did, she noticed how frozen and paralyzed her body became, and that she felt small and helpless. Her throat felt constricted, as if she were holding something back. Although Ellen had had several previous therapists and had talked about this event before, it still felt raw and unresolved. She had been unable to process and integrate it. I asked Ellen to focus on her throat and notice if there was a sound or a movement that she wanted to make. Ellen hesitated and then said that she felt there was a powerful scream in her throat that she had been keeping down for decades, too frightened to release it. We stayed with the fear that she would be hurt and severely punished if she made a sound, and I gently encouraged her to express any sounds that she wanted to make, reassuring her that I would be there for her and provide her with as much support as I could. Finally, Ellen was able to overcome her fear, and she let out a loud scream that reverberated for quite some time. This was the scream she had been too terrified to make as a young child and had held back for decades. Ellen's scream allowed her to release her fear, anguish, and anger at her father, empowering her to express her outrage and to protest as she moved from the role of victim to that of empowered survivor. The act of screaming is what Ogden calls an "act of triumph," (2015, 236) a shifting from victim to survivor. For the first time in her life, Ellen felt free.

Summary

This vignette illustrates the sensorimotor emphasis on using the principles of directed mindfulness with a present-moment focus on embodied experience that coexists with the narrative. It also exemplifies a phase-based treatment, starting with resourcing and stabilization, moving to the processing of trauma, and then to integration through an expressed "act of triumph"— thus completing a physical act that had been interrupted at the time of the traumatic event.

INTERNAL FAMILY SYSTEMS (IFS) THERAPY

The internal family systems (IFS) approach is based on earlier theories of object relations, Jungian psychology, and family systems theory (Schwartz 1995, 2013). The object-relations concept of internalized objects and internalized self/other interactions, the Jungian theory of archetypes, and the family systems theory of familial roles and relationships together form the underpinnings for the IFS theory of internal parts and the relationships among them. The notion of discrete internal parts of the mind has been associated with trauma, psychopathology, and a range of dissociative disorders as defined in the *DSM-V*, particularly in the case of dissociative identity disorder (DID). However, Schwartz, the founder of IFS, asserts that a system of internal parts is a normative structure to one degree or another, though it is often unconscious (Schwartz 2013; Schwartz and Sparks, 2015). For example, we all utilize many aspects of our personality and experiences and use different parts of ourselves to function in varied settings and with different people.

IFS draws on mindfulness practice in its emphasis on learning to relate to a turbulent inner experience from a calm, mindful place, not by attempting to eliminate it but instead by learning to accept and feel compassion for the pain and trauma of inner parts that have been "exiled" from awareness (Schwartz 2013). However, IFS goes further than acceptance and focuses on transforming inner conflict by developing an internal dialogue with and between one's inner parts. One of the important goals of IFS is to bring all the interior parts, or states of mind, into one's awareness, thus learning to be more accepting of the roles they play. Rather than challenging, ignoring, replacing, or changing thoughts and feelings, clients are encouraged to develop curiosity and compassion as they witness their painful traumatic memories and experiences, or as they learn to understand the roles of different protective parts, including the inner critic, the shaming self, or the angry part. The cultivation of compassion includes the acceptance of these self-protective aspects of the personality and the development of empathy toward the frightened and vulnerable inner selves that hold traumatic memories. According to the IFS perspective, the vulnerable parts, or "exiles," took on the burden of carrying the pain and trauma that are too destabilizing for the client to know and remember. Schwartz asserts that when clients connect directly to these inner parts instead of thinking about or interpreting what happened, the experience becomes more visceral, intense, and ultimately transformative (Schwartz 1995, Schwartz and Sparks 2015). Gradually, through a systematic processing that evolves into a procedure called "unburdening," the relationship among the different parts of the personality becomes more conscious and engaged, and the traumatic experiences can finally be communicated and then released. The client's compassionate witnessing, the retrieval of painful memories, and the freeing of protective parts from their habitual, maladaptive roles allow for release, integration, and internal reorganization.

THE SELF

Much like the mindfulness practices of loving-kindness, compassion, and moment-to-moment awareness, the IFS perspective focuses on the developing awareness of a mindful core self that intrinsically encompasses the qualities of wisdom and compassion. Mindfulness principles are integral to the theory and intervention of IFS in that the observing, holding, and regulating functions of the self are important factors in the therapeutic process, allowing clients to become more conscious and aware of the complex relationships among their different internal parts.

The therapist facilitates the process of cultivating and strengthening this core self so that the client may use it to organize and facilitate communication among the different parts without becoming destabilized or overwhelmed—what Schwartz terms "self leadership." Although mindfulness meditation and a loving-kindness practice can strengthen that core self, the therapist may also facilitate the process by encouraging the client to attend to their somatic and affective experience. The therapist helps the client to develop a witnessing perspective and to engage with their internal parts through compassion and understanding. Once more internal space has been created for the core self, Schwartz suggests that clients typically shift from states of fear, rage, or despair to curiosity, calm, and compassion (Schwartz 2013).

THE INTERNAL PARTS

Schwartz divides the internal parts into three primary levels: the core self, the protectors (divided into "managers" and "firefighters"), and the exiles. Each holds discrete memories, affects, developmental stages, and personality styles, and each has a different function of managing, protecting, or holding traumatic memories. The protectors are responsible for defending the system from the pain of traumatic memories and experiences. They include the managers, who are charged with functioning in the world and with presenting a facade of stability and organization that belies the pain and trauma residing in the exiles. The firefighters are the protector parts that use extreme measures to distract and prevent awareness of traumatic memories via addictive and impulsive behaviors such as alcohol and drug abuse, overeating, and sex. Other protectors typically intervene through states of shame, self-doubt, self-judgment, confusion, and anger. In essence, the protectors are tasked with shielding the system from remembering and reexperiencing the trauma. Finally, the exiles hold the burden of retaining traumatic memories and the somatic and affective experiences associated with the trauma; these parts are usually dissociated. The exiles are the deepest, most vulnerable, and often the youngest parts of the internal system (they have been described as the "inner child").

PRINCIPLES OF PRACTICE

The IFS therapy process is intended to help clients understand the function of each part, become more conscious of how and when their parts are triggered, and understand the parts' relationships with one another. Through this process, clients eventually develop some distance from identification with their parts, and are then able to contact the traumatic memory and "unburden" the trauma. This process of increasing awareness, internal communication, and unburdening brings about a transformative change in the client's internal system. The therapeutic process is collaborative in that both client and therapist develop greater awareness of and communication among their different parts. The IFS therapist models a stable, calm, and compassionate self by developing awareness of and communication with his or her own internal parts, and by strengthening his or her own self-leadership capacity, especially in the face of the clients' despair, hopelessness, suicidality, or shame. The goal is for the client (or the client's inner parts) to develop trust in the therapist and ultimately to unburden his or her pain and trauma.

Though IFS has been acknowledged as an evidence-based practice in the treatment of anxiety, phobia, and depression (Matheson 2015), research on IFS-based trauma treatment is still in its beginning stages. Current studies include IFS treatment of combat trauma (Lucero, Jones, and Hunsaker 2017) and sexual abuse (Wilkins 2007; Miller, Cardona, Harden 2006).

Clinical Vignette

The following vignette provides an example of treatment with a client presenting with childhood physical abuse by her father and other relatives. I will describe how IFS was applied to the client's dissociated traumatic experience.

Following a period of supportive therapy, I discovered that Mary was a survivor of extensive developmental trauma. Dissociated affects and self-states that Mary had silenced started to emerge. Mary had developed impressive competence in her academic and professional life and had been functioning quite well in school and in her jobs, an aspect of her internal system that IFS would describe as her inner "managers." However, she had also internalized her father's and other family members' negative judgments of her, as well as their view that she had to work hard for her family and others in order to be "good" and worthwhile. These negative inner voices grew loud after she was criticized, experienced a failure, or tried to be assertive with others. According to the IFS perspective, these judgmental parts were her "protectors," and Mary learned to push and motivate herself through harsh criticisms and self-judgments. Gradually we discovered that these protectors were also severely critical of her more vulnerable, frightened, and anxious states (her "exiles") and that they worked hard to silence those internal voices of fear and anxiety. Other protector states of shame and guilt emerged as well. The harsh internal voices flooded Mary whenever she tried to protest against her abusers or to disclose to me the mistreatment she had experienced by family members and others. We discovered that they prevented Mary from distancing from her family and ensured that she continued to be the "good daughter" in accordance with her family's traditional values. We recognized that Mary had difficulty disentangling from her internalized rage and harsh self-judgments, that her states of shame and self-hatred had a powerful pull on her, and that she had learned to motivate herself and keep her fear and rage under control through these protector parts.

As Mary's sense of self (or self-leadership function) became stronger and more trusting and secure with me, she started to tolerate greater access to her vulnerable states and felt less need to put herself down and indulge in criticism of her fear and vulnerability. One of the more significant "exiles" was the frightened, isolated little girl who didn't trust anyone and who preferred to hide in the pain and darkness with which she was familiar. I recognized the little girl part when Mary's voice softened and became childlike. She would hide under a shawl or cover her face in her hands, too embarrassed to have me witness her fear and vulnerability. During one of our sessions, I saw this child part emerging in Mary's voice and facial expression, and I asked her to tell me who she was. Mary answered, "We don't want you to know." Mary was shocked and embarrassed, clearly unaware of how alive this child self, or exile, was within her. As we processed the interaction, Mary became aware that she was protecting her child self from my intrusion and from potential harm. Her child part did not trust me; she was frightened of coming out and being seen by me. During a process that IFS calls "unburdening," Mary told me more about her abusive childhood memories and explained that her little girl self preferred to remain hidden in darkness, surrounded by familiar pain, where she was lonely but safe and secure. Pain was familiar and comforting, and Mary was afraid to believe that love and freedom were reliable or lasting. After every step toward freeing herself and loosening the bonds, the voice of the "protectors" became louder and more insistent. Mary was trained to dismiss and reject her fear and sadness, and she responded harshly to any sign of her own helplessness and vulnerability.

As Mary's relationship to more vulnerable parts of herself unfolded, she reported a gradual change in her relationship to others, for whom she now experienced greater empathy and compassion. She grew more aware of danger signals, becoming able to distance herself from toxic relationships and destructive interactions. With time, Mary learned to hold and accept states of fear and helplessness, and rather than reflexively withdraw into her familiar pain or punish herself with self-judgments, she learned to be more gentle and kind with herself, to comfort and soothe her little girl part, and to regulate a range of affects through greater self-awareness and empathic explorations between the two of us.

SUMMARY

The IFS procedure aims to help clients become more aware of their different part systems, the roles of the parts, and the relationships among them. The therapist helps to strengthen and stabilize self-leadership functions, to facilitate the process of unburdening and processing traumatic memories, and to transform old and often distorted protective functions into more mature and adaptive coping strategies.

Mary's vignette illustrates the application of IFS to the clinical process when addressing childhood trauma and dissociation. It illustrates the focus on strengthening the client's "self-leadership" core and on identifying the internal system of managers, protectors, and exiles. Initially the therapist must work to strengthen and stabilize the client's self-leadership system. This increases the capacity for wisdom, compassion, and grounding and enhances the ability to observe and facilitate relationships among the different parts. The therapist helps the client access the protector system of managers and firefighters, understand their functions, and facilitate acceptance and compassion between these parts and the core self, ultimately allowing the exile parts to emerge and "unburden" traumatic memories and affects. Finally, a new state of reorganization and increased awareness and compassion among the different parts is achieved.

CONCLUSION

Mindfulness practice has become more ubiquitous in everyday life. It is popular for managing chronic pain, terminal illness, and a range of mental disorders, including anxiety, depression, and borderline personality disorder. The practice of mindfulness has been successfully implemented in prisons, schools, and the military as a way to foster greater self-awareness, inner peace, and equanimity. As discussed in this chapter, mindfulness has also been integrated into a variety of clinical models, including CBT and psychodynamic practice.

I have addressed mindfulness-oriented trauma interventions, including acceptance and commitment therapy (ACT), sensorimotor psychotherapy, and internal family systems (IFS) therapy. I have discussed how certain mindfulness principles—including moment-to-moment awareness and acceptance of emerging thoughts, feelings, and sensory experiences without identifying with them—are fundamental components to each of these models. Clinical vignettes illustrated how each may be infused into clinical practice with survivors of trauma and dissociation.

Finally, it is important to keep in mind that mindfulness is not simply an intervention strategy but rather a holistic way of life that can permeate each moment and activity. It is an approach to living that can be cultivated outside the therapy office, transforming one's relationship to self, to others, and to the world.

REFERENCES

Arnsten, A. 2009. "Stress Signaling Pathways That Impair Prefrontal Cortex Structure and Function." *Nature Reviews Neuroscience* 10:410–422.

Brandchaft, B., S. Doctors, and D. Sorter. 2010. *Toward an Emancipatory Psychoanalysis: Brandchaft's Intersubjective Vision.* New York: Routledge.

Briere, J. 2015. "Pain and Suffering: A Synthesis of Buddhist and Western Approaches to Trauma." In *Mindfulness Oriented Interventions for Trauma,* ed. V. Follette, J. Briere, D. Rozelle, J. Hopper, and D. Rome, 11–30. New York: Guilford Press.

Brach, T. 2013. *True Refuge.* New York: Bantam.

Brach, T. 2015. "Healing Traumatic Fear: The Wings of Mindfulness and Love." In *Mindfulness Oriented Interventions for Trauma,* ed. V. Follete, J. Briere, D. Rozelle, J. Hopper, and D. Roma, 31–42. New York: Guilford Press.

Bromberg, P. 2011. *Awakening the Dreamer.* New York: Routledge.

Bucci, W. 1997. *Psychoanalysis and Cognitive Science: A Multiple Code Theory.* New York: Guilford Press.

Engle, J., and V. Follette. 2015. "Mindfulness and Valued Action: An Acceptance and Commitment Therapy Approach to Working with Trauma Survivors." In *Mindfulness Oriented Interventions for Trauma,* ed. V. Follete, J. Briere, D. Rozelle, J. Hopper, and D. Roma, 61–74. New York: Guilford Press.

Engler, J. 2003. "Being Somebody and Being Nobody: A Reexamination of the Understanding of Self in Psychoanalysis and Buddhism." In *Psychoanalysis and Buddhism,* ed. J. Safran, 35–79. Boston: Wisdom Publishing.

Epstein, M. 1995. *Thoughts Without a Thinker.* New York: Basic Books.

Epstein, M. 2007. *Psychotherapy Without the Self.* New Haven, Conn.: Yale University Press.

Fisher, J. 2011. "Sensorimotor Approaches to Trauma Treatment." *Advances in Psychiatric Treatment* 17:171–177.

Geller, S., and S. Porges. 2014. "Therapeutic Presence: Neurophysiological Mechanisms Mediating Feeling Safe in Therapeutic Relationships." *Journal of Psychotherapy Integration* 24 (3): 178–192.

Gene-Cos, N., J. Fisher, P. Ogden, and A. Cantrel. 2016. "Sensorimotor Psychotherapy Group Therapy in the Treatment of Complex PTSD." *Annals of Psychiatry and Mental Health* 4:1080.

Goldstein, J. 2013. *Mindfulness: A Practice Guide to Awakening.* Boulder, Colo.: Sounds True.

Haven, T. 2009. "That Part of the Body Is Just Gone: Understanding and Responding to Dissociation and Physical Health." *Journal of Trauma and Dissociation* 10:1529–1570. doi:10.1080./15299730802624569.

Hayes, S. C., K. D. Strosahl, K. G. Wilson. 2012. *Acceptance and Commitment Therapy: The Process and Practice of Mindful Change.* New York: Guilford Press.

Hiraoka, R., A. J. Cook, J. M. Bivona, E. C. Meyer, and S. B. Morissette. 2016. "Acceptance and Commitment Therapy in the Treatment of Depression Related to Military Sexual Trauma in a Woman Veteran: A Case Study." *Clinical Case Studies* 15:84–97.

Jennings, P. 2003. *Mixing Minds: The Power of Relationship in Psychoanalysis and Buddhism.* Boston, Mass.: Wisdom Publications.

Kulka, R. 2012. "Between Emergence and Dissolving: Contemporary Reflections on Greatness and Ideals in Kohut's Legacy." *International Journal of Psychoanalytic Self Psychology* 7 (2): 264–283.

Langmuir, J. I., S. G. Kirsh, and C. C. Classen. 2012. "A Pilot Study of Body-Oriented Group Psychotherapy: Adapting Sensorimotor Psychotherapy for the Group Treatment of Trauma." *Psychological Trauma: Theory, Research, Practice, and Policy* 4:214–220.

Levine, P. 1986. *Waking the Tiger: Healing Trauma.* Berkeley, CA: North Atlantic Books.

Lucero, R., A. C. Jones, and J. C. Hunsaker. 2017. "Using Internal Family Systems Theory in the Treatment of Combat Veterans with Post-Traumatic Stress Disorder and Their Families." *Contemporary Family Therapy: An International Journal.* doi.10.1007/s1059/-017-9424-2

Matheson, J. 2015. "IFS: An Evidence Based Practice." https://www.foundationifs .org/news-articles/79-ifs-an-evidence-based-practice.

McLean, C., and V. M. Follette. 2016. "Acceptance and Commitment Therapy as a Nonpathologizing Intervention Approach for Survivors of Trauma." *Journal of Trauma and Dissociation* 17:138–150.

Miller, B., J. R. Cardona, and M. Hardin. 2006. "The Use of Narrative Therapy and Internal Family Systems with Survivors of Childhood Sexual Abuse: Examining Issues Related to Loss and Oppression." *Journal of Feminist Family Therapy* 18 (4): 1–27.

Ogden, P. 2015. "Embedded Relational Mindfulness: A Sensorimotor Psychotherapy Perspective on the Treatment of Trauma." In *Mindfulness Oriented Interventions for Trauma*, ed. V. Follette, J. Briere, D. Rozelle, J. Hopper, and D. Rome, 227–242. New York: Guilford Press.

Ogden, P., and B. Goldstein. 2017. "Embedded Relational Mindfulness (ERM) in Child and Adolescent Treatment: A Sensorimotor Psychotherapy Perspective." *European Journal of Trauma and Dissociation* 1:171–176.

Ogden, P., and K. Minton. 2000. "Sensorimotor Psychotherapy: One Method for Processing Traumatic Memory." *Traumatology* 3:149–173.

Ogden, P., C. Pain, and J. Fisher. 2006. "A Sensorimotor Approach to the Treatment of Trauma and Dissociation." *Psychiatric Clinics of North America* 29:263–279.

Orange, D. 2011. *The Suffering Stranger.* New York: Routledge.

Orsillo, S. M., and S. V. Batten. 2005. "Acceptance and Commitment Therapy in the Treatment of Posttraumatic Stress Disorder." *Behavior Modification* 29:95–129.

Porges, S. W. 2001. "The Polyvagal Theory: Phylogenetic Substrates of a Social Nervous System." *International Journal of Psychophysiology* 42:123–146.

Porges, S. W. 2003. "The Polyvagal Theory: Phylogenetic Contributions to Social Behavior." *Physiology and Behavior* 79:503–513.

Porges, S. W. 2007. "The Polyvagal Perspective." *Biological Psychology* 74:116–143.

Ringel, S. 2018. "Integrating Mindfulness in the Psychoanalytic Treatment of Affect Dissociation." *Psychoanalysis, Self and Context* 13 (2): 119–131.

Safran, J. 2003. Introduction to *Psychoanalysis and Buddhism*, ed. J. Safran, 1–34. Boston: Wisdom Publications.

Schimmenti, A., and V. Caretti. 2016. "Linking the Overwhelming with the Unbearable: Developmental Trauma, Dissociation, and the Disconnected Self." *Psychoanalytic Psychology* 33 (1): 106–128.

Schore, A. 2011. "The Right Brain Implicit Self Lies at the Core of Psychoanalysis." *Psychoanalytic Dialogues* 21 (1): 75–100.

Schwabe, L., M. Joels, B. Roozendall, O. Wolf, and M. Oitzl. 2012. "Stress Effects on Memory: An Update and Integration." *Neuroscience and Biobehavioral Reviews* 36:1740–1749.

Siegel, D. 2007. *The Mindful Brain.* New York: Norton.

Smith, R. 2014. *Awakening.* Boston, Mass.: Shambhala.

Schwartz, R. 1995. *Internal Family System Therapy.* New York: Guilford Press.

Schwartz, R. C. 2013. "Moving from Acceptance Toward Transformation with Internal Family Systems Therapy (IFS)." *Journal of Clinical Psychology* 69:805–816.

Schwartz, R., and F. Sparks. 2015. "The Internal Family Systems Model in Trauma Treatment: Parallels with Mahayana Buddhist Theory and Practice." In *Mindfulness Oriented Interventions for Trauma*, ed. V. Follette, J. Briere, D. Rozelle, J. Hopper, and D. Rome, 125–139. New York: Guilford Press.

Stoddard, J., N. Afari, and S. Hayes. 2014. *The Big Book of ACT Metaphors: A Practitioner's Guide to Experiential Exercises and Metaphors in Acceptance and Commitment Therapy.* Oakland, Calif.: New Harbinger.

Twohig, M. P. 2009. "Acceptance and Commitment Therapy for Treatment-Resistant Posttraumatic Stress Disorder: A Case Study." *Cognitive and Behavioral Practice* 16:243–252.

van der Hart, O., E. Nijenhuis, and K. Steele. 2006. *The Haunted Self: Structural Dissociation and the Treatment of Chronic Traumatization.* New York: Norton.

van der Kolk, B. A. 2002. "Posttraumatic Therapy in the Age of Neuroscience." *Psychoanalytic Dialogues* 12:381–392.

van der Kolk, B. 2014. *The Body Keeps the Score: Brain, Mind, and Body in the Healing of Trauma.* New York: Penguin.

Warner, E., J. Koomar, B. Lary, and A. Cook. 2013. "Can the Body Change the Score? Application of Sensory Modulation Principles in the Treatment of Traumatized Adolescents in Residential Settings." *Journal of Family Violence* 28:729–738.

Warner, E., J. Spinazzola, A. Westcott, C. Gunn, and H. Hodgdon. 2014. "The Body Can Change the Score: Empirical Support for Somatic Regulation in the Treatment of Traumatized Adolescents." *Journal of Child and Adolescent Trauma* 7:237–246.

Wilkins, E. J. 2007. "Using an IFS Informed Intervention to Treat African American Families Surviving Sexual Abuse: One Family's Story." *Journal of Feminist Family Therapy* 19:37–53.

Williams, S. M., J. Teasdale, Z. Segal, and J. Kabat-Zinn. 2007. *The Mindful Way Through Depression: Freeing Yourself from Chronic Unhappiness.* New York: Guilford Press.

Woidneck, M. R., K. L. Morrison, and M. P. Twohig. 2014. "Acceptance and Commitment Therapy for the Treatment of Posttraumatic Stress Among Adolescents." *Behavior Modification* 38:451–476.

7

Cultural and Historical Trauma Among Native Americans

▸ SHELLY A. WIECHELT, JAN GRYCZYNSKI,
and KERRY HAWK LESSARD

> Even the seasons form a great circle in their changing, and always come back again
> to where they were. The life of a man is a circle from childhood to childhood, and so
> it is in everything where power moves.
> BLACK ELK, *Oglala Sioux holy man, quoted in Neihardt* ([1932] 2008)

BIOLOGICAL, PSYCHOLOGICAL, and social system processes affect individuals in how they perceive and function in the world. Complex interactions between these systems within individuals influence how they think, feel, and behave in relation to themselves and others. The individual's status reflects his or her lived experience. Traumatic events that occur in the lives of individuals have the potential to dramatically affect their functioning in terms of physical health, mental health, and social behavior.

Similarly, cultures embody complex processes that sustain and nourish them. Internal influences such as values, beliefs, symbols, and norms uphold cultures. External forces such as interactions with other cultures and the effects of nature may put pressure on a culture. To a certain extent external pressures may challenge a culture to change and grow. However, sudden and catastrophic pressures may overwhelm the cultural system's ability to cope and thus can be traumatic. Gradual pressures such as oppression and aggressive encroachment will stress a culture and the individuals and systems within it with potentially traumatic effects.

Native Americans have endured individual and cultural traumas that have profoundly affected their personal and communal lives. Some of these events occurred in the remote past, producing effects that have rippled across generations until today. Others have occurred more recently. The impact of cultural traumas from the remote past intermingle with the impact of recent traumas, resulting in a cumulative and compounding spiral of traumatic effects. In order to understand trauma in the lives of Native Americans and ways to promote healing, it is important to begin with a foundation in relevant concepts.

WHAT DOES *NATIVE AMERICAN* MEAN?

First, it is essential to understand to whom the term *Native American* refers. The term is misleading as it implies that a single group of indigenous people exists in the United States. In fact, hundreds of different tribes—each with its own origins, cultural rubrics, beliefs, and practices—exist in this country. There are 567 federally recognized tribes, many other tribes that are recognized at the state level, and tribes that are not recognized by the government (Bureau of Indian Affairs, n.d.; National Conference of State Legislatures 2016). The 2010 U.S. Census showed that 5.2 million individuals identified their race as American Indian or Alaska Native (AI/AN, defined as having origins in any of the original peoples of North, Central, or South America); 2.9 million of these individuals identified as AI/AN alone, and 2.3 million identified as AI/AN in combination with other races (Norris, Vines, and Hoeffel 2012). Of the total, 71 percent live in urban areas. Any reference to Native Americans in this chapter encompasses an array of diverse groups whose commonality is in their indigenousness to the continental land now known as the United States of America. Since the focus of this chapter is on the experience of indigenous people of the United States in general rather than on a specific tribal group, the term *Native American* is used despite its limitations. In many population statistics, the term *American Indian/Alaska Native* is commonly used as a racial designation. In this chapter, the terms *Native American* and *American Indian/Alaska Native* are used interchangeably.

TRAUMA

The current conception of trauma in Western cultures is largely based on the definition encompassed in the post-traumatic stress disorder (PTSD) criteria listed in the *Diagnostic and Statistical Manual of Mental Disorders*, fifth edition (*DSM-V*) (American Psychiatric Association 2013). Criterion A establishes that an individual has undergone a traumatic event or events. Essentially, a traumatic event is one that an individual directly experiences, witnesses, or learns that a close friend or family member has experienced. The event involves "actual or threatened death, serious injury, or sexual violence" (271). Individuals who undergo "repeated or extreme exposure to aversive details of a traumatic event(s)" also meet criterion A (271). Simply experiencing events such as those described in the *DSM-V* does not mean that an individual will perceive the event as being traumatic or will experience traumatic effects. Research suggests that pretrauma characteristics of the individual, peritraumatic distress, the nature and severity of the traumatic event, the individual's perception of the event, and post-trauma experiences interact in ways that determine the nature and severity of traumatic reactions or lack thereof to the event (Briere and Scott 2015).

In addition to criterion A, the *DSM-V* criteria for a diagnosis of PTSD include four symptom-based criteria known as clusters: (b) reexperiencing, (c) avoidance, (d) negative cognitions and mood, and (e) arousal and reactivity. The reexperiencing cluster includes intrusive symptoms such as thoughts and memories about the event, flashbacks (in which the individual feels as though they are reliving the event), nightmares related to the event, and psychological and physical reactions to stimuli that remind the individual of the event. The avoidance cluster involves symptoms that may be cognitive (i.e., avoiding thoughts and feelings related to the traumatic event) or behavioral (i.e., avoiding people, places, or situations that are connected to the traumatic event) in nature. The negative cognitions and mood cluster includes symptoms of numbing, negative thoughts, and negative emotions. The arousal and reactivity cluster includes symptoms indicating an exaggerated startle response, hypervigilance, irritability, and sleep disturbances. Individuals may experience various constellations of symptoms under criteria B, C, D, and E. (See American Psychiatric Association 2013, the *DSM-V*, for a detailed listing of the symptoms and minimum requirements to meet diagnostic criteria for PTSD.)

In addition to criteria A through E, individuals must experience the symptoms for more than one month (criterion F), they must experience clinically significant distress or impairment from their symptoms (criterion G), and their symptoms cannot be attributed to the effects of a substance or other medical condition (criterion H). Specifiers for dissociative symptoms and delayed expression of PTSD symptoms are available in *DSM-V*.

Although trauma reactions are often discussed in terms of PTSD and acute stress disorder (ASD; diagnosis less than one month after trauma exposure), individuals can experience reactions that meet criteria for other disorders alone or in tandem with PTSD or ASD, such as other trauma- and stressor-related disorders, depressive disorders, brief psychotic disorder, dissociative disorders, anxiety disorders, substance use disorders, adjustment disorders, conversion disorder, somatic symptom disorder, and personality disorders. Furthermore, individuals may experience trauma reactions that do not meet criteria as outlined by the *DSM-V*; they may exhibit symptoms that either do not fully meet or exist entirely outside the *DSM* criteria. Two issues to consider in this regard are complex PTSD and culture-bound trauma responses.

Herman (1992) coined the term *complex PTSD* (C-PTSD). She posited that individuals who experience prolonged repeated traumatic stressors (such as hostages; prisoners of war; and survivors of domestic violence, childhood physical abuse, childhood sexual abuse, or organized sexual exploitation) experience alterations in affect regulation, consciousness, self-perception, perception of the perpetrator, relations with others, and systems of meaning. Individuals who manifest this syndrome are often misdiagnosed with other disorders that may be pejorative in nature (e.g., borderline personality disorder) and may receive fragmented treatment that never addresses the underlying trauma. Complex trauma syndromes have been described extensively in the clinical literature using terminology such as *disorders of extreme stress not otherwise specified* (DESNOS) (Pelcovitz et al. 1997) and *developmental trauma disorder* (DTD) (van der Kolk 2005), but they were not included as a separate diagnostic category in *DSM-IV* or *DSM-V* despite considerable efforts on the part of some experts (Resick et al. 2012; Roth et al. 1997). Nevertheless, it is apparent that individuals who experience prolonged and repeated traumatic stress, particularly of an interpersonal or purposeful nature, present with a complex constellation of problems and have a variety of treatment needs.

As noted above, PTSD is a Western conception of a disorder that develops in response to a traumatic event that is in part contingent on the perceptions, characteristics, and environment of the afflicted person. Certainly, the constructed meanings of the event, ways of coping, and social and physical environments where the event takes place and where healing may occur vary by culture. It follows that what one perceives as being a traumatic event and how one reacts to it, even to the extent of exhibiting a pathologic response, is influenced by culture. The PTSD construct does not exactly fit all cultures, but it is useful in understanding traumatic experiences when care is taken to recognize ethnocultural differences (Friedman and Marsella 1996). The reexperiencing and arousal symptoms appear to be more consistent across cultures than the avoidance and numbing symptoms and likely have more of a biological basis (Marsella et al. 1996; McFall and Resick 2005). Marsella (2010) notes that even the universal biological arousal response is mediated by culture. Although the PTSD diagnosis may be applied across cultures, the symptom clusters should be considered in the context of the culture, and it should be recognized that the construction of what is traumatic as well as the trauma response may fall entirely outside the parameters of the PTSD diagnosis.

CULTURE

Culture is a complex concept that many have endeavored to define. The definition presented by Marsella (2005) incorporates the various facets of culture:

> Culture is a shared learned behavior and meanings that are socially transferred in various life-activity settings for purposes of individual and collective adjustment and adaptation. Cultures can be (1) transitory (i.e., situational even for a few minutes), (2) enduring (e.g., ethnocultural life styles), and in all instances are (3) dynamic (i.e., constantly subject to change and modification). Cultures are represented (4) internally (i.e., values, beliefs, attitudes, axioms, orientations, epistemologies, consciousness levels, perceptions, expectations, personhood), and (5) externally (i.e., artifacts, roles, institutions, social structures). Cultures (6) shape and construct our realities (i.e., they contribute to our world views, perceptions, orientations) and with this ideas, morals, and preferences.

> (657)

According to Marsella, the notion that cultures can be temporary or transitory is based on the fact that cultures can develop in all social settings (e.g., classrooms, youth gangs, etc.), and the cultures that emerge in such settings can be in conflict with others. The most salient point, however, is that "culture constructs our realities and shapes the way we perceive and experience reality" (Marsella et al. 2008, 5). Culture provides a structure and a context in which members can define themselves and make meaning of the events in their lives as well as in the collective. Cultures often contain a paradigm as to how the world operates in relation to a divine force. Rules for behavior and associated benefits and consequences are clear. Members of the culture understand the power hierarchy and know what characteristics and behaviors will gain them value and worth (Salzman 2001). The culture also creates a context for living in which goods and services can be produced and used. The structure and context of the culture create a sense of belonging, safety, and protection. The many facets of culture come together to buffer members from the effects of external stressors. Individuals and systems within a culture rely on it to provide them with the structure and context for their lives; the disintegration of a culture is thus traumatic (deVries 1996).

CULTURAL TRAUMA

It is difficult to determine when the concept of cultural trauma first appeared in the literature, but as early as 1925 the notion that a society could be damaged by dramatic social change was discussed (Sorokin [1925] 1967). Sorokin was one of the first to discuss damages to a culture as a result of traumatic actions on the culture itself. He argued that rampant societal damage caused by the political, economic, epistemological, and spiritual upheaval of the Soviet revolution included dramatic increases in poverty, violence, sexual assault, disease, psychological disorders, familial instability (increasing divorce rates and declining birth rates), death rates, and alcoholism. These changes, caused by the trauma of the revolution, contributed to an overall cultural decline and a period of "primitivization."

Sztompka (2000) suggests that the conditions for cultural trauma exist in an atmosphere of cultural disorientation that emerges when sudden and unexpected disruptions occur. Radical changes in technological, economic, or political conditions (e.g., revolution, market collapse, forced migration or deportation, genocide, terrorism, violence, assassination of a political leader, etc.) can affect core values, beliefs, and norms, creating cultural disorientation and possibly cultural trauma. As with PTSD, the experience of the event in and of itself is not traumatic; the interpretation and meaning that is attached to the event by a given culture influences whether or not it becomes traumatic for the culture. It is likely that the nature of the event, the social construction of the meaning of the event, and the degree to which the culture is able to resume its functions following the event affect the extent and severity of the trauma experience or lack thereof. For example, Bracken (2002) notes that in England during World War II, the expected rise in mental health problems and social problems associated with the effects of war in the homeland (e.g., bombing raids, food shortages, etc.) did not occur. The English people constructed the events as a time for solidarity and strength and came together in a culturally sustaining way rather than experiencing the events as traumatic, which would potentially have led to societal deterioration. Taken a step further, the meaning that the world made of the British stand against the Blitzkrieg was one of a courageous people standing against the Nazi evildoers. This type of narrative allows for memorialization and healing. If England had lost the war, a vastly different narrative may have been constructed. By contrast, others who have experienced violent assaults against their culture strive to have their voices heard and their experience validated in the eyes of the world, such as the Armenians, who struggle for recognition of the genocide they endured at the hands of the Turkish government in 1915, and Native Americans, who contend with a revisionist history that purports that massacres of their people by American forces were actually heroic battles won against a savage force.

In summary, cultural trauma is a complex concept whose components are discussed in a variety of ways in the literature. It is clear that when a culture is overwhelmed by trauma, it loses its ability to protect and support its members. Homeostatic mechanisms that normally operate within the culture fail to function, and the stress-buffering properties of the culture are diminished or destroyed (deVries 1996). Such has been the case with Native Americans and other ethnocultural groups subjected to widespread disturbances as a result of colonization, slavery, forced relocation, genocide, disease, war, or any number of events that cause an entire group of people to suffer tragically (Neal 1998).

THEORETICAL PERSPECTIVES ON CULTURAL TRAUMA

Alexander (2004) posits that "cultural trauma occurs when members of a collectivity feel they have been subjected to a horrendous event that leaves indelible marks upon their group consciousness, marking their memories forever and changing their future identities in fundamental ways" (1). Members of the collective do not need to directly experience the event to feel the dramatic loss of identity and meaning that the trauma causes. Nor does the trauma have to be a sudden event; it can be a slow process that works its way into the psyche of the collective. The *trauma process* as described by Alexander (2004) begins with a claim that a fundamental injury to a social group has occurred; the claim-making carrier groups within the collective struggle to make meaning out of the event. Once the members of the wounded group recognize their traumatization, the claim can be broadened to the wider social community. This meaning-making process takes account of the nature of the pain, the nature of the victim, the relation of the trauma victim to the wider audience, and attribution of responsibility. Social institutions in the domains of religion, law, science, aesthetics, mass media, and state bureaucracy affect the representational process and may constrain or expand claims based on their own interests or agendas, and they may themselves be agents of trauma. The distribution of power among these institutions is often uneven and affects how trauma is or is not represented in a culture. Once meaning is made from the traumatic experience it becomes incorporated into the collective identity, and a process of reparation, reconstruction, and healing can occur. When carrier groups lack the resources to disseminate trauma claims or social institutions constrain trauma claims, perpetrators of collective suffering can avoid assuming responsibility for the damage they have caused, and the healing components of the trauma process are stymied.

Salzman (2001) and Salzman and Halloran (2004) apply terror management theory (TMT) (see Greenberg, Solomon, and Pyszczynski 1997; Solomon, Greenberg, and Pyszczynski 2004) to the concept of cultural trauma, particularly among indigenous people. In essence, TMT contends that human beings' self-consciousness makes them aware of the inevitability of their own death, and thus they experience an underlying terror of personal annihilation. This fear of mortality would be immobilizing if not for the anxiety-buffering effects of self-esteem and cultural worldview. Culture provides the standards for success and makes meaning of life. Individuals who conform to cultural standards and are deemed successful enjoy both enhanced self-esteem and a meaningful world in which to live. The cultural worldview is essential for buffering anxiety. When a culture is threatened, members will coalesce to protect it from being diminished. When a culture experiences trauma and its cultural worldview is damaged, anxiety flourishes and serious psychological and behavioral effects emerge.

Stamm et al. (2004) developed a theory of cultural trauma and loss that is based on the idea of cultural clash, whereby a hegemonic "arriving" culture challenges the "original" culture and disrupts fundamental cultural, social, and economic processes. Colonialism is the clearest example of a context for such a clash to occur. However, it is also possible for cultural clash to occur within one culture where conflict exists between subgroups. In their model, the repercussions of cultural clash—characterized by disruptions such as expanded trade, intellectual innovations, epidemics, competition for scarce resources between the arriving culture and original culture, incongruent belief systems, and war—precede an era of cultural loss in which members of the challenged group, still struggling to adjust to the new social reality, continue to experience an erosion of their shared identity and the loss of familiar social structures (cultural memory, language, self-rule, place, family system, economic resources, and healing systems). By the time this era of continued cultural disintegration emerges, the arriving culture may have established itself as a powerful and overbearing social, political, and military force, institutionalizing its dominance and structuring the distribution of resources and benefits to the detriment of the original culture (see also Walters and Simoni 2002).

MULTIGENERATIONAL AND HISTORICAL TRAUMA

The recognition that trauma experienced by one generation could be passed on to later generations emerged when children of Nazi Holocaust survivors were found to be experiencing psychiatric symptoms seemingly related to their parents' traumatic experiences (Kansteiner 2004). The phenomenon responsible for these symptoms was termed *transposition*, meaning that the trauma experience was transposed from one generation to another, i.e., the children of Holocaust survivors relived the experiences of their parents in an unconscious way (Kestenberg 1989; Laub 2002). This transposition is thought to continue passing to subsequent generations, as even the grand-children of Holocaust survivors have been observed to experience traumatic effects. The notion of transposition has its critics, who suggest that the neg-ative effects experienced by the children are a result of poor parenting by traumatized parents rather than a direct effect of the past trauma, in this case the Holocaust (Kansteiner 2004). Rather than debating the merits of these arguments, Auerhahn and Laub (1998) point to their research, which suggests that "knowledge of psychic trauma weaves through the memories of several generations" and that "massive trauma has an amorphous presence . . . that shapes the internal representation or reality of several generations, becoming an unconscious organizing principle passed on by parents and internalized by their children" (22). Research indicates that al-though the trauma response is heterogeneous in terms of individual and collective constructions, it is likely that the multigenerational experience of trauma across groups who experienced mass trauma is a universal phenom-enon (see Danieli 1998).

Drawing from the literature on the intergenerational transmission of trauma among the descendants of Nazi Holocaust survivors and other mas-sively victimized populations, Maria Yellow Horse Brave Heart developed the theory of historical trauma and delineated the historical-trauma response as it occurs among Native American people (Brave Heart 2003; Brave Heart and DeBruyn 1998). Historical trauma is defined as "the cumulative emo-tional and psychological wounding, over the lifespan and across generations, emanating from massive group trauma experiences" (Brave Heart 2003, 7). The historical-trauma response occurs in reaction to historical trauma and involves an array of problems that may include substance misuse, self-destructive behavior, suicidal thoughts and gestures, depression, anxiety, low self-esteem, anger, difficulty recognizing and expressing emotions, sur-vivor guilt, intrusive trauma imagery, identification with ancestral pain, fix-ation to trauma, somatic symptoms, and elevated mortality rates (Brave Heart 2003, 2007). Historical unresolved grief is associated with the historical-trauma response. The unresolved grief is a result of a long history of personal, familial, and communal losses that could not be mourned. These include massacres; premature death due to disease, suicide, or poverty; loss of language; changes in spirituality and belief systems; and disrupted family structure due to forced repression of Native social systems and children's co-erced or forced attendance at boarding schools. Grief is a normal response to loss, and various cultures have ways of mourning and expressing their grief. Native Americans were often unable to mourn in traditional ways or were compelled to detach from the pain of tremendous grief by a hegemonic culture that delegitimized their lived experience (Brave Heart and DeBruyn 1998). This historical unresolved grief gets passed from generation to generation.

Evans-Campbell (2008) elaborated on historical-trauma theory by suggesting a multilevel framework for understanding the phenomenon that includes impacts at the individual, family, and community levels. She further suggested a dynamic interplay between direct trauma experiences and transgenerational trauma, proposing that high rates of current violence, victimization, and trauma among Native American populations are best understood against the backdrop of temporally distal patterns of collective harm.

NATIVE AMERICAN TRAUMA EXPERIENCE: HISTORY AND PRESENT DAY

Native Americans contend with present-day events that have the potential to be traumatic at the individual and cultural level at much higher rates than the general population and other racial groups. They also contend with the cumulative effects of cultural and intergenerational trauma from the past, which is conceptualized as historical trauma. In order to help the reader understand the magnitude of the trauma that is part of the Native American experience, we provide in this section an overview of the traumatic events that have occurred and continue to occur in the lives of Native Americans.

The era of European discovery and subsequent colonization of the Americas marked the beginning of great suffering for the indigenous people of the American continents. The Native American population decreased from greater than 5,000,000 in 1492 to 250,000 in the decade between 1890 and 1900 (Thornton 1987). This massive depopulation is attributed to a number of factors, including disease, genocidal acts, war, and subsistence-disrupting policies. Europeans brought with them an array of diseases, such as smallpox, that the Native American people had never encountered. With the population lacking the biological immunities that come with disease exposure, the introduction of European illnesses devastated many Native American tribes with recycling epidemics. The devastation of illness would be compounded by the destructions of war and displacement as Europeans spread throughout the continent.

As the European presence grew, peaceful relations with Native American tribes gave way to conflicts over land and resources. These conflicts escalated as the republic of the United States of America formed and expanded. The competition for land in the east and the Americans' belief in their "manifest destiny" led to the passage of the Indian Removal Act of 1830, which forced southeastern tribes (even those that were "civilized," i.e., had adopted White ways such as owning and farming land, entrepreneurialism, Christianity, and European-style governmental systems) to relocate to reservations in the west (Wilson 1998). Thousands of Native Americans died on brutal forced marches to the reservations, the most notorious of which is the Cherokee trail of tears. When tribes were forced to relocate from their homelands, a vital cultural connection to place was severed. As the young nation pushed further westward, it engaged in a series of conflicts that came to be known collectively as the "Indian Wars." Although the manifest social policy of the U.S. government toward the Native Americans was one of relocation, in actual practice the result was too often annihilation. Tribal groups that did not relocate from their lands to reservations were attacked and, in many instances, massacred. Those that did move to reservations were compelled to abandon traditional spiritual practices and adopt Christianity along with other White ways of being.

In addition to the ravages of disease, war, and forced removal from homelands, early U.S. government policies toward Native Americans often functioned under the implicit assumption that the White culture was superior to indigenous cultures. Practices aimed at "civilizing the savages" proliferated. Sometimes, such policies and practices were driven by benevolent motives, but nevertheless the message conveyed was one of Native Americans' cultural inferiority. A systematic pattern of policies evolved with the explicit goal of hastening Native American assimilation into the hegemonic culture, which was often pursued through force or coercion and involved attempts to destroy or suppress elements of Native American tribal cultural and traditional practices (Brave Heart and DeBruyn 1998; Johnson et al. 2008). One of the most damaging assimilation practices was forcing Native American children to attend boarding schools. The Carlisle Industrial Indian School, located in Carlisle, Pennsylvania, was founded in 1879 and served as a model for other Indian schools. The motto of Richard Pratt, founder of the Carlisle Indian School, was "kill the Indian, and save the man." This motto is emblematic of the notion that replacing Indian cultural practices among the children with skills and practices from the White culture would allow them to assimilate and somehow save them. To that end, Native American children were forced to discard their familiar traditional ways and adopt the ways of the Whites. They were compelled to adopt Christian names, cut their hair, wear uniforms, eat unfamiliar foods from the White culture, and speak only English. Children were severely beaten if they engaged in traditional behaviors or spoke their own language. Thousands of children died from disease and sheer loneliness (Luther Standing Bear cited in Wilson 1998). Boarding schools lasted well into the twentieth century, and many attendees report experiencing violence and victimization at the schools in the form of physical and sexual abuse.

After the Wounded Knee Massacre in 1890, in which three hundred men, women, and children along with Chief Big Foot were mowed down by the bullets of the U.S. Army and left lying on the frozen ground, the Indian Wars were over. However, the traumatization of the Native American people was not. Along with Native American children being sent to boarding schools, transracial adoptions were frequent until the passage of the Indian Child Welfare Act in 1978. Religious and cultural practices were squelched until the passage of the Indian Religious Freedom Act in 1978. The repression of Native American cultural practices has led to a number of cultural losses such as the loss of Native languages. Microaggressions such as offensive team mascots, offensive slogans depicting or referring to Native Americans, and use of the term *squaw* to refer to Native American women continue today (Walters et al. 2006). Additionally, many Native Americans still contend with poverty, prejudice, discrimination, and various other forms of oppression.

During the twentieth century, many Native Americans left reservation lands to migrate to urban settings in search of economic opportunities, and the U.S. government policies encouraged such urban relocation (Brave Heart and DeBruyn 1998; Johnson et al. 2008; Snipp 1992). The majority of Native Americans now live outside of AI/AN areas (reservations or other tribal areas) (Norris, Vines, and Hoeffel 2012), where they may have more limited access to the tribal culture and its attendant social support systems. Although many urban Native Americans have been successful in retaining ties to culture practices and cultural identity through various mechanisms (see Cheshire 2001; Snipp 1992), some urban Native American communities have experienced a loss of community and cultural cohesion that may have adverse impacts on health and well-being (Johnson, Gryczynski, and Wiechelt 2007).

Regardless of location in urban or rural communities, Native Americans experience systemic oppression and social inequities such as high rates of poverty and unemployment that place them at greater risk for general health and behavioral health problems (Gone 2013). Furthermore, such health problems may be associated with the embodiment of historical trauma across generations (Walters et al. 2011). The Indian Health Service (2015) reports that American Indians/Alaska Natives experience overall death rates that are 1.2 times higher than rates for all other races in the United States, and much higher death rates from certain diseases (5.5 times for tuberculosis, 4.7 times for chronic liver disease and cirrhosis, and 3.1 times for diabetes), substance misuse (6 times for alcohol-related deaths and 1.8 times for drug-related deaths), unintentional injuries (2.4 times), and suicide (1.6 times).

Currently, Native Americans experience very high rates of lifetime traumatic events. Rosay (2016) reports high rates of lifetime violence against AI/AN men and women: 84 percent of AI/AN women experience violence, including 56.1 percent who have experienced sexual violence and 55.5 percent who have experienced physical intimate-partner violence; 81.6 percent of AI/AN men experience violence, including 27.5 percent who have experienced sexual violence and 43.2 percent who have experienced physical intimate-partner violence. Most AI/AN who were victims of violence (97 percent of women and 90 percent of men) experienced acts of violence committed by an interracial perpetrator. The homicide rate for Native Americans is twice the rate for all other races in the United States (Indian Health Service 2015). American Indian/Alaska Native children experience elevated rates of exposure to adverse events in childhood, such as physical abuse, sexual abuse, neglect, witness of domestic violence, and community violence. Furthermore, children's exposure to multiple forms of violence increases the risk of post-traumatic responses, health issues, and mental health problems into adulthood (Dorgan et al. 2014; Warne et al. 2017).

REACTIONS TO TRAUMA

Given their high incidence of trauma exposure, it is not surprising that Native Americans experience high rates of PTSD (Basset, Buchwald, and Manson 2014; Beals et al. 2005). Nor is it surprising that they experience higher rates of substance use disorders (SUDs) than the general population (9.7 percent vs. 4 percent for past-year alcohol use disorders, and 4.1 percent vs. 2.9 percent for past-year illicit drug use disorders) given that SUDs are known to be associated with trauma and PTSD (Bailey and Stewart 2014; Substance Abuse and Mental Health Services Administration 2017). Native Americans have high rates of psychological distress and mental health problems in comparison to the general population as well as high rates of unmet needs for such problems (National Center for Health Statistics 2016). Additionally, studies suggest that depression and anxiety are commonly experienced by Native Americans, particularly as comorbid disorders with SUD or PTSD, and that depression may be expressed in atypical ways (Beals et al. 2005; B. Duran et al. 2004; Robin, Chester, and Goldman 1996). Readers should note that population studies typically do not include enough AI/AN to adequately assess their health and mental health experiences (Warne et al. 2017).

The PTSD classification fails to adequately incorporate symptoms of complex, prolonged, or multigenerational cumulative trauma that are so often experienced by indigenous people. The interpersonal, prolonged, and cumulative nature of the traumatic events that Native Americans endure may produce a trauma reaction that is more consistent with C-PTSD/DES-NOS rather than PTSD, as it is more inclusive of the broad range of psychological distress symptoms that Native Americans experience.

The heterogeneity of Native Americans in the United States is an important consideration in any effort to understand their life experience in general and their experience of mental health and substance use problems in particular. The mental health system and its associated epistemology in the United States are constructed in such a way that they reflect the dominant Western culture. Mental health and substance use problems as experienced by Native Americans may not fit neatly into mainstream constructions. For example, it is well known that standard measures of depression fail to detect depression in Native American individuals in many instances (Beals et al. 2005). Despair that is experienced in association with the loss of sacred places or intrusions on identity does not easily fit into hegemonic nosological systems, nor are they resolved by mainstream intervention strategies (Gone 2006; Robin et al. 1996). For Native Americans, the experience of trauma and trauma responses are likely much broader than those that are included in existing classification systems. Also, constructions of trauma and trauma effects are likely to have some variation by tribal group, gender, sexual orientation, reservation versus urban status, and degree of assimilation (Balsam et al. 2004; Beals et al. 2005; Cole 2006; B. Duran et al. 2004; Evans-Campbell et al. 2006). Current-life traumatic experiences and trauma reactions among Native Americans occur against a backdrop of cumulative cultural traumas whose effects were passed down across generations, albeit in different ways depending on the experiences of the various tribes.

CULTURAL TRAUMA AND ITS EFFECTS
ON NATIVE AMERICANS

The arrival of Europeans to North American soil launched an epoch of cultural trauma for the indigenous people. The Europeans viewed themselves as being on the right side of God and entitled to the newly found beautiful lands. Further, they believed that they had the right to civilize the "savage" inhabitants of the land and to eradicate those inhabitants who did not comply. The presence and attitudes of the colonizing force inevitably produced cultural clashes resulting in disease, war, forced relocation, and challenges to traditional belief systems as briefly outlined above. Such clashes would be reproduced over the course of several hundred years throughout the expanding country. Napoleon (1996) describes the effects of exposure to European disease (influenza) and the sudden death of 60 percent of the Yup'ik people to illustrate the process and effect of cultural trauma on indigenous people:

> The suffering, the despair, the heartbreak, the desperation, and confusion these survivors lived through is unimaginable. People watched helplessly as their mothers, fathers, brothers, and sisters grew ill, the efforts of the *angalkuq* [medicine men] failing. . . . Whether the survivors knew or understood, they had witnessed the fatal wounding of *Yuuraraq* ["way of being a human being," 4] and the old Yup'ik culture. . . . The Yup'ik world was turned upside down, literally overnight. Out of the suffering in confusion, desperation, heartbreak, and trauma was born a new generation of Yup'ik people. They were born into shock. They woke to a world in shambles, many of their people and their beliefs strewn around them, dead. Their medicine and their medicine men and women had proven useless. Everything they had believed in had failed. Their ancient world had collapsed. . . . The world

the survivors woke to was without anchor. They woke up in shock, listless, confused, bewildered, heartbroken, and afraid.

(10–11)

Today we know that efforts to restore a culture should be undertaken as soon as possible following a culturally traumatic event in order to promote healthy coping and to minimize the effects of traumatic stress and potential damage to the culture. To that end, deVries (1996) suggests that the following steps be taken after an event that is potentially traumatic to a culture:

- Employ remaining cultural structures to help victims manage horror.
- Facilitate rituals and customs that order emotions.
- Create self-help opportunities.
- Legitimize suffering.
- Bring order and continuity into the post-traumatic period.
- Incorporate rituals and places to carry them out into the rehabilitative processes.
- Reestablish symbolic places (churches, gathering, and other meeting places).
- Work to reinstitute traditional social relationships.

The Native American people received no such restoration. The focus of the dominant U.S. culture was to do away with the indigenous cultures whether by annihilation or assimilation. Thus, the Native people were left to struggle with each successive traumatic event. There were, of course, opportunities to relocate and to accept White ways of being, but these came at the great costs of loss of connection with the land, loss of connection with the spirit world, loss of identity, and loss of family structures and other familiar ways of being that were each in and of themselves traumatic. The disintegration of culture results in a diminished sense of trust, aggression, anxiety, and other negative affective states among individuals from within that culture. According to Salzman (2001), the decimation of a culture leaves its members with a shattered worldview and no prescribed way of living; they are left with no means for maintaining anxiety-buffering self-esteem, and they resort to other, often self-destructive, methods of managing their anxiety. The effects of cultural trauma continue to reverberate through the lives of Native Americans and their communities. Understanding cultural trauma and its impact on Native Americans is an essential building block in comprehending the multiplicative, complex effects of ongoing, cumulative individual and cultural traumas that are collectively known as historical trauma.

HISTORICAL TRAUMA: THE NATIVE AMERICAN EXPERIENCE

The theoretical literature on the phenomenon of historical trauma among Native Americans has encompassed a multipronged, transtemporal emphasis spanning the micro and macro levels. At the micro or individual level, the cumulative effects of intergenerational trauma manifest as a psychological response that can mimic the symptoms of PTSD and disrupt the individual's psychological functioning and coping systems. Brave Heart (2003) termed the range of maladaptive psychological and behavioral reactions to historical trauma the *historical-trauma response*, arguing that the established diagnostic criteria for PTSD do not sufficiently reflect the culturally and historically grounded traumas experienced by Native Americans. Early applications of the concept of intergenerational trauma to the Native American experience also suggested a link between temporally distal experiences of cultural loss and subjugation in the group's shared history and the collection of health and social problems that continue to affect Native Americans as a group in the modern era (Brave Heart 2003; Brave Heart and DeBruyn 1998). This explicit dual conceptualization of intergenerational trauma as affecting not only individuals' psychological processes but also population-level disparities in health and access to resources was a significant theoretical advance. More recently, scholars have continued to elaborate on these kinds of multilevel conceptualizations of historical trauma (see, for example, Evans-Campbell 2008; Sotero 2006; Walters et al. 2011).

Brave Heart and others have contended that the contemporary plights faced by the Native American population—as indicated by racial disparities in such domains as violent victimization, substance use disorders, domestic violence, and health outcomes—could be seen as a direct consequence of historical trauma through its role in shaping the social and cultural contexts in which individuals operate (Brave Heart and DeBruyn 1998; Evans-Campbell 2008; Sotero 2006; Whitbeck et al. 2004). Health disparities continue to be evident in Native American communities. Empirical research suggests that the theorized link between trauma and health disparities is a plausible one given the relationship between PTSD and illness. For example, research has found that PTSD is associated with a range of health problems (Sareen et al. 2007; Sledjeski, Speisman, and Dierker 2008). Moreover, the association between PTSD and chronic health conditions is explained by the number of traumatic events experienced during the life course (Sledjeski, Speisman, and Dierker 2008). Hence, there is evidence indicating that repeated exposure to traumatic events has a cumulative impact on the development of a range of chronic illnesses. If individuals internalize the cultural traumas endured by their ancestors, it is possible that both historical and contemporary traumas might exert a cumulative adverse impact on human health.

The concept of historical trauma, its vital components, and the theorized pathways by which it perpetuates health and resource disparities in the affected population resonates well with a parallel body of scholarship in the field of social epidemiology that has sought to develop more nuanced understandings of risk-shaping processes at multiple levels of social organization (see, for example, Berkman et al. 2000; Glass and McAtee 2006; Link and Phelan 1995). Historical trauma can be seen through the prism of what Link and Phelan (1995) describe as fundamental causes of disease. The fundamental-cause conceptualization shifts emphasis away from proximal risk factors and encourages researchers to "contextualize" risk factors by appreciating the role of social conditions in structuring resource disparities that give rise to such risks. Although Link and Phelan's conceptualization is by and large temporally static and fixed in the present, historical-trauma theory complements their approach to understanding what puts people "at risk of risks" by postulating a process and mechanism that generate risk for the health-demoting fundamental causes themselves. While it is admittedly an imperfect metaphor, the phenomenon of historical trauma and its intergenerational transmission can be seen as giving rise to the contemporary social conditions that structure risk for disease and social problems.

Working from a perspective of public health and social epidemiology, Sotero (2006) has outlined a comprehensive conceptual model of historical trauma that details the physiological, psychological, and social consequences resulting from primary exposure to a mass trauma experience. Sotero argues that intergenerational transmission of the trauma response can occur through multiple vectors, including genetics, environmental factors, psychosocial factors, social-economic-political systems, and discrimination. A key feature of enduring historical trauma is that some part of the mass trauma was perpetrated against the culture in a deliberate, purposeful way. Even though Native Americans experienced their share of unintentional disasters (e.g., large numbers of deaths from illness due to lack of immunity to European diseases), much of the shared mass trauma in the group's history emanates from human decisions and contact with other cultures (e.g., war; policies of forced or coerced assimilation; attempts to suppress cultural and religious practices of the Native American people by a powerful White majority). Native Americans faced a systematic and drawn-out series of injustices that were perpetrated on them by the colonizing forces and the U.S. government (Thornton 1987; Wilson 1998).

Historical status inequalities and group subjugation are often intergenerational phenomena that leave societal, cultural, and institutional legacies that are difficult to dismantle. Nevertheless, it is important to remember that an individual from a specific cultural group that has a shared history of mass trauma will not automatically exhibit a pattern of symptoms attributable to a historical trauma response. The degree to which an individual experiences problems in psychosocial functioning that can be linked to a historical-trauma response may vary depending on an array of considerations, including but not limited to cultural identification, cultural knowledge, existing support systems, connection to culture, and available outlets for cultural expression.

A graphical depiction of historical trauma and the pathways by which some of its effects may become manifest is shown in Figure 7.1. It draws from several sources (Brave Heart and DeBruyn 1998; Evans-Campbell 2008; Sotero 2006; Stamm et al. 2004) as well as our own understanding of the phenomenon. Mass cultural traumas experienced by one generation result in disruption of cultural roles and protective processes. These disruptions stifle culturally grounded opportunities for healing from the effects of acute PTSD. The trauma experience does not emanate from a singular event, but rather is characterized by a sequential collection of cultural traumas that generate momentum for processes of cultural loss and disintegration (which endure through subsequent generations). Policies and systems of subjugation—some intentionally designed to destroy or fundamentally transform the culture—are put in place by the new hegemonic order.

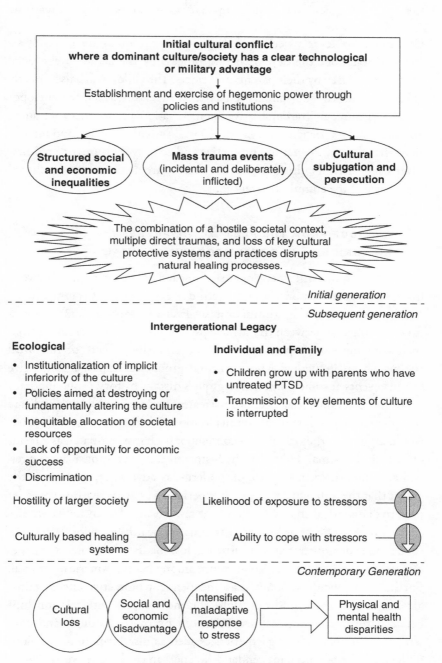

FIGURE 7.1 A model of the generational flow and consequences of historical trauma.

Children who never experienced the first set of traumas are adversely affected throughout the developmental process by the acute psychosocial problems endured by their parents and elders. The children are also directly affected by subsequent trauma events that are a feature of the new sociopolitical environment. The cumulative intergenerational experiences of trauma and cultural loss perpetuate legacies of social systems, policies, and institutions that disrupt the natural protective and adaptive features of a culture. Over time, critical cultural protective factors are displaced by the shared experience of the cumulative trauma.

A BRIDGE FROM THE PAST TO THE PRESENT: HISTORICAL AND CONTEMPORARY TRAUMAS

An interesting and still emergent area of research is the interaction between historical-trauma response and modern-day experiences of trauma, injustice, mistreatment, or discrimination (see Evans-Campbell 2008). It is useful to distinguish between the adverse psychosocial effects stemming from such contemporary experiences and the enduring effects of historical trauma on an individual whose cultural group was exposed to massive trauma events at some point in the group's distant history. Contemporary exposure to trauma, injustice, or mistreatment does not by itself indicate the presence of a historical-trauma response (although some theorists would argue that the risk of such contemporary harm is inflated as a result of historical trauma). However, the historical-trauma response may be reified and intensified in the face of modern-day adverse experiences to the extent that the individual views such experiences as fitting within a broader pattern of historical abuses. In one of the few advanced quantitative studies examining the effects of historical trauma on health behavior, Whitbeck et al. (2004) demonstrated that historical loss mediated the effects of experienced discrimination on alcohol abuse among Native American women. Furthermore, enculturation had an independent protective effect against alcohol abuse. These findings highlight the complex interrelationships between historical trauma (as experienced by the individual) and contemporary stress-producing experiences such as discrimination; they also underscore the potential for gender differences in the link between historical loss and the practice of health-demoting behaviors (see also Brave Heart 1999; Walters and Simoni 2002). Other protective factors such as family cohesion and connection to community have been identified (Wiechelt et al. 2012).

Native Americans as a group are at elevated risk for experiencing trauma, violence, and stress-inducing events (Basset, Buchwald, and Manson 2014; Johnson et al. 2008; Warne et al. 2017). Understanding the way that historical trauma or cultural loss shapes these experiences and prevents healing could have important implications for culturally focused intervention development and clinical work. If historical trauma plays a role in intensifying subjective experiences of stress and promulgating maladaptive behavioral responses, providing opportunities for the expression of healthy grieving processes and coping skills could presumably buffer against poor outcomes. Because historical trauma affects individuals, families, communities, and the broader Native American population, efforts to hasten healing through fostering empowerment, resiliency, and reclamation of cultural identity should target all these areas (Evans-Campbell 2008; Sotero 2006; Schultz et al. 2016).

HEALING

The complex and heterogeneous nature of trauma and trauma reactions among Native Americans as well as the heterogeneity that exists among Native Americans mean that there is not now, nor is there ever likely to be, an easy, prescribed, or uniform approach to resolving the effects of trauma among them. It is clear that multiple considerations regarding the individual are needed in the assessment and treatment-planning process. These include:

- the experience of traumatic event(s)
- the experience of PTSD and C-PTSD symptoms
- the experience of other psychiatric symptoms, e.g., depression and anxiety
- substance use behaviors
- the experience of psychological or spiritual distress that is not captured by DSM classifications
- the experience of health-related problems
- the degree to which the individual identifies with the Native culture
- the extent to which the individual engages in traditional practices and behaviors

- the awareness of and identification with cultural and historical trauma
- the economic, political, geographic, and cultural contexts in which he or she lives
- individual strengths and capacity for resilience
- connection with family and Native American community
- the capacity of the family or the community to support the healing process.

An individual's treatment needs are going to vary radically depending on his or her experiences relative to the above factors. For example, a Native American male who has PTSD symptoms related to his experiences in war and who resides on the Navajo reservation in Arizona, where he embraces traditional practices and feels a close connection to his family and community is likely to have very different needs and strengths than a woman of Cherokee descent residing in Baltimore, Maryland, who experiences C-PTSD symptoms related to a past history of long-term childhood physical abuse and is only vaguely aware of her Native American ancestry. In the first case, the integration of traditional healing practices with familial and community support would likely be extremely important early in the treatment process (see Manson 1997). In the second, efforts to integrate traditional healing practices early in the treatment process would likely be perceived as weird and perhaps even emblematic of prejudice or at least cultural insensitivity on the part of the clinician (if the clinician were not a Native American). However, in both cases historical trauma is likely to play a role. It possibly created the circumstances in which trauma occurred in the case of childhood physical abuse (via historic disruptions in family functioning and parenting practices), and it may have increased the vulnerability to developing PTSD and potentially amplified the trauma experience in either case (see Evans-Campbell 2008). In both cases, attention to historical trauma will be an important component of the healing process; the only questions are how and when.

A careful assessment of the individual's sense of Native American identity and cultural connection will be useful to the clinician in determining an appropriate course of action. Aragon (2006) suggests that the use of a genogram and a timeline diagram can provide useful insight into family connections and patterns and lifetime milestones and setbacks that will help to clarify the individual's status regarding culture and identity. In the case of the Cherokee woman described above, the assessment may reveal that she has assimilated into the dominant culture, and current mainstream strategies for addressing C-PTSD are indicated (Courtois and Ford 2009). Nevertheless, historic trauma may still be playing a role in her life, and the clinician should at least be cognizant of that possibility. As treatment progresses, deeper healing of the disengaged historical trauma may be possible by reconnecting her with her ancestral past in a slow and careful way (E. Duran 2006).

According to E. Duran (2006), the soul wound, now known as historical trauma, has long been acknowledged by Native American elders as a result of ancestral wounding of the people and the earth. He asserts that remedying the problems faced by Native Americans today (e.g., depression, anxiety, substance misuse, violence) occurs via a decolonizing process aimed at healing the soul wound. Clinicians who work with Native Americans must use care not to perpetuate the trauma of colonialism. Epistemological hybridism, whereby clinicians can understand and value the worldview of Native Americans in addition to their own, is needed for a clinician to practice in decolonizing ways. The helping process should "address the immediate problem and simultaneously set in motion the act of decolonizing" (14). An important component of the process is for the clinician to ask the client, "Who are you?" (i.e., Who is your tribe? Who is their God? What is their tribal creation story?). The clinician must also answer these questions for herself or himself, as being disconnected from one's own ancestral path makes it impossible to help others connect with theirs. The healing work in this model is aimed at making the connections between current life problems and historical trauma. E. Duran's model is instructive for all clinicians who work with Native Americans in that cultural competency, respect for different ways of knowing and being, and connection with oneself are necessary regardless of the specific therapeutic approach being used.

Clinicians who work with Native Americans may work with a particular tribal group on or near reservations or with an array of tribal groups in urban Indian centers. Additionally, since most Native Americans now live away from tribal lands, clinicians in any geographic area or type of practice setting may come into contact with Native Americans in their practice. Therefore, it is incumbent on all clinicians to have at least a basic understanding of the experience of Native Americans in the United States and the effects of historical trauma on behavioral and physical health (see Johnson et al. 2010; Johnson, Gryczynski, and Wiechelt 2007). Clinicians who work with a particular tribal group should be very familiar with the history and practices of that tribe. In order to be culturally competent practitioners with Native Americans, clinicians should go beyond simply acquiring knowledge and reflect on their own biases and the biases of the helping professions toward Native Americans, and they should redress those biases in their work with and on behalf of Native Americans (Weaver 1998).

Community-level healing is vital to ameliorating the effects of historical trauma over the long term. Salzman (2001) describes cultural recovery movements in which Native American people are identifying and making use of their traditional values and practices in association with political struggles to regain power. Such struggles restore the cultural worldview and the people's faith in their ways of being, thus restoring the anxiety-buffering properties of the culture. The Yup'ik people, whose dramatic cultural loss was briefly described above, are working to heal from historical trauma and have incorporated their traditions into behavioral health treatment (Mills 2003). More recently, Schultz et al. (2016) suggest that communal engagement with place and experiential learning promote health and healing in Native American communities. They point out that interventions rooted in indigenous ways of knowing and being (e.g., those that emphasize the interrelationships between all living things and promote active engagement with the natural world) are likely to be more effective than individually focused, indoor, Western-based approaches. Members of the Choctaw Nation who walked a portion of the trail of tears that their ancestors walked were physically engaged in the place where their ancestors struggled. By so doing, they both honored their ancestors and experientially learned to work to maintain their own health and the health of the tribe as a community.

There are many other interventions rooted in Native ways of knowing and being. Notably, Brave Heart (1998) developed the historical-trauma and unresolved-grief intervention, which addresses generational and lifespan trauma using empowerment principles in the context of the Lakota culture. Communal grieving and reconnection are key components of healing historical trauma and unresolved grief. The Lakota people also spiritually honor their ancestors and celebrate the strength of the Lakota people via the annual Bigfoot Memorial Ride (Weaver 1998). Tribal healing efforts emphasize interconnectedness to ceremony, culture, community, and place (Bigfoot, England-Aytes, and King 2017). Macro actions to redress social inequity and dismantle systems of oppression empower communities as well (Hartman and Gone 2014).

Native American tribes, communities, families, and individuals show tremendous resilience in the face of much historical and present-day adversity. Native communities hold a great deal of strength, knowledge, and wellness. These attributes can be drawn on to foster resilience in others. Shared narratives of strength, connection to history and place, and connection to community promote resilience (Reinschmidt et al. 2016). There are many tribes, many places, and many stories, and in each of them power moves.

CASE VIGNETTE

Joe is a sixty-two-year-old Native American male who is a member of the Lumbee tribe. He resides with his wife of forty years, who is also Lumbee. The couple has five adult children and seven grandchildren. Joe primarily grew up in Robeson County, North Carolina, where the Lumbee tribe is mainly located. His family of origin relocated to Baltimore, Maryland, when he was twelve in an effort to find a better source of income. (Some members of the Lumbee tribe began migrating to Baltimore in the late 1930s to seek work; the flow of migration peaked during the 1940s and 1950s. A large group of them and their offspring still reside there.) He reports that when he was a boy in North Carolina, segregation between Whites, Blacks, and "Indians" (the term Joe uses to describe himself) was commonplace. Thus, he only affiliated with other Lumbee people when he lived there; the school, church, and other parts of his community all comprised Lumbees. He found the relocation to Baltimore difficult because it meant he had to attend school and interact in an urban community with many fewer Indians and more Black and White people. Joe reports that even though people in North Carolina often treated the Lumbee people with disdain and discriminatory practices, they knew that they were Native Americans. In Baltimore, people were unsure what race the Lumbees were and often cast them as mixed-race people (i.e., a combination of Black and White). Joe reports that he grew up in impoverished conditions. Furthermore, both his parents had alcohol use disorders, and his father was physically violent toward his mother and also toward Joe and his siblings. When the family lived in North Carolina, the whole family picked cotton and tobacco in order to subsist economically. The family was financially better off once they settled in Baltimore, where Joe's father obtained work as a roofer. The Lumbee community in Baltimore lived in a certain area of the city's east side (Butcher's Hill) until recent years, when the area underwent economic development and gentrification. Joe recalls frequent community picnics and other activities, which he enjoyed.

Joe began using alcohol at age fourteen and drank heavily until he started to use heroin at age twenty-four. He developed an addiction to heroin and used it daily. He continued to drink alcohol, although less often because he was more interested in using heroin. Joe's alcohol and drug use caused him to be arrested and incarcerated on multiple occasions for crimes such as possession, public intoxication, and theft. He also got into numerous fights and has been both shot and stabbed. Joe primarily socializes at the "corner bar," which is frequented by members of the Lumbee community. Joe is currently unemployed but has worked under the table as a roofer for most of his adult life.

At first glance, Joe's experience of trauma and substance use is not atypical for individuals with substance use problems in Baltimore. However, when Joe's issues are considered in the context of what we know about historical and cultural trauma and the Lumbee experience, we get a better sense of what Joe needs to support his recovery efforts and help him to heal.

Dial and Eliades (1996) have written a history of the Lumbee Indians. A few of their key points are described here to help the reader get a sense of what might constitute historical trauma for the Lumbee people. The Lumbee strongly identify as Native Americans, but they adopted European ways so long ago that they are disconnected from their language and other cultural traditions. It is believed that the ancestors of the Lumbee tribe helped the members of the "Lost Colony" of Roanoke by allowing them to merge into the tribe. This merger likely resulted in the White and Native people exchanging cultural practices, which is a possible explanation for the Native group's early use of the English language and other European ways of being. The Lumbees' geographic isolation and degree of acculturation protected them from colonial aggression against Indians. As anti-Indian sentiment and fears of non-Whites in general grew in the southern United States during the 1800s, the Lumbee increasingly experienced race-based discrimination and oppression. Prior to 1952 the Lumbee were known as Croatan or the Indians of Robeson County. The Croatan name had become a source of derision and abuse; consequently, the tribe adopted the name "Lumbee" and petitioned the government to be recognized under their chosen name. The Lumbee are recognized as a Native American tribe by the state of North Carolina and the U.S. government. However, the federal recognition was not granted until 1956, and the language of the bill recognizing them contained the caveat that they would not receive federal Indian services as offered to other tribes. The Lumbee tribe continues to struggle for full recognition and eligibility for federal services. The Lumbee also struggle for full recognition as a Native American tribe with other Native Americans, who sometimes discount the Lumbees because of their assimilated history and lack of a distinct Native culture (e.g., language, dance, foods).

A review of Lumbee history makes it apparent that disconnection, diffusion, oppression, and mixed messages are core features of the tribal experience. They were assimilated and isolated enough to avoid being subjected to forced relocation to reservations in the nineteenth century, but Indian enough to be deprived of their basic rights and to be recipients of derision and discrimination. Nevertheless, the Lumbee people are strongly connected to one another, their homeland, and their spirituality and function as a unified force to retain and advance their community. This strong connectivity in the community has maintained the groups' Native American identity. The Lumbee of Baltimore retain strong ties with the main tribal group in North Carolina. To this day, many Lumbee Indians living in Baltimore still refer to Robeson County as home and frequently visit the area.

Joe experienced trauma as a child in the form of family violence and race-based oppression. He felt safe in Robeson County in the company of his tribal group. Moving to Baltimore and being disconnected from his identity and his cultural group were extremely disruptive. He also experienced a different kind of prejudice in Baltimore: Whites treated him poorly because he was Black in their eyes, and Blacks treated him poorly because they saw him as being White. He did not belong with either group, and his formerly prominent identity as an Indian had become invisible to those around him. The invisibility issue remained a problem throughout Joe's life in Baltimore because medical, social service, and justice-system personnel typically misidentified him and did not know how to interact with him. Joe's struggle to be seen and valued as a Native American person is consistent with the struggle of the Lumbee people to be seen and valued as a Native American tribe.

Joe's family history of alcoholism, exposure to childhood abuse and domestic violence, poverty, and social disruption all placed him at high risk to develop substance use problems. Violence and victimization are associated with substance use, and thus Joe's alcohol and heroin use placed him at high risk for the shooting and stabbing that he experienced. All of this occurred against the backdrop of the historical trauma endured by the Lumbee people, which sets up the context for violence, poverty, and a diffuse sense of self.

Joe sought help from a local agency whose mission is to work with the Native American community. Joe's physical health and substance use behaviors were initially the primary concerns. Joe distrusted the mainstream medical system and was reluctant to accept a referral. He was angry that he had been racially misclassified in the past and felt that medical personnel did not respect him or listen to his needs. Joe was referred to a clinic that provides services for physical health, mental health, and substance use. One of the case managers there is Native American and worked with Joe to help him negotiate the system and accept services. Through the clinic, Joe received medical treatment and enrolled in a methadone maintenance program. Simultaneously, he received ongoing treatment and case-management services from the Native American centered community agency. The agency worked with Joe to help him obtain economic resources and dental care. Joe joined a therapist-led weekly recovery group. He also attended educational groups on HIV/AIDS and hepatitis prevention and tobacco cessation. The groups at the agency are all designed for Native Americans and are particularly sensitive to the needs of the Lumbee community. The group format is used to facilitate community connections and draw on the strong affiliations that the Lumbee feel for one another. The recovery support group incorporates sober-living skills with an exploration of Lumbee identity and the establishment of non-drug-using community connections. The educational groups are delivered from a cultural-strengths perspective and incorporate Native American concepts, symbols, and worldviews into disease prevention and health maintenance. Joe benefits from these types of services because they allow him to feel respected as a Native American, help him feel connected to the community (prior disconnections were extremely upsetting to him), help him to explore his identity as a Native American and his connection to his tribe, and provide him with skills to address his substance use problems and trauma-related issues. The agency hosts activities that allow Joe to socialize with other Lumbees in a substance-free environment, thus reducing his need to affiliate at the corner bar.

This case illustrates the complex links between historical cultural trauma, family trauma, and individual trauma in Joe's life. It also highlights the importance of reconnecting Joe with the strength of his community and his own cultural identity. Given Joe's particular circumstances, services that are designed to foster that reconnection may help to keep him engaged in therapeutic interventions from which he stands to benefit. Joe's case reflects a typical case in a particular agency that serves Native Americans in Baltimore. All three of this chapter's authors are affiliated with the agency. The agency is staffed with both Native and non-Native personnel and provides culturally sensitive services. It is important to note that Joe hesitated to seek help because he felt disrespected and misunderstood by other social service and health care agencies from which he had sought help in the past. All helping professionals should be sensitive to the cultural identification of the individuals they serve and provide services in response to their particular needs.

CONCLUSION

Native American tribal groups have experienced cultural and historical traumas that play a role in the health and social problems that many Native Americans contend with today. It is incumbent on helping professionals to have an understanding of cultural and historical trauma and its interaction with current individual and communal life challenges in order to provide sensitive and effective services to Native Americans in both urban and rural settings. This chapter is designed to help readers develop a beginning understanding of how current life traumas and struggles among Native Americans may be related to cultural and historical trauma, and to recognize that pathways to healing come through a reconnection to the strength and resilience of the community. Native Americans are diverse in terms of their experience of current and historical trauma as well as in their reactions to such experiences. Therefore, care must be taken to understand the story of each person and each tribal group in order to provide meaningful healing pathways, services, and interventions that respect and honor the "who" of those sitting before you.

REFERENCES

Alexander, J. C. 2004. "Toward a Theory of Cultural Trauma." In *Cultural Trauma and Collective Identity*, ed. J. C. Alexander, R. Eyerman, B. Giesen, N. J. Smelser, and P. Sztompka, 1–30. Berkeley: University of California Press.
American Psychiatric Association. 2013. *Diagnostic and Statistical Manual of Mental Disorders*. 5th ed. Arlington, Va.: American Psychiatric Association.

Aragon, A. M. 2006. "A Clinical Understanding of Urban American Indians." In *Mental Health Care for Urban Indians: Clinical Insights from Native Practitioners*, ed. T. M. Witko, 19–31. Washington, D.C.: American Psychological Association. doi:10.1037/11422-001.

Auerhahn, N. C., and D. Laub. 1998. "Intergenerational Memory of the Holocaust." In *International Handbook of Multigenerational Legacies of Trauma*, ed. Y. Danieli, 21–41. New York: Plenum Press.

Bailey, K. M., and S. H. Stewart. 2014. "Relations Among Trauma, PTSD, and Substance Misuse: The Scope of the Problem." In *Trauma and Substance Abuse: Causes, Consequences, and Treatment of Comorbid Disorders*, 2nd ed., ed. P. Ouimette and J. P. Reed, 11–34. Washington, D.C.: American Psychological Association.

Balsam, K. F., B. Huang, J. M. Simoni, and K. L. Walters. 2004. "Culture, Trauma, and Wellness: A Comparison of Heterosexual and Lesbian, Gay, Bisexual, and Two-Spirit Native Americans." *Cultural Diversity and Ethnic Minority Psychology* 10:287–301. doi:10.1037/1099-9809.10.3.287.

Basset, D., D. Buchwald, and S. Manson. 2014. "Posttraumatic Stress Disorder and Symptoms Among American Indians and Alaska Natives: A Review of the Literature." *Social Psychiatry and Psychiatric Epidemiology* 49:417–433. doi:10.1007/s00127-013-0759-y.

Beals, J., S. M. Manson, N. R. Whitesell, P. Spicer, D. K. Novins, and C. M. Mitchell. 2005. "Prevalence of DSM-IV Disorders and Attendant Help-Seeking in 2 American Indian Reservation Populations." *Archives of General Psychiatry* 62:99–108. doi:10.1001/archpsyc.62.1.99.

Berkman, L. F., T. Glass, I. Brissette, and T. E. Seeman. 2000. "From Social Integration to Health: Durkheim in the New Millennium." *Social Science and Medicine* 51:843–857. doi:10.1016/S0277-9536(00)00065-4.

Bigfoot, D. S., K. England-Aytes, and P. J. King. 2017. "Application: Cultural Trauma in American Indian Populations." In *Social Psychology: How Other People Influence Our Thoughts and Actions*, ed. R. W. Summers, vols. 1 and 2, 539–557. Santa Barbara, Calif.: Greenwood.

Bracken, P. 2002. *Trauma: Culture, Meaning, and Philosophy*. London: Whurr Publishers.

Brave Heart, M. Y. H. 1998. "The Return to the Sacred Path: Healing the Historical Trauma and Historical Unresolved Grief Response Among the Lakota Through a Psychoeducational Group Intervention." *Smith College Studies in Social Work* 68:287–305. doi:10.1080/00377319809517532.

Brave Heart, M. Y. H. 1999. "Oyate Ptayela: Rebuilding the Lakota Nation Through Addressing Historical Trauma Among Lakota Parents." *Human Behavior in the Social Environment* 2:109–126. doi:10.1300/J137v02n01_08.

Brave Heart, M. Y. H. 2003. "The Historical Trauma Response Among Natives and Its Relationship with Substance Abuse: A Lakota Illustration." *Journal of Psychoactive Drugs* 35:7–13.

Brave Heart, M. Y. H. 2007. "The Impact of Historical Trauma: The Example of the Native Community." In *Trauma Transformed: An Empowerment Response*, ed. M. Bussey and J. B. Wise, 176–193. New York: Columbia University Press.

Brave Heart, M. Y. H., and L. M. DeBruyn. 1998. "The American Holocaust: Healing Historical Unresolved Grief." *American Indian and Alaska Native Mental Health Research* 8 (2): 60–82.

Briere, J., and C. Scott. 2015. *Principles of Trauma Therapy: A Guide to Symptoms, Evaluation, and Treatment.* 2nd ed., DSM-5 Update. Los Angeles: Sage.

Bureau of Indian Affairs. n.d. "About Us." Accessed April 16, 2019. https://www.bia.gov/about-us.

Cheshire, T. C. 2001. "Cultural Transmission in Urban American Indian Families." *American Behavioral Scientist* 44:1528–1535. doi:10.1177/0002764021956863.

Cole, N. 2006. "Trauma and the American Indian." In *Mental Health Care for Urban Indians*, ed. T. M. Witko, 115–130. Washington, D.C.: American Psychological Association. doi:10.1037/11422-006.

Courtois, C. A., and J. D. Ford. 2009. *Treating Complex Traumatic Stress Disorders: An Evidence-Based Guide.* New York: Guilford Press.

Danieli, Y., ed. 1998. *International Handbook of Multigenerational Legacies of Trauma.* New York: Plenum Press.

deVries, M. W. 1996. "Trauma in Cultural Perspective." In *Traumatic Stress: The Effects of Overwhelming Experience on Mind, Body, and Society*, ed. B. A. van der Kolk, A. C. McFarlane, and L. Weisaeth, 398–413. New York: Guilford Press.

Dial, A. L., and D. K. Eliades 1996. "The Only Land I Know: A History of the Lumbee Indians." Syracuse, N.Y.: Syracuse University Press.

Dorgan, B. L., J. Shenandoah, D. S. Bigfoot, E. Broderick, E. F. Brown, V. Davidson, . . . J. Keel. 2014. *Attorney General's Advisory Committee on American Indian and Alaska Native Children Exposed to Violence: Ending Violence So Children Can Thrive.* U.S. Department of Justice. November. https://www

.justice.gov/sites/default/files/defendingchildhood/pages/attachments/2014 /11/18/finalaianreport.pdf.

Duran, B., M. Sanders, B. Skipper, H. Waitzkin, L. H. Malcoe, S. Paine, and J. Yager. 2004. "Prevalence and Correlates of Mental Disorders Among Native American Women in Primary Care." *American Journal of Public Health* 94:71–77. doi:10.2105/AJPH.94.1.71.

Duran, E. 2006. *Healing the Soul Wound: Counseling with American Indians and Other Native Peoples.* New York: Teachers College Press.

Evans-Campbell, T. 2008. "Historical Trauma in American Indian/Native Alaska Communities." *Journal of Interpersonal Violence* 23:316–338. doi:10.1177 /0886260507312290.

Evans-Campbell, T., T. Lindhorst, B. Huang, and K. L. Walters. 2006. "Interpersonal Violence in the Lives of Urban American Indian and Alaska Native Women: Implications for Health, Mental Health, and Help-Seeking." *American Journal of Public Health* 96:1416–1422. doi:10.2105/AJPH.2004.054213.

Friedman, M. J., and A. Marsella. 1996. "Posttraumatic Stress Disorder: An Overview of the Concept." In *Ethnocultural Aspects of Posttraumatic Stress Disorder: Issues, Research, and Clinical Applications,* ed. A. J. Marsella, M. J. Friedman, E. T. Gerrity, and R. M. Scurfield, 11–32. Washington, D.C.: American Psychological Association. doi:10.1037/10555-001.

Glass, T. A., and M. J. McAtee. 2006. "Behavioral Science at the Crossroads in Public Health: Extending Horizons, Envisioning the Future." *Social Science and Medicine* 62:1650–1671. doi:10.1016/j.socscimed.2005.08.044.

Gone, J. P. 2006. "Mental Health, Wellness, and the Quest for Authentic American Indian Identity." In *Mental Health Care for Urban Indians: Clinical Insights from Native Practitioners,* ed. T. M. Witko, 55–80. Washington, D.C.: American Psychological Association. doi:10.1037/11422-003.

Gone, J. P. 2013. "Redressing First Nations Historical Trauma: Theorizing Mechanism for Indigenous Culture as Mental Health Treatment." *Transcultural Psychiatry* 50:683–706.

Greenberg, J., S. Solomon, and T. Pyszczynski. 1997. "Terror Management Theory of Self-Esteem and Cultural Worldviews: Empirical Assessments and Conceptual Refinements." In *Advances in Experimental Social Psychology,* ed. M. P. Zanna, vol. 29, 61–139. San Diego, Calif.: Academic Press.

Hartman, W. E., and J. P. Gone. 2014. "American Indian Historical Trauma: Community Perspectives from Two Great Plains Medicine Men." *American Journal of Community Psychology* 54:274–288.

Herman, J. L. 1992. *Trauma and Recovery.* New York: Basic Books.

Indian Health Service. 2015. *Trends in Indian Health: 2014 Edition.* Washington D.C.: U.S. Government Printing Office. https://www.ihs.gov/dps/includes/themes/responsive2017/display_objects/documents/Trends2014 Book508.pdf.

Johnson, J. L., J. Baldwin, J. Gryczynski, S. A. Wiechelt, and R. C. Haring. 2010. "The Native American Experience: From Displacement and Cultural Trauma to Resilience." In *Multiethnicity and Multiethnic Families: Development, Identity, and Resilience*, ed. H. McCubbin, 277–343. Honolulu: Le'a Publications.

Johnson, J. L., J. Baldwin, R. C. Haring, S. A. Wiechelt, S. Roth, J. Gryczynski, and H. Lozano. 2008. "Essential Information for Disaster Management and Trauma Specialists Working with American Indians." In *Ethnocultural Perspectives on Disaster and Trauma*, ed. A. J. Marsella, J. L. Johnson, P. Watson, and J. Gryczynski, 73–113. New York: Springer Science + Business Media.

Johnson, J. L., J. Gryczynski, and S. A. Wiechelt. 2007. "HIV/AIDS, Substance Abuse, and Hepatitis Prevention Needs of Native Americans: In Their Own Words." *AIDS Education and Prevention* 19:531–544. doi:10.1521/aeap.2007 .19.6.531.

Kansteiner, W. 2004. "Testing the Limits of Trauma: The Long-Term Psychological Effects of the Holocaust on Individuals and Collectives." *History of the Human Sciences* 17 (2/3): 97–123. doi:10.1177/0952695104047299.

Kestenberg, J. 1989. "Transposition Revisited: Clinical, Therapeutic, and Developmental Considerations." In *Healing Their Wounds: Psychotherapy with Holocaust Survivors and Their Families*, ed. P. Marcus and A. Rosenberg, 67–82. New York: Praeger.

Laub, D. 2002. "Testimonies in the Treatment of Genocidal Trauma." *Journal of Applied Psychoanalytic Studies* 4:63–87. doi:10.1023/A:1013937226642.

Link, B. G., and J. Phelan. 1995. "Social Conditions as Fundamental Causes of Disease." *Journal of Health and Social Behavior* (extra issue): 80–94. doi:10.2307 /2626958.

Manson, S. M. 1997. "Cross-Cultural and Multiethnic Assessment of Trauma." In *Assessing Psychological Trauma and PTSD*, ed. J. P. Wilson and T. M. Keane, 239–266. New York: Guilford Press.

Marsella, A. J. 2005. "Culture and Conflict: Understanding, Negotiating, and Reconciling Conflicting Constructions of Reality." *International Journal of Intercultural Relations* 29:651–673. doi:10.1016/j.ijintrel.2005.07.012.

Marsella, A. J. 2010. "Ethnocultural Aspects of PTSD: An Overview of Concepts, Issues, and Treatments." *Traumatology* 16 (4): 17–26.

Marsella, A. J., M. J. Friedman, E. T. Gerrity, and R. M. Scurfield. 1996. "Ethnocultural Aspects of PTSD: Some Closing Thoughts." In *Ethnocultural Aspects of Posttraumatic Stress Disorder: Issues, Research, and Clinical Applications*, ed. A. J. Marsella, M. J. Friedman, E. T. Gerrity, and R. M. Scurfield, 529–538. Washington, D.C.: American Psychological Association. doi:10.1037/10555-022.

Marsella, A. J., J. L. Johnson, P. Watson, and J. Gryczynski. 2008. "Essential Concepts and Foundations." In *Ethnocultural Perspectives on Disaster and Trauma: Foundations, Issues, and Applications*, ed. A. J. Marsella, J. L. Johnson, P. Watson, and J. Gryczynski, 3–13. New York: Springer Science + Business Media.

McFall, G. J., and P. A. Resick. 2005. "A Pilot Study of PTSD Symptoms Among Kalahari Bushmen." *Journal of Traumatic Stress* 16:445–450. doi:10.1023/A:1025702326392.

Mills, P. 2003. "Incorporating Yup'ik and Cup'ik Eskimo Traditions into Behavioral Health Treatment." *Journal of Psychoactive Drugs* 35:85–88.

Napoleon, H. 1996. *Yuuyaraq: The Way of the Human Being*. Fairbanks: University of Alaska Fairbanks, Native American Knowledge Network.

National Center for Health Statistics. 2016. *Health, United States, 2015: With Special Feature on Racial and Ethnic Health Disparities*. Washington, D.C.: U.S. Government Printing Office. https://www.cdc.gov/nchs/data/hus/hus15.pdf.

National Conference of State Legislatures. 2016. "Federal and State Recognized Tribes." http://www.ncsl.org/research/state-tribal-institute/list-of-federal-and-state-recognized-tribes.aspx.

Neal, A. G. 1998. *National Trauma and Collective Memory*. Armonk, N.Y.: M. E. Sharpe.

Neihardt, J. G. (1932) 2008. *Black Elk Speaks: Beginning the Life Story of a Holy Man of the Oglala Sioux*. Premiere ed. Albany: State University of New York Press.

Norris, T., P. L. Vines, and E. M. Hoeffel. 2012. *The American Indian and Alaska Native Population: 2010*. January. https://www.census.gov/prod/cen2010/briefs/c2010br-10.pdf.

Pelcovitz, D., B. A. van der Kolk, S. Roth, F. Mandel, S. Kaplan, and P. A. Resick. 1997. "Development of a Criteria Set and a Structured Interview for Disorders of Extreme Stress (SIDES)." *Journal of Traumatic Stress* 10:3–16.

Reinschmidt, K. M., A. Attakai, C. B. Kahn, S. Whitewater, and N. Teufel-Shone. 2016. "Shaping a Stories of Resilience Model from Urban American Indian

Elders' Narratives of Historical Trauma and Resilience." *American Indian and Alaska Native Mental Health Research* 4:63–85.

Resick, P. A., M. J. Bovin, A. L. Calloway, A. M. Dick, M. W. King, K. S. Mitchell, . . . E. J. Wolf. 2012. "A Critical Evaluation of the Complex PTSD Literature: Implications for DSM 5." *Journal of Traumatic Stress* 25:241–251. doi:10.1002/jts.21699.

Robin, R. W., B. Chester, and D. Goldman. 1996. "Cumulative Trauma and PTSD in American Indian Communities." In *Ethnocultural Aspects of Posttraumatic Stress Disorder: Issues, Research, and Clinical Applications*, ed. A. J. Marsella, M. J. Friedman, E. T. Gerrity, and R. M. Scurfield, 239–253. Washington D.C.: American Psychological Association. doi:10.1037/10555-009.

Rosay, A. B. 2016. "Violence Against American Indian and Alaska Native Women and Men." *National Institute of Justice Journal* 277:38–45.

Roth, S., E. Newman, D. Pelcovitz, B. A. van der Kolk, and F. S. Mandel. 1997. "Complex PTSD in Victims Exposed to Sexual and Physical Abuse: Results from the DSM-IV Field Trial for Posttraumatic Stress Disorder." *Journal of Traumatic Stress* 10:539–555. doi:10.1002/jts.2490100403.

Salzman, M. B. 2001. "Cultural Trauma and Recovery: Perspectives from Terror Management Theory." *Trauma, Violence, and Abuse* 2:172–191. doi:10.1177/1524838001002002005.

Salzman, M. B., and M. J. Halloran. 2004. "Cultural Trauma and Recovery: Cultural Meaning, Self-Esteem, and the Reconstruction of the Cultural Anxiety Buffer." In *Handbook of Existential Psychology*, ed. J. Greenberg, S. L. Koole, and T. Pyszczynski, 231–246. New York: Guilford Press.

Sareen, J., B. J. Cox, M. B. Stein, T. O. Afifi, C. Fleet, and G. J. G. Asmundson. 2007. "Physical and Mental Comorbidity, Disability, and Suicidal Behavior Associated with Posttraumatic Stress Disorder in a Large Community Sample." *Psychosomatic Medicine* 69:242–248. doi:10.1097/PSY.0b013e31803146d8.

Schultz, K., K. L. Walters, R. Beltran, S. Stroud, and M. Johnson-Jennings. 2016. "'I'm Stronger than I Thought': Native Women Reconnecting to Body, Health, and Place." *Health and Place* 40:21–28.

Sledjeski, E. M., B. A. Speisman, and L. C. Dierker. 2008. "Does Number of Lifetime Traumas Explain the Relationship Between PTSD and Chronic Medical Conditions? Answers from the National Comorbidity Survey-Replication (NCS-R)." *Journal of Behavioral Medicine* 31:341–349. doi:10.1007/s10865-008-9158-3.

Snipp, C. M. 1992. "Sociological Perspectives on American Indians." *Annual Review of Sociology* 18:351–371. doi:10.1146/annurev.so.18.080192.002031.

Solomon, S., J. Greenberg, and T. Pyszczynski. 2004. "The Cultural Animal: Twenty Years of Terror Management Theory and Research." In *Handbook of Experimental Psychology*, ed. J. Greenberg, S. L. Koole, and T. Pyszczynski, 13–34. New York: Guilford Press.

Sorokin, P. (1925) 1967. *The Sociology of Revolution*. New York: Howard Fertig.

Sotero, M. A. 2006. "A Conceptual Model of Historical Trauma: Implications for Public Health Practice and Research." *Journal of Health Disparities Research and Practice* 1 (1): 93–108.

Stamm, B. H., H. E. Stamm, A. C. Hudnall, and C. Higson-Smith. 2004. "Considering a Theory of Cultural Trauma and Loss." *Journal of Loss and Trauma* 9:89–111. doi:10.1080/15325020490255412.

Substance Abuse and Mental Health Services Administration. 2017. *Behavioral Health Barometer: United States,* vol. 4: *Indicators as Measured Through the 2015 National Survey on Drug Use and Health and National Survey of Substance Abuse Treatment Services.* HHS Publication NO. SMA-17-BarolUS-16. Rockville, Md.: Substance Abuse and Mental Health Services Administration.

Sztompka, P. 2000. "The Other Face of Social Change." *European Journal of Social Theory* 3:449–466.

Thornton, R. 1987. *American Indian Holocaust and Survival: A Population History Since 1492.* Norman: University of Oklahoma Press.

van der Kolk, B. A. 2005. "Developmental Trauma Disorder: Toward a Rational Diagnosis for Children with Complex Trauma Histories." *Psychiatric Annals* 35:401–408.

Walters, K. L., T. Evans-Campbell, A. Stately, and R. Old Person. 2006. "Historical Trauma, Microaggressions, and Colonial Trauma Response: A Decolonization Framework for HIV Prevention Efforts Among Indigenous Communities." Paper presented at Embracing Our Traditions, Values, and Teachings: Native Peoples of North America HIV/AIDS Conference, Anchorage, Alaska, May.

Walters, K. L., S. A. Mohammed, T. Evans-Campbell, R. Beltran, J. H. Chae, and B. Duran. 2011. "Bodies Don't Just Tell Stories, They Tell Histories." *Du Bois Review* 8 (1): 179–189.

Walters, K., and J. Simoni. 2002. "Reconceptualizing Native Women's Health: An Indigenest Stress-Coping Model." *American Journal of Public Health* 93:520–524. doi:10.2105/AJPH.92.4.520.

Warne, D., K. Dulacki, M. Spurlock, T. Meath, M. M. Davis, B. Wright, and K. J. McConnell. 2017. "Adverse Childhood Experiences (ACE) among American Indians in South Dakota and Associations with Mental Health Conditions, Alcohol Use, and Smoking." *Journal of Health Care for the Poor and Underserved* 28:1559–1577.

Weaver, N. H. 1998. "Indigenous People in a Multicultural Society: Unique Issues for Human Services." *Social Work* 43:203–211.

Whitbeck, L. B., X. Chen, D. R. Hoyt, and G. W. Adams. 2004. "Discrimination, Historical Loss, and Enculturation: Culturally Specific Risk and Resiliency Factors for Alcohol Abuse Among American Indians." *Journal of Studies on Alcohol* 65:409–418.

Wiechelt, S. A., J. Gryczynski, J. L. Johnson, and D. Caldwell. 2012. "Historical Trauma Among Urban American Indians: Impact on Substance Abuse and Family Cohesion." *Journal of Loss and Trauma* 17:319–336.

Wilson, J. 1998. *The Earth Shall Weep: A History of Native America*. New York: Grove Press.

8

Art Therapy with Traumatically Bereaved Youth

▸ *LAURA V. LOUMEAU-MAY*

ART THERAPY IS EFFECTIVE in the treatment of traumatized client populations. As a nonverbal, sensory-based, enactive modality that has narrative and
symbolic potential, the act of making art within a therapeutic relationship can
access aspects of trauma experiences that have evaded verbal processing.
Brain research supports art therapy as a treatment to promote hemispheric
integration—linking the verbal with the nonverbal. Specific techniques developed by art therapists include the Instinctual Trauma Response to work with
post-traumatic stress disorder (PTSD). Losing a parent or a sibling is traumatic
for children, even when it is anticipated. When death is sudden and violent, as
by accident, suicide, or murder, actual trauma is intensified, which complicates
the grieving process. The increase in societal violence (e.g., mass shootings) and
in catastrophic natural disasters has an impact not only on those directly affected but also on all children in terms of their perception of vulnerability to
danger. Art therapy in grief work with children is the focus of this chapter. The
author provides case examples from her work at Journeys, a youth bereavement
program in northern New Jersey; they illustrate the benefits of art therapy in
healing traumatizing aspects of loss. Names of clients have been changed.

THE USE OF ART THERAPY WITH POPULATIONS
AFFECTED BY TRAUMA

Art has long functioned as a response to trauma. While she was confined at
the Czech concentration camp Terezin during the Second World War, Friedl
Dicker-Brandeis taught children drawing and painting, activities that sus-

tained them (Potok and Volavková 1993; Wix 2009). Japanese Americans placed in relocation camps in the 1940s processed their experiences through art (Byers 1996; Gesensway and Roseman 1987). Globally, children's artwork provides testament to the horrors of war (Geist and Geist 2002). Communities erect ad hoc public shrines subsequent to the deaths of figures such as Princess Diana or tragedies such as 9/11 (Santino 2006).

Art therapy, a profession with roots in psychiatry, has been effective in treating trauma for more than forty years (Stember 1977). Many traumatized populations have been helped by art therapy, including burn and accident survivors (Chapman et al. 2001; Mallay 2002; Martin 2008; Russell 1999; Wald 1989), victims of natural disasters (Chilcote 2007; Lacroix et al. 2007; Orr 2007; Roje 1995), veterans (Collie et al. 2006; Lande et al. 2010; Morgan and Johnson 1995), and rape victims (Amir and Lev-Wiesel 2007; Cross 1993; Kaufman and Wohl 1992; Pifalo 2002, 2006, 2007, 2009; Serrano 1989; Spring 1993, 2004). Art therapists have "had boots on the ground" (and brushes in their hands) to respond to global natural disasters such as the tsunamis in Japan, hurricanes Katrina and Sandy in the United States, the Puerto Rican and Haitian hurricanes, and human-generated mass violence such as the many public and school shootings, 9/11, etc. (Goodman 2004; Loumeau-May et al. 2015)

Following the 1994 Los Angeles earthquake, Roje (1995) noted that art therapy "enabled children to express internal processes which they had no verbal awareness of and facilitated working through the defenses in order to identify underlying conflicts which hindered recovery" (243). After three months all the children had healed, except those who had preexisting trauma history. Collie et al. (2006) outlined the advantages of using art therapy with combat veterans experiencing post-traumatic stress disorder (PTSD). Benefits include the following:

- Reconsolidation of implicit and declarative memories
- Progressive symbolic exposure to stimuli perceived as threatening
- Externalization and distancing of the trauma narrative through visual form
- Reduction of arousal through the relaxing effects of art making
- Reactivation of positive emotion to counteract the numbing of trauma
- Enhancement of emotional self-efficacy
- Improved self-esteem

Pifalo conducted studies to evaluate the use of art therapy with sexually abused children (2002, 2006). She used the Brief Trauma Symptom Checklist for Children to measure symptoms before and after a ten-week art therapy group and conducted a follow-up study four years later. Both studies demonstrated a reduction in sexual abuse–identified symptoms subsequent to intervention. Spring (2004) conducted a thirty-year study of the graphic forms created by sexually abused women. Specific recurrent imagery was linked to documented experience of sexual assault. Other studies found that use of the Chapman Art Therapy Treatment Intervention, which was designed for "incident-specific, medical trauma," reduced acute stress symptoms (Chapman et al. 2001, 101).

FACTORS UNIQUE TO ART THERAPY
THAT ADDRESS TRAUMA

Areas of the brain that handle speech and cognition shut down during a traumatic event. Recalling events through words is difficult, but sensorial memory is strong, and flashbacks often occur. Flashbacks are primarily visual and are triggered by specific sensory cues.

FIGURE 8.1 As late as a year after his sister's death by drowning, Doug started to experience triggers based on catastrophic weather events in the news. He began to draw images of deluges and storms.

Art making enables a victim to represent his or her experience by externalizing it into a concrete form.

The image then enables the victim to describe the traumatic event through words, transforming the visual and sensorial memories. Tapping into visual recall should be handled cautiously by a trained art therapy professional with expertise in understanding the power of emergent imagery. One person may struggle to remember events clearly so they can heal through acknowledging the experience, whereas another may be emotionally overwhelmed by recall. Timing is essential and varies among clients according to their developmental levels, the severity of the trauma, and the strength of their defenses. Caution must be exercised not to encourage this process prematurely; however, in some cases recall is encouraged. Steele (2002) described

FIGURE 8.2 A teen sculpted the memory of his mother grasping her head during a fatal stroke. This helped him release and master the suppressed emotion of witnessing her death.

a boy who blocked his memory of the night his sister was raped and murdered. A year later he was demonstrating negative behavior with poor emotional and academic functioning. Using a series of drawings to re-create the tragic events, his therapist was able to help him unblock the memory and get him on the path to recovery.

Art making is sensory based. It employs visual, tactile, kinesthetic, and often olfactory and auditory sensations. It is a physical process involving motion, pressure, and rhythm to stimulate or to calm. Consider the difference between ripping and cutting versus blending and smoothing; these activities can both reflect emotion and evoke it. Art materials can be cold, wet, sharp, soft, sticky, rough, or smooth; they evoke sensations that trigger sensory-related memories which can be pleasant or negatively charged. Steele and Raider (2001) attributed the ability of making art to help access sensory memories to the fact that it is a psychomotor activity. In cases involving bodily trauma, such as physical abuse or burn trauma, the kinesthetic-sensorial aspect of working with art materials is particularly potent and can trigger as well as soothe. It is therefore important to choose materials carefully when working with clients who have experienced physical trauma or abuse.

During creative activity witnessed by the therapist, the artist-client is continually responding not only to internal images and feelings but also to the impact of embodied imagery as it develops in the artwork in progress and within the shared and reflective viewing of the therapist, who acts as a mirror and a safe container for intense affect. It is common for art therapy clients to rethink, change, or redo an image based on their own responses to it. Art making is a symbolic and metaphorical re-creation of experience; this is noticeable with young children who constantly change an image as they tell a story with it. A child's painting may begin as a representation of a beautiful day that dissolves into rain but later shines again as the sun reemerges and flowers blossom. Adolescents and adults are also affected by creating an artwork; the product may be so emotionally laden that they destroy, transform, or discard it. I have previously described the experience of Rachel, a ten-year-old girl who intended to make a mask to represent the face of her father, a victim of 9/11 (Loumeau-May 2008). While she was painting it, some of the red-orange pigment she used to re-create her father's hair color accidentally mingled with the coral pink she used for his flesh, evoking associations of fire, scarring, and burning. In response to this startling,

FIGURE 8.3 The sensorial qualities of glistening red, orange, and brown paint visually suggested burning and burial, two possible ways Rachel's father may have died. She chose to abandon her original plan for a portrait mask and explore these fears instead. It is crucial for the art therapist to be alert to the fact that art materials can trigger real or imagined memories and to provide a protective therapeutic environment that supports the client if and when this does occur. Additionally, it is critical to refrain from encouraging a client to imagine or remember traumatic events prematurely.

unplanned visual occurrence, the child discarded her original intention of creating a portrait and used the paint instead to portray burned flesh and mud burying the lower half of her father's face. The horrific image represented one of many possible scenarios of how he may have died. Empathic re-imagining of a loved one's death, especially in the case of traumatic loss, is not uncommon. The art-making process in this case was cathartic.

Rachel chose not to keep the mask, but she expressed relief at having been able to make a concrete image of her internal replay. To retain such an image, once it is created, is something clients often are not comfortable with. To do so may actually be retraumatizing. Schaverien (1992) observed clients' tendency to create toxic images and then discard them, or bequeath them to the therapist-witness who would honor and contain them. She named this the "Scapegoat Transference." This act of discarding a created image can be cleansing.

A seventeen-year-old whose father had been struck by lightning similarly reacted to the triggering visual effect of the mask she was creating. Diane had been sitting outside the room where doctors were attempting to resuscitate her father. She heard him code seven times as her mother begged the doctors to keep trying. Diane intended for the mask to be an elaborate and "royal" one, and she planned to work on it for many sessions. The mask was painted elegantly in gold, with the whites of the eyes carefully delineated prior to her adding jewels for the irises. She worked slowly. When the paint

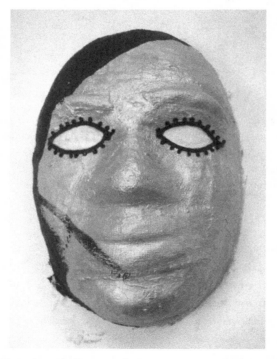

FIGURE 8.4 Diane's mask also seemed to trigger an emotional reaction. She viewed the image differently each time she returned to work on it. It was not until the third session that the pupil-less eyes startled her to the point where she abandoned her very controlled and elaborate plan and decided not to finish the mask.

was dry, she lined the eyes with finely laced black ribbon to represent eye-lashes. However, when returning to her project in the next session, she seemed startled by the intensity of the blank, white, pupil-less eyes. She began to paint over the gold with black paint, but finally abandoned the project altogether.

The Expressive Therapies Continuum, created by Kagin and Lüsebrink (1978) and further developed by Hinz (2009), is a conceptual model for understanding art dynamics and the use of media. A familiarization with the Expressive Therapies Continuum broadens the clinician's appreciation of art's therapeutic application to clinical goals. It analyzes four therapeutic levels of art making: kinesthetic/sensory, perceptual/affective, cognitive/symbolic, and creative. The kinesthetic level primarily utilizes motor discharge. Sensory exploration of materials grounds kinesthetic discharge and leads to the ability to form images. The perceptual level is externally focused and mediates relationships with the outside world. The affective level represents emotional involvement with expression. It can deepen and enrich the art-making process or can overwhelm, leading to regression. The cognitive level involves structured, intellectually focused, nonspontaneous work, such as visual problem solving. According to Lüsebrink and Hinz (2016), "Information processing on the right side permits exposure through Affective and/or Symbolic channels; processing on the left side provides containment and restructuring through perceptual and cognitive functions" (49). The symbolic level is characterized by intuitive work and metaphor and may augment therapy by amplifying the client's interpretation of personal experience. If defenses are worked through by repeated symbolic confrontation, transformation of their emotional value can occur (Lüsebrink 1990). This stage is usually original and expansive, similar to Schaverien's (1992) definition of the embodied image, wherein works created often have power that may defy verbal exploration.

The imagery basis of art therapy is evocative. Images have emotional impact and re-create experiences imagined or real. They operate on both symbolic and abstract levels. One image may encompass a multitude of actual, implied, or potential meanings, including conscious and unconscious intent. An image shows the client's conscious intent or plan while also indicating what the client is not yet prepared to explore. The art product is a tangible record that can be revisited at various times during therapy to reexamine its meaning and glean whatever insight it may contain. The image becomes an external, concrete form that distances it from the creator, thereby providing potential for objectivity and detachment. The client can contemplate it, which empowers the healing process; the client is no longer controlled by the emotional impact of the image but has achieved some distance and is in control of it.

The fact that art therapy occurs within a relational context is essential. Creative engagement is active rather than passive; the client is doing and making something that requires intent, planning, action, and appraisal. The enactive aspect of the creative process empowers the creator (Steele 2001). Clients are imaging, learning, and practicing actions that relieve anxiety, improve self-esteem, and enable them to visualize themselves functioning in the context of transformed lives and worldviews. According to Buk (2009), "on both physiological and psychological levels, the bodily and life-affirming activities of the artist making art can remediate the feelings of helplessness, passivity, and annihilation experienced during the trauma" (62). Creating an actual product in the presence of the art therapist encodes the image more effectively than using words or mental rumination alone. The therapist's attention and active interest in the art-making process—along with the client and therapist's mutual contemplation of the finished object, which encompasses both contingent and marked mirroring (Springham and Huet 2018)—are essential to validating the client's experience and helping the client recontextualize it.

Enactment can precede and stimulate remembrance. Embodied simulation, linked with the mirror neuron system, enhances the artist's ability to symbolically re-create experiences and the observer's ability to empathize with images produced and their emotional content (Buk 2009). Through companioned viewing, acknowledgment, and containment of dissociated memory images and metaphoric response, the art therapist assists in recall, recognition, and reintegration of intolerable affect-laden memories. In addition to the production of recognizable images, production of nonfigurative symbolic art such as mandalas (circular designs that have both a calming effect and symbolic potential for psychic integration) is frequently used in art therapy and has resulted in significant reduction in PTSD symptoms (Henderson, Mascaro, and Rosen 2007).

Finally, the use of art enhances the narrative aspect of trauma recovery. Although the story can be told with words alone, it is enriched and embodied in visual and material form. It can be presented directly in chronological order as it occurred or indirectly through allegory if the client is not ready for the former. Moreover, various alternative endings can be considered until the client is able to accept the reality of actual events. Art expression and play therapy techniques such as sand tray and puppetry are not merely play; they provide enactment opportunities to master and transform traumatic experience.

Mark, a nine-year-old, discovered the body of his father, who had died of a heart attack in his sleep. For many weeks Mark brought his large collection of well-articulated wrestling figures and a few superhero figures to session, preferring to obsessively re-create elaborate fights between them than to use art materials. Mark had been wrestling with his father the night before he died. In session, he focused much of his time on explaining the backstories of the superheroes and the wrestlers; in nearly all the scenarios, the heroes changed roles and altered their moral compasses following the death of a loved one—often realizing that they had been the cause of it. Eventually, Mark accepted my offer of clay. Clay is a potent medium due to its malleability, which invites aggressive actions and offers multiple transformations. Mark immediately created comic father-and-son characters who were being threatened by gigantic robots and dinosaurs. He played with these creations as he had with his action figures, but he also physically transformed one character into another—many times. Consistent with the psychoanalytic concept of repetition compulsion, Mark re-created the trauma repeatedly. However, as he did, he revised the symbolism of the relationship between father and son. The father sacrificed part of his physical (clay) body to save the son, and vice versa. They became caretakers and extensions of each other, until the metaphor was one of identification and transition of power.

Alan, age nine, created time machines in drawing, painting, and clay. He imagined going back in time to prevent his father from committing suicide. After many symbolic creations, he was able to let go of this fantasy, stating that he realized that unless he could have been with his father every minute of every hour, he would not have been able to stop the suicide. He understood that the locus of control had been with his father and not himself.

HOW TRAUMA AFFECTS THE BRAIN

People who have suffered traumatic events are often unable to express in words the details of their experience. Alexithymia, the inability to understand, describe, and process emotions, couples with post-traumatic dissociation, a disruption in conscious thought or psychological functioning. According to Lester, Wong, and Hendren, "It is hypothesized that patients with PTSD have difficulty restructuring recollections of traumatic histories due to the decreased activity of Broca's area, an area responsible for language processing and higher cognitive functioning" (2003, 264). There is a suppression of function of the hippocampus during traumatic experience (van der Kolk 2006). According to Buk (2009), "this leads to context-free, fearful memories and associations of the trauma that are encoded in implicit, sensorimotor form, are difficult to locate in place and time, and are therefore often impossible to verbally articulate" (62).

Neuroimaging research findings by Jakowski et al. (2009) indicate that permanent structural changes to the brain, notably in prefrontal/frontal lobe volumes, as well as alteration in neurotransmitter systems, have been found in chronically maltreated children. This implies that early repeated trauma may lead to permanent brain changes associated with psychopathology such as depression. Early neglect and deprivation can result in impairment to the limbic system and critical neuronal cell death, linked with future aggressive behavior and affective dysregulation (Schore 2003). Rapid increase of dopamine under discrete or prolonged stress can cause DNA mutations in brain tissue.

ART THERAPY AND THE BRAIN

The benefits of treating trauma victims with art therapy are reinforced by findings in neuroscience and psychology (Hass-Cohen and Carr 2008). Techniques in neuroimaging, specifically functional positron emission tomography and magnetic resonance imaging methods, illuminate our understanding of the way in which the different tasks and structures of the brain process information (Lüsebrink 2004). In a 1996 study, Rausch et al. reported that during victims' exposure to scripts of their traumatic experiences, their brain scans displayed arousal in the right hemisphere, particularly the amygdala, concurrent with a lack of left-brain activity in Broca's area (Tripp 2007).

Brain research supports art therapy as a treatment that promotes hemispheric integration, linking the verbal with the nonverbal functions while containing affect (Gantt and Tinnin 2009). Right-hemisphere activity is fully operant from birth. It affects the way implicit memory is stored, responding to and organizing incoming sensory experience. Early secure attachment is optimal for emotional development as well as for maximizing left-brain development and cognitive functioning. Even when verbally accessible, all explicit memories are retrieved through sensory and visual imagery associations. Implicit sensorial memories are processed by the amygdala in the right hemisphere before being sent to the hippocampus for storage and retrieval through explicit means.

By using visual and somatosensory processing, art therapy treats trauma symptoms with directives that reach areas of the brain that elude explicit thought. When an art therapist asks a client to create an image, the visual representation supersedes words to portray events and emotions. Art making activates the nonverbal (right) brain to reveal the pain and provide a foundation for the verbal (left) brain to express and externalize the traumatic experience, thereby reducing dissociation and alexithymia and generating cognitive and symbolic aspects of memory. Images reveal traumatic experiences and can be described, providing insight to how the experiences have affected thoughts and behavior, thus leading to mental, emotional, and physical healing (Lüsebrink 2004). With this approach, the trauma victim is able to recontextualize to make the events addressable and promote health and well-being.

Hass-Cohen (2016) states, "Therapeutic experiences happen through the continued process of reactivation, re-encoding, and reconsolidation of memories. Through this process, new rules or schemas (internal working models) will be updated, allowing clients more flexible ways of engaging with autobiographical narratives" (128).

SIX ART THERAPY PROTOCOLS DEVELOPED FOR MANAGING TRAUMA

The following are specific trauma-focused approaches developed by art therapists. Cohen and Cox (1995) proposed a model based on drawing content and style for recognizing and understanding the imagery produced by clients with dissociative identity disorder. These clients experienced prolonged, continual, sexual and/or physical abuse during childhood, usually by primary caregivers on whom the victims were dependent. Ongoing abuse is distinct from single-incident trauma in that hyperarousal symptoms are amplified as a result of the ongoing repetition of trauma (Herman 1992). These victims' adaptation strategies, such as dissociation, persist long after the abuse has ceased and are more difficult to recover from.

The integrative approach developed by Cohen and Cox (1995) for analyzing artwork focuses on structural elements of visual communication. The dissociative identity disorder model lists ten picture types: system, chaos, fragmentation, barrier, threat, induction, trance, abreaction, switching, and alert. Artwork in each category corresponds to clients' psychological or behavioral states. Identifying the category of drawings, especially when repeated, deepens clients' understanding of their experiences and can point toward appropriate therapeutic interventions that will help integrate personalities that have become dissociated.

Appleton (2001) created the Art Therapy Trauma Intervention and Assessment Paradigm, which identifies four progressive stages (impact, retreat, acknowledgment, and reconstruction) experienced by adolescents recovering from burn traumas. Her model can be applied to other forms of trauma. These stages support clients as they cope with initial regression, damage to body image, loss of function, and the need to reconstruct world views.

For each stage Appleton (2001) identified psychological issues, therapeutic goals, and art and graphic features that typically emerge. During the impact stage, burn patients experience shock, depersonalization, disbelief, and the pain associated with their burns. Spontaneous art making is encouraged; clients may tell the trauma story indirectly through metaphor. Relaxation techniques help clients cope with pain and anxiety. Art directives related to the trauma that may lead to catharsis are avoided at this stage as they cause retraumatization.

The retreat stage is characterized by resistance and development of defenses as full understanding of the permanent effects of the trauma emerges. The therapeutic goal is to build alliance through support. By helping patients use art materials, the therapist assists victims to develop coping mechanisms as well as trust. Encouragement of free exploration of imagery is more effective than the use of directives, which may be met with superficiality or resistance. More success is achieved with nondirective work in which clients have choices and autonomy.

As patients express painful feelings, including anger, they reach the acknowledgment stage. Their comfort level with the therapist through art making becomes a foundation for treatment. During this stage, active mourning happens, and clients are able to use media to express feelings and explore issues related to the loss. If clients do not do this spontaneously, relevant directives to facilitate exploration may be employed. Clients are capable of sustaining longer periods of focus on art making and will create more complex pieces.

In the reconstruction stage, clients integrate coping skills and insights and begin to accept life changes. This stage is marked by a search for the meaning of the trauma and the establishment of new directions in life. More complex directives and projects are possible. Patients are able to review life changes stemming both from the loss and from the internal growth they are undergoing. Memorial projects are appropriate, as are directed activities, such as creating timelines, that can help clients view life from different perspectives.

Rankin and Taucher (2003) provide a task-focused plan for addressing the psychological needs of trauma. They recommend appropriate art therapy directives that focus on recovery. These directives embrace the goals of safety planning, self-regulation, trauma narrative, grieving trauma-associated losses, self-concept, worldview revision, self-development, and relational development. Structured collage and writing techniques identify physical and psychic dangers while establishing safety plans early on; these offer a more secure base of cognitive control. Soothing art tasks such as the creation of mandalas, bodywork, and visualization will help clients regulate intense emotions and become grounded during flashbacks. Trauma narrative, essential to recovery, is encouraged when clients feel ready. Integrating imagery into storytelling activates sensations, emotions, and cognitions of the actual trauma, aiding recall. Narration is structured to provide closure through media or ritual, minimizing negative effects. Extensive trauma or loss may be divided into segments to prevent overwhelming clients. The final stage involves revising clients' worldviews and concepts of self. A contextual sense of continuity of the self following trauma is achieved through projects such as lifelines. Reframing techniques will help clients acknowledge self-growth resulting from processing trauma.

Goodman (2004) used an art therapy protocol that integrated cognitive-behavioral and client-centered approaches when working with families victimized by 9/11 at New York University's Child Study Center. The cognitive-behavioral approach employed structured interventions to address trauma-related affects in specific ways. Self-regulating techniques such as systematic relaxation supported gradual exposure to traumatic events during personal narrative, so as not to retraumatize children by encouraging premature recall, including triggers, before they were psychologically prepared to handle frightening memories. These techniques helped children manage their anxiety both in and outside the therapy sessions. The client-centered aspect of treatment incorporated active-listening techniques and acceptance, which addressed the individual needs of the client; clients themselves determined the content and direction of therapy. Combining both approaches has strengths in the treatment of traumatic grief: the first focuses on the trauma quickly, providing concrete skill-building techniques, and the second is gentler, respects clients' defenses, and increases self-determination, which empowers the child.

The Instinctual Trauma Response (ITR), a theory developed by Gantt and Tinnin (2007), analyzes typical reactions to trauma and provides a task-oriented treatment using imagery to process the trauma narrative. This method, Intensive Trauma Therapy, or ITT (Gantt and Tripp 2016), helps resolve dissociation as well as victim mentality. Human responses to trauma, as described by the ITR, are similar to the survival strategies animals use when attacked, namely,

- startle
- thwarted intention
- freeze
- altered state of consciousness
- body sensation
- state of automatic obedience
- self-repair.

Using the ITT method, clients draw "graphic narratives" to narrate each of the seven stages, beginning with a "safe place." In this way, they bring implicit memory into conscious awareness. The series of drawings includes before and after pieces that frame the traumatic experience within the context of clients' ongoing lives. Bilateral stimulations such as the butterfly hug, a tapping on both arms while they are folded, are used to enhance the visual and verbal process. It is only when the complete narrative is integrated sequentially with a beginning, middle, and end that closure can be brought to the trauma. The unification of memory fragments into a coherent story is made possible by the sensorial images that enhance the re-creation of subjective experiential states; through their externalization and representation they become accessible to explicit memory. Once the graphic narrative is complete, the art therapist verbally re-presents the trauma narrative to the client by describing the pictures. The client's next task is to have an external written dialogue with their narrative, writing with both their dominant and nondominant hands. They use their dominant hand to cognitively address those parts of the trauma they wish to explore further and their nondominant hand to respond on an emotional level, thus activating and integrating the two hemispheres of the brain. This treatment aims to resolve dissociation. The symbolic act of creation inherent by art making is instrumental in rewriting "victim mythology" into a reempowered view of self in which trust in personal safety is restored.

McNamee (2003, 2004), Talwar (2007), and Tripp (2007) have developed bilateral stimulation techniques based on eye movement desensitization and reprocessing that they combine with art making to transform traumatic memory. These processes stimulate memories from both sides of the brain and promote integration. McNamee directs clients to draw alternately with their dominant and nondominant hands in response to the processing of emotions and conflicts that they themselves identify. Talwar intensifies the aesthetic sensory experience by using paint rather than drawing and combines this with the physical stimulation of standing and moving around the room to select colors during the art making. Tripp has clients create scribble drawings of emotions and cognitions related to traumatic memories while wearing headphones that produce bilaterally alternating tones, music, and sounds as well as pulsating devices placed under each knee. The art therapist carefully monitors and processes the resultant images with the clients; recommended subsequent images build on emerging feelings or are based on a cognitive restructuring of events and perceptions.

DEVELOPMENTAL ISSUES IN PROCESSING PARENTAL LOSS IN CHILDREN

By age fifteen, 5 percent of American children have experienced the death of a parent. It is crucial to note that both anticipated loss and actual loss of parents during childhood can be considered traumatic due to developmental and dependency factors. Parentally bereaved youth are immediately at risk for psychological disturbance, health problems, poor academic performance, increased delinquency, and lower self-esteem. Long-term consequences of untreated childhood bereavement may include clinical depression, substance dependence and poor object relations related to fear of emotional bonding. However, with support, most bereaved youth can develop coping skills and do not suffer long-term psychological impairment (Dowdney et al. 1999; Sandler et al. 2003; Silverman, Nickman, and Worden 1995; Thompson et al. 1998).

Grief is experienced differently at each stage of maturation. Although infants do not yet have the ability to encode this information explicitly, they undergo emotional trauma if there is a change in their primary caregivers. Depending on the severity of the remaining parent's grief and the availability of alternate caregivers, the death of one parent during a child's infancy can cause significant disturbance to the relational bonding critical to early brain development and hemispheric integration. Infants and toddlers may exhibit regression in feeding, toileting habits, sleep disturbances, and clinging behavior. Until about age five, most children do not understand that death is permanent. Some may expect the deceased parent to be "fixed" by God and sent back to them. Focus and attention spans are limited; brain structures are not developed sufficiently to self-regulate. Younger children will exhibit extreme distress one moment and cheerfulness the next. This can lead caregivers, who are grieving themselves, to believe that the children are not affected.

From ages five through seven, school-aged children have greater social exposure. They identify as part of an intact family and compare themselves to peers as a measure of normality. Their understanding of death is incomplete. Children of this age may grasp the concept of permanency yet retain magical thinking regarding what causes death or whether it is contagious. Despite increasing ability to negotiate the world outside their homes, they are still quite dependent and necessarily egocentric about how the death will affect their lives. They may display regressive tendencies such as fear of sleeping alone. Somatic symptoms may mimic those of the deceased parent.

From seven to eleven years, children become "scientific" in their reasoning. They will express interest in the biological, moral, and spiritual aspects of death. However, grief may take the form of forgetfulness and inability to concentrate in school. Because they understand its finality, they are more capable of realizing that death can happen to anyone—and therefore display fear for themselves and their remaining parent. As they approach adolescence, their ambivalence about sharing feelings and receiving comfort versus being mature and independent increases. Children's peers are often very supportive, even curious, immediately after the death, but then they quickly want their friends to be their "normal" selves again. Occasionally, bereaved children and adolescents will switch friends, seeking out others who have experienced loss and will therefore understand.

Teens that lose parents are in more danger of becoming "parentified," that is, assuming some duties of the deceased parent. This gives them responsibility and provides support for the surviving parent. Yet this premature adulthood belies their emotional vulnerability and incomplete maturity. Teens are more capable of risk-taking behavior and may act out in dangerous and self-destructive ways. Promiscuity may offer a false sense of intimacy, or substance abuse may numb emotional pain. Rebellion against parental authority is a developmental norm. However, to lose a parent during this stage deprives teens of the opportunity to resolve normal defiance and distancing, leaving them with unresolved relational issues and guilt. The handling of intense emotions is challenging, and defense against regressive dependency becomes even stronger.

Secondary losses, such as the financial impact death has on the family and the redistribution of parenting roles, compound grief for all ages. A stay-at-home parent may have to return to work; another may have to hire caregivers. The energy level, stress, and emotional availability of the remaining parent are compromised in the early stages of grief. Family routines such as meals and bedtimes change. Children may go into after-school care for the first time. Rules, expectations, and approaches to discipline will be different. Homes may be sold; children may have to move in with extended family, forcing them to change schools and distancing them from their peer support network.

An important factor that also impacts a child's grief process is "death awareness," a concept discussed by Bluebond-Langner (1978) and Worden (2002). A child's understanding of death is determined by individual and social factors through maturity and experience. How they attribute meaning to the death and how they incorporate the loss into their identity, evolving belief system, and visions of their own future are all affected by their direct and indirect experience. Normal developmentally based cognition has been discussed in this section. Additionally, other factors may come into play, such as prior firsthand exposure to death, trauma, or life-threatening

FIGURE 8.5   Bird's Nest Assessment Drawing (Kaiser and Deaver 2009), created by Connor, a boy who had been internationally, interracially adopted after having been abandoned for more than a year in a Vietnamese orphanage. This dramatic image with many bizarre and seemingly unrelated elements incorporates aspects of extreme early relational trauma that interfere with secure attachment, specifically his adaptation to new relationships and situations. His early trauma became reactivated, despite healthy reparative bonding with his adoptive parents, when his (adopted) paternal grandmother died (Loumeau-May and Fallat 2017).

illness (Councill 2012; Loumeau-May and Fallat 2017), secondary exposure through intergenerational narrative (Dekel and Goldblatt 2008; Denham 2008; Kidron 2003; Niemeyer 2001; Schaverien 1998; Walsh 2003), religious and spiritual constructs, cultural attitudes, media, and societal exposure such as increasing incidents of mass shootings as well as evolving existential un-derstanding of mortality (Loumeau-May et al. 2015; Speert 1989; van der Kolk 2005).

Even indirect exposure to societal violence affects a child's sense of vul-nerability. Personally bereaved children not only process their own grief, but also place it in the context of the world as they know it. One young boy who had lost his sister to cancer understood more acutely that children can die too. He became focused on how many people, including children, were dying in catastrophic events on the news, and he started to refer to himself as someone who had "survived my childhood so far." A six-year-old girl whose father had died suddenly wondered what it would be like if one of her friends "had been the shooter" in a recent school shooting.

ANTICIPATED VERSUS SUDDEN GRIEF

Responses to debilitating terminal illness and death contain aspects of trauma. These responses vary according to the developmental stage of the child. Anthony (1973) discussed fear of abandonment in the young child. He suggested that parental relationships root, mirror, protect, and define a child. The younger the child, the more his or her existence is based on connection with the parent; emotional and physical needs must be met for survival. When one parent is ill, typically both are absent; one may be in the hospital being treated while the other is visiting or transporting the ill parent. Despite the provision of alternative caregivers, the child feels abandoned. This is exacerbated by the child's sense of the anxiety that the adults are experiencing.

Many aspects of an illness itself are potentially traumatic to children. Most significant are the physical and behavioral changes in the parent resulting from illness or side effects of its treatment. These include weight and hair loss, memory loss, vomiting, falls, the results of surgery, and others. Some children and teens may be physically repulsed by these changes yet feel guilty about not wanting to touch the sick parent. Younger children may believe that touching their parent will cause harm, or they may fear contagion. Children also have fears associated with the treatment their parent is undergoing. One five-year-old boy, Johnny, had repeated nightmares, envisioning his father being chained to the wall of a cave with a vampire approaching while at the same time a laser beam was pointed at the father's head. The child was afraid to talk about his dream until after he had sketched a picture of it. The therapist asked the boy to tell what happens at the doctor visits. Johnny described how his father would have a blood test and then get radiation therapy. Without directly interpreting the image, the therapist reflected to Johnny that maybe his father's treatment was even scarier than knowing he had cancer, an illness Johnny did not yet fully comprehend, especially since his concept of death was not fully developed. Johnny was able to acknowledge his fear that certain medical procedures were making his father sick.

Older children and teens understand the permanency of death and the implications of a cancer diagnosis more fully. When the diagnosis is revealed to them, it traumatically shatters their assumptions of a secure family life and a continuing relationship with the ill parent. A twelve-year-old girl used a photo collage to depict such a moment. She placed a picture of two girls sitting on a couch (as she and her sister had been when told the news) inside the open mouth of a shark to convey the devastating impact the news had on her. In addition to trauma experienced or witnessed, children are more apt to vividly imagine unobserved aspects of the trauma. Jennifer, an eight-year-old whose father had died suddenly two years earlier, was understandably fearful when her mother was scheduled for a mastectomy. She drew how she pictured her mother's surgery. The image featured home and hospital side by side, effectively separating mother and daughter, who were each encapsulated within one of the structures. The buildings were similarly sized and mound-shaped with pointed roofs, and they were colored a brownish-pink,

FIGURE 8.6 Jennifer's drawing of her mother in surgery unconsciously depicts fear of losing her remaining parent, longing, ambivalence about the surgical procedure, and her identification with her mother as she approaches puberty herself.

resembling the breasts her mother was about to lose. In the hospital portion of Jennifer's drawing, the surgeon appeared as a magician levitating Jennifer's prone mother while simultaneously raising a blade as if to saw her in half.

Younger children may experience magical thinking related to causality and undoing. Some children feel that the noise they made while playing when told not to disturb an ailing grandparent or the fact that they wished they did not have a younger sibling who always got into their toys is what ultimately caused the death. Johnny, mentioned above, prayed every night that God would give him cancer to take it away from his father. When he developed a benign tumor on his knee, he thought his prayers had been answered.

When a parent's death is sudden, unanticipated, and violent, as in an accident, suicide, or murder, actual trauma intensifies and complicates the grieving process for the child or adolescent. Thompson et al. (1998) noted that studies on grief indicate that the ability to prepare for an anticipated death usually results in improved coping. Additional factors of violence, proximity to danger, and witnessing or discovering death further intensify the trauma, putting children at risk for childhood traumatic grief (Cohen, Mannarino, and Deblinger 2006), which is characterized by the coexistence of unresolved grief and PTSD symptoms. It is theorized that the presence of significant PTSD symptoms is more predictive of future psychiatric and behavioral conditions such as substance abuse, major depression, or borderline personality disorder than the parental loss by itself.

When trauma and grief coexist, trauma must be addressed before grieving can begin. It is not unusual for pleasant memories of the deceased to segue into horrific images of the death. This was true in Rachel's case, cited earlier, when her attempt to paint her father's portrait reverted instead into a dreadful image of how he may have died. In traumatic death, external factors such as media coverage, police investigation, and litigation may intrude on the family's life, further traumatizing and delaying the grief process. Survivors of accidents may be hospitalized and have to undergo surgery or other medical procedures. One ten-year-old boy remained in intensive care for two weeks after he survived the car accident that killed his mother. Shards of glass remained in his cheeks and chest, painful reminders of both his own survival and his mother's death.

Causality of a violent and sudden death is a complicating factor in traumatic loss. Guilt and blame, typical in the emotional experience of grief, occur even when there is no source for blame. When there is a perpetrator or negligent cause, justification and intensification of blame are amplified. Accident, homicide, and suicide contain specific complicating aspects that exacerbate the grief process. With accidental death, there is an arbitrariness that defies reason and challenges potential spiritual meaning-making for survivors. In the case of homicide, often the perpetrator is known to the victim. This has relational consequences for the grieving family, especially when anger and blame have a valid target such as the other parent, on whom the child has also been dependent (Lev-Wiesel and Sampson 2001). A family environment characterized by anger, violence, and fear may have led up to the murder. The presence of mental illness or family dysfunction further complicates the ability to process grief. Where suicide has been the cause of death, unique factors in the grieving process include self-blame, anger toward the deceased, loss of idealization of the beloved parent, and the experience of stigma and shame (Kuramato, Brent, and Wilcox 2009). Children whose parents commit suicide may be biologically at a higher risk for mental illness if that was a factor in the parent's suicide. Many are aware of this as they struggle with identity issues following the death. Anxiety related to inheriting bipolar illness from his father was a preoccupation for Alan, cited earlier. Kuramato Brent, and Wilcox state, "These offspring may have undergone considerable emotional distress prior to parental suicide compared to individuals who experienced other types of parental loss" (2009, 148).

Death caused by political or mass violence entails a wide variety of factors affecting grief. The 9/11 attacks claimed nearly three thousand lives on a single day. Individual grief was overshadowed by national grief. The deaths, which were intentional, extremely violent, and targeted at the entire country, attracted continuous media coverage. Mass shootings also receive unwanted media attention and curiosity that interfere with families' intimate mourning. National focus on such attacks takes the sanctuary of privacy away from the families of the victims. All these factors play significant roles in the grief process for surviving family members.

USING ART THERAPY TO TOLERATE MEMORIES
OF ACTUAL AND IMAGINED HORROR

Traumatically bereaved children are vulnerable to nightmares and flashbacks that may reveal aspects of the loss. Teens Andrew and Monique were settling down for the night when their father had a fatal heart attack. Monique had recurring memories of the paleness of her father's face when she ran into his bedroom at the sound of her mother's screams. Visualization techniques coupled with the act of painting this memory helped her to achieve emotional mastery of the image. Her brother, Andrew, conversely, was adept at using intellectualization as a defense. He described numbness and depersonalization associated with his loss. Andrew expressed a desire to remember all the details; he did not want to forget what had occurred. After leading him through a relaxation exercise, I used guided imagery to encourage him to remember, instructing him to focus on the sounds, smells, and images he could recall. Andrew then painted a diagram of his home, color coding stick-figure people and objects to re-create the chaotic events of the evening: his sister getting him out of the shower to assist his mother, administering CPR, letting a priest (to administer last rites) and emergency personnel into the home, witnessing their exit with his father's body, and noticing his sister and grandfather huddled together on the couch downstairs. Remembering the details helped him embody the event and reconnect with his emotions.

Diane, the teen whose father was struck by lightning, had flashbacks to her real and imagined memories of his death, yet she managed to function well at school and in her extracurricular activities. She declined to discuss most aspects of what happened for many months because it was too painful and frightening. As her therapist, I allowed her to be self-directed, doing occasional relaxation exercises with her. However, when Diane felt stuck or asked for guidance, I encouraged her to use media with flow, such as painting, which stimulates emotions and unconscious processes. Not too long after Diane abandoned the mask project, she created an image that resembled both a bolt of lightning and an EKG printout, symbolizing the many times her father had coded before lifesaving measures were abandoned. An image rather than words allowed her to speak the unspeakable.

As stated earlier, aspects of death from long-term illness can be internally and externally traumatic, especially to younger children who witness physical and behavioral changes that they do not understand. However, with maturity

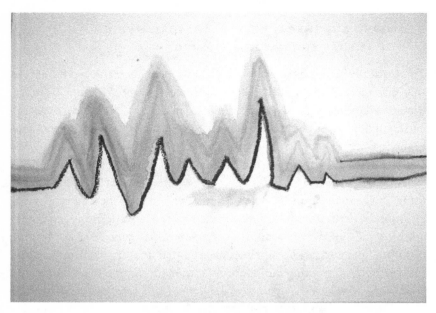

FIGURE 8.7   As with her mask, Diane did not finish this drawing made with water-soluble oil pastels—a medium with which she typically created flowing, colorful imagery. The zigzag line resembled an EKG graph. The yellow glow above the upper gray line also suggested a bolt of lightning turned on its side.

and a capacity for empathy, older children and teens may experience some internal trauma from imagining and identifying with the disease process a loved one is experiencing. Another teen, Kara, whose father died of brain cancer, chose watercolor paint as her primary medium of choice in self-directed individual work. For many sessions she painted visions of dying and rotting vegetation, which seemed to arise spontaneously from her mind and brush as she worked.

She joked that she was depleting my supply of black paint. Kara was unsure why she continued to dream of dying trees and visualize decaying plants. Nonetheless these images were the ones that came unbidden, and she trusted her intuitive process. One week she decided to paint a portrait of her father. As she started to re-create his image, she instinctively returned to the black paint. The image of his face that she was creating changed into a chaotic image of the tumor taking over his brain; the thought of how that process affected her father as it took his life had been dreadful to her, but she had

FIGURE 8.8   One of Kara's many watercolor paintings of decaying plants. Kara did not understand why these images came to her each time she sat down to paint in her art therapy sessions.

pushed it out of her conscious mind while he was still alive in order to be emotionally present and support him. This final image, which resulted from allowing herself to create and process the earlier images, helped her release her horror and pain while understanding how important it had been to avoid thinking about that at a time when she wanted to be there for him.

Following this insight, her artwork and media choices changed as she started to focus on happier memories and to explore how her family was grieving and finding ways to adjust to their loss.

USING ART THERAPY TO REDUCE STRESS
WITH RELAXATION TECHNIQUES

Mandalas have been discussed in relation to their relaxation potential. Making a mandala aids in self-regulation, but as with other creative processes it can also lead to symbolic insight. During her second session, I instructed

FIGURE 8.9 Several sessions later, Kara tried a mandala in order to center herself. Again, her compulsion to use the black paint took over and burst through the symmetry of the circular image, distorting it. The next week, she decided to paint a portrait of her father. As she painted his smiling face, she placed a yellow circular shape between his eyes. She realized that this was where his tumor had been located. With the black paint and her newly gained insight, she depicted swirls of the cancer taking over his brain, realizing that her previous images represented her suppressed visualizations of his disease process.

seven-year-old Maia, whose father had died suddenly in an accident, how to create a mandala, giving her instructions to approach the process mindfully. The rationale for this intervention was the fact that Maia, a child who loved to draw and paint, was having difficulty finishing any image she started. I provided her with a "formula" that was meditative, relaxing, and also potentially insightful. The structure fully engaged Maia. She was able to draw and paint the mandala to completion and her satisfaction. In the center she drew an eye, which, she informed me, represented her father's eye watching over her at night. She took the image home and placed it over her bed to help her sleep.

FIGURE 8.10 The formal structure of a mandala and the meditative approach involved in creating one led Maia to envision the watchful eye of her father protecting her after he died. Whereas some might consider this image fearsome, for Maia it answered her spiritual questions about where her father resided in the universe following his death and assuaged her sense of vulnerability regarding no longer having a father to keep her safe.

Although Johnny's father's cancer went into remission for five years, he had a recurrence and eventually died. In the months prior to the death, Johnny witnessed his father's seizures and falls as the disease progressed. Now a ten-year-old, Johnny felt a strong sense of responsibility for his father and was anxious about going anywhere without him. This interfered with his ability to concentrate in school and to enjoy peer activities such as overnight scout camp; he was afraid his father would have a seizure and die when he was not there. When he returned to the Journeys youth-bereavement program, a primary aspect of his therapy was to help him manage his anxiety prior to his father's death so that he could function in normal, age-appropriate

FIGURE 8.11 Visualization techniques, reinforced by creating actual images, can be helpful to reduce anxiety. In this stamp picture, Johnny used his favorite sport, basketball, as a metaphor for "dunking" the anxiety he felt related to his father's brain tumor.

activities. A two-part art therapy exercise proved beneficial to him. In one, he was asked to visualize a situation in which he felt safe, relaxed, empowered, and joyful. Johnny created a picture of himself playing basketball.

His next task was to practice imagining that the basketball represented thoughts about his father's tumor, and whenever he dunked it through the net, those thoughts would disappear. Johnny was advised to try to practice this exercise and to use his internal image whenever he became anxious about his father. This successfully reduced his anxiety.

As his father's death grew near, Johnny had sleep difficulties. Together with his art therapist (myself) and his mother, Johnny recorded a relaxation tape using his own vision, script, and music to use at bedtime. By being a cognitive and creative agent in this project, Johnny empowered himself to manage his fears.

USING ART THERAPY TO BUILD VOCABULARY
TO CONNECT SENSORIAL MEMORIES WITH WORDS

When traumatic memory is encoded, both memory and affect can be blocked from discursive recall. This is true for many children who witness their loved ones' sudden deaths. Douglas was playing with friends in the backyard when his three-year-old sister fell into the pool and drowned. Creating spontaneous as well as loss-related imagery can enable a child to select words for the visually revealed affect. Douglas was numb to his feelings and had avoided discussing or portraying his loss for several months in therapy. He had attended therapy individually, with his mother, and in a peer group. After a conference, his mother and I decided to discharge him until he felt more ready to deal with his emotion-laden memories. He returned to therapy a year later, after he had seen news coverage of a Tsunami in Indonesia and became anxious about weather disasters. He was intrigued by a picture of Stonehenge hanging in the art room. I showed him a book titled *Earthworks and Beyond* (Beardsley 1984), which he studied and used to inspire his sketches. Employing nature elements as a metaphor, he created detailed pictures of earth sculptures, water, and rainstorms. With each, he became increasingly articulate in discussing emotional equivalents to visual metaphors. Finally he was able to draw his most painful memory—his sister as she lay in her coffin. It is important to note that Douglas's ability to respond creatively to his triggers and to process them occurred about a year after his sister's death, and following months of establishing emotional safety through therapy and community support.

Materials and art-making processes can potentiate the emergence of emotions. As described in Mark's case, clay is a medium that is quite effective. Ned, a fourteen-year-old whose father also died suddenly of a heart attack, initially reacted in shock and pain when his mother informed him of the death, but then shut down and refused to talk about it with anyone. Understanding the fragility of his defenses, I encouraged self-direction and choice of medium; this made it possible for me to observe his primary reactions. Early in therapy, Ned chose clay. After creating and recycling many potential images, he developed a somewhat hard to discern but definite fist, modeling it after the clenched fist of his dominant hand. The physical processes demanded by the physicality of working

FIGURE 8.12 Doug drew this poignant memory of his sister in her coffin after over a year of work. Although it was an extremely painful memory, he drew the picture as carefully, precisely, and lovingly as he could, taking time to include every detail and gently coloring it. It was his idea to draw the image. After he had, he felt he had faced his most painful associations and no longer needed formal bereavement support.

with this material, which are metaphorically aggressive, enabled his anger to emerge.

USING ART THERAPY CLUES TO ASCERTAIN DEFENSES
AND PACE THERAPEUTIC PROCESS

Ned was vulnerable to his emotions and in touch with his denial; he was able to admit that although his father's death was painfully real, it sometimes felt as if it could not have happened. His ambivalence was exemplified by a bridge drawing he completed early in treatment.

FIGURE 8.13 Although Ned was very guarded and avoided accessing the full intensity of his emotions, the aggressive processes involved in working with clay helped him to express his restrained anger. This image of Ned's clenched fist is hard to discern, as were his emotions to him early in his grief process.

The bridge drawing is an assessment (Hays and Lyons 1981) that can indicate a client's goals, their feelings about their past, present, and future, the amount of support they feel they have, etc. Ned's father died at the end of the summer, following an enjoyable family vacation. Ned's drawing depicts a bridge leading to the vacation destination with a horse standing in the water underneath the bridge. The most relevant factors to note are the weakness of the bridge, the amount of perseveration in the arrow, which goes back and forth from present to past, the fact that Ned placed the X representing himself in the past, and most importantly, the fact that the choice of black paper with the use of color (light blue surrounds the horse, linking water and sky) evokes the expression "deer caught in the headlights"—a shocked creature that is frozen in fear and cannot go backward or forward. In discussing the drawing, Ned gained some insight into the amount of anxiety he had experienced in accepting the reality of father's death.

We continued to work very slowly, touching on ideas, sentimental memories, and abstract emotion-identification techniques. After a couple of months, I offered an exercise in relaxation and guided imagery to evoke an

FIGURE 8.14 Ned's bridge drawing. The bridge lacks any supports and is barely discernable due to the back-and-forth travel lines, which look like a gash severing the light blue color that surrounds the bridge.

image of a safe place. My intention was to use the image to help Ned gradually explore his more difficult memories of the night his father died. Ned drew a detailed portrayal of his living room from the perspective of sitting on the couch, the exact same view his father had had at the moment of his fatal heart attack.

Ned did not consciously realize the connection and spoke at length about the many happy memories he had enjoyed in the living room. This posed a therapeutic challenge because Ned retained a strong positive emotional investment in this particular place. It would take a while before he was able to consciously explore the fact that the sense of security he associated with the living room was potentially threatened by the loss that had occurred there. Ned's creation of the image, as well as his earlier bridge drawing, reaffirmed to me that the pace of work must continue in a slow and gentle manner, until Ned showed signs that he was able to face painful memories more directly.

FIGURE 8.15 The living room, where Ned's father died, was also the room he associated with his safest and happiest memories.

USING SYMBOLIC LANGUAGE AND PLAY
TO TELL THE TRAUMA NARRATIVE

Many art therapy directives help children relate their stories of trauma or loss. Sometimes they will depict the death when they are asked to draw, paint, or sculpt a difficult memory. Others will avoid or block a traumatic memory until they are able to face it. When this occurs, metaphoric or symbolic play images can allude to events, or aspects of traumatic imagery may appear in drawn images. Such was the case with many children of 9/11 victims, who, although consciously avoiding the images in their art making, unconsciously created plane-like shapes or depicted the penetration of buildings (Loumeau-May 2008, 102; Loumeau-May et al. 2015, 215).

Elsa, five years old, was frightened by memories of seeing her "Poppy" in the coffin at the wake. In her first session she shook visibly when the therapist gently explained to her that she was coming to art therapy because her grandfather had died. Her first picture, in response to a request to draw

FIGURE 8.16 Two years after the 9/11 attacks, a child drew this picture of her family home. Without realizing it, she had created an image of wind that seems to move through the structure of the building.

anything she wanted, was a boarded-up house. Next, Elsa asked to play with the dollhouse for the remainder of the session. Rearranging every piece of furniture and every doll in the house, she re-created her experience of the wake, the repast, and the house full of relatives that characterized the family rituals following the death.

USING ART THERAPY TO RESTORE POSITIVE MEMORIES OF THE LOST OBJECT

Children can ascribe damage to the lost parental object when the death has been tragic. This can take several forms: an internalized image of the physical disfigurement the parent sustained, experiencing the parent as no longer invincible but rather as a victim, or, if the death was self-inflicted, seeing the parent as an unloving monster. This last example was true in the case of Alan, who felt secure in his father's love and had

FIGURE 8.17 Too upset to even call her "Poppy" (grandfather) by his name, Elsa carefully set up the dollhouse to feature many relatives sleeping over, the viewing line at the wake, and the restaurant where they ate after the services.

a normal, idealized memory of his father prior to learning that his father had killed himself. Alan struggled with newly ambivalent feelings toward his father before he could grieve. In one drawing he depicted a many-headed grief monster hovering nearby as he prayed at his father's grave. Alan was torn between feeling anger and forgiveness toward his father.

Alan's identification with his father was strong. He also acknowledged anxiety about how his loss would ultimately affect the person he would become. A major focus in Alan's therapy, after he had worked through rage, despair, and fear, was to repair his memory of his father. His final project was a symbolic still-life painting in which he depicted objects that had been precious to his father and that represented the memories Alan valued and wanted to retain. It helped him internalize positive aspects of his father's life as well as his love for his father.

FIGURE 8.18 Elsa propped up a grandfather doll in a bathtub, which represented an open coffin, and arranged adult dolls in a long line as they wait to pay their respects. Note the grandmother figure standing to the side, watching.

In contrast, for children who lost parents on 9/11, the damaged memory in the early stages of grief involved the physical embodiment of their parents. The idea that their parents had been burned, been crushed, or disintegrated was unfathomable. As discussed earlier, in the beginning stages of therapy, Rachel could not erase from her imagination the probable circumstances of her father's death. This resulted in the disintegration of a portrait mask into the terrifying image that existed in her mind. Toward the end of therapy, she was ready to make a portrait painting of her father as she wanted to remember him based on a favorite photograph.

FIGURE 8.19 While the family is at the funeral home, a chef prepares a meal at a restaurant for the gathering afterward. The rituals associated with death and mourning were new to Elsa, who was experiencing them for the first time.

USING ART THERAPY TO MASTER AFFECTIVE EXPERIENCE THROUGH (COMPANIONED) ACTION

The creative act involves not merely catharsis or release of emotional expression. Its potency lies in mastering and redirecting emotional energy. The act of vicariously and symbolically re-creating authentic affective-laden experience in an art product requires cognition for the planning, construction, and evaluation of the product. Artwork produced within the context of an art therapy session involves symbolic communication from client to therapist, who serves as a witness. Internal experience is relived through imaginative recall within a supportive relationship wherein the client's reality is validated. It is transformed and mastered through the ability to portray and share it, and through the opportunity to distance oneself from the experience afforded by contemplation of the finished product. I have previously compared the art therapy process when used in trauma and bereavement

FIGURE 8.20 In a group art therapy directive, Alan drew a fictional monster to symbolize his struggle with his own grief process. He depicted a three-headed beast, which included an evil image of his father as someone who took his own life, a tiny image of himself emerging from an enormous ghost, and a split face representing his father's bipolar illness. In a corner of the picture, Alan depicted himself as a loving son, taking flowers to his father's grave.

work to Campbell's analysis of the hero's journey (Campbell 1949; Loumeau-May 2006). Key features of heroic transformation include a precipitating crisis, deep suffering and questioning, initiative of the hero to search for meaning or reparation, endurance of trials, performance of tasks, companionship, failure (of ego alone) that necessitates the acceptance of help, and acquisition of treasure (which is usually internal change, insight, or a restructured worldview)—a progression that can be considered a model for resiliency. Thus, healing involves a combined ability to endure the pain of reality, accept help, and act by completing grief-related tasks.

The clinical vignettes in this chapter illustrate this process. In these examples, the creation of an image was instrumental in mastering the affect associated with it. However, facing the pain associated with loss is only part of the heroic journey. Additional grief-related tasks are accomplished through art therapy. Among these are identifying coping skills, evaluating positive family adjustments, symbolically internalizing the strengths of the deceased

FIGURE 8.21 Much of the complex grief work that Alan did focused around regaining a positive image of his father, which had almost been destroyed by the betrayal of father's chosen death. As termination of our work together approached, we discussed a final project that would be symbolic and meaningful. Alan had already created a biographical scrapbook about his father by obtaining mementoes and letters from many people who had known him. Now he chose to do a portrait of his father depicting special objects, each of which represented his father's passions and hobbies.

in revised self-images, and comparing past, present, and future to explore new views of life.

With these goals in mind, memorialization projects such as memory boxes, books, or quilts are done toward the end of treatment.

CONCLUSION

Art therapy is uniquely suited to the treatment of trauma. Although more research is indicated, evidence-based practices and current brain research support its use in accessing memories and regulating affect. Trauma-focused techniques developed by art therapists have been successful. Applied to grief, art therapy is effective. Its advantages include the fact that it is an

FIGURE 8.22 In a final portrait of her father, Rachel was able to restore her image of him as a healthy, intact person. However, in the checkered shirt pattern and the small marks on his neck, there remains an unconscious suggestion of a building disintegrating.

action-based, sensorily evocative modality with narrative and symbolic properties that bypass and complement speech. As highlighted in this chapter, bereavement work with youth who have experienced traumatic loss, as well as with those who are coping with traumatic aspects of anticipated death, is a good application of art therapy. Specific treatment areas of focus might include visual desensitization, building an expressive vocabulary, symbolic reparation of the damaged object, and narration.

When one is working with traumatically bereaved children, the initial goal of treatment must be the establishment of safety and comfort. Soothing art activities that offer control and opportunity for metaphor will help children and teens use their defenses effectively while building confidence. This will later yield to expression of feelings and reworking of the experience of the loss. Creative activity stimulates unconscious imagery and affective

FIGURE 8.23 Memorial quilts and cushions are a comforting way to create a "transitional object." In some instances, photographs of loved ones can be transferred onto the cloth, and objects such as articles of clothing that belonged to the deceased can be sewn on.

FIGURE 8.24 Memory scrapbooking can include photographs, writing, and original artwork depicting special times with a loved one. Here, a girl remembers her older brother meeting her at the bus stop and helping her with her homework, and also tucking her in at night and counting sheep with her.

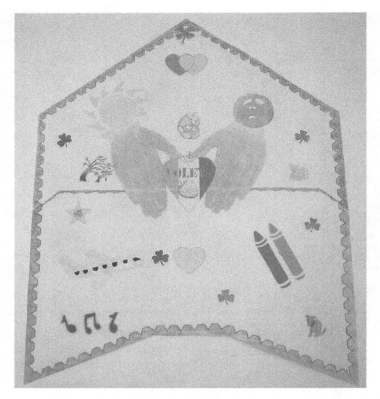

FIGURE 8.25   One girl created a family crest to represent two grandparents who had died. Before decorating it, she made a list of the qualities she wanted to remember from each and what might symbolize them.

arousal. Understanding the psychological aspects of the creative process as well as visual vocabulary and symbolism, the experienced art therapist will recognize when a client is ready for deeper exploration, or if the process, material, or imagery has the potential to overwhelm. The therapist can then intervene or help the client manage the affect, avoiding retraumatization. The author cautions against the use of the methods described in this chapter by non-art therapists. Employing these techniques may inadvertently retraumatize the client if the therapist fails to recognize when the art-making process is disinhibiting or reveals material that the client is not yet ready to explore.

   It is in the middle stage described in this chapter that more intense trauma and grief work is accomplished. The final stages of such work include strengthening coping skills, memorializing the loss, and establishing new goals and a revised worldview. Creating objects that honor the memory of the deceased is empowering and sustains closure.

REFERENCES

Amir, G., and R. Lev-Wiesel. 2007. "Dissociation as Depicted in the Traumatic Event Drawings of Child Sexual Abuse Survivors: A Preliminary Study." *The Arts in Psychotherapy* 34 (2): 114–123.

Anthony, E. J. 1973. "Mourning and Psychic Loss of the Parent." In *The Child in His Family: The Impact of Disease and Death*, ed. E. J. Anthony and C. Copernic, vol. 2, 255–264. New York: Wiley.

Appleton, V. 2001. "Avenues of Hope: Art Therapy and the Resolution of Trauma." *Art Therapy: Journal of the American Art Therapy Association* 18 (1): 6–13.

Beardsley, J. 1984. *Earthworks and Beyond*. New York: Abbeville Press.

Bluebond-Langner, M. 1978. *The Private Worlds of Dying Children*. Princeton, N.J.: Princeton University Press.

Buk, A. 2009. "The Mirror Neuron System and Embodied Simulation: Clinical Implications for Art Therapists Working with Trauma Survivors." *The Arts in Psychotherapy* 36 (2): 61–74.

Byers, J. G. 1996. "Children of the Stones: Art Therapy Interventions in the West Bank." *Art Therapy: Journal of the American Art Therapy Association* 13 (4): 238–243.

Campbell, J. 1949. *The Hero with a Thousand Faces*. New York: Bollingen Foundation.

Chapman, L., D. Morabito, C. Ladakakos, H. Schreier, and N. M. Knudson. 2001. "The Effectiveness of Art Therapy Interventions in Reducing Post-Traumatic Stress Disorder (PTSD) Symptoms in Pediatric Trauma Patients." *Art Therapy: Journal of the American Art Therapy Association* 18 (2): 100–104.

Chilcote, R. 2007. "Art Therapy with Child Tsunami Survivors in Sri Lanka." *Art Therapy: Journal of the American Art Therapy Association* 24 (3): 156–162.

Cohen, B., and C. Cox. 1995. *Telling Without Talking: Art as a Window Into the World of Multiple Personality*. New York: Norton.

Cohen, J. A., A. P. Mannarino, and E. Deblinger. 2006. *Treating Trauma and Traumatic Grief in Children and Adolescents*. New York: Guilford Press.

Collie, K., A. Backos, C. Malchiodi, and D. Spiegel. 2006. "Art Therapy for Combat-Related PTSD: Recommendations for Research and Practice." *Art Therapy: Journal of the American Art Therapy Association* 23(4): 157–164.

Councill, T. 2012. "Medical Art Therapy with Children." In *Handbook of Art Therapy*, 2nd ed., ed. C. A. Malchiodi, 222–240. New York: Guilford Press.

Cross, D. 1993. "Family Art Therapy and Sexual Abuse." In *Art Therapy with Families in Crisis*, ed. D. Linesch, 104–127. New York: Brunner/Mazel.

Dekel, R., and H. Goldblatt. 2008. "Is There Intergenerational Transmission of Trauma? The Case of Combat Veterans' Children." *American Journal of Orthopsychiatry* 78 (3): 281–289.

Denham, A. R. 2008. "Rethinking Historical Trauma: Narratives of Resilience." *Transcultural Psychiatry* 45:391–414.

Dowdney, L., R. Wilson, B. Maughan, M. Allerton, P. Schofield, and D. Skuse. 1999. "Psychological Disturbance and Service Provision in Parentally Bereaved Children: Prospective Case-Control Study." *British Medical Journal* 319:354–373.

Gantt, L., and L. Tinnin. 2007. "The Instinctual Trauma Response." In *Art, Angst, and Trauma*, ed. D. B. Arrington, 168–174. Springfield, Ill.: Charles C. Thomas.

——. 2009. "Support for a Neurobiological View of Trauma with Implications for Art Therapy." *The Arts in Psychotherapy* 36 (3): 148–153.

Gantt, L., and T. Tripp. 2016. "The Image Comes First: Treating Preverbal Trauma with Art Therapy." In *Art Therapy, Trauma and Neuroscience*, ed. J. L. King, 67–99. New York: Routledge.

Geist, A. L., and P. N. C. Geist. 2002. *They Still Draw Pictures: Children's Art in Wartime from the Spanish Civil War to Kosovo*. Urbana: University of Illinois Press.

Gesensway, D., and M. Roseman. 1987. *Beyond Words: Images from America's Concentration Camps*. Ithaca, N.Y.: Cornell University Press.

Goodman, R. 2004. "Treatment of Childhood Traumatic Grief: Application of Cognitive-Behavioral and Client-Centered Therapies." In *Mass Trauma and Violence: Helping Children and Families Cope*, ed. N. Webb, 77–99. New York: Guilford Press.

Hass-Cohen, N. 2016. "Secure Resiliency: Art Therapy Relational Neuroscience Trauma Treatment Principles and Guidelines." In *Art Therapy, Trauma, and Neuroscience*, ed. J. L. King, 100–138. New York: Routledge.

Hass-Cohen, N., and R. Carr, eds. 2008. *Art Therapy and Clinical Neuroscience*. London: Jessica Kingsley Press.

Hays, R. E., and S. J. Lyons. 1981. "The Bridge Drawing: A Protective Technique for Assessment in Therapy." *The Arts in Psychotherapy* 8:208–217.

Henderson, P., N. Mascaro, and D. Rosen. 2007. "Empirical Study on the Healing Nature of Mandalas." *Psychology of Aesthetics, Creativity, and Art* 1 (3): 148–154.

Herman, J. L. 1992. *Trauma and Recovery.* New York: HarperCollins.

Hinz, L. 2009. *Expressive Therapies Continuum.* New York: Routledge.

Jakowski, A. P., C. M. de Araújo, A. L. T. de Lacerda, J. de Jesus Mari, and J. Kaufman. 2009. "Neurostructural Imaging Findings in Children with Post-Traumatic Stress Disorder: Brief Review." *Psychiatry and Clinical Neurosciences* 63:1–8.

Kagin, S., and V. B. Lüsebrink. 1978. "The Expressive Therapies Continuum." *Art Psychotherapy* 5 (4): 171–179.

Kaiser, D. H., and S. Deaver. 2009. "Assessing Attachment with the Bird's Nest Drawing: A Review of the Research." *Art Therapy: Journal of the American Art Therapy Association* 26 (1): 26–33.

Kaufman, B., and A. Wohl. 1992. *Casualties of Childhood: A Developmental Perspective on Sexual Abuse Using Projective Drawings.* New York: Brunner/Mazel.

Kidron, C. A. 2003. "Surviving a Distant Past: A Case Study of the Cultural Construction of Trauma Descendant Identity." *Ethos* 31:513–544. doi:10.1525/eth.2003.31.4.513.

Kuramato, S. J., D. A. Brent, and H. C. Wilcox. 2009. "The Impact of Parental Suicide on Child and Adolescent Offspring." *Suicide and Life-Threatening Behavior* 39 (2): 137–151.

Lacroix, L., C. Rousseau, M.-F. Gauthier, A. Singh, N. Giguère, and Y. Lemzoudi. 2007. "Immigrant and Refugee Preschoolers' Sandplay Representations of the Tsunami." *The Arts in Psychotherapy* 34 (2): 99–113.

Lande, R. G., V. Tarpley, J. L. Francis, and R. Boucher. 2010. "Combat Trauma Art Therapy Scale." *The Arts in Psychotherapy* 37 (1): 42–45.

Lester, P., S. W. Wong, and R. L. Hendren. 2003. "The Neurobiological Effects of Trauma." *Adolescent Psychiatry* 27:259–282.

Lev-Wiesel, R., and T. Sampson. 2001. "Long-Term Effects of Maternal Death Through Parental Homicide Evidenced from Family of Origin Drawings." *The Arts in Psychotherapy* 28 (4): 239–244.

Loumeau-May, L. 2006. "Death and the Hero Quest: Adolescent Bereavement and the Development of Self." Paper presented at the conference of the American Art Therapy Association, New Orleans, November 16.

——. 2008. "Grieving in the Public Eye: Art Therapy with Children Who Lost Parents at the World Trade Center September 11, 2001." In *Creative Interventions with Traumatized Children*, 1st ed., ed. C. Malchiodi, 81–111. New York: Guilford Press.

Loumeau-May, L., and Fallat, L. November 2017. "'Little Red Bird on the Lonely Moor': Metaphor and Early Attachment Trauma." Paper presented at the conference of the American Art Therapy Association, Albuquerque, N.M.

Loumeau-May, L., E. Siebel-Nicol, M. P. Hamilton, and C. A. Malchiodi. 2015. "Art Therapy as an Intervention for Mass Terrorism and Violence." In *Creative Interventions with Traumatized Children*, 2nd ed., ed. C. Malchiodi, 94–125. New York: Guilford Press.

Lüsebrink, V. B. 1990. *Imagery and Visual Expression in Therapy*. New York: Plenum.

——. 2004. "Art Therapy and the Brain: An Attempt to Understand the Underlying Processes of Art Expression in Therapy." *Art Therapy: Journal of the American Art Therapy Association* 21 (3): 125–135.

Lüsebrink, V. B., and L. D. Hinz. 2016. "The Expressive Therapies Continuum as a Framework in the Treatment of Trauma." In *Art Therapy, Trauma, and Neuroscience*, ed. J. L. King, 42–66. New York: Routledge.

Mallay, J. N. 2002. "Art Therapy, an Effective Outreach Intervention with Traumatized Children with Suspected Brain Injury." *The Arts in Psychotherapy* 29 (3): 159–172.

Martin, E. S. 2008. "Medical Art and Play Therapy with Accident Survivors." In *Creative Interventions with Traumatized Children*, ed. C. Malchiodi, 112–131. New York: Guilford Press.

McNamee, C. 2003. "Bilateral Art: Facilitating Systematic Integration and Balance." *The Arts in Psychotherapy* 30:283–292.

——. 2004. "Using Both Sides of the Brain: Experiences That Integrate Art and Talk Therapy Through Scribble Drawings." *Art Therapy: Journal of the American Art Therapy Association* 23 (3): 136–142.

Morgan, C. A., III, and D. R. Johnson. 1995. "Use of a Drawing Task in the Treatment of Nightmares in Combat-Related PTSD." *Art Therapy: Journal of the American Art Therapy Association* 12 (4): 244–247.

Niemeyer, R.A. 2001. "Meaning Reconstruction and Loss." In *Meaning Reconstruction and the Experience of Loss*, ed. R. A. Niemeyer, 1–9. Washington, D.C.: American Psychological Association

Orr, P. 2007. "Art Therapy with Children After a Disaster: A Content Analysis." *The Arts in Psychotherapy* 34 (4): 350–361.

Pifalo, T. 2002. "Pulling Out the Thorns: Art Therapy with Sexually Abused Children and Adolescents." *Art Therapy: Journal of the American Art Therapy Association* 19 (1): 12–22.

———. 2006. "Art Therapy with Sexually Abused Children and Adolescents: Extended Research Study." *Art Therapy: Journal of the American Art Therapy Association* 23 (4): 181–185.

———. 2007. "Jogging the Clogs: Trauma Focused Art Therapy with Sexually Abused Children." *Art Therapy: Journal of the American Art Therapy Association* 24 (4): 170–175.

———. 2009. "Mapping the Maze: An Art Therapy Intervention Following the Disclosure of Sexual Abuse." *Art Therapy: Journal of the American Art Therapy Association* 26 (1): 12–18.

Potok, C., and H. Volavková. 1993. . . . *I Never Saw Another Butterfly* . . . : *Children's Drawings and Poems from Terezin Concentration Camp, 1942–1944*. New York: Schocken Books.

Rankin, A., and C. Taucher. 2003. "A Task-Oriented Approach to Art Therapy in Trauma Treatment." *Art Therapy: Journal of the American Art Therapy Association* 20 (3): 138–147.

Rausch, S., B. A. van der Kolk, R. Fisler, S. Orr, N. M. Alpert, C. R. Savage, . . . R. K. Pittman. 1996. "A Symptom Provocation Study of Posttraumatic Stress Disorder Using Positron Emission Tomography and Script Driven Imagery." *Archives of General Psychiatry* 53:380–387.

Roje, J. 1995. "LA '94 Earthquake in the Eyes of Children: Art Therapy with Elementary School Children Who Were Victims of Disaster." *Art Therapy: Journal of the American Art Therapy Association* 12 (4): 237–243.

Russell, J. 1999. "Art Therapy on a Hospital Burn Unit: A Step Toward Healing and Recovery." In *Medical Art Therapy with Children*, ed. C. Malchiodi, 133–152. London: Jessica Kinglsey.

Sandler, I. N., T. S. Ayers, S. A. Wolchik, J.-Y. Tein, O.-M. Kwok, R. A. Haine, . . . W. Griffin. 2003. "The Family Bereavement Program: Efficacy Evaluation of a Theory-Based Prevention Program for Parentally Bereaved Children and Adolescents." *Journal of Consulting and Clinical Psychology* 71 (3): 587–600.

Santino, J. 2006. *Spontaneous Shrines and Public Memorialization of Death*. New York: Palgrave Macmillan.

Schaverien, J. 1992. *The Revealing Image: Analytical Art Psychotherapy in Theory and Practice*. London: Jessica Kingsley.

———. 1998. "Jewish Identity, Art Psychotherapy Workshops, and the Legacy of the Holocaust." In *Arts Therapists, Refugees, and Migrants: Reaching Across Borders*, ed. D. Dokter, 155–173. London: Jessica Kinglsey Publishers.

Schore, A. N. 2003. "Early Relational Trauma, Disorganized Attachment, and the Development of a Predisposition to Violence." In *Healing Trauma: Attachment, Mind, Body, and the Brain*, ed. M. F. Solomon and D. J. Siegel, 107–167. New York: Norton.

Serrano, J. S. 1989. "The Arts in Therapy with Survivors of Incest." In *Advances in Art Therapy*, ed. H. Wadeson, P. Durkin, and D. Perach, 114–125. New York: Wiley.

Silverman, P. R., S. Nickman, and J. W. Worden. 1995. "Detachment Revisited: The Child's Reconstruction of a Dead Parent." In *Children Mourning, Mourning Children*, ed. K. J. Doka, 131–148. Washington, D.C.: Hospice Foundation of America.

Speert, E. 1989. "Beyond Psychic Numbing: Art Therapy and the Nuclear Taboo." *Art Therapy: Journal of the American Art Therapy Association* 6 (3): 106–112.

Spring, D. 1993. *Shattered Images: Phenomenological Language of Sexual Trauma*. Chicago: Magnolia Street.

——. 2004. "Thirty-Year Study Links Neuroscience, Specific-Trauma PTSD, Image Conversion, and Language Translation." *Art Therapy: Journal of the American Art Therapy Association* 21 (4): 200–209.

Springham, N., and V. Huet. 2018. "Art as Relational Encounter: An Ostensive Communication Theory of Art Therapy." *Art Therapy: Journal of the American Art Therapy Association* 35 (1): 4–10.

Steele, W. 2002. "Using Drawing in Short-Term Trauma Resolution." In *Handbook of Art Therapy*, ed. C. Malchiodi, 139–151. New York: Guilford Press.

Steele, W., and M. Raider. 2001. *Structured Sensory Intervention for Traumatized Children, Adolescents, and Parents*. Lewiston, N.Y.: Edwin Mellen Press.

Stember, C. J. 1977. "Printmaking with Abused Children: A First Step in Art Therapy." *American Journal of Art Therapy* 16 (3): 104–109.

Talwar, S. 2007. "Accessing Traumatic Memory Through Art Making: An Art Therapy Trauma Protocol (ATTP)." *The Arts in Psychotherapy* 34 (1): 22–35.

Thompson, M., N. Kaslow, A. Price, K. Williams, and J. Kingree. 1998. "Role of Secondary Stressors in the Parental Death–Child Distress Relation." *Journal of Abnormal Child Psychology* 26 (5): 357–366.

Tripp, T. 2007. "A Short Term Therapy Approach to Processing Trauma: Art Therapy and Bilateral Stimulation." *Art Therapy: Journal of the American Art Therapy Association* 24 (4): 176–183.

van der Kolk, B. 2005. "Developmental Trauma Disorder: Towards a Rational Diagnosis for Chronically Traumatized Children." *Psychiatric Annals* 35 (5): 401–408.

——. 2006. "Clinical Implications of Neuroscience Research in PTSD." *Annals of the New York Academy of Sciences* 1071:277–293.

Wald, J. 1989. "Severe Head Injury and Its Stages of Recovery Explored Through Art Therapy." In *Advances in Art Therapy*, ed. H. Wadeson, J. Durkin, and D. Perach, 181–203. New York: Wiley.

Walsh, F. 2003. "Family Resilience: A Framework for Clinical Practice." In *Family Process* 42 (1): 1–18.

Wix, L. 2009. "Aesthetic Empathy in Teaching Art to Children: The Work of Friedl Dicker-Brandeis in Terezin." *Art Therapy: Journal of the American Art Therapy Association* 26 (4): 152–158.

Worden, W., ed. 2002. *Grief Counseling and Grief Therapy: A Handbook for the Mental Health Practitioner.* 3rd ed. New York: Springer.

9

The Effects of Bullying on Schoolchildren

▸ *JUN SUNG HONG and JEOUNG MIN LEE*

BULLYING IS A PERVASIVE problem that has probably occurred in schools since schools have existed. However, it was not until the Columbine High School shootings in 1999 that school bullying began to receive a considerable amount of media attention in the United States. Since that time, many concerned parents, school teachers, school officials, and lawmakers have gradually become more determined to take action to prevent and stop bullying in schools. Over the years, scholarship on school bullying has proliferated in the United States, and presently, school districts in all fifty states are mandated to have anti-bullying policies and programs in place. Despite the significant attention and scrutiny from scholars and lawmakers and the amount of federal and state monies invested in prevention and intervention programs and strategies, 23 percent of students in K–12 schools nationwide report being bullied by their classmates and peers (Robers et al. 2015).

This chapter will provide an overview of school bullying and peer victimization among children and adolescents. The various types and psychosocial outcomes of bullying will be reviewed. Types of bullying include *direct bullying* (physical and verbal bullying), *indirect bullying* (rumor spreading, social exclusion), and *cyberbullying* (use of electronic technology to threaten, harass, or damage reputations). Research demonstrating adverse psychosocial outcomes of bullying will also be reviewed, with a particular emphasis on traumatic experiences. Finally, two case examples will be presented to highlight the importance of validation and attunement by adults to prevent or diminish the likelihood that a child or adolescent will experience bullying as traumatic.

DEFINITION AND TYPES OF BULLYING

Generally, the definition of human aggression involves the intention to cause harm to others (Archer and Coyne 2005); however, there appears to be significant variation both in how bullying is defined and in the specific types of bullying involving children and adolescents. This section provides a definition of bullying and outlines the different types of bullying and victimization involving children and adolescents in school.

Definition of Bullying

Pioneering work on bullying has been done by Dan Olweus, a scholar in Norway who characterized a bully as someone who "chronically harasses someone else either physically or psychologically." He also wrote that a "student is being bullied or victimized when he or she is exposed, repeatedly and over time, to *negative actions* on the part of one or more other students" (Olweus 1993, 9). Olweus's conceptualization of "bullying" behavior in schoolchildren has been adopted by many American scholars (Atlas and Pepler 2001; Juvonen, Graham, and Schuster 2003; Nansel et al. 2001; Pellegrini 2002; Twemlow, Sacco, and Williams 1996). It is evident from Olweus's definition that bullying comprises negative actions that are repeated and intentional, and that involve a power differential between the bully and the victim. However, a growing body of research suggests that the way students themselves define and conceptualize bullying is inconsistent with this widely adopted definition (Espelage and De La Rue 2012).

It was not until 2014 that a clear and standard definition of *bullying* was established (Espelage, Rao, and De La Rue 2013). In 2014, the Centers for Disease Control and Prevention, in partnership with the Department of Education and the Health Resources and Services Administration, developed a uniform definition of *bullying* for research and surveillance. They define it as "any unwanted aggressive behavior(s) by another youth or group of youths who are not siblings or current dating partners that involves an observed or perceived power imbalance and is repeated multiple times or is highly likely to be repeated. Bullying may inflict harm or distress on the targeted youth including physical, psychological, social, or educational harm" (Gladden et al. 2014, 7).

Types of Bullying

Researchers have identified major characteristics of bullies, which encompass several subcategories. As described above, Olweus (1993) characterized a bully as someone who deliberately causes, or attempts to cause, fear, discomfort, or injury to another person. Olweus made a distinction between indirect and direct forms of bullying. He categorized indirect or "verbal" aggressors as those who engage in teasing, taunting, threatening, name calling, and spreading rumors, and direct or "physical" aggressors as those who engage in pushing, shoving, hitting, kicking, or restraining. Some researchers have distinguished between "overt" (physical fighting and verbal threats) and "covert" in which verbal aggression is displayed through name calling and rumor spreading) acts of bullying (see Crick, Casas, and Ku 1999; Espelage and Horne 2008). Others have found that boys are more likely to engage in direct (or overt) forms of bullying while girls are more likely to engage in indirect (or covert) forms, particularly relational aggression (see Espelage and Swearer 2003; Varjas, Henrich, and Meyers 2009). Still others, however, found no sex differences in bullying; boys and girls were equally likely to be engaged in both direct and indirect forms of bullying (e.g., Barboza et al. 2009).

Bullying and aggressive behavior have been further categorized as "reactive" ("a defense reaction to a perceived threat, which is accompanied by some visible form of anger") or "proactive" (an "unprovoked aversive means of influencing or coercing another person" that is "more goal-directed than reactive aggression") (Camodeca, Goossens, Terwogt, and Schuengel 2002; Price and Dodge 1989, 456; Salmivalli and Nieminen 2002). Camodeca and colleagues (2001) found that bullies were overrepresented among children who were both reactively and proactively aggressive. Other scholars categorized bullying as either "overt" aggression (confrontational behavior toward another individual or a group of individuals, such as physical attack, verbal threats, property destruction, or self-harming behavior) or "relational" aggression (indirect or covert aggression that is aimed at damaging a social relationship) (Griffin and Gross 2004). Relational aggression involves socially excluding the target from a peer group, spreading rumors about the target, keeping secrets from the target, or humiliating the target in a social setting (Griffin and Gross 2004). Some researchers have focused on relational aggression (Goldstein, Young, and Boyd 2008; Murray-Close, Ostrov, and Crick 2007). The concept of relational aggression was introduced by Crick and Grotpeter (1995), who subsequently defined it as "behaviors that harm other through damage (or threat to damage) to relationships or feelings of acceptance, friendship, or group inclusion" (Crick, Werner, et al. 1999, 77). Relational aggression is found to contribute to social anxiety (Crick, Ostrov, and Werner 2006; Loukas, Paulos, and Robinson 2005; Storch, Brassard, and Masia-Warner 2003), depressive symptoms (Crick, Ostrov, and Werner 2006; Prinstein, Boergers, and Vernberg 2001), and aggressive behaviors (Cillessen and Mayeux 2004; Crick, Ostrov, and Werner 2006).

Types of Victims

Fewer studies have identified types of bullying victims. Besag (1989) categorized them into four types: passive victims, vicarious/surrogate victims, perpetual victims, and false victims. Passive victims, a group that encompasses most victims of bullying, are those who do not directly provoke bullies; these youth lack social skills and have few (or no) friends. They are often lonely and depressed and are frequently anxious when confronted with new social situations. Vicarious (or surrogate) victims witness or hear about bullying at school and are fearful of possibly becoming targets of bullying. Perpetual victims are those who have been victimized all their lives and through such experiences have developed a "victim mentality." False victims are those who complain (often without justification) about being victims of bullying to seek attention or sympathy from their teachers or other students.

Cyberbullying

As the number of children and adolescents utilizing the internet and social media has grown rapidly within the past decade, a new form of aggression, "cyberbullying," has emerged (Tokunaga 2010). Although traditional bullying and cyberbullying share similar constructs, such as an aggressive act, cyberbullying mainly differs in the reach of the perpetrator (Tokunaga 2010). Mindful of the lack of a uniform and consistent definition of *cyberbullying*, Tokunaga (2010), in his review of the literature on the topic, defined it as "any behavior performed through electronic or digital media by individuals or groups that repeatedly communicates hostile or aggressive messages intended to inflict harm or discomfort on others. . . . In cyberbullying experiences, the identity of the bully may or may not be known. Cyberbullying can occur through electronically-mediated communication at school; however, cyberbullying behaviors commonly occur outside of school as well" (Tokunaga 2010, 278). Tokunaga (2010) also identified several differences between cyberbullying and traditional bullying. He noted that unlike traditional bullying, cyberbullying can be perpetrated anonymously. In addition, there is a lack of supervision in electronic media (see Patchin and Hinduja 2006), and the victim is accessible at any time (Patchin and Hinduja 2006; Slonje and Smith 2007), which make a cyberbullying victim a relatively easy target.

PSYCHOSOCIAL IMPACT OF BULLYING VICTIMIZATION ON CHILDREN

Many empirical studies have documented the impact of being bullied on youths' lives and whether it can be harmful to their mental health. This section examines psychosocial outcomes and traumatic responses, including PTSD.

Psychosocial Outcomes

Adverse experiences of bullying victimization disrupt children's and adolescents' interpersonal relationships. Bullying victims may feel lonely and isolated from their peers at school, and may as a result feel a sense of low self-worth. Such negative emotions and attitudes about themselves can have the effect of elevating their psychosocial distress, which, in turn, may lead to depression, anxiety, or low self-esteem. These sequelae may subsequently be linked to adverse outcomes such as risk-taking behaviors (e.g., alcohol and drug use), criminal offenses (e.g., delinquent behaviors), and suicidal ideation as well as frank suicidal attempts. Moreover, the negative outcomes associated with being bullied can have far-reaching effects, subverting development across the life span, as studies have shown (Lereya et al. 2015; Wolke et al. 2013). Because adverse psychosocial outcomes of bullying are detrimental to children's and adolescents' physical and mental health, a large body of research has explored the link between bullying victimization and psychosocial and behavioral problems (Kaltiala-Heino, Frojd, and Marttunen

2010; Kim, Boyle, and Georgiades 2018; Kim et al. 2018; Schneider 2012; Shen et al. 2016; Stewart et al. 2017; Williams et al. 2017; Wolke et al. 2013; Wolke, Lee, and Guy 2017).

Study findings consistently reveal the negative impact of bullying and cyberbullying victimization on victims' psychosocial and physical health. A study by Kim et al. (2018) of 31,148 students in grades six to twelve in Canada found that victims of physical bullying reported behavioral problems (e.g., physical fighting, stealing, and breaking into houses), while victims of social and verbal bullying experienced emotional problems (e.g., depression and anxiety). Victims of cyberbullying had experienced both emotional and behavioral problems during the preceding six months. In a sample of 233 ninth graders, Williams and colleagues (2017) found that compared to nonvictims, female victims of verbal bullying, social bullying, and cyberbullying were at higher risk of depression, and cyberbullying victims were at significantly higher risk of suicidal ideation and attempts. Male victims of verbal and social bullying were at a higher risk of depression, suicidal ideation, and suicide attempts than victims of physical bullying and cyberbullying. Moreover, females are more likely than males to communicate with their peers or express their emotions by using technologies, which may increase their likelihood of cyberbullying victimization. Another study (Stewart et al. 2017) examined suicidal ideation and behaviors among 340 adolescents ages thirteen to nineteen with depressive symptoms. They found that victims of overt bullying and relational aggression were more likely to report having attempted suicide.

Studies have supported the proposition that since adolescence is considered a vulnerable epoch in development, exposure to bullying victimization may increase the risks of psychological and behavioral problems. Kim, Boyle, and Georgiades (2018) examined how cyberbullying victimization affects the health of individuals age fifteen and older among 31,907 Canadians. Their results showed that adolescents (ages fifteen to eighteen) reported the highest prevalence of cyberbullying victimization (12.2 percent), poorer mental health, more binge drinking, and more drug use than other groups (older than eighteen). Likewise, Wolke and colleagues' (2013) longitudinal research examined the effects of bullying victimization in childhood on life difficulties in adulthood. Youth who reported chronic bullying victimization at ages nine, eleven, and thirteen experienced a higher risk of psychological and physical health problems (e.g., psychiatric disorders and regular smoking), decreased financial and educational outcomes, and interpersonal problems in young adulthood than those who had been uninvolved in bullying. Another longitudinal study (Kaltiala-Heino, Frojd, and Marttunen 2010) found that victims of bullying at fifteen years of age reported depressive symptoms, which continued through age seventeen.

Several studies have investigated the co-occurrence of bullying and cyberbullying and the effect of multiple forms of victimizations on victims' psychosocial outcomes. Schneider and colleagues (2012) conducted a study of 20,406 students in grades nine to twelve; they found that youth who experienced both school bullying and cyberbullying victimization exhibited more depressive symptoms, suicidal ideation, self-injury, and suicide attempts than those who were victims of only cyberbullying or school bullying. A study by Wolke, Lee, and Guy (2017) of 2,745 adolescents ages eleven to sixteen in the United Kingdom also found that youth who endured multiple forms of victimization (i.e., co-occurrence of direct bullying, relational bullying, and cyberbullying) were likely to display lower self-esteem and behavioral difficulties, including hyperactivity, emotional symptoms, peer problems, and conduct problems. To illustrate, victims of bullying and cyberbullying may "act out" in their classroom, refusing to perform assigned tasks such as homework, and may also frequently get into fights in school. Consequently, such adolescents may do poorly in school and may drop out as a result. They may also develop problems in adulthood in their relationships with friends, peers, coworkers, and romantic partners. Given that youth who are chronically victimized are likely to experience adverse health, wealth, and social functioning in adulthood, such victimization needs to be assessed and monitored by clinicians and school officials early.

Trauma and Posttraumatic Stress Disorder

Post-traumatic stress disorder (PTSD) can occur when people have experienced or witnessed a traumatic event, such as a natural or unnatural disaster, a severe accident, war, rape, or other violent assault (American Psychiatric Association 2013). Children's and adolescents' chronic exposure to bullying victimization can be considered traumatic, which can reinforce symptoms of PTSD and disrupt the development of brain functioning, gradually resulting in physical difficulties. Children and adolescents who face bullying victimization can experience cognitive, emotional, and behavioral problems that can last a lifetime (Cook et al. 2005). Many studies have found a link between bullying victimization and PTSD symptoms (Chen et al. 2018; Idsoe, Dyregrov, and Idsoe 2012; Karsberg, Armour, and Elklit 2014; Ranney et al. 2016; Shen et al. 2016; Sourander et al. 2010). PTSD is likely to manifest if the trauma from bullying reinforces feelings of helplessness. For instance, a bullying victim is required to attend school and is forced to encounter his tormentors on a daily basis. The victim may be picked on for days, weeks, months, or years, potentially culminating in a sustained experience of trauma. As a consequence, the victim may attempt to avoid school altogether.

Studies suggest that the development of PTSD is a common result of bullying victimization and impairs the victim's daily functioning. Depression, suicidal thoughts, and suicide attempts have been positively correlated with PTSD; thus, victims of bullying are at heightened risk of such behavior. Ranney and colleagues (2016) examined mental health symptoms and risk behaviors among adolescents ages thirteen to seventeen who were patients at a level-1 trauma center's pediatric emergency department. They found that, in the previous year, 23.2 percent had reported symptoms of PTSD, 13.9 percent had reported depressive symptoms, and 11.3 percent had reported suicidal thoughts. The case of Tyler Clementi serves as an illustration. Clemente, a freshman at Rutgers University, ended his life by jumping off the George Washington Bridge shortly after undergoing humiliation and trauma by his roommate, who had secretly videotaped his sexual activity with another man and streamed it on the internet for public viewing.

In other studies, childhood experiences of physical bullying and cyberbullying victimization were found to be significant predictors of future PTSD symptoms in adolescence and adulthood. Using a national sample of 963 students in grades eight and nine in Norway, Idsoe, Dyregrov, and Idsoe (2012) reported that PTSD symptoms from bullying victimization were higher for girls than for boys, which seems to suggest that traumatic stress affects the brain differently in male and female adolescents. Girls may have greater vulnerability to stress symptoms than boys after experiencing trauma, which is not surprising given that girls are more likely than boys to experience internalizing problems such as depression and anxiety (Angold and Rutter, 1992). Anti-bullying intervention and prevention programs need to consider whether gender differences exist in strategies for coping with bullying. Practitioners might also conduct an initial assessment to determine whether a child is manifesting an internalizing problem, such as depression or anxiety. Practitioners are encouraged to consider an intervention strategy that teaches children healthy ways to cope with bullying victimization.

Spending a significant time on the internet may provide greater exposure to negative information on self-harm and suicidal thoughts. Cyberbullying victimization was found to be positively linked to PTSD, depression, physical and mental health, deliberate self-harm, and suicidal ideation in one study of 18,341 Chinese students ages fifteen to seventeen (Chen et al. 2018). In another study, Shen and colleagues (2016) examined the effects of multiple types of bullying victimization on mental health and behaviors among 6,233 fourth-grade students in Taiwan. The study found that PTSD symptoms (e.g., upsetting thoughts, avoidance, insomnia) were the most prevalent outcome among those experiencing multiple victimizations. Another study (Sourander et al. 2010) of 2,215 Finnish adolescents ages thirteen to sixteen found that victims of cyberbullying experienced psychosomatic problems such as headaches, recurring abdominal pain, and sleeping difficulties; high levels of perceived difficulties; emotional and peer problems; and feeling unsafe in school.

CASE EXAMPLES

In this section, two fictitious case scenarios, based on common varieties of bullying, illustrate the psychologically debilitating impact of bullying on children and teenagers.

Case of Leroy

Danny and Alex, both fifteen, created a false email account using their classmate Leroy's information. The two boys thought it would be hilarious if they told other students that "Leroy is gay and is infatuated with all the football players in the school." Danny and Alex emailed the football players using the false account and displayed the messages to their classmates. Shortly after the email was widely circulated, students began tormenting Leroy, and his friends excluded him from their social gatherings. Because of the cruel prank, Leroy developed severe depressive symptoms and incapacitating anxiety and eventually attempted suicide. He is currently undergoing counseling. During the counseling sessions, it was revealed that Leroy had been struggling with loneliness and low self-esteem shortly after transitioning from middle school to high school. He was not interested in football and did poorly in his gym class. The other boys frequently made fun of him, calling him "gay" and "homo" for not measuring up to other students. Though fully aware of the situation, the coach made no effort to stop or even mitigate the behavior of Leroy's classmates. When the rumor about his being gay circulated via the internet, he grew afraid to show up at the gym. Leroy's counselor settled on a cognitive-behavioral treatment approach, which has been widely used to treat depressive symptoms linked to such stressors. The strategy, which aims to change Leroy's thought patterns to help facilitate a mood shift, improved his ability to cope with bullying and harassment (see Mor and Haran 2009).

Case of Tamara

Tamara, age fourteen, was hesitant to undress in the locker room during physical education. Compared to other girls her age, she was a "late bloomer." She had always been self-conscious about her chest being underdeveloped. Whenever she changed clothes before or after PE class, the other girls would stare and point at her, mocking her and calling her "flat tire" and "girly boy." One day, a group of girls took pictures of her undressing and showed them to many other students online. Tamara, mortified, locked herself in her room. Feeling utterly humiliated and depressed, she refused to eat or sleep, and she skipped school. Three days later, she ended her life by ingesting an entire bottle of sleeping pills.

In such a case, the school social workers, in collaboration with teachers and administrators, might decide that the school's anti-bullying and zero-tolerance policies were insufficient to prevent such incidents. It is important for school social workers and practitioners to assess the climate at school to determine whether it might reinforce bullying behavior directed against students who are or appear to be different from others. The social worker might also work with teachers and other school personnel in a more didactic or psychoeducational manner, helping them not only to recognize the signs of bullying but also to identify and respond effectively to specific situations.

DISCUSSION AND CONCLUSION

Cases like Leroy and Tamara clearly suggest that bullying is a serious problem that can be psychologically debilitating to the victims. School bullying can have the potential to leave lasting scars. A growing body of research documents the serious consequences of bullying victimization, including drug and alcohol use, depression and anxiety, low self-esteem, and suicidal thoughts and ideations (Hinduja and Patchin 2010; Ttofi et al. 2016; Wang et al. 2010; Wang, Nansel, and Iannotti 2011). It is also important to emphasize that trauma associated with bullying episodes may affect not only the victims who are directly involved but also bystanders who witness the events. Moreover, retrospective and longitudinal studies reveal that experiences in bullying during childhood can reinforce trauma during adulthood (e.g., Nielson et al. 2015). Based on a recognition of the serious impact of bullying in schools, numerous efforts have been made to address and reduce bullying. Considerable time and energy have been devoted to bullying prevention with the assumption that the effort will create a safer school climate for all students (Gruber and Fineran 2008). Regrettably, the effectiveness of school-bullying prevention and intervention programs has been modest (Evans, Fraser, and Cotter 2014; Richard, Schneider, and Mallet 2012). Although programs such as those adopting the whole-school approach have shown promise in some school districts, it is imperative that schools also consider programs that reinforce students' social-emotional learning. Social-emotional learning (SEL) refers to a "process through which children and adults acquire and effectively apply the knowledge, attitudes, and skills necessary to understand and manage emotions, set and achieve positive goals, feel and show empathy for others, establish and maintain positive relationships, and make responsible decisions" (Collaborative for Academic, Social, and Emotional Learning 2017). It emphasizes the development of self-concept, a sense of competence, and self-regulation. It teaches skills in remaining calm and focused and in following directions. Recent studies have found that SEL can be effective in reducing bullying, fighting, and problem behaviors in schools and in promoting children's prosocial behavior (e.g., see Espelage, Rose, and Polanin 2015; Smith and Low 2013). For programs such as SEL to be effective, it is important for schools to integrate and reinforce the skills into teachers' daily interactions and practices with their students (Jones and Bouffard 2012).

The serious psychological impact of bullying victimization highlights the importance of early school-based interventions that are designed to prevent bullying. The immediate and long-term adverse outcomes of children's traumatic experiences are multifaceted; however, children who are exposed to traumatic episodes are likely to have impaired self-regulation and interpersonal relationships (Cook et al. 2005). Victims as well as bystanders who are traumatized by bullying episodes can benefit from programs and activities that promote self-care and provide information on how to handle trauma (Carney 2008). Further, effective and sustainable interventions for children who are traumatized as a result of bullying require developing or restoring individual resilience (Kinniburgh, Blaustein, and Spinazzola 2005). Most important, improving the quality of mental health services in schools is paramount (Kataoka et al. 2003) as that is where a great deal of mental health care for children is delivered (Burns et al. 1995). School-based mental health services, such as trauma-informed training and curricula, are powerful tools for school officials interested in reducing students' trauma, fostering prosocial behavior, and promoting academic success (Day et al. 2015; Wiest-Stevenson and Lee 2016).

REFERENCES

American Psychiatric Association. (2013). *Diagnostic and Statistical Manual of Mental Disorders* (5th ed.). American Psychiatric Association: Washington, D.C.

Archer, J., and Coyne, S. M. (2005). An integrated review of indirect, relational, and social aggression. *Personality and Social Psychology Review, 9*, 212–230.

Atlas, R. S., and Pepler, D. J. (2001). Observation of bullying in the classroom. *The Journal of Educational Research, 92*, 86–99.

Barboza, G. E., Schiamberg, L. B., Oehmke, J., Korzeniewski, S. J., Post, L. A., and Heraux, C. G. (2009). Individual characteristics and the multiple contexts of adolescent bullying: An ecological perspective. *Journal of Youth and Adolescence, 38*, 101–121.

Besag, V. E. (1989). *Bullies and Victims in Schools*. Milton Keynes, England: Open University Press.

Burns, B. J., Costello, E. J., Angold, A., Tweed, D., Stangl, D., Farmer, E. M. Z., and Erkanli, A. (1995). Children's mental health service use across service sectors. *Health Affairs 14* (3), 147–159.

Camodeca, M., Goossens, F. A., Terwogt, M. M., and Schuengel, C. (2002). Bullying and victimization among school-age children: Stability and links to proactive and reactive aggression. *Social Development, 11* (3), 332–345.

Carney, J. V. (2008). Perceptions of bullying and associated trauma during adolescence. *Professional School Counseling, 11,* 179–188.

Chen, Q., Lo, C. K. M., Zhu, Y., Cheung, A., Chan, K. L., and Ip, P. (2018). Family poly-victimization and cyberbullying among adolescents in a Chinese school sample. *Child Abuse and Neglect, 77,* 180–187.

Cillessen, A. H. N., and Mayeux, L. (2004). From censure to reinforcement: Developmental changes in the association between aggression and social status. *Child Development, 75,* 147–163.

Collaborative for Academic, Social, and Emotional Learning. (2017). "What is SEL?" Accessed April 2019. http://www.casel.org/what-is-sel/.

Cook, A., Spinazzola, J., Ford, J., Lanktree, C., Blaustein, M., Cloitre, M., . . . van der Kolk, B. (2005). Complex trauma in children and adolescents. *Psychiatric Annals, 35* (5), 390–398.

Crick, N. R., Casas, J. F., and Ku, H. C. (1999). Relational and physical forms of peer victimization in preschool. *Developmental Psychology, 35,* 376–385.

Crick, N. R., and Grotpeter, J. (1995). Relational and overt aggression in preschool. *Developmental Psychology, 33,* 579–588.

Crick, N. R., Ostrov, J. M., and Werner, N. E. (2006). A longitudinal study of relational aggression, physical aggression, and children's social-psychological adjustment. *Journal of Abnormal Child Psychology, 34* (2), 127–138.

Crick, N. R., Werner, N., Casas, J., O'Brien, K., Nelson, D., Grotpeter, J., et al. (1999). Childhood aggression and gender: A new look at an old problem. *Nebraska Symposium on Motivation, 45,* 75–141.

Day, A. G., Somers, C. L., Baroni, B. A., West, S. D., Sanders, L., and Peterson, C. D. (2015). Evaluation of a trauma-informed school intervention with girls in a residential facility school: School perceptions of school environment. *Journal of Aggression, Maltreatment and Trauma, 24* (10), 1086–1105.

Espelage, D. L., and De La Rue, L. (2012). School bullying: Its nature and ecology. *International Journal of Adolescent Medicine and Health, 24* (1), 3–10.

Espelage, D., and Horne, A. (2008). School violence and bullying prevention: From research based explanations to empirically based solutions. In S. Brown and R. Lent (Eds.), *Handbook of Counseling Psychology* (4th ed., pp. 588–606). Hoboken, NJ: John Wiley and Sons.

Espelage, D. L., Rao, M. A., and De La Rue, L. (2013). Current research on school-based bullying: A social-ecological perspective. *Journal of Social Distress and the Homeless, 22* (1), 7–21.

Espelage, D. L., Rose, C. A., and Polanin, J. R. (2015). Social-emotional learning program to reduce bullying, fighting, and victimization among middle school students with disabilities. *Remedial and Special Education, 36* (5), 299–311.

Espelage, D. L., and Swearer, S. M. (2003). Research on school bullying and victimization: What have we learned and where do we go from here? *School Psychology Review, 32* (3), 365–383.

Evans, C. B. R., Fraser, M. W., and Cotter, K. L. (2014). The effectiveness of school-based bullying prevention programs: A systematic review. *Aggression and Violent Behavior, 19* (5), 532–544.

Gladden, R. M., Vivolo-Kantor, A. M., Hamburger, M. E., and Lumpkin, C. D. (2014). *Bullying Surveillance Among Youths: Uniform Definitions for Public Health and Recommended Data Elements, Version 1.0.* Atlanta, GA: National Center for Injury Prevention and Control, Centers for Disease Control and Prevention and U.S. Department of Education.

Goldstein, S. E., Young, A., and Boyd, C. (2008). Relational aggression at school: Associations with school safety and social climate. *Journal of Youth and Adolescence, 37,* 641–654.

Griffin, R. S., and Gross, A. M. (2004). Childhood bullying: Current empirical findings and future directions for research. *Aggression and Violent Behavior, 9,* 379–400.

Gruber, J., and Fineran, S. (2008). Comparing the impact of bullying and sexual harassment victimization on the mental health of adolescents. *Sex Roles, 59* (1/2), 1–13.

Hinduja, S., and Patchin, J. W. (2010). Bullying, cyberbullying, and suicide. *Archives of Suicide Research, 14,* 206–221.

Idsoe, T., Dyregrov, A., and Idsoe, E. C. (2012). Bullying and PTSD symptoms. *Journal of Abnormal Child Psychology, 40* (6), 901–911. doi:10.1007/s10802-012-9620-0.

Jones, S. M., and Bouffard, S. M. (2012). Social and emotional learning in schools: From programs to strategies. *Society for Research in Child Development Social Policy Report, 26,* 1–33.

Juvonen, J., Graham, S., and Schuster, M. A. (2003). Bullying among young adolescents: The strong, the weak, and the troubled. *Pediatrics, 112* (6), 1231–1237.

Kaltiala-Heino, R., Frojd, S., and Marttunen, M. (2010). Involvement in bullying and depression in a 2-year follow-up in middle adolescence. *European Child and Adolescent Psychiatry, 19* (1), 45–55.

Karsberg, S., Armour, C., and Elklit, A. (2014). Patterns of victimization, suicide attempt, and posttraumatic stress disorder in Greenlandic adolescents: A latent class analysis. *Social Psychiatry and Psychiatric Epidemiology, 49* (9), 1389–1399.

Kataoka, S. H., Stein, B. D., Jaycox, L. H., Wong, M., Escudero, P., Tu, W., Zaragoza, C., and Fink, A. (2003). A school-based mental health program for traumatized Latino immigrant children. *Journal of the American Academy of Child and Adolescent Psychiatry, 42* (3), 311–318.

Kim, S., Boyle, M. H., and Georgiades, K. (2018). Cyberbullying victimization and its association with health across the life course: A Canadian population study. *Canadian Journal of Public Health, 108* (5–6), e468–e474.

Kim, S., Colwell, S. R., Kata, A., Boyle, M. H., and Georgiades, K. (2018). Cyberbullying victimization and adolescent mental health: Evidence of differential effects by sex and mental health problem type. *Journal of Youth and Adolescence, 47* (3), 661–672.

Kinniburgh, K. J., Blaustein, M., and Spinazzola, J. (2005). Attachment, self-regulation, and competency: A comprehensive intervention framework for children with complex trauma. *Psychiatric Annals, 35* (5), 424–430.

Lereya, S. T., Copeland, W. E., Costello, E. J., and Wolke, D. (2015). Adult mental health consequences of peer bullying and maltreatment in childhood: Two cohorts in two countries. *The Lancet Psychiatry, 2* (6), 524–531.

Loukas, A., Paulos, S. K., and Robinson, S. (2005). Early adolescent social and overt aggression: Examining the roles of social anxiety and maternal psychological control. *Journal of Youth and Adolescence, 34*, 335–345.

Mor, N., and Haran, D. (2009). Cognitive-behavioral therapy for depression. *Israel Journal of Psychiatry and Related Sciences, 46* (4), 269–273.

Murray-Close, D., Ostrov, J. M., and Crick, N. R. (2007). A short-term longitudinal study of growth of relational aggression during middle childhood: Associations with gender, friendship intimacy, and internalizing problems. *Development and Psychopathology, 19*, 187–203.

Nansel, T. R., Overpeck, M. D., Pilla, R. S., Ruan, W. J., Simons-Morton, B., and Scheidt, P. (2001). Bullying behaviours among U.S. youth: Prevalence and association with psychosocial adjustment. *Journal of the American Medical Association, 285* (16), 2094–2100.

Nielson, M. B., Tangen, T., Idsoe, T., Matthiesen, S. B., and Mageroy, N. (2015). Post-traumatic stress disorder as a consequence of bullying at work and at school: A literature review and meta-analysis. *Aggression and Violent Behavior*, *21*, 17–24.

Olweus, D. (1993). *Bullying at School: What We Know and What We Can Do*. Oxford: Blackwell.

Patchin, J. W., and Hinduja, S. (2006). Bullies move beyond the schoolyard: A preliminary look at cyberbullying. *Youth Violence and Juvenile Justice*, *4*, 148–169.

Pellegrini, A. D. (2002). Bullying, victimization, and sexual harassment during the transition to middle school. *Educational Psychologist*, *37*, 151–163.

Price, J. M., and Dodge, K. A. (1989). Reactive and proactive aggression in childhood: Relations to peer status and social context dimensions. *Journal of Abnormal Child Psychology*, *17*, 455–471.

Prinstein, M. J., Boergers, J., and Vernberg, E. M. (2001). Overt and relational aggression in adolescents: Social-psychological adjustment of aggressors and victims. *Journal of Clinical Child and Adolescent Psychology*, *30*, 479–491.

Ranney, M. L., Patena, J. V., Nugent, N., Spirito, A., Boyer, E., Zatzick, D., and Cunningham, R. (2016). PTSD, cyberbullying and peer violence: Prevalence and correlates among adolescent emergency department patients. *General Hospital Psychiatry*, *39*, 32–38.

Richard, J. F., Schneider, B. H., and Mallet, P. (2012). Revisiting the whole-school approach to bullying: Really looking at the whole school. *School Psychology International*, *33* (3), 263–284.

Robers, S., Zhang, A., Morgan, R. E., and Musu-Gillette, L. (2015). *Indicators of School Crime and Safety: 2014* (NCES 2015-072/NCJ 248036). Washington, D.C.: National Center for Education Statistics, U.S. Department of Education, and Bureau of Justice Statistics, Office of Justice Programs, U.S. Department of Justice.

Salmivalli, C., and Nieminen, E. (2002). Proactive and reactive aggression among school bullies, victims, and bully-victims. *Aggressive Behavior*, *28* (1), 30–44.

Schneider, S. K., O'Donnell, L., Stueve, A., and Coulter, R. W. (2012). Cyberbullying, school bullying, and psychological distress: A regional census of high school students. *American Journal of Public Health*, *102* (1), 171–177. doi:10.2105%2FAJPH.2011.300308.

Shen, A. C. T., Feng, J. Y., Feng, J. Y., Wei, H. S., Hsieh, Y. P., Huang, S. C. Y., and Hwa, H. L. (2016). Who gets protection? A national study of multiple victimization and child protection among Taiwanese children. *Journal of Interpersonal Violence*, 1–25. doi:10.1177/0886260516670885

Slonje, R., and Smith, P. K. (2007). Cyberbullying: Another main type of bullying? *Scandinavian Journal of Psychology, 49*, 147–154.

Smith, B. H., and Low, S. (2013). The role of social-emotional learning in bullying prevention efforts. *Theory into Practice, 52* (4), 280–287.

Sourander, A., Brunstein Klomek, A., Ikonen, M., Lindroos, J., Luntamo, T., Koskelainen, M., . . . Helenius, H. (2010). Psychosocial risk factors associated with cyberbullying among adolescents: A population-based study. *Archives of General Psychiatry, 67* (7), 720–728.

Stewart, J. G., Valeri, L., Esposito, E. C., and Auerbach, R. P. (2017). Peer victimization and suicidal thoughts and behaviors in depressed adolescents. *Journal of Abnormal Child Psychology, 46* (3), 581–596.

Storch, E. A., Brassard, M. R., and Masia-Warner, C. L. (2003). The relationship of peer victimization to social anxiety and loneliness in adolescence. *Child Study Journal, 33*, 1–18.

Tokunaga, R. S. (2010). Following you home from school: A critical review and synthesis of research on cyberbullying victimization. *Computers in Human Behavior, 26*, 278–287.

Ttofi, M. M., Farrington, D. P., Losel, F., Crago, R. V., and Theodorakis, N. (2016). School bullying and drug use later in life: A meta-analytic investigation. *School Psychology Quarterly, 31*, 8–27.

Twemlow, S. W., Sacco, F. C., and Williams, P. (1996). A clinical and interactionist perspective on the bully-victim-bystander relationship. *Bulletin of the Menninger Clinic, 60*, 296–313.

Varjas, K., Henrich, C. C., and Meyers, J. (2009). Urban middle school students' perceptions of bullying, cyberbullying, and school safety. *Journal of School Violence, 8*, 159–176.

Wang, J., Iannotti, R., Luk, J. W., and Nansel, T. R. (2010). Co-occurrence of victimization from five subtypes of bullying: Physical, verbal, social exclusion, spreading rumors, and cyber. *Journal of Pediatric Psychology, 35*, 1103–1112.

Wang, J., Nansel, T. R., and Iannotti, R. J. (2011). Cyber and traditional bullying: Differential association with depression. *Journal of Adolescent Health, 48*, 415–417.

Wiest-Stevenson, C., and Lee, C. (2016). Trauma-informed schools. *Journal of Evidence-Informed Social Work, 13* (5), 498–503.

Williams, S. G., Langhinrichsen-Rohling, J., Wornell, C., and Finnegan, H. (2017). Adolescents transitioning to high school: Sex differences in bullying victimization associated with depressive symptoms, suicide ideation, and suicide attempts. *Journal of School Nursing, 33* (6), 467–479.

Wolke, D., Copeland, W. E., Angold, A., and Costello, E. J. (2013). Impact of bullying in childhood on adult health, wealth, crime, and social outcomes. *Psychological Science, 24* (10), 1958–1970.

Wolke, D., Lee, K., and Guy, A. (2017). Cyberbullying: A storm in a teacup? *European Child and Adolescent Psychiatry, 26* (8), 899–908.

10

Combat Trauma

▸ KATHRYN BASHAM

WAR AND ARMED conflict involve a combination of combat and deployment stressors that affect service members and their families in myriad ways. Without doubt, war is horrific and devastating for everyone involved. Wars have existed since the beginning of humanity, and regrettably they continue with a disturbing predictability. In this chapter, I will primarily address the challenges and rewards facing U.S. service members, Veterans and their families as they navigate combat trauma while integrating back home. Many service members and Veterans have also experienced traumatic events during childhood and adulthood of the types featured in other chapters of this text. (The term Veteran is capitalized in this chapter because when General Shinseki was the director of Veterans Affairs, he requested that written communications would use the capital "V" as a sign of respect.) The effects of layers of traumatic events on worldviews and coping abilities are influenced by counterbalancing forces of risk and protective factors. Since the 9/11 attacks on the United States, 2.77 million troops have served in the armed forces, with one-third of troops engaged in multiple deployments. Following 9/11, 6,251 service members have died in combat, 4,471 of those in Iraq (McCarty 2018). This number is lower than the number of casualties reported in the Vietnam War (58,000). Yet many post-9/11 Veterans have survived deployment with devastating physical and mental health disabilities. In fact, compared with any previous war era, more Veterans from Operation Enduring Freedom (OEF, in Afghanistan), Operation Iraqi Freedom (OIF), and Operation New Dawn (OND, in Iraq) have applied for disability benefits. Furthermore, uncounted numbers of combatants and civilians have died in Iraq, Afghanistan, and other war zones in the past seventeen years.

A strictly voluntary military organization (the draft for military service ended in 1973), the U.S. Armed Forces comprises the branches of Army,

Navy, Marines, Air Force, and Coast Guard. The current number of service members stands at 1.29 million or less, encompassing .5 percent of the U.S. population. Most members of the military come from middle-income neighborhoods, the majority from California, Texas, Florida, Georgia, and New York. The average age of members of the National Guard and Air Force is greater than those of the other branches; Marines skew younger, with 84 percent of troops age twenty or younger. Among enlisted recruits, 43 percent of men and 56 percent of women self-identify as Hispanic or a racial minority; overall, female recruits are consistently more racially diverse than the civilian population. In general, the number of women in the military has increased; they constitute 16 percent of all enlisted service members and 18 percent of officers. In the Army there are nearly as many black women (40 percent) as white women (45 percent). The Marine Corps is the only service where the percentage of black men is lower than it is in the civilian labor force (Reynolds and Shendruk 2018).

I will open the chapter with a brief historical account of central themes that have emerged throughout the history of war, in particular in the United States. Next I will introduce a definition of combat trauma in the context of various types of trauma. Third, I will discuss distinguishing features of combat trauma, including rewards, challenges, and paradoxes that emerge during reintegration back home (Castro, Kintzle, and Hassan 2015). Fourth, the role of sociocultural factors and social context will be addressed in relation to how they shape responses to combat trauma. Sociocultural factors include gender, race, ethnicity, language of origin, sexual orientation, and religion, among others. Fifth, aftereffects and resilience following exposure to combat trauma will be discussed. Sixth, general guidelines in mental health practice will be outlined for combat Veterans and their families. Seventh, I will describe specific evidence-based clinical approaches, including psychodynamic, cognitive-behavioral, family, and complementary and alternative medicine. Clinical vignettes based on a case composite will illustrate the fundamental guiding principles of a "relationship-based, culturally-responsive, anti-racism-grounded, theoretically-supported, and research informed" clinical social work practice with a de-identified fictitious combat Veteran couple, the Hernandezes (Basham 2014). References to empirical and conceptual literature will be woven throughout the chapter.

Many combat Veterans harness remarkable resilience and often report experiences of efficacy, mastery, and accomplishment both during and following deployment. Feelings of satisfaction and pride are often associated with strong military values, including a commitment to the "larger good" of a mission and to loyalty and camaraderie within a unit. In contrast, other Veterans describe alienation from partners, children, and other family members, distrust of civilians in the community, hypervigilance, intense mood swings, a lack of purpose, moral injury, and survivor guilt. These symptoms and issues do not necessarily reflect a major mental health disorder. In the assessment of all military and Veteran clients, it is important to carefully differentiate between criteria for post-traumatic stress disorder (PTSD) and indicators of post-traumatic stress that are normal responses to abnormal, life-threatening, traumatic events (Shaw 2005; Shay 1994). Efforts have been made to consider these responses to traumatic and nontraumatic combat stressors as contributing to post-traumatic stress injuries rather than as a disorder. For example, if a soldier has lost a leg in an IED (improvised explosive device) blast, we would recognize a major physical injury rather than labeling it "a missing leg disorder." Along similar lines, with mental health responses to combat, would we consider a Marine's profound grief and moral injury a sign of PTSD or a psychological injury of war? Even though the service member might be suffering from post-traumatic stress, he doesn't automatically meet criteria for PTSD. Most, if not all, service members are likely to experience some post-traumatic stress responses that do not lead to a primary mental health disorder. Only a discrete number of combat Veterans grapple with trauma-related and affective mental disorders. This distinction is important as a way to normalize understandable, ordinary responses to extraordinary circumstances.

Waves of service members returning from Iraq, Afghanistan, and other regions ("hot spots") have reintegrated with their families and communities in the past decade and a half. We need to understand more thoroughly the unique stressors and rewards facing them. More than 50 percent of all post-deployed U.S. Veterans do not seek out any services through the Veterans Administration Medical Centers; still, we hold a responsibility as professional mental health and health providers to thoroughly understand the many ways that these Veterans navigate the complex effects of combat trauma in the context of reentry back home (Basham 2012a, 2012b). A vast number of Veterans "bring the war home" with them.

HISTORICAL CONTEXT FOR WAR-RELATED TRAUMA

What do we mean by *trauma*? Our understanding has changed dramatically over the years, often influenced by the sociopolitical forces that support or invalidate the reality of trauma that affects individuals, families, and communities. In 1656, the word *traumatic* appeared in the *Oxford English Dictionary*. Greek in origin, it indicated a situation associated with wounds or the cure of an injury (Basham 2014; Dass-Brailsford 2007). Two centuries later, the term started to be used to denote events that were emotionally disturbing or distressing. In 1866, Dr. John Erichsen, a London surgeon, addressed the effects of witnessing a railway accident, which often led to psychological injuries to the nervous system, resulting in "railway spine" (Morris 2015). He compared the phenomenon to a "magnetized horseshoe that has had its force jarred, shaken or concussed" (Morris 2000, 62). Early on, then, experts noted that witnessing a traumatic event could lead to debilitating neurobiological symptoms, anticipating our current emphasis on the neurobiology of traumatic stress. The notion of traumatic shock entered the conversation.

Throughout history, war and combat have generated much of our discourse around trauma. In a compelling autobiographical account, David J. Morris, a journalist and former Marine, offered that PTSD as a condition does not capture an intrinsic unity (2015). Rather, it came together by "practices, technologies and narratives with which it is diagnosed, studied, treated and represented . . . and by the institutions and moral arguments that mobilized these efforts" (62). Some of the themes related to PTSD are timeless; individuals have expressed pain, sadness, fear, and loss associated with distressing events for many centuries. Yet the actual constructs of the PTSD diagnosis have only existed within the past several decades (Basham 2014). Young (1995) elaborates on the origins of trauma apparent in prehistorical hunter-gatherer societies in Siberia and the Huichol tribe of central Mexico. In the latter context, tribal members needed to survive a life-threatening event to qualify as an esteemed shamanic healer. Such veneration of survivorship prefigured what is now referred to by Calhoun and Tedeschi (2008) as "post-traumatic growth," which recognizes as the first theme individuals' capacity to transform the legacies of trauma into positive, life-enhancing phenomena. A second important universal theme is the alternating pattern of intermittent awareness and denial of a traumatic event. Jonathan Shay, an eminent psychiatrist dedicated to the healing of Vietnam Veterans, wrote eloquently about the psychological, physical, and moral injuries suffered by Greek warriors and drew comparisons with the sagas reported by Vietnam Veterans (1994). Similar symptoms of hyperarousal, heart palpitations, disturbed sleep, and breathing problems were also reported in the Civil War, when they were referred to as "irritable heart" or the "Da Costa" syndrome (Morris 2015, 84). A half century later, WWI Veterans experienced amnesia, blindness, mutism, and tremors reminiscent of what was described in the early narratives of Civil War Veterans. Although these debilitating symptoms were initially thought to have been caused by the deafening sounds of exploding shells, experts became aware of the psychological origins of these combat-trauma-related responses. Treatment often involved a combination of nursing, respite care, and supportive psychotherapy.

The ravages of widespread war resurfaced only two decades later. Many WWII Veterans described intense alternating episodes of hyperarousal and detachment and terrorizing nightmares, which were referred to collectively as "battle fatigue" or "combat exhaustion." Decades later, thousands of drafted and enlisted Vietnam Veterans once again suffered similar physical and psychological responses of acute traumatic stress. It was not until 1980, several years after the war had ended, that the syndrome *post-traumatic stress disorder* (PTSD) was formally recognized in the *DSM-III*, which allowed Veterans to access mental health services for the condition (American Psychiatric Association 2013).

DEFINITIONS OF COMBAT TRAUMA

According to Figley (1995), trauma involves a state of discomfort and extreme stress in the presence of experiences or memories of a catastrophic event. Severe (traumatic) stressors are imposed with exposure to actual or threatened death, serious injury, or sexual violation. In her groundbreaking work, Herman (1992) expanded on this definition to include events that overwhelm an ordinary system of care that gives people a sense of control, connection, and meaning in the world. Trauma disrupts attachments and relationships. In everyday conversations, the word *trauma* is often used freely, yet incorrectly, as a synonym for *stress*. A distinguished authority on stress, Bruce McEwen, writes persuasively about a continuum of stress (e.g., the experience of discomfort) that moves from mild to moderate to severe (traumatic) in terms of intensity (1999). Stress is typically triggered by an internal or external event (stressor) whose intensity also ranges along a continuum of mild to moderate to severe (traumatic). The range of stressors leads to a variety of consequences and outcomes. McEwen (1999) notes that we all have a certain psychological and neurobiological equilibrium that ensures *allostasis*, or a sense of stability. If new stressors impinge on an individual, his or her *allostatic load* increases, burdening the person and undermining equanimity, leading to an overload of stress with negative outcomes. Even so, several mediating factors affect the nature of outcomes, including any preexisting mental health vulnerability, resilience, co-occurring stressors, and social context. An important point to emphasize is that exposure to traumatic events does not automatically lead to mental health problems. Depending on various mediating influences, a combat Veteran with noteworthy resilience would experience milder responses. For example, a Veteran who confronts a traumatizing, life-threatening event may experience only mild to moderate stress based on protective factors that strengthen resilience, such as constitutional hardiness, efficacy, social support, and respect for command.

Combat trauma involves a unique brand of horror that often encompasses exposure to violent and life-threatening events combined with experiences of mastery, accomplishment of the mission, and powerful bonds with others, fueling an incendiary cauldron of complex emotions, thoughts, and actions. Although an event that happens during combat may, according to Terr's typology (1999), be considered a type I trauma (i.e., a single, discrete life-threatening event), the lengthy nature of deployments and the reality of multiple consecutive deployments can involve ongoing trauma exposure consonant with Terr's type II trauma (e.g., the chronic and repetitive physical, sexual, or emotional abuses of childhood). Many combat Veterans entered the military with previous experiences of childhood trauma, including physical, sexual, and emotional abuses; they often did so with the aim of seeking a more consistent and healthy environment. Finally, many troops from targeted racial and ethnic identities have been subjected to cultural or racial trauma, which is understood as chronic, pernicious, bigoted threats that undergird psychological and physical safety (Allen 1998; DeGruy 2005; de Jong et al. 2005; Edgerton 2009). Although the Department of Defense has reversed the "don't ask don't tell" policy (IOM 2014, 2010; Nicholson 2012), LGBTQ service members are frequently subjected to overt and covert

discrimination, or cultural trauma, both while deployed and upon returning home.

What Is a Combat Zone?

The term *combat zone* typically refers to a particular geographic area, designated by executive order, where U.S. troops are actively engaged in military
operations. As of June 2018, Afghanistan, the Arabian Peninsula, and the
Kosovo area were identified as combat zones characterized by armed conflict. These areas typically involve both safe and unsafe spaces. In the center
of Baghdad, Iraq, the International Zone has served as the Iraqi governmental headquarters for various regimes. In 2003, this district was taken over
by U.S. military forces and referred to as the "Green Zone." Post-9/11
Veterans and service members describe the Green Zone as a relatively safe
installation that was protected by high cement walls and barbwire fences;
it was where military officials and international visitors were housed. Yet
even with external fortifications, the Green Zone failed to provide safety to
our troops. For example, high rates of military sexual harassment and military sexual trauma occurred there, increasing the risk of life-threatening
assault. When service members ventured to other areas, referred to as the
"Red Zone," they encountered active combat, erupting mines, and experiences of attacking and being attacked.

Post-9/11 service members who have served in Iraq and Afghanistan have
reported an experience of 24/7 danger. Similarly, Veterans of the first Gulf
War described a pervasive feeling of apprehension and a constant threat to
safety. Since troops in Desert Storm lacked appropriate helmets and other
protective gear, they were continuously vulnerable to harm. One combat Veteran described his unit's mission as "sacrificial, where soldiers served as
speed bumps to slow down and hold off the onslaught of Iraqi forces headed
to the oil fields in Riyadh" (personal communication, 2012). In contrast, during WWII and the Korean War, long periods of calm were intermittently
interrupted by violent assaults and attacks (Adler et al. 2011).

Exposure to combat is one of the greatest stressors a person can experience (Hoge 2010; 2011). In the more recent conflicts in Afghanistan and Iraq,
traumatic stressors have included roadside IEDs, suicide bombers, sniper fire,
and an indistinguishable insurgency (IOM 2013, 2014). As one combat Veteran reported, "Without warning, we would be surrounded by exploding

vehicles, a blanketing of body parts strewn across the ground, putrid, sickening smells of burning flesh and gasoline, and cacophonous sounds." Another noted, "These unrelenting assaults chip away at whatever resilience we have left—this is a 360 degree 24–7 war without any relief" (Tripp 2008).

Many service members witnessed the deaths and extreme physical injuries of their unit buddies and consequently suffer unresolved grief and moral injury (Taneilian and Jaycox, 2011). Shay (1994) introduced the notion that moral injury—or murder of the soul—explained the symptoms and beliefs of Vietnam Veterans. When service members encountered unethical actions taken by commanding officers or when they were directly involved in such events, serious self-doubt related to moral corruption overwhelmed them. Shay (1994) vividly describes what he refers to as the "psychological injury to the soul and character." During combat, a whole new set of skills and strengths alters the way service members relate to the world, especially if they have suffered disillusionment. Shay states that soldiers learn first to control their fears, and then learn the art of deception and cunning to find ways to survive. They develop a capacity to respond immediately and instantly with violent, lethal force. They maintain a watchful stance at all times, prepared to respond to danger. Physical strength, courage, endurance, and quickness are cultivated. Finally, they may challenge the fixed rules of hierarchy in order to survive (Shay 1994). Fighting and killing are inevitable features of warfare. Yet even if they are notably resilient, many service members feel overwhelmed by the ravages of combat. They may experience a bracing awareness of moral dissonance when the "justness" of killing to protect oneself or others may be questioned, or when decisions ordered by a commanding officer are deemed unethical. Another common moral dilemma relates to questioning the purpose and meaning of a U.S. military presence in a combat zone. Any of these experiences may cause a service member to feel overwhelmed with moral injury and with associated shame and guilt.

Tick (2005) has assisted Vietnam Veterans with their healing by accompanying them on voyages to the original locations of their military service in Vietnam. The treatment aims to reconcile the moral conflicts and injuries that occurred in the war zones, helping the Veteran move toward expiation of guilt and shame, acceptance of forgiveness, and social vindication. William Nash, an esteemed retired Naval psychiatrist with thirty years of military service, has developed a scale to determine if an active-duty service member has suffered moral injury (Nash et al. 2017). Nash and his colleagues saw a high incidence of moral injury while embedded with troops, and in response they developed an effective clinical intervention, the Adaptive Disclosure Method, which addresses exposure to traumatic events and moral injury in the field (Litz et al. 2017). Moral injury accounts for many reports by service members of hopelessness, self-hatred, shame, and a loss of meaning and purpose.

In the past decade, clinicians and researchers have been focused on expanding the narrow definition of PTSD as caused primarily by a fear response. The empirically supported trauma-treatment methods that are deemed to hold the strongest evidence for efficacy (e.g., prolonged exposure [PE], cognitive-processing therapy [CPT], and cognitive-behavioral therapy [CBT]) are based on the explanation that fear associated with a threat to safety is the primary source of post-traumatic stress symptoms. Since these treatment models suffer very high dropout rates, we need to look beyond one explanation for the complex responses. Many service members do not report fear connected to their military service. Instead, they are burdened by a combination of moral injury that engenders shame, guilt, and unresolved grief.

In a combat zone, physical conditions can be harsh. Service members may encounter extremes of heat and scorching temperatures, blinding sandstorms, and life-threatening scorpions and insects. Hoge, Castro, and Messer (2004) conducted a study using postdeployment surveys of 2,856 Army and 2,815 Marine combat infantry troops. Data analysis revealed that 92 percent of Operation Iraqi Freedom (OIF) soldiers were attacked or ambushed; 95 percent received small-arms fire; 94 percent saw dead bodies or human remains; 89 percent received incoming artillery, rocket, or mortar fire; 86 percent knew someone who was killed or seriously injured; and 57 percent reported being responsible for the death of an enemy combatant. The major noncombat stressor was consistently reported to be separation from family and friends. Operation Enduring Freedom (OEF) service members often reported similar experiences with combat exposure yet usually were sent on missions to outposts away from the central base, which posed even more extreme safety risks.

PSYCHODYNAMIC PERSPECTIVES

From a psychoanalytic perspective, Shaw (2005) comments on the "acute traumatic moment" in war: the sudden awareness of intense and devastating feelings of helplessness that surface before the fear of injury and death.

This overwhelming moment leads to the collapse of the following world-views: (1) the ego ideal, with specific narcissistic defenses associated with the idealized self; (2) the illusion of safety; and (3) the mechanisms of denial (23). Shaw shares a vivid example of this profound narcissistic injury:

> A 24-year-old corporal who was a petrol truck driver with an armored unit advanced on the first day of the war. He had forgotten to take his flak jacket. As his unit advanced on the eastern front, they came under attack. There was no place to hide. And the corporal felt "alone, helpless and angry." Experiencing panic, he both hugged and hid under a cardboard box. He had terrible fears that he was going to be killed and shifted into a hysterical stupor. When the doctor arrived, the solder was described as being in a state of shock, with mutism and amnesia.
>
> (26)

In this case and others, the combat Veteran experienced a sudden awareness of his vulnerability and the fragility of human life after having lived with a sense of invulnerability. An ego ideal that provided assurances of invincibility and survival was shattered, resulting in his feeling alone and unprotected from the threat of injury and death.

Carr (2011) suggests that combat trauma does not relate solely to the traumatic incident per se, but also to how overwhelmed the Veteran feels in tolerating and dealing with the intense emotions associated with trauma. Drawing upon the writings of Stolorow with an intersubjective theoretical stance, Carr writes, "We all want our traumatic experiences to be understood and so we cling to those who have experienced similar trauma" (477). As Stolorow (2007) suggests, our common finitude and traumatic experiences leave all of us desiring an "existential kinship-in-the-same-darkness" (49).

Kudler (2007), a psychodynamically informed psychiatrist, writes extensively about the principles of outreach to combat Veterans and their families. Although PTSD is generally understood in biological and medical terms, the biopsychosocial-spiritual issues facing Veterans and their families are better understood in psychodynamic terms. Following WWII, Grinker and Speigel (1945), in their text titled *Men Under Stress*, challenged the notion that a "broken brain" was the main cause of post-traumatic stress. Instead, they asserted that anyone could break under enough stress, and that the psychological processes associated with such responses require steadfast attention. The needs of OIF and OEF Veterans are complex and do not fit a traditional medical model. The processes of meaning-making, reconciling complex identities, navigating grief and loss, and restoring connections with family and friends are central and warrant an exploratory psychodynamic approach (Bragin, 2010)

Sherman (2005) writes eloquently about what she terms "stoic warriors," based on ancient Greek and Roman philosophies that recognize the importance and usefulness of controlling and concealing emotions at certain critical moments, not only during combat. She believes that emotions can be consciously managed rather than assuming that they will unavoidably erupt. Several authors assert that the horrors of attacking, being attacked, killing, and witnessing killing inevitably change a person (Grossman and Christensen 2008; Grossman 2009; Sherman 2005).

Survivor guilt and unresolved grief over many losses may also plague service members. Grieving may be thwarted by tenacious feelings of guilt, self-depreciation, and unworthiness at being alive in the face of tragic death. As one OIF soldier who lost a revered unit leader repeatedly expressed the wish that he had been the one to die. He was convinced that he did not deserve to be alive.

In a combat situation, a service member may feel like a victimizer, a victim, or a bystander, reflecting the trauma triangle addressed by several authors (Basham 2014; Herman 1992; Staub 1989). If a service member endured physical, sexual, or emotional abuse during childhood, he may have internalized voices and ideas from others. Introjection has been defined as a process, later defined as a defense, wherein an individual replicates in oneself the behaviors, attitudes, and affectively charged fragments of the surrounding world, primarily from people (Ogden 1982). During fighting and killing, if a service member maintains an internal world populated with these negative introjections, additional traumatic stressors may intensify the new negative experiences. Consider an interior army of saboteurs, whether they are victimizing abusers, helpless victims, or detached bystanders (Fairbairn 1943).

In a psychotherapy framework, these roles are played out in transference/ countertransference enactments through intersecting projective identification processes, wherein both the service member and the clinician alternate between roles (Ogden 1982). After returning home, combat Veterans may continue to see their world through the scenarios of "victim-victimizer-bystander," even when death and killing have been sanctioned aspects of their designated roles in a mission.

REWARDS AND CHALLENGES: THE PARADOXES OF COMBAT TRAUMA

Castro and Hoge assumed the lead in codeveloping *Battlemind Training*, which for a decade was the primary resilience-building model for soldiers, their partners, and their clinicians. It aimed to understand the stressors and rewards soldiers experience during predeployment, deployment, and post-deployment (Castro and Kintzle 2017; Castro and Adler 2011; Castro et al. 2006).

Certain modes of coping that were enormously useful during deployment may be less effective once combat Veterans return to their families and communities. Hypervigilance, for instance, is needed to respond to dangerous situations during deployment, where it may be affirmed and admired. In contrast, family members may feel frightened by similar behavior back home. During deployment, driving fast can minimize life-threatening attacks. A twenty-eight-year old OIF Veteran, Sgt. Miller, experienced a flashback of an attack launched by adolescent combatants who lobbed an IED onto the truck he was driving. Although he escaped physical harm, the iconic traumatic memory was engraved in his brain. Back home, when he was driving on a major freeway, he started to accelerate when he saw a bridge in the distance that spanned the highway. Vividly seeing potential threat from people standing on the bridge, he careered forward, recklessly changing lanes. He pushed his wife under the dashboard, yelling, "Get down!" Once they had passed under the bridge, Sgt. Miller pulled onto the shoulder of the highway and expressed great relief that danger had passed. In contrast, his wife expressed intense anger and fear, having been subjected to the terrorizing effects of her husband's reliving wartime events.

PARADOXES

Castro, Kintzle, and Hassan (2015) introduced a model to understand the range of responses a Veteran faces following a return home from deployment. It lists twelve paradoxes: simultaneous yet contradictory thoughts, emotions, and behaviors that create a double-binding outcome. See table 10.1.

TABLE 10.1   Combat Veteran Paradoxes

PARADOX	SIMULTANEOUS THOUGHTS, EMOTIONS, AND BEHAVIORS
Modesty	
My service and sacrifice should be recognized.	Don't thank me, I was doing my job.
I'm proud of my service.	I don't want to discuss my service.
People don't want to help veterans.	I want to be left alone.
Don't talk about self; "it was my team."	Everyone wants me to talk about my service.
Emotions	
I'm happy to be home.	I am angry a lot.
	I am withdrawn a lot.
	I am often sad.
Back there	
I should share my feelings with family/friends.	I don't want to feel hurt again.
I want to be home.	I want to return to deployment.
I miss my family.	I want to be with the "guys."
There is no purpose here.	I want to be there, "where it matters."
Kanji	
I'm happy to be alive.	Better men were killed. I don't deserve to be here.
	I should have saved him/her.
Morpheus	
I am physically and mentally exhausted.	I cannot sleep.
	I cannot calm down.
Courage	
I proved courage and strength in combat.	People will think I am weak if I ask for help.
	Showing emotions is a sign of weakness.
	Apologizing to loved ones signals weakness.
Aschalasia	
I want to enjoy life.	I cannot relax.
I wish I could clear my mind and enjoy work.	Everything matters. People die following mistakes.

TABLE 10.1   *(Continued)*

PARADOX	SIMULTANEOUS THOUGHTS, EMOTIONS, AND BEHAVIORS
Intimacy	
Begin tight with unit members is important.	Keeping distance from family and loved ones is important.
It feels good to be loved.	I can't show emotions; I can't take another loss.
Safety	
Nothing can harm me.	The world is an unsafe place.
I am not afraid of death.	I never turn my back to anyone.
Silence	
No one understands what it is like.	I don't want to talk about it.
I need to get this "out of my head."	I don't even know how to describe it.
Risk taking	
Never take unnecessary risks (in combat).	When your time is up, it is up.
I mattered over there.	Nothing matters here.
Meaning in life	
I appreciate the important things in life.	I cannot let go of the little things.
Enjoy life.	Why live? For what purpose?

(Castro, Kintzle, and Hassan 2015, 301)

These thought processes capture the tensions that affect active-duty service members during deployment. Despite the fact that they are normative during combat, service members who are returning home can benefit from preventive psychoeducational and relationship-based counseling to help them integrate the contradictions. If Veterans and family members fail to recognize and understand the paradoxes, they might intensify, leading to mental health disorders. Typically, service members engage in substantive basic training that prepares them for military service by immersing them in military values, knowledge, and skills. In contrast, troops who are leaving the service frequently describe their "out-processing," or transition back to the civilian world, as foreshortened and superficial. The procedures to discharge service members are designed to do so as efficiently and quickly as possible; as a result they neglect training in how to identify and address these paradoxes, which can deeply affect the combat Veteran and family members (Basham 2012b; Castro and Adler 2011a).

The rest of this section describes the paradoxes in more detail to provide a greater understanding of the psychosocial challenges facing combat Veterans, their partners, children, parents, peers, colleagues, and other family members during reintegration into their community. I have organized the paradoxes into four domains: emotional responses, physical responses, meaning-making, and relationships and communication.

Emotional Responses

The *mixed-emotions paradox* refers to a full range of intense emotions, often contradictory, that Veterans experience during deployment and the return to civilian life. Veterans may be happy, enthusiastic, joyful, and proud upon returning home while simultaneously feeling angry about circumstances endured during combat, such as feeling betrayed or angered by a commanding officer. Anger may surface related to feeling misunderstood or invalidated by family and friends, or from resentment or envy toward a partner who competently managed parenting and household responsibilities while the Veteran was on active duty. Frustration and distrust between a Veteran and her partner may alternate with tender, loving feelings, often leading to emotional dysregulation for the partners and other family members. Many family members find these emotional shifts frightening and disorienting since they do not know which intense emotions might erupt at any moment. Intense stressors contribute to the higher rates of divorce among Veteran couples compared to the national civilian average (IOM 2014). These unstable emotional states call for a neurobiological explanation. When traumatic stressors affect a service member during deployment, the sympathetic and parasympathetic nervous systems are activated, leading to a traumatic stress response, alternating between hyperarousal (characterized by elevated heart rate, irritability, and a release of the natural stimulant epinephrine) and hypoarousal (decreased heart rate, lethargy, detachment, a release of the natural suppressor norepinephrine). For Veterans and their partners who enter psychotherapy, treatment goals should include demonstrating greater emotional balance, affect regulation, and an optimal zone of arousal midway between hyperarousal and hypoarousal (Cozolino 2010). The *courage paradox* refers to a need to mobilize courage during deployments, which is necessary for combat readiness, while simultaneously fearing being viewed as weak and cowardly for expressing vulnerable feelings of worry, fear, and sadness. These contradictory views often set the stage for wariness about seeking help for health and mental health concerns, creating major roadblocks to accessing care. The question arises "How can I be strong and courageous during combat but now accept vulnerability, which looks like weakness and cowardice?"

Physical Responses

The *Morpheus paradox* refers to the gifts granted to the Greek god of dreams, who exerts power over sleep. It is not uncommon for service members to sleep only four to six hours per night for the entire time they are deployed. Such a pattern is typical during combat in keeping with the goal of maintaining vigilance and alertness. However, diminished sleep relies on a continuous state of hyperarousal, which has long-term consequences upon returning home. As many Veterans have reported, you cannot turn the "hypervigilance switch" off and on at will.

In order to regain emotional regulation, clear judgment, and attentiveness, combat Veterans need to find ways to "upregulate" and "downregulate" their levels of arousal (Siegel, 2007). Without that modulation of affect, many combat Veterans have difficulty sleeping. They may try to self-medicate with alcohol and other drugs, which may lead to addictions. Or they may decide to sleep alone, potentially alienating their partner. Insomnia and disrupted sleep are major problems for many Veterans and their partners. When a Veteran awakens yelling in the middle of a flashback, it can be terrifying for partners, children, and other family members. The Veteran may feel strong remorse following such episodes. Castro and Kintzle (2014) refer to sleep disruption as one of many expected "occupation-related" traumas arising from combat, similar to what is experienced by humanitarian workers and uniformed service members (police officers, firefighters, correctional officers) (Castro and Adler 2011).

The *Aschalasia paradox* refers to the inability to relax. The very state of hyperarousal that helps with survival in combat can cause a full range of disturbances in civilian life, making it impossible to calm oneself and rest.

Meaning-Making

This set of paradoxes focuses on shifts in meaning-making and worldviews. First, the *Kanji paradox* focuses on the desire to feel happy, which is counterbalanced by not feeling justified in having positive feelings because others have perished in war. Emotions of shame and guilt activate moral injury and lead to questions such as "Why should I be alive when these other soldiers died? What could I have done to make the difference?" An overburdened sense of responsibility can immobilize a Veteran who is struggling with this moral dilemma. (Dombo, Gray, and Early 2013).

The *safety paradox* is central for survival during combat and symbolically relevant during postdeployment. Combat Veterans have a sense of indestructibility based on their having survived many life-endangering situations. This certainty may have a defensive quality in warding off feelings of vulnerability or fear. Veterans may begin to think of death as inevitable. Even though there may be considerably reduced risk of harm back home, combat Veterans may anticipate danger in large crowds, stadiums, and rooms that lack windows or easy access to doors. Their instinctual responses are activated to detect danger, fight back, and protect. The resulting fear feels disabling for them and their partners. One Veteran OIF couple talked about needing to check out a concert space by visiting the venue in advance of the event and planning their seating close to the exits to ensure protection and speed of escape.

A related paradox is the *risk-taking paradox*. During deployment, service members approach their life-threatening environment with caution and precision. After returning home they often still feel compelled to engage in high-risk activities such as reckless driving and excessive drug consumption. Some report an adrenalin rush upon engaging in these activities that may be related to regulating the highs and lows of a recurring traumatic stress response. Others express fatalistic views or a need to seek a dangerous distraction.

Relationships and Communication

Relationship paradoxes include the intimacy paradox, the back-there paradox, the modesty paradox, and the silence paradox.

The *intimacy paradox* reflects the need for combat Veterans, their partners, and others to recognize that everyone has changed during the Veteran's deployment. There is no way to recapture the exact relationship that existed prior to deployment. Exposure to combat may also have dampened trust between the Veteran, who worries about rejection and estrangement, and his or her partner. Relationships with fellow Veterans are very important because they can serve as protective factors in mediating possible outcomes of depression, poor self-esteem, and suicidal thoughts (Castro and Kintzle, 2014; Castro, Kintzle, and Hassan 2015; Japucak and Varra 2011).

Struggles with intimacy are also associated with the *back-there paradox*, in which a combat Veteran experiences alienation, emptiness, and an absence of purpose at home and wishes to be back in the region where she had been deployed. Some Veterans yearn for the sense of connectedness engendered by the powerful relationships they enjoyed with their military buddies and command. Their civilian partners often feel jealous of these strong attachment bonds among "bands of brothers" or "bands of sisters."

The *modesty paradox* reflects the fact that many combat Veterans seek recognition for their service but are irritated or embarrassed by expressions of gratitude from civilians. Humility may prevent some Veterans from being able to embrace the appreciation they seek.

Finally, the *silence paradox* can create frustrating conflicts when a Veteran seeks understanding and recognition of their experiences during deployment yet may not want to talk about them. A strong belief that civilians cannot possibly comprehend the magnitude of their experiences prevents some Veterans from breaking the silence and talking about feelings and reflections related to their assignments.

SOCIOCULTURAL FACTORS

Cultural Relativity of Diagnosis and Neurobiology

Although cultural factors influence responses to trauma and different modes of expressing trauma-related symptoms and beliefs, several researchers have noted some universality in neurobiological reactions to traumatic stressors. Extensive research in neuroscience has deepened our understanding of the effects of trauma on the body and has direct applicability to clinical practice (Appelgate and Shapiro 2005; Cozolino 2010; Levine 2005; Ogden, Minton, and Pain 2006; Porges 2011; van der Kolk 2003; Siegel 2010). A traumatic event during combat stimulates blood pressure and heart rate and

increases perspiration. A pendulum of intense emotions is set in motion: exuberance, excitement, anger, and frustration alternate with sadness, hopelessness, and emptiness (Porges 2011). The service member takes in auditory,
tactile, olfactory, and visual stimuli through the thalamus. When these
messages register as threatening rather than benign, a fight-flight-freeze
response takes over. First, the sympathetic regulatory system excites the
amygdala, which serves as the brain's "alarm system" and is activated to alert,
defend, and protect. The amygdala hijacks the usual information-processing
system, signaling full-blown distress. A cascade of physiological responses
overwhelms the body, and the hippocampus is flooded with affectively laden
stimuli that interfere with storing logical and rational memories. Instead,
the emotionally saturated experiences are laid down as body memories
(Basham 2014; van der Kolk 2003). The parasympathetic regulatory system
is activated concurrently. Opiates are released in the brain, creating a state
of numbness. Increases in cortisol, decreases in blood pressure, and flatten-
ing of emotions lead to an emotional "freezing." When the sympathetic and
parasympathetic systems are activated simultaneously, two opposing forces
collide, contributing to the fight-flight-freeze scenario.

Differences exist, even across cultures, in the ways that trauma-related
symptoms are expressed. Researchers have observed that Southeast Asian
refugees and immigrants may tend to experience dissociation in such situations, while some Latinx individuals may demonstrate a "pause-collect"
response, not uncommon in collectivist societies where an instinct to care for
others may be activated during the traumatic-stress response. This means
that some traumatized individuals, rather than switching into fight-flight-
freeze mode, may seek out loved ones to protect. Practitioners need to
recognize that feelings, behavior, and meaning-making associated with
post-traumatic stress are culturally determined (de Jong et al 2005). For example, a 38 year-old Filipino-American Corporal in the Army returned from
deployment to Los Angeles where he entered a program to improve his command of English as a second language and was totally incapable of taking
in new information. He literally could not make sense of what was being
said to him as he froze in a dissociative state. When he emerged from his
safe space of mutism, he described haunting flashbacks of observing a fellow soldier burn to death while he stood by helplessly.

Cultural and Racial Trauma

As noted earlier, in the past two decades the constructs of racial and cultural trauma have entered the social discourse (Allen 1998). Miller and Garran (2010) assert that daily verbal (and, at times, physical) racist assaults hurled at people of color perpetuate the legacies of slavery. They point out that the abusive language feels like psychological death via a thousand paper cuts. Such verbal attacks are described as "microaggressions," and they function in the same way as Terr's type II trauma—chronic, repetitive, and corrosive.

The psychologist DeGruy (2005) has advanced the notion that intergenerational legacies of slavery are revealed in African American youth and adults. They describe diminished self-esteem, hopelessness, and anger arising from being the daily object of hurtful, bigoted remarks. These assaults, rooted in racial hatred, are perpetrated against individuals who may already be marginalized by their socioeconomic status, gender, ethnicity, religion, sexual orientation, or ability. For example, a 35 year-old biracial Pakistani-American OEF Veteran received disability compensation due to severe hearing loss in both ears, an amputated leg and scarring from burns that injured his face and neck. In a group counseling session, rather than receiving compassion, three bullying group members yelled bigoted remarks about his Muslim faith, brown, scarred skin and tentative walking. Hatred showed no bounds at this moment of "othering" this young man, until other group members challenged the abuse.

Historical and intergenerational trauma contribute to the multiple layers and types of trauma that service members, Veterans, and their families withstand. The ways that Veterans cope with multiple traumatic events must be understood in the context of protective factors that build resilience. Brave Heart (1999) introduced the idea of "historical trauma response": a constellation of clinical features that includes dwelling on ancestors and past events, survivor guilt, intrusive dreams, and depression. Native American communities, in addition to having suffered intergenerational loss, endure the highest rates of traumatic events, including interpersonal violence, child abuse and neglect, and bombardment of racial stereotypes (Evans-Campbell 2009). Combat Veterans with Native American heritage are not spared these additional traumatic stressors, which further complicate their reentry to their communities. Several innovative indigenous healing methods for PTSD have been successful in remediating symptoms and providing renewed meaning-making associated with adversity during combat (Evans-Campbell 2009). (See chapter 7 for more on this topic.)

AFTER-EFFECTS AND RESILIENCE FOLLOWING EXPOSURE TO COMBAT TRAUMA

Each war produces its own set of signature injuries, and in the case of post-9/11 combat Veterans, unique injuries are associated with distinctive weapons that inflicted very specific damage. Improvised explosive devices (IEDs), used in Iraq, caused physical and psychological devastation. Research data indicate a high incidence of co-occurring conditions in combat Veterans who served in Iraq. No single mental health disorder advances to the foreground; instead, there are high rates of post-traumatic stress (PTS) or post-traumatic stress disorder (PTSD), depression and suicidal thinking, traumatic brain injury, substance misuse, and intimate partner violence (IOM 2014; Yarvis 2011; Yarvis and Schiess 2008). Disturbingly, there is a one in four chance that female service members will be victimized by sexual assault in the overall population of female military service members (IOM 2014).

Lengthy separations from loved ones are described as the second-most-intense deployment stressor, even above the immediate threat to safety (IOM 2013). Although many service members deeply miss their loved ones, they have learned to control fears, suppress emotions, carefully disguise information, and parse words (O'Brien 1990; Tripp 2008). These capacities are helpful while deployed, yet they alienate other people at home, interfering with the reestablishment of a loving and trusting attachment.

A Veteran's untreated acute stress disorder or PTSD can deeply hurt family members and increase the stressors faced by the Veteran and his or her family members (Finley 2011). Known risk factors that heighten the possibility of developing a mental health problem include female gender; lower socioeconomic status; lower rank; absence of peer, social, and family support; and a preexisting history of unresolved childhood trauma (Basham and Miehls 2004; Finley 2011). Among Vietnam Veterans, various sociocultural factors served as mediating factors that increased PTSD. Many Veterans of color were assigned the most dangerous duties and subjected to outright discrimination from command, leading to more intense combat trauma exposure.

Many troops and their families harness a shared resilience to navigate a smooth reunion postdeployment (MacDermid and Riggs 2010). What are the protective factors that guard against developing psychopathology or mental health conditions? Current research literature focuses on constitutional hardiness, including strong physical health, sound mental health, and innate intelligence. In addition, a positive outlook, strong internal locus of control, belief in the purposefulness of one's actions, and an "esprit de corps" serve as protective factors (IOM 2013). Emotional support from family and friends, a hospitable welcome home from communities of origin, and thorough education about postdeployment adjustments also help with reintegration. During deployment, respectful and consistent leadership provides salutary effects, as do a clear-headed vision and adequate training. When wars are waged for ambiguous or questionable reasons, resulting in a loss of meaning and purpose, traumatic experiences increase.

GENERAL GUIDELINES FOR CLINICAL PRACTICE WITH COMBAT VETERANS AND THEIR FAMILIES

A question arises: how can we as clinical social workers be most effective in assisting combat Veterans and their families with their transitions home? What values, clinical knowledge, and skills are most relevant in our work? Throughout the years, I have distilled central principles that guide my practice. Basic parameters include following a "relationship-based, culturally responsive, antiracism-grounded, theoretically supported and research informed" approach (Basham 2009). Behavioral-health clinicians may or may not agree with these recommendations, but clinical social workers need to abide by the social work code of ethics, which privileges a respectful, nonjudgmental treatment alliance grounded in research and a synthesis of psychological and social theories (Coll, Weiss, and Yarvis, 2011). Moreover, cultural responsiveness, cultural humility, and an antiracism stance resonate with a professional commitment to social justice. This section examines each of these guidelines.

Relationship-Based

Clinicians, regardless of theoretical orientation, generally recognize the importance of a relationship-based treatment model since research evidence reveals that a sound therapeutic alliance represents a common factor promoting positive outcomes. Practice with combat Veterans and their families calls for a relationship-based approach, especially given the disruptions to attachment activated by exposure to ordinary stressors and traumatic events during deployment (Basham 2012a). Establishing effective engagement with military and Veteran clients requires the clinician to convey respect for and a familiarity with military culture. Most combat Veterans and their families express a wish for the treatment plan to be customized based on their particular biopsychosocial-spiritual needs. They often feel alienated when faced with an exclusive reliance on manualized treatment protocols that address specific diagnoses and symptom clusters. As one Veteran client noted, "I do not want to be viewed as a collection of body parts that requires a one-size-fits-all approach for all combat Veterans" and their families. Such an inflexible clinical stance can reinforce the "military/civilian divide," wherein service members feel objectified and misunderstood for the totality of their experiences. Within the context of a therapeutic alliance, clinicians, whether holding military or civilian status, need to focus on meaning-making related to loss of a military identity, losses and gains in reentry, and estrangement from family and community. Unlike the notion of a unidirectional relationship, the therapeutic alliance is bidirectional and mutually interactive. Just as we may influence our clients, our clients affect us. The work can be transformative for both client and clinician. We must also track transference/countertransference themes in order to address countertransference enactments and repair therapeutic ruptures.

Clinical Vignette and Discussion

Sgt. Maria Hernandez, a thirty-eight-year-old Honduran American Army reservist with a nursing degree, has served in the military for the past twelve years, including an eight-month tour of duty in Afghanistan. At the age of thirteen, she immigrated with her mother to the United States to escape political conflict, leaving behind many cherished family members and a father who had inflicted sexual abuse on her for five years starting when she was seven. She has been married for seventeen years to Jose, a third-generation Cuban American and a college-educated accountant. They have three children: Pablo, age sixteen; Delia, age seven; and Anna, age four. Prior to Sgt. Hernandez's first deployment, family life had been stable and fulfilling, with a sound network of social support consisting of extended family, spiritual community, friends, and colleagues.

While deployed, Sgt. Hernandez worked as a medic. She treated many service members who had suffered both devastating physical injuries and less apparent, "invisible" injuries. One day, Sgt. Hernandez and her unit sustained an IED blast that felled a beloved eighteen-year-old private whom she had "taken under wing," trying to relieve his fears when she first sensed his naiveté. She cradled him in her arms as he stopped breathing and died. She felt devastated that she could not have prevented the loss.

Following her return home, although Sgt. Hernandez expressed pride in what she had accomplished during her tour of duty, she also experienced insomnia, intense headaches, frightening flashbacks to scenes of death and carnage, and estrangement from her husband, children, and other family members. Numbness and detachment characterized her emotional state, alternating with roller-coaster outbursts of moods. Feelings of despair and hopelessness burdened her daily. She said, "I should be dead since I should have been able to save Private Gerson's life. I do not deserve to be alive." In arguments with her husband, the two alternated between yelling and berating each other and becoming noncommunicative, with long periods of detachment. Sgt. Hernandez said, "I have lost everything. I am a terrible mother, a useless wife, a failure as a soldier, and an incompetent medic." Her adolescent son frequently skipped school and fought with friends; Delia complained of stomachaches and bedwetting; Anna shunned her mother.

Not only did Sgt. Hernandez experience shame and guilt about witnessing the violent death of a beloved soldier; she also felt estranged from her husband and children. Pervasive anxiety, tension, and alienation disrupted the secure attachments that had existed within this family prior to deployment. The combined effects of separation, loss, and reunion were significant. Sgt. Hernandez's family practitioner recommended that she receive benzodiazepines for sleep and meet with a civilian psychologist who would provide a CBT protocol to address her symptoms of post-traumatic stress and depression. After meeting with the psychologist four times, she reported having trouble completing her homework assignments, charting her moods, and writing in a journal. Feelings of failure and ineptness consumed her. She did not believe that her shame related to the death of the young solder involving distorted thinking/cognitions or faulty attributions. The therapist commented that Sgt. Hernandez seemed avoidant and noncompliant with the protocol. Sgt. Hernandez quit treatment and sank deeper into a vegetative, depressed state, sleeping fifteen hours a day and remaining silent for hours at a time. When awake, she would swallow her medication with several glasses of vodka.

Was her worsened state a sign of reluctance to engage? Or was it an iatrogenic effect of incorrectly timed treatment? When a clinician attends solely to symptoms of PTS and depression, she ignores the total person within that person's complex social context. Who is Sgt. Hernandez in the context of her relations with her partner, children, parents, military buddies, and colleagues? How has she navigated the multiple losses of military identity and important relationships "back there, downrange"? What meaning does she make of the major changes that she and others have undergone in the past eight months?

Sadly, although Sgt. Hernandez presented with distinct symptoms of post-traumatic stress and depression, neither the family practitioner nor the psychologist engaged her and her husband in a thorough biopsychosocial-spiritual assessment. After returning to the primary care physician with heightened suicidal thoughts, she was referred to the local VA Medical Center, where she was assigned a graduate student in social work who would provide an extensive assessment and engage in a therapeutic relationship. Under the careful guidance of a supervisor, the student clinician met with Sgt. Hernandez on several occasions to conduct a complete review of the relevant biopsychosocial-spiritual factors affecting her. The work they did together identified strengths and vulnerabilities in the sociocultural/institutional, interpersonal, and intrapersonal realms.

In the sociocultural/institutional realm, Sgt. Hernandez and her husband revealed distinct resilience with a strong shared commitment to family, bilingualism, cultural pride, successful careers, stable finances, commitment to a faith-based community, emotional and sexual intimacy, and physically and psychologically healthy children. However, postdeployment, several of these strengths were undermined by financial challenges related to interference with work, conflicts within the extended family and faith-based community, distance from her Army unit, and cultural and racial trauma.

On an interpersonal level, the couple's strengths included sound problem-solving around parenting, stable finances, and shared goals and interests. Vulnerabilities included harsh verbal fighting, poor communication, and mutual disengagement from sexual and emotional intimacy.

On an intrapersonal level, Sgt. Hernandez's strengths include constitutionally sound physical health and "earned secure attachment" during predeployment. Her vulnerabilities included symptoms and patterns of PTS, depression, substance abuse, and mild traumatic brain injury. During deployment and postdeployment, Sgt. Hernandez demonstrated an insecure-preoccupied internal working model of attachment, and her husband evinced a disrupted working model of attachment (insecure-ambivalent). Prior to deployment, both of them had demonstrated capacities for secure attachment with each other and their children. Sgt. Hernandez expressed quandaries consonant with all twelve of the paradoxes discussed earlier in the chapter (Castro, Kintzle, and Hassan 2015).

Cultural Responsiveness

Cultural responsiveness goes beyond the more static concept of cultural competence, which relates to developing knowledge, values, and skills. Cultural responsiveness involves a dynamic interchange between client and clinician to explore the meaning-making processes related to race, ethnicity, gender, sexual orientation, and other sociocultural factors. We presume that a client self-defines a complex nexus of social identities that shape worldviews and internalized self-images. Efforts should be made to avoid stereotypical assumptions while inviting discussion about these issues.

More specifically, how does cultural responsiveness, or cultural humility, relate to issues of diversity with combat Veterans' postdeployment? First, to practice effectively with combat Veterans and their families, it is important to know the values, customs, and hierarchical structure of the military. Values of responsibility, duty, courage, self-sacrifice, loyalty, and an "esprit de corps" provide scaffolding for the lives of military families. These families commit to a set of rules and directives aimed to protect the well-being and safety of others. Typically, the military stresses the notion of "oneness" and homogeneity, the antitheses of diversity and heterogeneity. As service members bond with each other and emphasize their common goals in accomplishing a mission, they often experience a sense of brotherhood or sisterhood. This is not usually the time to emphasize individuality; a shared purpose is vital to ensuring safety and effectiveness. Yet what occurs at the end of a day, when service members return to their domiciles and share meals? Individual differences inevitably emerge, requiring recognition and an appreciation for diversity.

The following excerpt from Sgt. Hernandez's case file illustrates her and her family's strengths and vulnerabilities in this area:

> [The couple's shared] primary language of origin (Spanish) and spiritual belief system (Catholicism), mutual pride in ethnic heritage, and fluent bilingualism emerged as central positive influences in their lives. Resilience was evident for Sgt. Hernandez up until the middle of her deployment, when combat trauma intensified and the family back home experienced the gradual erosion of all of these strengths. Sgt. Hernandez was reared in a home that strongly valued the primacy of children and elders, although she fiercely challenged the constraints of patriarchy and disempowerment, especially the negative effects of sexual abuse from her birth father. Her military identity is very strong yet shaken by what she considers her "perceived errors" in failing to save the life of a beloved fallen soldier. Although she embraced her roles as a mother, wife, and daughter, she also expressed deep loyalty to her fellow soldiers. In both her individual and couple therapy, the clinicians validated these important relationships and assisted Sgt. Hernandez in reconnecting with important members of her Army unit. These renewed relationships appeared to hold genuine importance in healing the attachment ruptures within the family.

Antiracism Grounded

The third principle that undergirds effective clinical social work involves an antiracism commitment. This theme starts with identifying the effects of racism in individual, interpersonal, and institutional frameworks. An antiracism stance requires recognizing and appreciating multiple social identities while foregrounding race and antiracism. Identifying and addressing abuses of power and privilege are woven into the context of the therapeutic alliance.

Sgt. Hernandez at age thirteen entered a new school in a racially and culturally homogeneous urban environment. She was bullied by three adolescent girls, who hurled mean, racialized comments about her skin color and her accented English. When she was a combat Veteran, one of her officers in command shouted racialized and misogynistic slurs against her on a regular basis. After she spoke up, she was reprimanded for "insubordinate re-marks." While talking about this memory from her deployment, she remembered the earlier racialized bullying from high school, which had damaged her emerging self-esteem. In discussing the corrosive effects of cul-tural and racial trauma, she started to regain more agency and hopefulness while reasserting pride in her ethnic identity. The social work student clini-cian and Sgt. Hernandez explored the policies and procedures at the VA Medical Center that addressed issues of racism. On the internal and interpersonal levels, distinct progress was made, while on an institutional level, slow progress unfolded in identifying needs for a pro-social-justice agenda within the outpatient behavioral health unit.

Martin Luther King Jr. reminded us that "we will remember not the words of our enemies, but the silence of our friends." Holding a values-based, antiracism commitment and implementing constructive interventions can meaningfully inform any clinical social work practice.

Theoretically Supported

Once a relationship-based and culturally responsive therapeutic alliance is established between client and clinician, reviewing the utility of various the-oretical models provides a conceptual framework that serves as both an-chor and compass for the multimodal treatment plan. Several social and psychological theories support the current psychotherapeutic approaches for treating combat Veterans and their families. Contemporary psychodynamic and attachment theories are very useful in their attunement to meaning-making, transference/countertransference phenomena, and reparative therapeutic alliances focused on rebuilding secure attachments during the postdeployment period. Many of the empirically supported clinical models that aim to treat PTSD, depression, and substance abuse are grounded in a cognitive-behavioral framework. Other deeply relevant practice models may also be supported by clinical evidence.

Interventions with the Hernandez family called for a synthesis of mod-els. Current psychodynamic relational theories shed clarity on the internal-ization processes of negative introjections that fuel the shame-based moral injury and low self-esteem that are often associated with responses to com-bat exposure and cultural and racial trauma. Trauma theories offer in-depth neurobiological understanding of the traumatic-stress response and methods to promote affect regulation and to attain an "optimal" zone of arousal. Attachment theories provide a perspective for examining the "working models" forged in early years that reveal similar or changed structure based on the availability of "earned attachment security." Important racial and feminist theories contribute significant perspectives to a thorough and complex biopsychosocial-spiritual assessment, which, in turn, guides the development of a coherent practice plan.

Sgt. Hernandez and her husband entered couple therapy with disrupted attachment patterns of interaction related to the corrosive forces of deployment and combat stressors. Although Sgt. Hernandez had developed an insecure attachment working model in childhood, prior to deployment she benefited from the love, consistency, and earned attachment in her marriage. The foundational years of the marriage were aided by the fact that her partner expressed a relatively secure working model of attachment. The construct of the "circle of security" is also relevant here. It focuses on a developmental process in which children, adolescents, and adults have primary attachment figures whom they turn to in times of uncertainty and distress. Although the Hernandezes had attained a circle of security within their marriage and in their immediate and extended family, these bonds were shattered during and following deployment (Basham 2008). Within a couple therapy framework, Sgt. Hernandez, her husband, and their children were able to reconstruct sound circles of security.

Research-Informed

Finally, clinical social workers need to determine the best practices available based on research-informed evidence. Making the decision is strengthened by completing a comprehensive biopsychosocial-spiritual assessment to shape the practice plan. Empirically supported practice models for mental health disorders are typically subjected to randomized, controlled research trials with different populations (often considered the gold standard for efficacy).

When Sgt. Hernandez reported more stability in her physical health, with sound sleep, fewer nightmares, relief from suicidal thoughts, and enhanced support from her parents and friends, the phase I trauma-informed therapy tasks of safety, self-care, and stabilization were realized (see the section that follows). At this point Sgt. Hernandez felt prepared to address the tragic loss of the young private killed in the IED blast—which had also caused both physical wounds and "invisible injuries associated with PTSD" to Sgt. Hernandez herself. In addition to continuing with couple and individual therapy, she entered a twelve-session cognitive-processing therapy protocol, a manualized treatment program for PTSD that is focused on building tolerance to bear the feelings associated with horrific traumatic events.

Although many of the primary treatment models recommended for military and Veteran clients focus on symptom relief, the drop-out rates are very high (Carr 2011). Therefore, we must also turn to alternative models that are supported by emerging evidence, such as brief psychodynamic therapy, attachment-based practice, complementary and alternative medicine (e.g., EMDR, sensorimotor processing), mindfulness-based stress reduction (MBSR), and couple and family therapy (Basham 2008, 2014; Fredman, Monson, and Adair 2011; Johnson 2002).

PSYCHOTHERAPY MODELS

This section describes a range of psychotherapeutic approaches grounded in various theoretical frameworks (e.g. psychodynamic, trauma, cognitive-behavioral, family) and diverse modalities (e.g., individual, group, and couple/family) that can be used in working with military and Veteran clients.

Individual Psychotherapy

Individual psychotherapy models that address the effects of combat trauma are typically designed in three phases (Basham 2014; Monson and Fredson 2012; Fredson, Monson, and Adair 2011). These phases, summarized both here and in the subsection on couple and family therapy (below), provide a scaffolding for all modalities. Phase I focuses on self-care, stabilization, safety, and building a context for change. Veteran clients work on attending to physical and mental health concerns, rebuilding important attachments, establishing a safe home environment, and developing affect-regulation skills. With the explosion of literature related to the mind-body connections associated with trauma, various somatic treatment approaches have been utilized effectively to balance emotions (Basham 2014). For example, somatic experiencing (Levine 2005), sensorimotor processing therapy (Ogden, Minton, and Pain 2006) and mindfulness-based stress reduction (Kabat-Zinn 2005) address both affect regulation and stress reduction. Many traumatized Veterans heal within community by building relationships among Veteran peers (Basham 2014; Herman 1992; Tick 2005).

Once a Veteran client has stabilized in phase I therapy, she may start to discuss the effects of traumatic events in her everyday life, which constitutes phase II. The focus is on narrating the trauma, reflecting on its meaning and legacies, and addressing unresolved grieving. After gaining perspective on how traumatic events have affected relationship development in the client's inner and outer worlds, the therapist will also want to devote attention to the client's intersecting social identities. Phase III involves transitioning from an identity exclusively defined by trauma to one of greater creativity, agency, and engagement, with post-traumatic growth (Tedeschi and Calhoun 2004).

Group Psychotherapy

Kingsley (2007) strongly asserts the need to provide psychodynamically focused group therapy that facilitates the building of trust and connections for combat Veterans, who often feel alone and alienated from everyone. When the membership of a therapy group includes fellow Veterans, group members may find it far easier to address their reintegration into civilian life. In discussing their stories and concerns, they feel understood by others who have shared similar experiences. Not only does the group modality offer a phase-oriented entry into other therapeutic approaches; it also serves vital functions in restoring a sense of attachment and reconnection to valued others.

Couple and Family Therapy

Couple and family therapy with combat Veterans focuses on a range of themes. Psychodynamic and attachment-based models attend to rebalancing disrupted affect regulation, promoting mentalization, strengthening attachments that have been dismantled by deployment, and reconnecting with partners, children, and other family members during reintegration (Basham 2008). In contrast, cognitive-behavioral conjoint therapy for PTSD addresses relational patterns as well as cognitive distortions. Integrative behavioral couple therapy presents psychoeducation and interventions that change faulty cognitive attributions (Basham 2014). The phase-oriented attachment-based couple therapy model for postdeployed service members involves three phases, touched on above. Phase I tasks include: (1) ensuring safety; (2) developing self-care; (3) improving affect regulation; and (4) establishing a context for change. Phase II tasks include: (1) reflecting on the trauma narratives; (2) grieving multiple losses and identities; (3) exploring current and intergenerational legacies of the "victim-victimizer-bystander" trauma triangle through projective identification processes; and (4) developing mentalization. Phase III tasks include: (1) consolidating new perspectives, attitudes, and behaviors; (2) expanding exploration of intersecting social identities; (3) enhancing empathy and capacities for mentalization; (4) strengthening emotional and sexual intimacy; and (5) achieving social vindication (Basham 2008, 2012a, 2012b).

Phase II work with Sgt. Hernandez and her husband involved addressing the interchanging roles of the victim-victimizer-bystander trauma scenario (Basham 2008; Staub 1989). After completing phase I tasks, the couple discussed the pernicious pattern of each partner enacting the role of a helpless, ignored, invalidated, and mistreated "victim" alternating with that of an irritable, rejecting, hostile, verbally abusive "victimizer." At other times, each partner would shift into the role of "detached bystander." Since both partners were exposed to childhood abuses and cultural and racial trauma, each of them has introjected "negative shame-based objects" that fuel the dynamic movement of this shifting, repetitive drama. As each partner gained more awareness of this destructive process, they developed stronger empathy for the other and vowed to work actively to disrupt this circular relational pattern.

Add two clinicians to the mix, and we bring our own personal and professional perspectives to the "trauma triangle." The student clinician noted her rescuing tendencies and became able to modulate her responses and access her disavowed aggression. As the couple therapist, I often felt drawn into an irritable, frustrated, "victimizing" stance or into that of an ineffective victim. The ongoing scrutiny of these intersecting, projective identification processes enabled both clinicians to "hold" and "contain" disavowed feelings as well as possible while strong affects emerged for both the clinicians and the clients. These countertransference responses were not actively discussed in sessions. Instead, the feelings and thoughts were observed, noted, and reflected on in clinical consultation to minimize potential enactments and allow the couple to openly talk about their disavowed feelings and behaviors.

Overall, this couple demonstrated distinct progress in remediating symptoms of post-traumatic stress, building self-care and stress-reduction methods, clarifying and challenging destructive relational patterns, opening communication with their children, and restoring connections with their extended families, faith-based community, and Veteran's outreach group.

SUMMARY

This chapter defines combat trauma, places it in historical context, discusses types of trauma, and outlines the distinguishing features of combat trauma. The role of sociocultural factors in shaping trauma-related symptoms, risk factors, protective factors, and outcomes is discussed. As many Veterans have told me, they recognize the horrors of war yet are able to come to terms with their actions in the context of accomplishing a mission. They are often spared negative aftereffects. Yet, when their senses of purpose and meaning-making are challenged, Veterans are faced with intense internal conflicts. Typical responses to deployment and combat stressors are outlined in the discussion of paradoxes as developed by Castro, Kintzle, and Hassan (2015).

Because responses to combat trauma vary a great deal during reintegration, many service members, Veterans, and their families benefit from a relationship-based, culturally responsive, antiracism-grounded, theoretically supported, research-informed, and phase-oriented clinical social work practice model. Vignettes based on the case of Sgt. Hernandez and her family illustrate ways of adapting to deployment and combat trauma stressors with noteworthy resilience. Complex issues related to post-traumatic stress, depression, moral injury, relational conflicts, and heightened anxiety among the children are also addressed.

A statement made by the couple in their last session offers a poignant message: "Although eight months ago we had lost all love for each other, feeling like total strangers in the same home, now we have accepted that each of us has changed during this past deployment and reentry, yet we have finally reclaimed hope that we can navigate any tough path together!" A capacity to restore caring connections amid personal and relational turmoil represents impressive perseverance and energetic striving.

REFERENCES

Adler, A. B., Britt, T. W., Castro, C., McGurk, D., and Bliese, P. D. (2011). Effect of transition home from combat on risk-taking and health-related behaviors. *Journal of Traumatic Stress, 24* (4), 381–389.

Allen, I. A. (1998). PTSD among African-Americans. In A. J. Marsalla, M. J. Friedman, E. T. Gerrity, and M. Scrufield (Eds.), *Ethnocultural Aspects of Posttraumatic Stress Disorder: Issues, Research and Clinical Implications* (pp. 209–238). Washington, DC: American Psychological Association.

American Psychiatric Association. 2013. *Diagnostic and Statistical Manual of Mental Health Disorders* (5th ed.). Arlington, VA: American Psychiatric Association.

Appelgate, J. S. and Shapiro, J. R. (2005). *Neurobiology for clinical social work: Theory and practice.* New York: Norton.

Basham K. (2008). Homecoming as safe haven or the new front: Attachment and detachment in military couples. *Clinical Social Work Journal, 36* (1), 83–96. DOI:10.1007s10615-007-0138-9.

——. (2009). Commentary on keynote lecture Jonathan Shay 6/29/09. The trials of war: Odysseus returns from Iraq and Afghanistan. *Smith College Studies in Social Work, 3/4,* 283–286.

——. (2012a). Couple therapy for redeployed military and Veteran couples. In A. Rubin, E. L. Weiss, and J. E. Coll. *Handbook of Military Social Work* (pp. 443–465). Hoboken, NJ: Wiley.

——. (2012b). Facilitators and barriers in effective clinical practice with redeployed military and Veteran couples. *Military Behavioral Health Journal, 1,* Los Angeles: Center for Innovative Research with Military and Veteran Families Publications.

——. (2014). Returning servicewomen and Veterans. In A. Gitterman (Ed.), *Handbook of Social Work Practice with Vulnerable and Resilient Populations* (pp. 441–461). New York: Columbia University Press.

Basham, K. K., and Miehls, D. (2004). *Transforming the Legacy: Couple Therapy with Survivors of Childhood Trauma.* New York: Columbia University Press.

Bragin, M. (2010). Can anyone here know who I am? Co-constructing meaningful narratives with combat veterans. *Clinical Social Work Journal, 38,* 316–326.

Brave Heart, M. Y. H. (1999). Gender differences in the historical response among the Lakota. *Journal of Health and Social Policy, 10* (4), 1–21.

Calhoun, L. G., and Tedeschi, R. G. (2008). The paradox of struggling with trauma: Guidelines for practice and directions for research. In L. G. Calhoun and R. G. Techeschi (Eds.), *Trauma, Recovery and Growth: Positive Psychological Perspectives on Posttraumatic Stress* (pp. 325–337). Hoboken, NJ: Wiley.

Carr, R. B. (2011). Combat and human existence: Toward an intersubjective approach to combat-related PTSD. *Psychoanalytic Psychology, 28* (4), 471–496.

Castro, C. A., and Adler, A. B. (2011). Military mental health training: Building resilience. In S. M. Southwick, B. T. Litz, D. Charney, and M. J. Friedman (Eds.), *Resilience and Mental Health: Challenges Across the Lifespan* (pp. 323–339). Cambridge: Cambridge University Press.

Castro, C. A., Hoge, C. W., Milliken, C. W., McGurk, D., Adler, A. B., Cox, A., and Bliese, P. D. (2006). *Battlemind Training: Transitioning Home from Combat*. Silver Spring, MD: Walter Reed Army Institute of Research Division of Psychiatry and Neuroscience.

Castro. C. A., and Kintzle, S. (2014). Suicides in the military: The post-modern combat Veteran and the Hemingway effect. *Current Psychiatry Reports, 16*, 460. http://dx.dol.org/101007/s11920-014-0460-1.

——. (2017). *The State of the American Veteran: The San Francisco Study*. Los Angeles: USC Suzanne Dworak-Peck School for Social Work Center for Innovation and Research on Veterans and Military Families.

Castro, C. A., Kintzle, S. and Hassan, A. M. (2015). The combat Veteran paradox: Paradoxes and dilemmas encountered with reintegrating combat Veterans and the agencies that support them. *Traumatology, 21* (4), 299–310.

Coll, J. E., Weiss, E. L., and Yarvis, J. S. (2011). No one leaves unchanged: Insights for civilian mental health care professionals into the military experience and culture. *Social Work in Health Care, 50* (7), 487–500.

Cozolino, L. (2010). *The Neuroscience of Psychotherapy: Healing the Social Brain*. New York: Norton.

Dass-Brailsford, P. (2007). *A Practical Approach to Trauma: Empowering Interventions*. Thousand Oaks, CA: Sage.

DeGruy, J. (2005). *Post-Traumatic Slavery Syndrome: American Legacy of Ending Injury and Healing*. Milwaukee, WI: Uptone Press.

De Jong, J. T. V. M., Komproe, I. H., Spinazzola, J., van der Kolk, B. S., and van Ommeren, M.H. (2005). DESNOS in three post-conflict settings: Assessing cross-cultural construct equivalence. *Journal of Traumatic Stress, 28* (1), 13–21.

Dombo, E. A., Gray, C., and Early, B. P. (2013). The trauma of moral injury: Beyond the battlefield. *Journal of Religion and Spirituality in Social Work: Social Thought, 32*, 197–210.

Edgerton, R. B. (2009). *Hidden Heroism: Black Soldiers in America's Wars*. New York: Westview Press.

Evans-Campbell, T. A. (2009). Social work practice with Native Americans. In A. Roberts (Ed.), *Social Work Desk Reference* (pp. 949–954). New York: Oxford University Press.

Fairbairn, R. (1943). The war neuroses: Their nature and significance. *The British Medical Journal 1* (4284), 183–186.

Figley, C. (1995). *Compassion Fatigue: Coping with Secondary Stress Disorder in Those Who Treat the Traumatized.* New York: Bruner/Mazel.

Finley, E. P. (2011). *Fields of Combat: Understanding PTSD Among Veterans of Iraq and Afghanistan.* Ithaca, NY: Cornell University Press.

Fredman, S. J., Monson, C., and Adair, K. C. (2011). Implementing cognitive-behavioral conjoint therapy with the recent generation of Veterans and their partners. *Journal of Clinical Psychology, 18* (1), 120–135.

Grinker, R., and Spiegel, J. P. (1945). *Men Under Stress.* London: Pickle Partners Publishing Press.

Grossman, D. (2009). *On Killing: The Psychological Cost of Learning to Kill in War and Society.* New York: Little, Brown and Company.

Grossman, D., and Christensen, L. W. (2008). *On Combat: The Psychology and Physiology of Deadly Conflict in War and in Peace* (3rd ed.). Millstadt, IL: Human Factor Research Group Inc. Publications.

Herman, J. (1992). *Trauma and Recovery.* New York: Basic Books.

Hoge, C. W. (2010). *Once a Warrior Always a Warrior: Navigating the Transition from Combat to Home—Including Combat Stress, PTSD, and mTBI.* Guilford, CT: Globe Pequot Press.

——. (2011). The paradox of PTSD: Bridging gaps in understanding the improving treatment. *VVA Veteran, 31,* 29–31.

——. (2011). Interventions for war-related posttraumatic stress disorder meeting Veterans where they are. *Journal of the American Medical Association, 306* (5), 461–568.

Hoge, C. W., Castro, C. A., Messer, S. C. (2004). Combat duty in Iraq and Afghanistan, mental health problems and barriers to care. *New England Journal of Medicine, 351,* 13.

IOM (Institute of Medicine). (2013). *Returning Home from Iraq and Afghanistan: Assessment of Readjustment Needs of Veterans.* Washington, DC: National Academy of Sciences.

——. (2014). *Treatment for Posttraumatic Stress Disorder in Military and Veteran Populations: Final Assessment.* Washington, DC: National Academy of Sciences.

Japucak, M. and Varra, E. M. (2011). Treating Iraq and Afghanistan war Veterans who are at high risk for suicide. *Cognitive and Behavioral Practice, 18,* 85–97.

Johnson, S. (2002). *Emotionally Focused Couple Therapy with Trauma Survivors: Strengthening Attachment Bonds.* New York: Guilford Press.

Kingsley, G. (2007). Contemporary group treatment of combat-related posttraumatic stress disorder. *Journal of the American Academy of Psychoanalysis and Dynamic Psychiatry*, *35* (1), 51–71.

Kudler, H. (2007). The need for psychodynamic principles in outreach to new combat Veterans and their families. *Journal of the American Academy of Psychoanalysis and Dynamic Psychiatry*, *35* (1), 39–50.

Levine, P. (2005). *Healing Trauma: A Pioneering Program for Recognizing the Wisdom of Your Body*. Boulder, CO: Sounds True.

Litz, B. T., Lebovitz, L., Gray, M. J., and Nash, W. (2017). *Adaptive Disclosure: A New Treatment for Military Trauma, Loss and Moral Injury*. New York: Guilford Press.

MacDermid, S. M., and Riggs, D. (Eds.) (2010). *Risk and Resilience in Military Families*. New York: Springer.

McCarty, N. (2018). 2.77 million served since 9/11. *Forbes* (March 20, 2018).

McEwen, B. S. (1999). Allostasis and allostatic load: Implications for neuropsychopharmacology. *Neuropsychopharmacology*, *22* (2), 10–24.

Miller, J., and Garran, A. M. (2010). *Racism in the U.S.: Implications for the Helping Professionals*. Pacific Grove, CA: Brooks Cole Publications.

Morris, D. J. (2015). *The Evil Hours: A Biography of Posttraumatic Stress Disorder*. New York: Houghton Mifflin Harcourt.

Nash, W., Carper, T. L., Mills, M., Au, T., Goldsmith, A., and Litz, T. (2013). Psychological evaluation of the moral injury events scale. *Military Medicine*, *178* (6), 646–652.

Nicholson, A. (2012). *Fighting to Serve: Behind the Scenes in the War to Repeal "Don't Ask–Don't Tell."* Chicago: Chicago Review Press.

O'Brien, T. (1990). *The Things They Carried*. New York: Houghton-Mifflin.

Ogden, P., Minton, K., and Pain, C. (2006). *Trauma and the Body: A Sensorimotor Approach to Psychotherapy*. New York: Norton.

Ogden, T. (1982). *Projective Identification and Psychotherapeutic Technique*. New York: Jason Aronson.

Porges, S. W. (2011). *The Polyvagal Theory: Neurophysiological Foundations of Emotions, Attachment, Communication and Self-Regulation*. New York: Norton.

Reynolds, G. M., and Shendruk, A. (2018). Demographics in the U.S. military. *Council on Foreign Relations CNA Population Representation in the Military Services: Fiscal year 2016 Summary Report*. April 24. http://www.cfr.org/article/demographics-us-military.

Shaw, J. A. (2005). The acute traumatic moment—psychic trauma in war: Psycho-analytic perspectives. *Journal of the American Academy of Psychoanalysis and Dynamic Psychiatry, 35* (1), 23–38.

Shay, J. (1994). *Achilles in Vietnam: Combat Trauma and the Undoing of Character.* New York: Scribner.

Sherman, N. (2005). *Stoic Warriors: The Ancient Philosophy Behind the Military Mind.* New York: Oxford University Press.

Siegel, D. (2007). *Mindful Brain: Regulation and Attunement in the Cultivation of Well-Being.* New York: Norton.

——. (2010). *The Mindful Therapist.* New York: Norton.

Staub E. (1989). *The Roots of Evil: The Origins of Genocide and Other Group Violence.* New York: Cambridge University Press.

Stolorow, R. D. (2007). *Trauma and Human Existence: Autobiographical, Psychoanalytic, and Philosophical Reflections.* New York: Analytic Press.

Tanelian, T., and Jaycox, L. H. (2008). (Eds.). *Invisible Wounds of War: Psychological and Cognitive Injuries, Their Consequences, and Services to Assist Recovery.* Santa Monica, CA: RAND Corporation.

Terr, L. (1999). Childhood trauma: An outline and review. *American Journal of Orthopsychiatry, 148,* 10–20.

Tick, E. (2005). *War and the Soul: Healing Our Nation's Veterans from Posttraumatic Stress Disorder.* Wheaton, IL: Quest Books.

Tedeschi, R. G., and Calhoun, L. G. (2004). *Post-Traumatic Growth: Conceptual Foundation and Empirical Evidence.* Philadelphia, PA: Lawrence Erlbaum.

Tripp, E. F. (2008). *Surviving Iraq: Soldier's Stories*, Northampton, MA: Olive Branch Press.

van der Kolk, B. A. (2003). Posttraumatic stress disorder and the nature of trauma. In M.F. Solomon and D.J. Siegel (Eds.), *Healing Trauma: Attachment, Mind, Body and Brain* (pp. 168–195). New York: Norton.

Yarvis, J. S. (2011). A civilian social worker's guide to the treatment of war-induced PTSD. *Social Work in Health Care, 50* (1), 51–72. DOI:10.1080/00981389.2010.518856.

Yarvis, J. S., and Schiess, L. (2008). Subthreshold posttraumatic stress disorder (PTSD) as a predictor of depression, alcohol use, and health problems in Veterans. *Journal of Workplace Behavioral Health, 23* (4), 395–424.

Young, A. (1995). *Harmony of Illusion: Inventing PTSD.* Princeton, NJ: Princeton University Press.

11

Trauma and Incarceration: Historical Relevance and Present-Day Significance for African American Women

▸ LAVERNE D. MARKS

MORE THAN TWO MILLION men and women are incarcerated in U.S. prisons and jails, more than in any other nation. The call for law and order is in contest with demands to end a system that has been enormously destructive to the social, political, and economic well-being of this society. An aspect of mass incarceration that is of deep concern but somewhat hidden from public view is the psychological toll that this country's brutal criminal justice system takes on individuals, families, and communities. One of the most overlooked populations bearing the brunt of this inhumane system is African American women, who are overrepresented among justice-involved individuals. The Sentencing Project (2018) reported that in 2016 the rate of imprisonment for African American women was 96 per 100,000. That is two times the rate of imprisonment for White women, which is 49 per 100,000 (2). Latinx women were incarcerated at 1.4 times the rate of White women, or 67 per 100,000. Marc Mauer (2013) of The Sentencing Project observes that this 2016 rate is a decrease from a high in 2000 of Black women's incarceration at six times the rate of White women.

Understanding the history of African American women within the criminal justice system helps to clarify how the U.S. penal system functions as a tool of race, class, gender, and economic domination. Knowing this history also gives a fuller picture of the treatment of Black women in America and enhances our understanding of societal expressions of punishment, shaming, personal responsibility, and ideas about Black women. Berzoff has pointed out that applying a psychodynamic lens to these issues reminds us that "race, social class, ethnicity, culture and transgenerational transmission of trauma are factors that figure into who we are" (2012, 8). Black women's involvement in the criminal justice system is a neglected part of that history. To know the history is to understand the racism and trauma that justice-involved Black women experienced in the past and continue to struggle against today. Understanding brings awareness of the psychological damage that present-day dehumanizing practices of mass incarceration inflict on millions of individuals.

This chapter explores the history of Black women in the U.S. criminal justice system and the trauma that has been inflicted by this system. One particular focus will be on shame, a pernicious aspect of trauma engendered by the prison experience, and how it uniquely affects Black women. Comments are included from formerly incarcerated Black women about their experience of incarceration and about shame. They offer suggestions for more effective clinical work with this nontraditional population.

RACE, GENDER, AND THE HISTORY OF PUNISHMENT

The history of brutal punishment of Black women stretches back to their enslavement. Activist and political theorist Angela Y. Davis (2003) said of the condition of enslaved Black women, "As slaves, they were directly and often brutally disciplined for conduct considered perfectly normal in a context of freedom" (67). The memoir of Harriet Jacobs ([1861] 1987), a formerly enslaved woman, offered a powerful narrative account of this brutality. Jacobs described how an enslaved woman who had recently given birth was separated from her newborn child at auction. In response to her tearful plea for mercy the slave owner replied, "You have let your tongue run too far, damn you." Jacobs wrote that "she had forgotten that it was a crime for a slave to tell who was the father of her child" (13).

Enslaved individuals were most often punished by whipping because it was not cost-effective for the slave owner to lose productive labor through confinement. Whippings, often done publicly, were also a powerful means of intimidation. Whippings were inflicted for such offenses as running away (seeking freedom), refusing to become the sexual partner of a man selected by the slave owner or of the slave owner himself, failing to meet a production quota, or talking back. Enslaved individuals could be whipped for the slightest offense or for no reason at all. Enslaved females were not spared the brutality of the lash. Formerly enslaved Elizabeth Sparks (1994) said of her owner, "Beat women! Why sure he beat women. Beat women just like men. Beat women naked and wash them down with brine" (28).

Following emancipation in 1865, the South instituted Black Codes, a legal means to control the movements and actions of the newly freed population (Bennett 1961; Blackmon 2008; Litwack 1979; Quarles 1964). Formerly enslaved individuals needed passes to leave their place of employment, were fined or imprisoned if they were unemployed, needed a license to preach, and could be fined or imprisoned for what was deemed an insulting act or gesture. Enforcement of the Black Codes, coupled with the need for the bankrupt South to rebuild its economic base, swept many formerly enslaved men and women into a hellish system that terrorized, killed, and maimed thousands of them. Described by Blackmon in his book *Slavery by Another Name* (2008), this was the convict lease system.

Under convict lease, a private contractor paid a commission to the state to lease an imprisoned person for use as a laborer. The leased individuals built levees, cleared swampland, laid railroad tracks, grew cotton, mined coal, and worked in turpentine camps and sawmills. W. E. B. DuBois (1901) described convict lease as "slavery in private hands of persons convicted of crimes and misdemeanors in the courts" (738). Of the women caught in the system, he said, "Women were mingled indiscriminately with the men, both working and sleeping, and dressed often in men's clothing" (741). This was a system where brutality knew no limits, and murder of prisoners was carried out with impunity. Mancini (1996) summed up the discounting of the worth of these human beings in the title of his book: *One Dies, Get Another*.

A critical missing piece of the history of convict lease is the full story of the presence of Black women who were imprisoned under this system. The omission was addressed by historian Talitha L. LeFlouria in her book *Chained in Silence: Black Women and Convict Labor in the New South* (2015), in which she meticulously documented the inhumane treatment of imprisoned Black women under the lucrative convict lease system in Georgia from 1868 to 1908. She exposed the "terrifying social encounters, demoralizing living conditions, inhumane violence, and astonishing work-related abuses Black female convicts endured in the New South" (7). LeFlouria noted that Black women represented 98 percent of the female prison population. In addition to working alongside the men plowing, felling trees, sawing lumber, digging ditches, firing bricks, forging iron, and building roads, they bore the additional gendered burden of cooking, cleaning, and washing and mending clothes.

Under convict lease, punishments were tantamount to torture. The women were subjected to such barbaric practices as *bucking*, in which a partially or completely nude woman was made to lie across a log and viciously beaten. They could be forced to *ride the blind pig*, which involved hoisting them up so that their feet barely touched the ground and then leaving them hanging for hours. They could be put in the *sweat box*, a small wooden crate that was left in the hot sun, or they might be given the *water cure*, which called for a hose to be turned on the face until water filled the nostrils and mouth, flowed into the lungs, and ran out the ears. LeFlouria noted the sexual overtones of many of these punishments. She wrote, "During these sexualized attacks that, in many ways, animated white men's perceptions about black female licentiousness, women prisoners were ordered to strip (usually from the waist down), while others were whipped 'stark naked.' With their bosoms, buttocks, and vaginas exposed, captives were beaten mercilessly, in the presence of their jailed counterparts—male and female" (71).

Sarah Haley (2016) also documented the story of Black women imprisoned in the convict lease system in Georgia in the latter third of the nineteenth century and the early twentieth century. She recounted how "overseers directed and choreographed naked whipping rituals before a mixed audience of other prisoners, producing a spectacle of gendered racial terror. Rape was sometimes exacted in view of other prisoners in the open structure of the camp" (92). The level of trauma and shame that must have resulted from these practices is hard to imagine.

Black women have always been disproportionately represented among those confined in U.S. prisons and jails. Leslie Patrick-Stamp (1995) researched the presence of Black women in Philadelphia's Jail and Penitentiary House at Walnut Street, which in 1790 became the nation's first state prison. Her review of prison records and census data revealed that in 1820, Black women were 3 percent of Pennsylvania's female population but 52.9 percent of the female population at the Walnut Street Jail. White

women, who were 97 percent of the state's female population, formed
47.1 percent of the female prison population. A decade later Black women
were still 3 percent of the state's female population but 70 percent of the
female prison population.

Patrick-Stamp noted that larceny was the largest category of offenses for
which both Black women and Black men served time. She wrote, "It is generally accepted that there is a correlation between poverty, race, and crime
that leads to imprisonment" (1995, 128)

This finding of nonviolent economic crimes being a central factor in Black
women's imprisonment was supported by Anne M. Butler's (1997) research
of Black women's incarceration in nineteen Western states from 1865 to 1915.
Butler reported that "in every geographical region, including the West, African American women incarcerated relative to the area's demography, sur-
passed that of any other group, including black males" (92). The majority of
crimes committed were property crimes or nonviolent crimes and "tended
to reflect the limited economics of their lives" (92).

As Butler did, Cheryl D. Hicks (2010) used the U.S. census of 1910 to
highlight the disproportionate rate of Black women's imprisonment. Her research centered on New York State. She wrote, "In 1910, the U.S. census
noted that Black people comprised just 1.5 percent of the state population,
but in that same year Black women represented 40 percent of the Auburn
prison population. . . . This trend would continue throughout the prison's
existence, even when black women's numbers dropped in certain years"
(131–132).

The media promoted ideas of Black women who broke the law as being
inherently violent, deviant, dangerous to polite society, and in need of
containment. Haley noted that Black women were "subjected to vicious
journalistic representations." They were referred to as "crazy negresses,"
"leather-skinned negresses," and "jet black negresses" (2016, 36).

This language is comparable to that found in the degrading stereotype
of the "Colored Amazon," a term that was used throughout the United
States in reference to Black justice-involved women from the late eighteenth
through the early twentieth centuries. Historian Kali N. Gross (2006)
researched the condition of Black women lawbreakers in Philadelphia between 1880 and 1910. She reported how this stereotype was used to paint a
picture of incarcerated Black women as threatening, violent criminals who
needed to be removed from society. She stated that the Colored Amazon

was considered to be "large, dark, dangerous and hypersexual." Although those early terms to describe justice-involved Black women are no longer used, vestiges of the stereotype live on. One of the ugliest stereotypes that leaves Black women exposed to sexual violence both inside and beyond the prison walls is that of the hypersexual woman, the Jezebel. This myth has been used as a cover for rape since the days of slavery. Modern versions of the stereotype are evident in the use of such terms as "hot mammas," "video hos," and "skanks."

INCARCERATED WOMEN AND THE PRESENCE OF SEXUAL ABUSE

Davis (2003) stated, "Ideologies of sexuality—particularly the intersection of race and sexuality—have had a profound effect on the representations of and treatment received by women of color both within and outside prison" (79). Davis pointed out that this hypersexual stereotype is used to justify prison sexual assaults by guards who receive few, if any, consequences.

A study conducted by Browne, Miller, and Maguin (1999) examined the results of two national surveys and four local studies and concluded that "the six studies published over the past ten years suggested a substantial prevalence of physical or sexual assault among incarcerated women" (307). Browne, Miller, and Maguin conducted their own study by interviewing 150 women incarcerated at Bedford Hills Maximum Security Facility in Bedford Hills, New York. The participants ranged in age from eighteen to fifty-nine years, and 49 percent were African American. The authors stated, "'These findings suggest that violence across the lifespan for women incarcerated in the general population of a maximum security prison is pervasive and severe" (316). They also noted that "82 percent of the sample reported experiencing severe parental violence and/or childhood sexual abuse before reaching adulthood" (317).

Blackburn, Mullings, and Marquart (2008) reported similar findings in "Sexual Assault in Prison and Beyond: Toward an Understanding of Lifetime Sexual Assault Among Incarcerated Women." The study comprised a sample of 436 women incarcerated in minimum, medium, and maximum prisons in the South. The women's ages ranged from twenty to seventy-three years, and African American women were 39.2 percent of the participants.

The authors found that 68.4 percent of the participants had experienced "life-time sexual victimization" (365).

A 1996 report by the Human Rights Watch Women's Rights Project documented sexual abuse of women prisoners at eleven state prisons in various parts of the United States. The report declared, "Our findings indicate that being a woman prisoner in U.S. state prisons can be a terrifying experience. If you are sexually abused you cannot escape your abuser. Grievance or investigatory procedures, where they exist, are often ineffectual, and correctional employees continue to engage in abuse because they believe that they will rarely be held accountable, administratively or criminally" (1).

Besides sexual assault, there are numerous ways that incarcerated women are violated, disrespected, dismissed, and demeaned. A woman may be viewed by a male guard in a state of undress or while using the shower. She may have to go to a male to request sanitary supplies and encounter ridicule or have to justify her need, which can be a humiliating experience. One of the most demeaning practices for both men and women is the strip search. Strip searches can happen upon returning to the prison after court, a medical appointment, a work detail, a visit, or if there is a suspicion of contraband. For female survivors of sexual assault, this practice is often retraumatizing, especially if conducted within view of a male guard. For women in general, it is a shaming experience.

SHAME

One of the most psychologically damaging consequences of sexual assault is the resulting shame. Clinician and educator Jon G. Allen (2005) noted that "shame is a common facet of trauma." Basham and Miehls (2004) asserted that such shame is "often profound" (41). Shame is described by many clinicians as an affective state that can be the source of great psychic pain (Brown 2007; DeYoung 2015; Kaufman 1989; Leary 2005; Lewis 1971; Morrison 1989; Nathanson 1992; Nussbaum 2013; Tangney and Dearing 2011). Some generally agreed upon aspects of shame are that:

- shame is a painful affect that may feel overwhelming;
- shame can engender a feeling of exposure or nakedness;
- the shamed person feels unworthy and worthless;

- shame implies the acceptance of a standard or measure, causing the shamed person to feel inferior; and
- the shamed person believes that s/he *is* bad, as opposed to the guilty person, who believes that s/he has *done* something bad.

Shame has been categorized in several ways. One definition is *state shame*, when a person experiences shame as an acute, transient feeling in certain situations. It has also been called *normal shame*. Schieff and Retzinger (1997) stated that normal shame can signal "a moral trespass or inappropriate distance from other(s)" (149). The authors noted that normal shame can serve to regulate social distance and be a key to understanding all social relationships. Judith Lewis Herman (2011) wrote, "Mild experiences of shame are part of ordinary social life . . . Through ordinary experiences of shame, individuals learn the boundaries of socially acceptable behavior" (264).

A more wounding form of shame is called pathological or *trait shame*, when one experiences shame in a pervasive, internalized, and painful manner and feels a fundamental sense of incompetence and inferiority. Trait shame is linked to poor self-concept, low self-esteem, self-doubt, insecurity, diminished self-confidence, and feelings of worthlessness (Kaufman 1989; Lewis 1971). This experiencing of the whole self as bad or worthless is the form of shame referred to here.

The first comprehensive and empirical study of shame was done by Helen Block Lewis (1971), a psychoanalyst and research psychologist who detailed both the pervasiveness and the hidden nature of shame. "Pervasiveness" refers to two interrelated phenomena: (1) how global the affect is for the individual, for example, even to the point that the whole self is unworthy and bad, and (2) how prevalent shame is, not only among seekers of mental health services but in society at large. The "hidden nature" of shame is reflected in how it can be masked by rage, depression, narcissism, or anxiety, and can be so successfully repressed that it is not even recognized by the individual. Lewis pointed out that guilt and shame may be present at the same time. Thus, incarcerated individuals may be struggling with both the weight of their transgressions and the debilitating feelings of shame.

Lewis's findings linked proneness to shame to persons who are more field-dependent, that is, sensitive to cues in the environment. Lewis wrote, "Shame is an experience in which a source in the field seems to scorn, despise or ridicule the self. The source in the field may be a specific 'other' or it may be an ill-defined source" (39). It may range from family members and friends to an undefined "they" or society at large.

The linking of shame to field dependency is relevant for women because research points to women having a relational style of interacting (Chodorow 1989; Gilligan 1982; Jordan 1997; Miller 1991; Surrey 1991). Relationality is particularly relevant for Black women, who have a long history of bonds of sisterhood and mutual support. This mutual support is also historically a life-line to survival for the Black community at large.

Piers (1953), in viewing shame through a psychodynamic lens, described shame as "a tension between the Ego and the Ego-Ideal" (23). He pointed out that shame indicates a shortcoming, a kind of failure. Piers asserted that shame can be revealed later in life through an individual's function in his or her social role, and that this later identification is still rooted in the concept of the ego-ideal. He emphasized that the images that go into the formation of the developmentally later parts of the ego-ideal need not be parental images. The fear behind shame is the fear of contempt, which Piers associated on a societal level to "social expulsion, like ostracism" (29).

Lansky (1995) also examined shame psychodynamically and, as Piers did, connected shame to the ego-ideal. The sense of self that is affirmed by the other can be shamed by the feeling that one fails to meet the standards of the ego-ideal. Lansky wrote, "Shame signals danger to the sense of self—that is, of rejection or relegation to inferior status" (1081).

Morrison (1989) pointed out that shame occurs not only in a relational context but can also be felt by a person in isolation because the contents of the ego-ideal have been internalized. The external source of expectations (e.g., the parent) is no longer required. On the societal level, Morrison observed, "In our own country, there is little doubt that the relationship of social class and racism to shame is among the most potently destructive influences on our society, having led to severe social upheaval and destruction" (187).

Racial shaming is a particular form of shame that targets people of color. Leverenz (2012) observed:

As noun and verb, shame gives race its negative meaning, because light-skinned people use shaming and humiliation to make race feel like shame. The two states of self-perception become equivalent, except for those who claim whiteness, which confers honor as well as dominance. Such shaming carries its own shame, since it springs not from prowess or goodness but from white people's fears of losing superiority. These fears aren't usually acknowledged.

(3)

Generations of shaming, often accompanied by violence, have marked this country's treatment of people of color. Notions of Black people as less than human, legal systems of segregation, laws on miscegenation, Whiteness promoted as the ideal of beauty and purity, and portrayals in the media of Black people as criminal, unintelligent, and immoral are foundational elements of racial shaming.

The historical roots of the shaming of African American women can be traced to chattel slavery. On the auction block, enslaved women were subjected to being disrobed and touched at will by men who were potential buyers. Enslaved women were stripped naked and whipped. The ultimate degradation of rape was an ever-present danger. Hooks (2003) named shaming as a tool of enslavement. She observed, "Mocking, ridiculing, and labeling black bodies as animalistic were all the ways a system of psychological terrorism was put in place before actual interracial contact. White colonizers encountering Africans during the slave trade were ready to enact shaming as a strategy of colonization" (35–36). A shocking example of how the shaming of Black women has persisted into the present involved the director of a nonprofit agency who referred to the first African American First Lady of the United States, Michelle Obama, as an "ape in heels." Hooks (2003) observed that the effects of this history of shaming are embedded in the sensitivity of African Americans to rejection due to skin color, hair texture, and the body. This privileging of lighter skin and White features as the standard of beauty is defined as "*colorism* . . . an intra-racial system of inequality based on skin color, hair texture, and facial features that bestows privilege and value on physical attributes that are closer to white" (Wilder and Cain, 2011, p. 578). The benefits bestowed on lighter-skinned African Americans with more European features include access to better jobs, more ready acceptance in white society, and being more appealing to some Black men. The heartbreak for many African Americans is that colorism is often practiced in families. A darker skinned sibling can grow up shamed by her own family, receiving the message, both overtly and covertly, that she is not as attractive or desirable as her lighter skinned sister. Colorism is one example of the transgenerational transmission of the psychologically wounding legacies of slavery.

Joy DeGruy (2005) adapted the theory of transgenerational transmission of trauma to develop her theory of what she terms "post-traumatic slave syndrome," which she defines as "a condition that exists when a population has experienced multigenerational trauma resulting from centuries of slavery and continues to experience oppression and institutionalized racism today. Added to this condition is a belief (real or imagined) that the benefits of society in which they live are not accessible to them" (125). She continues, "The slave experience was one of continual, violent attacks on the slave's body, mind and spirit. Slave men, women and children were traumatized throughout their lives and the violent attacks during slavery persisted long after emancipation. In the face of these injuries, those traumatized adapted their attitudes and behaviors to simply survive, and these adaptations continue to manifest today" (14).

DeGruy contends that shame is another legacy of the intergenerational transmission of trauma in the African American community. She wrote, "This subject of shame is particularly significant when it comes to African Americans. It is as though people live with a constant fear of being exposed. . . . I only know that this fear is something a number of us live with, a collective knowing of sorts, the details about which have been long forgotten" (163).

Gump (2017) wrote about the legacy of the traumas of slavery she encountered in doing therapy with African Americans. She contended that "the traumas of slavery and their transmission are thus relevant to the therapy of all African Americans, whether made explicit or not" (161). Gump detailed the erasure of the sense of self, the rupture of attunement between child and caregiver, the destruction of agency, and the prohibition against displaying affects or expressing desire. In her vignettes she described how the effects of these traumas were transmitted to later generations. Gump wrote of repeatedly encountering voids and absences of emotional capacity in her patients and concluded that the parents of these patients had experienced a void of emotional connection, which she describes as "a terrible nothingness." She stated, "This absence is transmitted to children, as it had been transmitted to them" (177).

PSYCHOLOGICAL EFFECTS OF INCARCERATION

Not only do incarcerated African American women have to contend with racialized shaming and the legacy of slavery, but they also must deal with what Erving Goffman (1961) defined as the mortification that results from being confined in a "total institution." Goffman described prison as an institution that "is organized to protect the community against what are felt to be intentional dangers to it, with the welfare of the persons thus sequestered not the immediate issue" (4–5). Goffman wrote that the individual's sense of self "is systematically, if often unintentionally, mortified." The mortification of the incarcerated person is brought about through "a series of abasements, degradations, humiliations and profanations of self" (14).

Goffman defined this mortification as the loss of "self-determination, autonomy and freedom of action." He noted that "a failure to retain this kind of adult executive competency, or at least the symbols of it, can produce in the inmate the terror of feeling radically demoted in the age-grading system" (43). Psychologist Craig Haney (2003, 2006) referred to the alteration of the self in service of survival in the harsh prison environment as *prisonization*, which he defined as "the incorporation of the norms of prison life into one's habits of thinking, feeling, and acting." He noted that the psychological mechanisms employed to survive in the unnatural milieu of prison can gradually become internalized, and when the individual is released these mechanisms are detrimental to his or her readjustment to the home environment. Prisonization can include the following psychological adaptations:

- A gradual diminution of autonomy and independent thinking, which is replaced by dependence on a system that dictates what you do and when you do it
- A hypervigilance and distrust of those around you
- Psychological distancing, a lack of spontaneity, and an emotional flatness that is self-protective and does not promote healthy relationships
- A lack of meaningful or prosocial activities that can lead to engagement in negativity
- Internalized feelings of low self-worth and spoiled identity
- Development of post-traumatic stress disorder resulting from the psychologically painful experience of incarceration and exposure to trauma

These negative adaptive mechanisms can make it hard to reestablish relationships, to take responsibility for finding critically needed employment and housing, and to resume the role of parent. For many formerly incarcerated individuals, there is also the threat of relapsing into drug addiction as a response to becoming overwhelmed, becoming discouraged, or reconnecting with negative associates. Many individuals who are in need of drug treatment while imprisoned fail to receive such treatment. Once released, they are at risk of relapse.

IMPACT OF THE WAR ON DRUGS

Drug involvement is a major factor contributing to the high numbers of Black women behind bars. The War on Drugs, launched in 1982 by President Ronald Reagan, led to large numbers of Black women going to prison. According to Mark Mauer (2013) of the Sentencing Project, "Women were particularly affected by the policies of the 'war on drugs.'" In noting that in 2000 Black women were incarcerated at a rate six times that of White women, Mauer pointed out that "law enforcement practices, particularly related to the drug war, targeting black neighborhoods, and, more limited access to treatment and alternatives to incarceration for low-income women were influencing factors." Indeed, a hallmark of the War on Drugs was the handing down of draconian sentences for even minor drug offenses. Legal scholar Michelle Alexander (2010) noted that detainees are pressured to plea bargain to avoid "sentences for minor drug crimes that are higher than many countries impose on convicted murderers" (88).

Andrea James (2013), a lawyer who ran afoul of the law and served twenty-four months in federal prison, wrote about serving time with women who had been in prison for "decades for non-violent drug offenses." She described a woman who at seventy years old was in her twenty-second year of a thirty-year sentence for selling cocaine. With the abolishment of parole in the federal system, her only hope for early release was a pardon.

Alexander (2010) also pointed out how the shame of incarceration can spread throughout a community. She cited ethnographic research by David Braman which found that "mass incarceration, far from reducing the stigma associated with criminality, actually creates a deep silence in communities of color, one rooted in shame. Imprisonment is considered so shameful that many people avoid talking about it, even within their own families" (161).

BLACK FEMINIST THOUGHT

Black feminist thought empowers formerly incarcerated African American women to speak out and tell their stories. As Patricia Hill Collins (1990) wrote, "I suggest that Black feminist thought consists of specialized knowledge created by African-American women which clarifies a standpoint of and for Black women. In other words, Black feminist thought encompasses theoretical interpretations of Black women's reality by those who lived it" (12). This standpoint considers African American women's responses and experiences within historical, political, cultural, socioeconomic, and relational contexts and acknowledges the uniqueness of African American women's experience—one marked by racism, trauma, gender discrimination, devaluation, and invisibility.

Acknowledgment of the importance of voice is a fundamental tenet of Black feminist thought (Collins 1990, hooks 1989, 1993, 2003; King 1988; Omolade 1994; Phillips and McCaskill 1995; Waters 2007). Hill Collins (1998) defined two goals for the voices of Black women in generating "knowledge produced by, for, and/or in behalf of African American women." She wrote, "One goal is the goal of self-definition, or the power to name one's reality. Self-determination, or aiming for the power to decide one's own destiny, is the second fundamental goal" (45).

A QUALITATIVE STUDY

In 2015 I held a series of focus groups with thirty-six formerly incarcerated African American women. I met with them so I could hear from them directly and gain understanding of the challenges faced by Black women in the criminal justice system. Women who ranged in age from twenty-five to sixty-nine came together to share their thoughts and feelings. I asked about the impact that incarceration had had on their lives and the lives of their families, and I asked if they had experienced shame as a result of their imprisonment. The aim of the project was to increase my understanding of the psychological toll that prison takes on formerly incarcerated African American women. Lessons learned were used to engage in more sensitive and effective clinical work with this population.

The most frequently mentioned, and most painful, source of shame for the participants was facing how their incarceration had affected their families. The effects on their children were particularly painful. One informant said, "I still hold a lot of guilt and shame about the way I treated my daughter when she was—she's a good kid. I just wasn't there for her like I should have been. So, that's one of my biggest things. I always get teary-eyed when I think of it."

Another of my informants spoke about her struggle to be free of the notion of Whiteness as the internalized standard of beauty and to learn to value her Black body and features. She had the following revelation at forty-eight years old:

> You know, for me, I am just learning how to love myself in order to let myself—it doesn't matter what you think of me, right, it's you know, what do I think about me. And learning how to embrace that, embrace my full lips, you know, my bigger nose, or whatever the case may be, you know my nappy or bald head, whatever. I needed to know that I was beautiful. My skin was brown and it was beautiful, you know, because there's the lies that build up over the years.

Several women spoke about their trauma, both before and after incarceration. One woman said, "I know the trouble for me is when I was using. I got hurt real, real bad, and I was beaten half to death, left to die in the alleyway. But when I went to jail—I was tough out here after that happened, but when I went to jail I shut down. When people are trying to get close to me, I can't accept that, just because of that, you know, because I was traumatized so bad."

Another shared her story of trauma before incarceration: "I think, for me, and I'm just speaking for myself, right, coming from an all-black school in the South and going to an all-white school in the North, right, was a culture shock. And even before that, like at the age of ten, I watched my mother's sister get shot in the head from her husband, and just blanked it out. So clearly, I had some trauma at that age and never really knew it."

Yet another woman revealed:

> Me, it was like the age of—I can't remember when. I was an abused child, physically, sexually and mentally. But the anger from me being abused as a kid I wasn't allowed to speak. . . . If I get in an argument or confrontation, I'm ready to lash out real quick. So I think they labeled me as PTSD, post-traumatic stress and depression. People are not even doing nothing to me, and I just wanted to hurt them because I was in so much pain.

A respondent talked about the trauma she experienced inside prison:

It's not just we were in there, it was being a woman. It's waking up in a single room at eighteen [years old] where a CO [corrections officer] is touching your titty and you look up at him, and he looks down at you, and you just close your eyes and he walks out of the room and nobody says nothing ever about it. Or going to the doctor where everybody knows the gynecologist tickles your clitoris when he finishes, and that's not how you give a pap. You see what I'm saying? There's other dynamics in there that just add to the trauma that you already going in there with, so you come out, you're like f*** everybody. It's no wonder that people turn around bad, because, like, what do you do?

In reflecting on where they drew their strength to survive the harsh and punishing conditions of prison, most of the women said they drew their strength from God and their family. One woman said:

If it wasn't knowing who God was in my life, I think I would have killed myself. I really don't think that I would be here. I used to always say, "God says he's not going to give you more than you can bear." I didn't want to bear that. But I thank God for seeing me through it, because he said he'd never leave us and won't forsake us. He helped me not feel alone in those dark spaces that I was in through that time. But my mother helped me a lot, too. Like I said, she was my biggest supporter. Which I guess—just being around my family helps because I've been away from them for so long. They're a big support system for me. But definitely my mother. She's the biggest supporter I have besides God.

In response to what would be clinically helpful to women returning home from prison, many of the women shared that they either were currently in therapy or had been in therapy. One respondent added, "Now, I know about resources and all that kind of stuff. But there needs to be a place where when women get out of jail they can meet and talk about their experiences and how they feel, and deal with the shame, and maybe have some mentors, and people in place—therapists, and different people in place to help deal with a lot of these things that we maybe never dealt with."

A woman who shared her trauma history spoke about her own therapy: "I have a therapist. I just saw her actually. And being near her is just so calming. She brings stuff out from me that makes me talk. Because sometimes with that trauma you don't know how to come out to talk about it."

In supporting the idea of therapy, the women added the caveat that they needed to be able to trust the therapist. They expressed their concern about confidentiality, and several of the women said there was "a need for the therapist to relate to me." Another concern was that they not feel judged.

PSYCHODYNAMICALLY ORIENTED CLINICAL WORK
WITH NONTRADITIONAL POPULATIONS

The notion of doing psychodynamically oriented clinical work with nontraditional populations is an idea that can be traced back to Sigmund Freud. Elizabeth Ann Danto (2005) wrote about this early work in *Freud's Free Clinics: Psychoanalysis and Social Justice 1918–1938*. In 1918, Freud called for free clinics where his revolutionary mental health treatment known as psychoanalysis would be available to working class people. The first free clinic, the Berlin Poliklinik, was opened in 1920. At least twelve free mental health clinics were established throughout Europe. Danto wrote, "At least one fifth of the work of the first and second generation of psychoanalysts went to indigent urban residents" (2). The work was promoted and carried out by such luminaries as Karl Abraham, Alfred Adler, Bruno Bettelheim, Helene Deutch, Eric Erikson, Otto Fenichel, Sandor Ferenzi, Anna Freud, Frieda Fromm-Reichmann, Karen Horney, Edith Jacobson, Ernest Jones, Melanie Klein, and Ernst Simmel. This dynamic activism and commitment to social justice set a precedent early on for providing psychoanalysis and psychodynamically oriented mental health treatment to people from all walks of life. In keeping with this commitment to inclusion and accessibility, clinical work is being done in prisons, in homeless shelters, in school-based clinics, with refugee populations, in war zones, and in low-income communities.

THERAPY WITH FORMERLY INCARCERATED
AFRICAN AMERICAN WOMEN

Participants in my focus groups testified to the benefits they experienced from therapy and offered several suggestions for establishing a mutually respectful therapeutic relationship. Several women noted that a therapist's not having been to prison did not mean that the therapist would be unable to relate to them, citing their own therapies as examples. One respondent summed it up by saying, "To me the counseling comes when you can connect, when you can feel comfortable enough with talking to somebody." This comment underscores how essential the relationship between therapist and client is, regardless of what form of therapy is employed.

Also essential to effective therapy is understanding the context of the individual. The context of formerly incarcerated African American women includes awareness of the history and culture of people of African descent in the United States, and their long and brutal history of racism and overrepresentation in the criminal justice system. It includes being mindful of the presence of racialized shaming and the uneasy relationship that many Black women have with their physical selves in the face of being portrayed in the media as unfeminine, emasculating, violent, hypersexualized, and inherently criminal. Besides the shame of being identified as a criminal and the stigma that endures long after release, there are the shaming stereotypes that adhere to Black women. Psychologist Jessica H. Daniel calls racism "a reality-based and repetitive trauma in the lives of African American women" (126).

In addition, therapists need to appreciate the strengths that have allowed African American women to thrive and develop a healthy self-esteem in spite of the challenges discussed here. Black women have a strong spirit of sisterhood. They have always displayed resilience and determination, and as my informants articulated, family and God have comforted and supported them. Even when families of origin are dysfunctional or unavailable, the Black community has a tradition of extended family, fictive kin, and "other mothers" who step in. These traditional coping measures have been strained mightily given the problems that plague the Black community, such as drugs, crime, poverty, systemic racism, and mass incarceration, but they have not disappeared.

Mental health services for formerly incarcerated individuals are woefully lacking. With 650,000 to 700,000 individuals coming home from prisons and jails each year, there is a critical need for clinicians who can assist in healing the psychological damage inflicted by a system of punishment that exacerbates existing trauma and inflicts its own. I believe that understanding the psychological toll that prison takes on formerly incarcerated African American women is one important step toward correcting this problem.

REFERENCES

Alexander, M. (2010). *The new Jim Crow: Mass incarceration in the age of colorblindness.* New York: The New Press.

Allen, J. G. (2005). *Coping with trauma: Hope through understanding.* Washington, DC: American Psychiatric Publishing.

Basham, K., and Miehls, D. (2004). *Transforming the legacy: Couple therapy with survivors of childhood trauma.* New York: Columbia University Press.

Bennett, L., Jr. (1961). *Before the* Mayflower: *A history of black America.* New York: Penguin Books.

Berzoff, J. (2012). Why we need a biopsychosocial perspective with vulnerable, oppressed, and at-risk clients. In J. Berzoff (Ed.), *Falling through the cracks: Psychodynamic practice with vulnerable and oppressed populations* (pp. 1–39). New York: Columbia University Press.

Blackburn, A. G., Mullings, J. L., and Marquart, J. W. (2008). Sexual assault in prison and beyond: Toward an understanding of lifetime sexual assault among incarcerated women. *Prison Journal, 88* (3), 351–377.

Blackmon, D. A. (2008). *Slavery by another name: The re-enslavement of black Americans from the Civil War to World War II.* New York: Doubleday.

Brown, B. (2007). *I thought it was just me: Women reclaiming power and courage in a culture of shame.* New York: Gotham Books

Browne, A., Miller, B. and Maguin, E. (1999) Prevalence and severity of lifetime physical and sexual victimization among incarcerated women. *International Journal of Law and Psychiatry, 22* (3–4), 301–322.

Butler, A. M. (1997). *Gendered justice in the American West: Women prisoners in men's penitentiaries.* Chicago: University of Illinois Press.

Chodorow, N. (1989). *Feminism and psychoanalytic theory.* New Haven, CT: Yale University Press.

Collins, P. H. (1990). *Black feminist thought: Knowledge, consciousness, and the politics of empowerment.* New York: Routledge

Daniel, J. H. (2000). The courage to hear: African American women's memories of racial trauma. In. L. Jackson and B. Greene (Eds.), *Psychotherapy with African American women: Innovations in psychodynamic perspectives and practice* (pp. 126–144). New York: Guilford Press.

Danto, E. A. (2005). *Freud's free clinics: Psychoanalysis and social justice 1918–1938.* New York: Columbia University Press.

Davis, A. Y. (2003). *Are prisons obsolete?* New York: Seven Stories Press.

DeGruy, J. D. (2005). *Post traumatic slave syndrome: America's enduring legacy of injury and healing.* Milwaukie, OR: Uptone Press.

DeYoung, P. A. (2015). *Understanding and treating chronic shame A relational/ neurobiological approach.* New York: Routledge.

Du Bois, W. E. B. (1901). The spawn of slavery: The convict-lease system in the south. *Missionary Review of the World,* 24, 737–745.

Gilligan, C. (1982). *In a different voice: Psychological theory and women's development.* Cambridge, MA: Harvard University Press.

Goffman, E. (1961). *Asylums: Essays on the social situation of mental patients and other inmates.* Garden City, NY: Anchor Books.

Gross, K. (2006). *Colored Amazons: Crime, violence and black women in the city of brotherly love 1880–1910.* Durham, NC: Duke University Press.

Gump, J. P. (2017). The presence of the past: Transmission of slavery's traumas. In A. Harris, M. Kalb, and S. Klebanoff (Eds.), *Demons in the consulting room: Echoes of genocide, slavery and extreme trauma in psychoanalytic practice.* New York: Routledge.

Haley, S. (2016). *No mercy here: Gender, punishment, and the making of Jim Crow modernity.* Chapel Hill: University of North Carolina Press.

Haney, C. (2003). The psychological impact of incarceration: Implications for postprison adjustment. In J. Travis and M. Waul (Eds.), *Prisoners once removed: The impact of incarceration and reentry on children, families, and communities* (pp. 33–66). Washington, DC: the Urban Institute Press.

——. (2006). *Reforming punishment: Psychological limits to the pains of imprisonment.* Washington, DC: American Psychological Association.

Herman, J. L. (2011). Posttraumatic stress disorder as a shame disorder. In R. L. Dearing and J. P. Tangney (Eds.), *Shame in the therapy hour* (pp. 261–275). Washington, DC: American Psychological Association.

Hicks, C. D. (2010). *Talk with you like a woman: African American women, justice, and reform in New York, 1890–1935.* Chapel Hill: University of North Carolina Press.

hooks, b. (1989). *Talking back: Thinking feminist thinking black.* Boston: South End Press.

——. (1993). *Sisters of the yam: Black women and self-recovery.* Boston: South End Press.

———. (2003). *Rock my soul: Black people and self-esteem.* New York: Atria Books.

Human Rights Watch Women's Rights Project. (1996). *All too familiar: Sexual abuse of women in U.S. state prisons.* New York: Human Rights Watch.

Jacobs, H. (1987). *Incidents in the life of a slave girl written by herself.* Cambridge, MA: Harvard University Press. (Original work published 1861.)

James, A. C. (2013). *Upper bunkies unite: And other thoughts on the politics of mass incarceration.* Boston: Goode Book Press.

Jordan, J. V. (1997). Relational development: Therapeutic implications of empathy and shame. In J. V. Jordan (Ed.), *Women's growth in diversity: More writings from the Stone Center* (pp. 138–161). New York: Guilford Press.

Kaufman, G. (1989). *The psychology of shame.* New York: Springer.

King, D. K. (1988). Multiple jeopardy, multiple consciousness: The context of a black feminist ideology. *Signs, 14* (1), 42–72.

Lansky, M. R. (1995). Shame and the scope of psychoanalytic understanding. *American Behavioral Scientist, 38* (8), 1076–1090.

Leary, J. D. (2005). *Post traumatic slave syndrome: America's legacy of enduring injury and healing.* Milwaukie, OR: Uptone Press.

LeFlouria, T. (2015). *Chained in silence: Black women and convict labor in the new south.* Chapel Hill: University of North Carolina Press.

Leverenz, D. (2012). *Honor bound: Race and shame in America.* New Brunswick, NJ: Rutgers University Press.

Lewis, H. B. (1971). *Shame and guilt in neurosis.* New York: International Universities Press.

Litwack, L. F. (1979). *Been in the storm so long: The aftermath of slavery.* New York: Alfred A. Knopf.

Mancini, M. J. (1996). *One dies, get another: Convict leasing in the American south 1866–1928.* Columbia: University of South Carolina Press.

Mauer, M. (February 27, 2013). The changing racial dynamics of women's incarceration. http://www.sentencingreport.org/doc/publications/rd_Changing%20Racial%20Dynamics%202013.pdf.

Miller, J. B. (1991). The development of women's sense of self. In J.V. Jordan, A.G. Kaplan, J. B. Miller, I. P. Stiver and J. L. Surrey (Eds.), *Women's growth in connection: Writings from the Stone Center* (pp. 11–26). New York: Guilford Press.

Morrison, A. P. (1989). *Shame: The underside of narcissism.* Hillsdale, NJ: Analytic Press.

Nathanson, D. L. (1992). *Shame and pride: Affect, sex, and the birth of the self.* New York: Norton.

Nussbaum, M. C. (2004). *Hiding from humanity: Disgust, shame, and the law.* Princeton, NJ: Princeton University Press.

Omolade, B. (1994). *The rising song of African American women.* New York: Routledge.

Patrick-Stamp, L. (1995). Numbers that are not new: African Americans in the country's first prison, 1790–1835. *The Pennsylvania Magazine of History and Biography,* 19 (1/2), 95–128.

Phillips, L., and McCaskill, B. (1995). Who's schooling who? Black women and the bringing of the everyday into academe, or why we started "The Womanist." *Signs* 20 (4), 1007–1018.

Piers, G., and Singer, M. B. (1953). *Shame and guilt: A psychoanalytic and a cultural study.* Springfield, IL: Charles C. Thompson.

Quarles, B. (1964). *The Negro in the making of America.* New York: Collier Books.

Schieff, T. J., and Retzinger, S. M. (1997). Helen Block Lewis on shame: Appreciation and critique. In M. R. Lansky and A. P. Morrison (Eds.), *The widening scope of shame,* (pp. 139–154). Hillsdale, NJ: Analytic Press.

The Sentencing Project. (2018). *Incarcerated women and girls 1980–2016.* May 10. https://www.sentencingproject.org/publications/incarcerated-women-and -girls.

Sparks, E. (1994). Interview by Claude J. Anderson. In. B. Hurmence (Ed.), *We lived in a little cabin in the yard.* Winston-Salem, NC: John E. Blaire.

Surrey, J. L. (1991). Relationship and empowerment. In J. V. Jordan, A. G. Kaplan, J. B. Miller, I. P. Stiver and J. L. Surrey (Eds.), *Women's growth in connection: Writings from the Stone Center* (pp. 162–180). New York: Guildford Press.

Tangney, J. P., and Dearing, R. L. (2011). Introduction: Putting shame in context. In J.P. Tangney and R.L. Dearing (Eds.), *Shame in the therapy hour* (pp. 3–19). Washington, DC: American Psychological Association.

Waters, K. (2007). Some core themes of nineteenth-century black feminism. In K. Waters and C. Conaway (Eds.), *Black women's intellectual traditions: Speaking their minds* (pp. 365–392). Burlington: University of Vermont Press.

Wilder. J. and Cain, C. (2011). Teaching and learning color consciousness in black families: Exploring family processes and women's experiences with colorism. *Journal of Family Issues,* 32 (5), 577–604.

12

Working with LGBTQIA+ Clients in the Context of Trauma, with a Focus on Transgender Experiences

▸ *DAVID BYERS, KAI Z. THIGPEN, and SARA WOLFSON*

TRAUMATIC EXPERIENCE CAN INVOLVE a disorganization of identity, a jostling of fragmented parts of the self, and a disconnection from social supports. These effects can be more destabilizing when gender and sexual identities and experiences are unrecognized, contested, split off, or understood as etiologically tied to the traumatic experience. Trauma treatment with clients with diverse genders and sexualities can therefore be a fraught but important opportunity for reimagining how parts of the self might come to fit together with each other and in relation to community.

Gender and sexual identificatory processes operate not only at the individual level but also in relationship to the group or community, a basis for what social psychologists call social identity (Hornsey 2008). Little attention has traditionally been paid in psychodynamic theory to the meaning of social identity or its role in treatment. Social identity is a way of symbolizing self-concept in relation to a group or groups through internalization and assimilation. It is different from traditional conceptions of personal subjectivity in psychodynamic theory, including Freud's more mechanistic conception of the ego and Kohut's more essentialist understanding of the self (Minolli 2004). In trauma treatment, attending to social identity can be particularly important when it has been disavowed or isolated, either within the individual, socially, or both.

Today, the expanding acronym of LGBTQIA+ represents a spectrum of gender and sexual identities that diverge from heterosexual and cisgender norms, including lesbian, gay, bisexual, transgender/gender nonbinary, queer, intersex, and asexual, as well as emergent identity categories such as pansexual, polysexual, and demisexual.[1] It can also include people who may engage in sexual- and gender-variant activities but do not identify with any of the above labels (Galupo et al. 2014; Walton, Lykins, and Bhullar 2016). The ongoing evolution of the acronym points to the ways in which conceptions of gender and sexual minority identities continually evolve. They are socially contingent, taking on different meanings in different places and times. They intersect with each other and with other dimensions of social identity, including race, class, religion, and ability. They can represent a confrontation with earlier identity constructs, what Goldman (2017) has referred to as "generational identity," a declaration of new and differentiated generational self-understandings. At the same time, the conceptualization of an expanding LGBTQIA+ coalition reflects an uneasy collective identification imbued with political strategy, a shared sense of marginality, and aspirations—shared by many—for a queer "community in difference" (Muñoz 2009). This orientation to queer identities calls on clinicians to attend to individual and local interactions of meaning rather than static and essentialized identity constructs.

In this chapter, we begin by discussing the complex relationship between trauma and LGBTQIA+ identities. Next, we trace some of the ways these correlations have been used to raise etiological questions about LGBTQIA+ identities, especially with queer children and adolescents. Speculations about the causes of LGBTQIA+ identities are often the basis for pathologizing them, and they need to be understood within a historical and prevailing context of clinical aggression toward LGBTQIA+ people. This backdrop of clinical aggression means that trauma treatment today is never safely distinct from homophobia and transphobia, making it difficult for clinicians and clients to explore the ways gender and sexuality can also sometimes be informed by trauma and recovery. In the final section, we focus on clinical attention to traumatic fragmentation related to gender and sexual identities and experiences. Parts of the self and identity can be dissociated, projected, and introjected in transference and countertransference, in particular through victim-victimizer-bystander dynamics (Basham 2004, 2016; Davies and Frawley 1992; Herman [1992] 2015) and the client's experiences of homophobic and transphobic hostility. A queer-affirmative clinical stance to traumatic fragmentation often involves the clinician's reflexive use of self as a reparative and affirming object. We discuss two case examples—a fifteen-year-old transgender girl and her family, and an eighteen-year-old transgender woman—to demonstrate and elaborate on our points. They reflect only two among many intersectional LGBTQIA+ social identity experiences that have been both underrepresented and misrepresented in the clinical literature.

TRAUMA AND LGBTQIA+ IDENTITIES AND EXPERIENCES

Population and epidemiological research has demonstrated that people who are gender and sexual minorities endure much higher rates of potentially traumatic experiences throughout life than cisgender and heterosexual people (Austin et al. 2008; Balsam, Rothblum, and Beauchaine 2005; Herek 2009; James et al. 2016; Jones et al. 2016; Mizock and Lewis 2008; NYCAVP 2015; Parent and Ferriter 2018; Roberts et al. 2010). Experiences that are potentially traumatic do not of course always lead to the development of symptoms, but LGB people are more likely than heterosexual people to develop a range of related medical and mental health problems, including post-traumatic stress disorder (PTSD) as defined in the American Psychiatric Association's fifth edition of the *Diagnostic and Statistical Manual* (Roberts et al. 2010). Research is much more limited that focuses specifically on survivors of potentially traumatic experiences who are transgender and gender nonbinary (James et al. 2016), intersex (Jones et al. 2016), and asexual (Parent and Ferriter 2018). Bisexual and transgender women of color may face particularly high rates of violence, including physical assaults, threats, and police violence (NYCAVP 2015). These types of findings can be important for recognizing the scale of violence against people with marginalized identities and for organizing far-reaching programmatic interventions to address population needs.

It is also important to attend to less recognized forms of traumatic stress for gender and sexual minorities, including the following: (1) complex trauma (Courtois 2004), which results from sustained abuse or neglect rather than one identifiable traumatic event; (2) microaggressions (Nadal 2013; Woodford et al. 2014), defined as subtle expressions of explicit or implicit hostility toward marginalized groups, which can have traumatic effects over time;

(3) collective, intergenerational, and historical trauma (Brave Heart et al. 2011; Primm et al. 2010; Quiros and Berger 2015; Tummala-Narra 2007), which are cumulative injuries affecting whole communities over time; and (4) additional forms of minority stress (Alessi and Martin 2017; Hatzenbuehler 2009; Meyer 2003), which may manifest in a range of anxiety, mood, and psychosomatic responses rather than as a symptom cluster consistent with PTSD.

The minority-stress model posits that both external effects of oppression, such as discrimination and microaggressions, and internal effects, such as internalized oppression and the anticipation of external oppressive experiences, can have a deleterious effect on the mental health of people in affected populations (Alessi and Martin 2017; Hatzenbuehler 2009; Meyer 2003). These stressors can exacerbate emotional dysregulation, interpersonal difficulties, and cognitive processes such as hopelessness and rumination, and can be a driver of negative mental and physical health outcomes (Mereish and Poteat 2015; Meyer 2003). The link between minority stress and mental and physical health may be mediated by tenuous interpersonal connections, low engagement with community, and feelings of shame and loneliness (Mereish and Poteat 2015). These frameworks are vital to keep in mind in clinical assessment, as Alessi (2014) demonstrates with a two-step model for examining experiences of minority stress as well as coping and resilience.

At the same time, medical and mental health clinicians can run into trouble with basic logical fallacies when attempting to apply findings from large population samples to the experiences of individuals in clinical practice. Overly simplistic deductions are especially evident when public health reports—such as the ones described at the start of this section of the chapter—urge clinicians to assess more carefully LGBTQIA+ clients for histories of abuse, neglect, or violent victimization based on their social identities. Traumatic stress and its impacts on individuals should be understood as mediated by complex biopsychosocial interactions rather than on more predictable correlations (Keenan 2010). Moreover, the relationship between trauma and identity, even in large data sets, is extremely complex and multidirectional: traumatic experiences can influence experiences of identity, and identity can influence experiences of trauma and the potential for posttraumatic growth (Alessi and Martin 2017; Berman 2016; Meyer 2010). In practice, using epidemiological data to speculate about the mental health of marginalized individuals can perpetuate a recursive circular reasoning about the etiology of LGBTQIA+ identities (Cvetkovich 2003; Ovenden 2011).

In other words, we caution clinicians against speculating based on a client's genders and sexualities about the possibility that he/she/they may have endured traumatic experiences rather than asking every client as part of collaborative, ongoing assessment work. Moreover, as we will discuss in the next section, we encourage skepticism and scrutiny of questions about the causes of gender and sexual variance in clients, particularly in the context of trauma treatment, where such questions often seem to arise and to turn on specious conceptualizations of queer identities in psychopathological terms.

CLINICAL AGGRESSION AND ETIOLOGICAL RHETORIC

When we use the term *clinical aggression*, we are referring to the ways that clinicians have pathologized differences based on gender and sexuality and have attempted to alter clients' gender identities and sexual orientations, in the past and present (Drescher 1998; Vider and Byers 2015). It is what Saketopoulou (2011) has described as "blood that stains our clinical hands" (193), and it should be understood as part of every treatment—even if the clinician is explicitly aware of and attentive to inevitable dynamics of homophobia and transphobia.

Questions about the etiology of LGBTQIA+ identities often seem most urgent with reference to queer children and adolescents. The assumption that childhood trauma can trigger situational gender and sexual variance remains deeply embedded in clinical practice in the United States and elsewhere. In the following case of short-term trauma treatment with the parents of a transgender adolescent, the parents had initially expected their child to be the primary focus of treatment.

Sara, a Fifteen-Year-Old

Sara,[2] a fifteen-year-old, Muslim, South Asian, transgender girl, came for consultation at a community mental health clinic with a referral from her high school guidance counselor because she was experiencing bullying and seemed suddenly very unmotivated in classes. She was accompanied to the consultation by her parents, Rawdha, a nursing student, and Fahad, a taxi driver with a degree in accounting. They had moved to the United States from India just before Sara was born. The clinician—a White, cisgender, and queer-identified man—felt eager to connect with Sara and both her parents; however, he was unsure how they would relate to him. From the start, the clinician, parents, and Sara seemed to encounter each other with politeness and a conscientious if businesslike demeanor. Psychotherapy was not new to the family, and Rawdha kept a notebook open on her lap, ready to take notes. Sara had been diagnosed in early childhood with mild autism, and they had grown accustomed to accessing more didactically oriented therapies and psychosocial services through the school and community.

Sara had begun to wear girls' pants and a shirt at home about a year before, and Rawdha and Fahad had mainly ignored it. From a young age, Sara would lie on the bed and watch her mother wrap her head in a brightly colored hijab, sometimes wondering aloud when she could have her own. They grew very concerned, however, when the school guidance counselor told them that Sara was being bullied, and they worried that Sara might be "confused" about her gender because she was on the autism spectrum. Her friends from middle school had all been boys of Indian descent, but they had recently begun to target Sara with harassing name calling. Sara had more recently become friends with a group of cisgender White girls from an older grade. The guidance counselor's concern resonated initially with Rawdha, who explained, "Sometimes she doesn't know who she is until someone tells her that this is how people need to be. She learns very quickly from people around her. When she was little, if I told her to take a shower, I would tell her to take a shower for fifteen minutes, to use soap and shampoo, to wash it off, to dry off, to get dressed in pajamas after. If I didn't say each step like the doctors told me, she wouldn't do it. But when I would say it, she would do it perfectly." Her concern, then, was that Sara might have "learned to be a girl" because she had suddenly made new friends at school who were girls.

Some recent studies suggest a limited correlation between gender variance and autism (Glidden et al. 2016), which was enough for the guidance counselor and Rawdha to speculate that Sara might be attempting to act (or be) like her new friends, just as she had attempted to conform to bewildering patterns of social behavior throughout childhood with the help of behavioral coaches and classroom aids. "I don't want to be the unaccepting kind of mother," Rawdha said, "but I do want to know, is this really true that she is transgender, or is this just confusion with everything going on and the bullying?"

Asked whether she had any concerns herself, Sara explained that her parents were the main problem. They were too protective, and Sara wanted to be allowed to wear gender-affirming clothing and a backpack to school. A few months earlier, a terrorist bombing had occurred in the city in which two young men detonated homemade explosives they were carrying in their school backpacks. The clinician felt suddenly nauseous hearing reference to the bombing but noticed in himself an attempt to remain unreactive. He nodded awkwardly and tried to look casual. Everyone in the city had shared an experience of terror, but—as he started to realize for the first time in session, and later in supervision—he did not want to seem or feel affected himself, at least not with these clients. Rawdha, Fahad, and many other Muslim people of color had less opportunity for denial as they were faced with an immediate and ongoing threat of Islamophobic backlash and violence.

This traumatic event became the center of the work for Rawdha and Fahad, while Sara was referred for her own therapy. The aim of Rawdha and Fahad's therapy turned to helping them process and grieve what had happened and how it had activated a rigid and vigilant focus on their child. They had insisted that Sara never go outside with a backpack and felt afraid of Sara making White friends—friends who might mean well, they said, but who would not know what to do if Sara was targeted by police or other students. The clinician wondered if they might feel similarly about him. In subsequent sessions, the parents explained that they had stopped attending their mosque because of both their fearfulness about the bombing and their apprehension about how others might respond if they heard that their child was transgender.

The dynamic between the clinician and the parents began to shift when the clinician started to recognize his own denial of grief and vulnerability in the wake of the bombing. He grew more responsive to them and less distant, and they began to feel increasingly trusting and open. Rawdha and Fahad gradually started to reflect on the ways their anxiety about Sara's gender related to their own difficulties adjusting, and they grieved these unexpected changes in how they thought about their child. It took a few months of weekly treatment for Rawdha and Fahad to recognize how they were displacing their own traumatized reactions to the bombing onto Sara's mostly separate experience of queer adolescence. Their child had become a convenient container for their feelings of marginality and vulnerability in a country that characteristically fails to acknowledge its aggression toward people of color and queer people. Without Sara to hold those fears, they began to recognize them in their relationship to the clinician. Fahad discussed a sense of fondness and care for the clinician, a desire to invite him for dinner, but at the same time a sense of ambivalence and pain in relationship to the clinician's Whiteness. Discussing their social identities gradually became a means of thinking together about Rawdha and Fahad's anxious reactions to Sara's White friends.

Rawdha and Fahad's urgent inquiry about the causes for Sara identifying as transgender was an unconscious attempt to steady themselves with a sense of control, to deny the losses and transitions ahead for their child, themselves, their community, and their chosen city and country. This recognition allowed them to reflect differently on Sara's strengths, resilience, and development. In a separate treatment with a different clinician, Sara was free to focus on her experience of the conflicting messages from her parents, the ways she internalized and incorporated objects from outside her family, and what she really was seeking for herself. She joined her parents' treatment occasionally to check in.

It is not hard to imagine Rawdha, Fahad, and Sara finding different treatment in clinics across the United States. The focus could have remained exclusively on Sara, and on "correcting" her confusion or teaching her to conform to prescriptions of gender identity and expression using cognitive or behavioral approaches. So-called "conversion therapies" have recently been rebranded as "sexual orientation change efforts" (S.O.C.E.). They have been condemned by the Council on Social Work Education, the National Association of Social Workers, the American Psychological Association, and the American Psychiatric Association, among others. The Council on Sexual Orientation, Gender Identity, and Expression (CSOGIE) has developed a range of resources pointedly challenging the lasting foothold of conversion therapies in clinical education (see CSOGIE, n.d.), yet the ideas persist in all clinical fields, and clinicians can still use S.O.C.E. in most states with both children and adults (Byers and Coburn 2015; Vider and Byers 2015).

In a more mundane fashion, efforts to diagnose and control gender and sexual variance in children and adolescents are quite common, even in work with clinicians who attempt to practice in ways to affirm gender and sexual diversity. A colleague working in an adolescent group home recently sought consultation on a case of a cisgender White woman who seemed to be "turning lesbian" in an effort to fit in with others, given the violence she had experienced in her last group home. Another colleague consulted on a case of a cisgender, White, male, and heterosexually identified client who she thought might have experienced a trauma in the past because he had recently begun exploring sexual contact with another man. These conceptualizations are erroneous and homophobic, but they are also common and understandable given that we practice in a heterosexist society. Similarly, it is easy to imagine how treatment of Sara, Rawdha, and Fahad, even within the same clinic, could have remained defensively anchored in Rawdha's initial line of questioning about whether Sara is "really" transgender or else confused.

Distinguishing "real" LGBTQIA+ identities in adolescence from experiences of gender and sexuality associated with trauma reflects a classical Freudian idea that children are inherently bisexual and become heterosexual as they "mature" and develop fixed and stable gender identities and sexual object orientations (Blos 1967). Some "gay affirmative" clinical models have until recently retained the idea of developing a true or fixed sexual orientation as a sign of health, working to resolve "bisexual panics" among adolescent clients who they thought were truly, ultimately heterosexual if not for trauma-related confusion (Isay 1989). Sedgwick (1991) points out that the third edition of the *Diagnostic and Statistical Manual*, published in 1980, was the first following the removal of "Homosexuality"[3] as a diagnosis, but it also included a new diagnosis of "Gender Identity Disorder of Childhood." The substitute, she contends, reveals a vision of "healthy" homosexuality (male, adult, and associated with masculine gender expression) as distinguished from pathological expressions, which are understood as feminine, especially effeminacy in boys. In this way, patriarchal aggression found a new target in the indeterminacy of queer children—who are often, though certainly not exclusively, the continuing targets of clinical aggression against gender and sexual minorities. The historical and prevailing context of clinical aggression toward LGBTQIA+ people calls on clinicians today to use a higher level of caution with regard to etiological questions about marginalized gender and sexual identities and experiences.

The need for caution can make it difficult to explore with clients the ways that experiences of gender and sexuality can also convey pain and distress (Corbett 2008; Saketopoulou 2011). Saketopoulou (2011) provides a challenging example through her work in an inpatient hospital with a Black, ten-year-old, transgender client named DeShawn, who used male pronouns. DeShawn's mother and other family members lived with mental illness. DeShawn was suicidal, had attempted to murder his sister, had assaulted a peer, and presented with disordered thinking. He repeatedly made sexually aggressive comments to hospital staff. The cisgender, female, and White clinician worked to support DeShawn in wearing and exploring gender-affirming clothing and wigs and in playing with dolls, but his experience of gender was not without pain and conflict. DeShawn's gender exploration was frequently rejected by other staff, particularly those who were people of color, leading Saketopoulou to reflect on the ways DeShawn seemed forced to choose between racial and gender identities. At one point DeShawn grabbed the clinician's long hair, refusing to release it, and screamed, "I swear, I'll pull all your hair out" (193) in a violent expression of envy.

Saketopoulou (2011) reasons that in the context of highly regulated binary gender norms for children, DeShawn's nonconformity was impossible for him to make sense of and integrate into his ego-ideal without conflict, particularly given his experiences of psychosis and his mother's mental health challenges during critical periods in his development. She is careful to point out that she is working to "explore" rather than "fix" DeShawn's gender, but she maintains that "for such patients, encouraging the exploration of the meanings of gendered experience and offering the opportunity to metabolize affective reactions and unconscious fantasies becomes a matter of psychic life or death, psychosis and its containment" (198). Others have difficulty understanding and connecting with DeShawn due to his subversion of binary and unitary identity constructs—an aspect of DeShawn's emergent gender identity that may express both his resilience and distress at once. As Corbett (2008) has similarly suggested, "slipping the symbolic, and stepping out of regulatory norms, can happen through freedom as well as alienation" (852). DeShawn's capacity to work with a clinician to see parts, or fragments, of himself in conversation with the clinician and with other groups of people is limited by the regulatory violence in the larger society of racism, misogyny, and transphobia. Exploration of these parts and their meanings seems, as Saketopoulou suggests, an important component of her work with DeShawn.

Still, a key question remains whether clinicians can learn to pay attention to the dynamics of gender and sexuality without pathologizing variance—that is, without repeating the regulatory violence and abuse of clinical aggression. This would involve the clinician taking an affirmative yet open and exploratory stance toward a client's marginalized and contested identities and experiences of gender and sexuality without neglecting to attend to the ways they can be inflected through trauma, too. It is the challenge, as Corbett (2008) puts it, of "listening to gender now" (851).

A QUEER-AFFIRMATIVE CLINICAL STANCE
IN THE CONTEXT OF TRAUMATIC FRAGMENTATION

In this section we discuss the clinician's role in working with traumatic fragmentation with attentiveness to variant genders and sexualities, which can be dissociated at individual, dyadic, and community/social identity levels simultaneously. Significant attention has been paid in contemporary clinical theory and research to intrapsychic traumatic fragmentation for individuals (Bromberg 1996; Charles 2015), to the recognition and holding of fragmented parts of the self in relational clinical work (Benjamin [1988] 2013; Bromberg 2003; Ringel 2018; Tummala-Narra 2011), and to multifaceted mesolevel programming to promote community-affirming resources of resilience for LGBTQIA+ clients (Craig 2013; Craig and Furman 2018). It is important for clinicians to consider how these different levels of dynamic process can interrelate in treatment with clients with variant genders and sexualities.

Whereas in postmodern psychodynamic conceptions the self is understood to be a collection of parts, rather than unitary (as discussed elsewhere in this volume), parts can be further dissociated or dislocated in the context of traumatic experience. This presents challenges and opportunities for thinking about identity with LGBTQIA+ clients in trauma treatment. Although fashioning queer selves with agency in the context of trauma is sometimes romanticized by queer- and cultural-studies theorists (Cavitch 2016), Butler (2002) has described the pain and sense of precarity of living outside recognized and valued categories of social identity in a manner that might resonate more with lived experiences of traumatic fragmentation. There is an opportunity in post-traumatic growth for creative queer self-expression and new connections to LGBTQIA+ community, but moving outside categories where peers can provide resources of recognition and support can also mean further isolation and retraumatization. As Butler explains, "These are not precisely places where one can choose to hang out, subject positions one might opt to occupy. These are nonplaces in which one finds oneself in spite of oneself: indeed, these are nonplaces where recognition, including self-recognition, proves precarious if not elusive, in spite of one's best efforts to be a subject in some recognizable sense" (2002, 20).

Many clients can and do locate a sense of agency in finding and learning to play with fragmented parts of the self in the context of trauma work, exploring indeterminacy and moments of feeling seen in therapy and in the world outside, yet the pain and often terror of traumatic fragmentation cannot be minimized (Layton 1995). Clinicians can work with clients to explore how various parts might be in dialogue with each other and with others.

Kate, an Eighteen-Year-Old

Kate—an eighteen-year-old, White, heterosexual, and transgender woman in her senior year of high school—presented for therapy two months after witnessing her mother die by heroin overdose. Kate had felt close to her mother, but during Kate's childhood her mother had been unable to accurately mirror many aspects of Kate's emergent sense of self or experience, in part due to recurrent patterns of substance use and depression. She also had not known that Kate was transgender and had never considered the possibility. Kate deeply regretted not finding a way to come out to her mother before her death. At the same time, Kate was a high-achieving honor student and very involved with youth organizing and activism related to supporting other LGBTQIA+ youth.

The clinician—a White, queer, and cisgender-identified woman—noticed early on that she liked Kate and looked forward to her appointments. She admired Kate's work as an activist and community organizer and enjoyed hearing about Kate's public-speaking engagements in schools and other organizations. Kate spoke with a sense of wisdom beyond her years. "Your role as a leader seems very important to you, Kate," the clinician said early in the treatment. Kate responded, "Yeah, it's definitely better to not just sit around waiting and hoping that people won't be ignorant or mean."

Kate described how she hated asking for help or getting sympathy from others in the wake of her mother's death. The one exception, she said, was that boys at school she had crushes on were suddenly talking to her because they felt bad for her. She was excited about their attention but also felt deep ambivalence for secretly desiring them sexually. She experienced a sense of rage toward her peers, who—while supportive generally—she knew were unable to see her as a sexual being. "I'm like a transgender mascot to them," she said. She often described violent fantasies of getting revenge on others, and she once anonymously targeted online another student, a cisgender lesbian she knew from a queer youth group who had just begun dating another woman. She folded into herself, bending her head over her lap and covering her eyes, saying she felt like "a monster," like "a freak," and "disgusting," for both her sexual desires and her feelings of resentment. The clinician privately wondered whether Kate might similarly feel resentment toward her that might be difficult to acknowledge. She also considered the ways that Kate's anger might feel dangerous to her. Kate had described feelings of rage toward her mother when she was using heroin, secretly fantasizing that she would die yet waking up repeatedly to make sure she was breathing, still watching television late into the night.

The clinician was attentive to parts of Kate's experience that seemed to stay separated. She was her mother's caretaker and an activist; someone ashamed, furious, sad, afraid; someone with a range of emergent sexual desires; someone with a longing to be cared for but great discomfort with this potential; someone alone and terrified; an adolescent who had to know and explain herself before anyone else could; someone who felt surprised and ashamed of her rage and impulsive retaliatory actions. Through supervision, the clinician also began to notice in her countertransference different parts of herself in various interactions with Kate. She reluctantly acknowledged a part of herself that wanted Kate's acceptance as queer and aligned with her in some way, though she often felt rejected and dismissed by Kate. Noticing her frustrated desire for a mutual identification through queerness, the clinician was able to reflect on the ways she minimized differences between Kate and herself and relegated aspects of Kate's experience that the clinician found challenging and unlikable, such as Kate's aggressive and punitive desires. As many others had done in the past in relation to Kate, the clinician was valuing fragments of Kate's experience and devaluing others, attending to her selectively.

The dynamic of selection and exclusion of parts in the countertransference was fueled by Kate's conscious and unconscious work to regulate how deeply the clinician could know her. Sometimes in the context of psychotherapy, transgender clients and others with contested identities experience a strong need for empathy and mirroring as reassurance that the clinician can see them as they need to feel seen (Fraser 2009). Kate, however, needed to titrate the clinician's empathy and capacity to see her. When she wanted to test that the clinician was able to pay attention, Kate would challenge her with provocations such as, "Looks like you've been drinking or something—like you're too out of it to even listen." Alternatively, she would push back against closeness with admonitions such as, "Whoa, calm down, take care of yourself, don't worry so much on me, I'm fine." Kate often missed appointments or came late, explaining that she had public-speaking engagements or peer groups to run, which led the clinician to again feel rejected and resentful. Sometimes Kate would ask to speak with her chair turned away from the clinician.

Many people who have survived trauma experience themselves and others as victims, victimizers, and bystanders, a projective trauma triangle that can emerge interpersonally (Staub 1989; Herman [1992] 2015) as well as intrapersonally and dyadically in treatment (Basham 2004, 2016; Davies and Frawley 1992). A client's different parts may simultaneously observe past and present interactions from these three important but dislocated and projective perspectives—as when Kate projected herself as both a victim and victimizer of her peers and perceived her clinician as a hapless bystander. For Kate, these projections refracted experiences of shame, rage, and neglect that she had experienced as a child.

At the same time, these fragments took on particularly charged meaning in interaction with the clinician's countertransference. The clinician needed support in supervision to recognize how her dynamic with Kate resembled Kate's relationship with her mother—marked at once by care and resentment, frailty and resilience, affection and fear, rage and shame, longing to be seen and feeling misrecognized. The clinician grew able to guide the treatment toward better recognition of Kate's emergent selves, but first she needed to see how her own experience of herself resonated at times with Kate's projection of her as a bystander. She frequently felt helpless and useless as a cisgender-identified clinician in relation to Kate. The client's sense of caution toward the clinician as another ineffectual bystander needed to be acknowledged as understandable and warranted. In this newly attentive and responsive relationship, Kate was able to feel noticed with queer-affirmative complexity and care.

Queer-affirmative trauma treatment must manage recognition and appreciation for difference and openness to exploration. The clinician's transparent, nonpunitive, reflective responses to projective enactments in the transference and countertransference is critical to repair within the relationship (Russell 2006). The clinician can serve as an actively affirming reparative object, attentive and responsive to victim-victimizer-bystander dynamics and to other expectations of environmental hostility and indifference. Byers (2013, 2016) has argued that peers (not just clinicians, teachers, or parents) can also learn to take up this function in response to potentially traumatic bullying in adolescence.

The clinician's use of self as an affirmative, reparative object involves mirroring the client's pain and pleasure, vulnerability and resilience, and divergent parts and complexity with a high degree of credibility and authenticity. Clinical credibility in the context of trauma treatment cannot be assumed. It does not depend on sharing the same intersections of social identities; however, it does rely on the clinician's capacity for empathy from marginalized positions, for recognition of mutual differences in the treatment, for openness to learning through often difficult enactments in ongoing supervision and peer consultation, and for evident investment in the client's well-being with reflexive attention to power and social identity. Taking a queer-affirmative stance in trauma treatment should not and cannot mean providing a perfect mirror for all of a client's complexity as fragments of the self emerge, shift, and grow. Rather, it means working to understand the intricacies of another person in relation to community in the context of trauma. It means feeling and conveying empathy in both solidarity and difference.

NOTES

1   For a recent popular discussion of gender and sexual identity terms and their definitions, see Gold 2018.

2   Case material throughout this chapter uses pseudonyms and removes identifying information.

3   The American Psychiatric Association voted to remove the diagnosis of "Homosexuality" in 1973. The third edition of the *Diagnostic and Statistical Manual* reflected this change, as Sedgwick (1991) points out; however, it also added a new diagnosis of "Ego Dystonic Homosexuality" to address unwanted, unhappy same-sex sexual desire.

REFERENCES

Alessi, E. J. (2014). A framework for incorporating minority stress theory into treatment with sexual minority clients. *Journal of Gay and Lesbian Mental Health* *18*, 47–66.

Alessi, E., Martin, J. (2017). Intersection of trauma and identity. In K. L. Eckstrand and J. Potter (Eds.), *Trauma, Resilience, and Health Promotion in LGBT Patients* (pp. 3–14). Cham, Switzerland: Springer.

Austin, S. B., Jun, H. J., Jackson, B., Spiegelman, D., Rich-Edwards, J., Corliss, H. L., and Wright, R. J. (2008). Disparities in child abuse victimization in lesbian, bisexual, and heterosexual women in the Nurses' Health Study II. *Journal of Women's Health 17* (4), 597–606.

Basham, K. (2004). Transforming the legacies of childhood trauma in couple therapy. *Social Work in Health Care 39* (3/4), 263–285.

——. (2016). Trauma theories and disorders. In J. Berzoff, L. M. Flanagan, and P. Hertz (Eds.), *Inside Out and Outside In: Psychodynamic Clinical Theory and Psychopathology in Contemporary Multicultural Contexts* (pp. 481–517). Lanham, MD: Rowman and Littlefield.

Balsam, K. F., Rothblum, E. D., and Beauchaine, T. P. (2005). Victimization over the life span: A comparison of lesbian, gay, bisexual, and heterosexual siblings. *Journal of Consulting and Clinical Psychology 73* (3), 477.

Benjamin, J. (1988, 2013). *The Bonds of Love: Psychoanalysis, Feminism, and the Problem of Domination.* New York: Pantheon.

Berman, S. L. (2016). Identity and trauma. *Journal of Traumatic Stress Disorders and Treatment 5* (2), 1–3.

Blos, P. (1967). The second individuation process of adolescence. *The Psychoanalytic Study of the Child 22* (1), 162–186.

Brave Heart, M. Y. H., Chase, J., Elkins, J., and Altschul, D. B. (2011). Historical trauma among indigenous peoples of the Americas: Concepts, research, and clinical considerations. *Journal of Psychoactive Drugs 43* (4), 282–290.

Bromberg, P. M. (1996). Standing in the spaces: The multiplicity of self and the psychoanalytic relationship. *Contemporary Psychoanalysis 32* (4), 509–535.

Bromberg, P. M. (2003). One need not be a house to be haunted: On enactment, dissociation, and the dread of "not-me"—a case study. *Psychoanalytic Dialogues 13* (5), 689–709.

Butler, J. (2002). Is kinship always already heterosexual? *differences: A Journal of Feminist Cultural Studies 13* (1), 14–44.

Byers, D. S. (2013). "Do they see nothing wrong with this?": Bullying, bystander complicity, and the role of homophobic bias in the Tyler Clementi case. *Families in Society 94* (4), 251–258.

Byers, D. S. (2016). Recognition of social pain among peers: Rethinking the role of bystanders in bullying and cyberbullying. *Smith College Studies in Social Work 86* (4), 335–354.

Byers, D. S., and Coburn, J. (2015). The APA issued "aspirational" guidelines for transgender care. What can they accomplish? Slate. August 28. http://www.slate.com/blogs/outward/2015/08/28/new_apa_guidelines_for_transgender_care_do_they_go_far_enough.htm.

Cavitch, M. (2016). "Do you love me?": The question of the queer child of psychoanalysis. *Psychoanalysis, Culture, and Society 21* (3), 256–274.

Charles, M. (2015). Trauma, fragmentation, memory, and identity. In M. O'Loughlin and M. Charles (Eds.), *Fragments of Trauma and the Social Production of Suffering* (pp. 25–44). Lanham, MD: Rowman and Littlefield.

Corbett, K. (2008). Gender now. *Psychoanalytic Dialogues 18* (6), 838–856.

Courtois, C. A. (2004). Complex trauma, complex reactions: Assessment and treatment. *Psychotherapy: Theory, Research, Practice, Training 41* (4), 412–425.

Craig, S. L. (2013). Affirmative supportive safe and empowering talk (ASSET): Leveraging the strengths and resiliencies of sexual minority youth in school-based groups. *Journal of LGBT Issues in Counseling 7* (4), 372–386.

Craig, S. L., and Furman, E. (2018). Do marginalized youth experience strengths in strengths-based interventions? Unpacking program acceptability through two interventions for sexual and gender minority youth. *Journal of Social Service Research 44* (2), 168–179.

CSOGIE (Council on Sexual Orientation, Gender Identity, and Expression of the Council on Social Work Education). (n.d.). CSOGIE Resources. https://www.cswe.org/About-CSWE/Governance/Commissions-and-Councils/Commission-for-Diversity-and-Social-and-Economic-J/Council-on-Sexual-Orientation-and-Gender-Identity/CSOGIE-Resources.

Cvetkovich, A. (2003). *An Archive of Feelings: Trauma, Sexuality, and Lesbian Public Cultures*. Durham, NC: Duke University Press.

Davies, J. M., and Frawley, M. G. (1992). Dissociative processes and transference-countertransference paradigms in the psychoanalytically oriented treatment of adult survivors of childhood sexual abuse. *Psychoanalytic Dialogues 2* (1), 5–36.

Drescher, J. (1998). *Psychoanalytic Therapy and the Gay Man*. Hillsdale, NJ: Analytic Press.

Fraser, L. (2009). Depth psychotherapy with transgender people. *Sexual and Relationship Therapy 24* (2) 126–142.

Galupo, M. P., Davis, K. S., Grynkiewicz, A. L., and Mitchell, R. C. (2014). Conceptualization of sexual orientation identity among sexual minorities: Patterns across sexual and gender identity. *Journal of Bisexuality 14* (3–4), 433–456.

Glidden, D., Bouman, W. P., Jones, B. A., and Arcelus, J. (2016). Gender dysphoria and autism spectrum disorder: A systematic review of the literature. *Sexual Medicine Reviews 4* (1), 3–14.

Gold, M. (2018). The ABCs of L.G.B.T.Q.I. *New York Times.* June 21. https://www.nytimes.com/2018/06/21/style/lgbtq-gender-language.html.

Goldman, D. (2017). *A Beholder's Share: Essays on Winnicott and the Psychoanalytic Imagination.* New York: Routledge.

Hatzenbuehler, M. L. (2009). How does sexual minority stigma "get under the skin"? A psychological mediation framework. *Psychological Bulletin 135* (5), 707–730.

Herek, G. M. (2009). Hate crimes and stigma-related experiences among sexual minority adults in the United States: Prevalence estimates from a national probability sample. *Journal of Interpersonal Violence 24* (1), 54–74.

Herman, J. (2015). *Trauma and Recovery: The Aftermath of Violence, from Domestic Abuse to Political Terror.* New York: Basic Books. (Originally published 1992.)

Hornsey, M. J. (2008). Social identity theory and self-categorization theory: A historical review. *Social and Personality Psychology Compass 2* (1), 204–222.

Isay, R. A. (1989). *Being Homosexual: Gay Men and Their Development.* New York: Giroux.

James, S. E., Herman, J. L., Rankin, S., Keisling, M., Mottet, L., and Anafi, M. (2016). *The Report of the 2015 U.S. Transgender Survey.* Washington, DC: National Center for Transgender Equality.

Jones, T., Carpenter, M., Hart, B., Ansara, G., Leonard, W., and Lucke, J. (2016). *Intersex: Stories and Statistics from Australia.* London: Open Book Publishers.

Keenan, E. K. (2010). Seeing the forest and the trees: Using dynamic systems theory to understand "Stress and coping" and "Trauma and resilience." *Journal of Human Behavior in the Social Environment 20* (8). 1038–1060.

Layton, L. (1995). Trauma, gender identity and sexuality: Discourses of fragmentation. *American Imago 52* (1), 107–125.

Mereish, E. H., and Poteat, V. P. (2015). A relational model of sexual minority mental and physical health: The negative effects of shame on relationships, loneliness, and health. *Journal of Counseling Psychology 62* (3), 425–437.

Meyer I. H. (2003). Prejudice, social stress, and mental health in lesbian, gay, and bisexual populations: Conceptual issues and research evidence. *Psychological Bulletin 129* (5), 674–697.

Meyer I. H. (2010). Identity, stress, and resilience in lesbians, gay men, and bisexuals of color. *Counseling Psychology 38* (3), 442–454.

Minolli, M. (2004). Identity and relational psychoanalysis. *International Forum of Psychoanalysis 13* (4), 237–245.

Mizock, L., and Lewis, T. K. (2008). Trauma in transgender populations: Risk, resilience, and clinical care. *Journal of Emotional Abuse 8* (3), 335–354.

Muñoz, J. E. (2009). *Cruising Utopia: The Then and There of Queer Futurity*. New York: New York University Press.

New York City Anti-Violence Project, National Coalition of Anti-Violence Programs. (2015). Lesbian, gay, bisexual, transgender, queer, and HIV-affected hate violence in 2014. http://avp.org/wp-content/uploads/2017/04/2014_HV_Report-Final.pdf.

NYCAVP. See New York City Anti-Violence Project, National Coalition of Anti-Violence Programs.

Ovenden, G. (2011). Complicating trauma connections: Lesbian and queer survivor experiences. *Gay and Lesbian Issues and Psychology Review 7* (3), 191–204.

Parent, M. C., and Ferriter, K. P. (2018). The co-occurrence of asexuality and self-reported post-traumatic stress disorder diagnosis and sexual trauma within the past 12 months among US college students. *Archives of Sexual Behavior 47*, 1277–1282.

Primm, A. B., Vasquez, M. J. T., Mays, R. A., Sammons-Posey, D., McKnight-Eily, L. R., Presley-Cantrell, L. R., McGuire, L. C., Chapman, D. P., and Perry, G. S. 2010. The role of public health in addressing racial and ethnic disparities in mental health and mental illness. *Preventing Chronic Disease 7* (1), 1–7.

Quiros, L., and Berger, R. (2015). Responding to the sociopolitical complexity of trauma: An integration of theory and practice. *Journal of Loss and Trauma 20* (2), 149–159.

Ringel, S. (2018). Integrating contemplative practice and embodied awareness in the treatment of dissociative anxiety. *Psychoanalysis, Self and Context 13* (2), 119–131.

Roberts, A. L., Austin, S. B., Corliss, H. L., Vandermorris, A. K., and Koenen, K. C. (2010). Pervasive trauma exposure among US sexual orientation minority adults and risk of posttraumatic stress disorder. *American Journal of Public Health 100* (12), 2433–2441.

Russell, P. L. (2006). The theory of the crunch. *Smith College Studies in Social Work* *76* (1–2), 9–21.

Saketopoulou, A. (2011). Minding the gap: Intersections between gender, race, and class in work with gender variant children. *Psychoanalytic Dialogues 21* (2), 192–209.

Sedgwick, E. K. (1991). How to bring your kids up gay. *Social Text 29*, 18–27.

Tummala-Narra, P. (2007). Conceptualizing trauma and resilience across diverse contexts: A multicultural perspective. *Journal of Aggression, Maltreatment and Trauma 14* (1–2), 33–53.

Tummala-Narra, P. (2011). A psychodynamic approach to recovery from sexual assault. In T. Brynt-Davis (Ed.), *Surviving Sexual Violence: A Guide to Recovery and Empowerment* (pp. 236–255). Lanham, MD: Rowman and Littlefield.

Vider, S., and Byers, D. S. (2015). A half-century of conflict over attempts to "cure" gay people: The history of treatment of homosexuality shows that psychiatry may need a cure of its own. *Time.* February 12. http://time.com/3705745/history -therapy-hadden/.

Walton, M. T., Lykins, A. D., and Bhullar, N. (2016). Beyond heterosexual, bisexual, and homosexual: A diversity in sexual identity expression. *Archives of Sexual Behavior 45* (7), 1591–1597.

Woodford, M. R., Han, Y., Craig, S., Lim, C., and Matney, M. M. (2014). Discrimination and mental health among sexual minority college students: The type and form of discrimination does matter. *Journal of Gay and Lesbian Mental Health 18* (2), 142–163.

13

The Effects of Trauma Treatment on the Therapist

▸ BRIAN RASMUSSEN

FOR THE CLINICIAN, therapy with individuals who have experienced trauma firsthand frequently provides rewarding experiences. Facilitating individuals' healing and growth offers a glimpse into the strength and resiliency of the human spirit and people's capacity for overcoming some of life's most cruel and tragic events. Inspiring stories abound regarding people's courage to face unimaginable assaults and personal indignities. Indeed, some evidence suggests that therapeutic work with people who have been traumatized may have growth-producing effects for the therapist (Linley and Joseph 2007; Sacco and Copel 2018). Nonetheless, therapists who bear witness to the traumatic suffering of others may, as is true of the people they treat, suffer negative effects. Repeated stories of physical assaults, rape, torture, hate crimes, war, incest, shootings, and emotional cruelty, to mention just a few possible traumatic events, potentially affect the self of the therapist. How does this occur? What impact does it have on the clinician? Does it change the therapist? Are any of these possible changes lasting? How are the effects encapsulated in familiar terms such as *burnout* or *countertransference*? Do all therapists who treat trauma survivors experience negative effects? What are the mechanisms or processes that facilitate potential negative effects? What empirical evidence supports the constructs that have been developed to understand these effects? What impact do the effects have on the clinical process? What can be done to mitigate the possible negative effects? A growing body of literature is helping us to answer these questions—but the answers remain far from certain or straightforward. Although psychotherapy can be a rewarding and meaningful, if not personally enriching, career, it nonetheless can exact a toll on therapists (Kadambi and Ennis 2004), particularly those helping the traumatized.

This chapter examines the concept of vicarious trauma (VT) and, more broadly, the effect of therapeutic work with people who have been traumatized on the therapist. It also examines some related ideas, including the ideas of compassion fatigue (CF), burnout, and countertransference. Each of these concepts is distinct yet similar, and indeed they are interrelated. Distinguishing among them is important for both research and clinical practice because the proliferation of terms has resulted in conceptual confusion (Canfield 2005; Newell, Nelson-Gardell, and MacNeil 2016). I will also review some of the empirical support for VT, a body of literature that has grown ever more complex. The implications of VT will be addressed, particularly as they influence the therapeutic relationship and the treatment process. Finally, the chapter examines the need for self-care and effective organizational responses that hold potential for mitigating the deleterious effects of trauma treatment. Case examples will be selectively employed to highlight the concepts and processes involved.

VICARIOUS TRAUMA

McCann and Pearlman (1990) first coined the term *vicarious trauma* almost thirty years ago. Since that time there has been a great deal of attention paid to ill effects on therapists who work with trauma survivors. In their groundbreaking article they wrote:

> While an extensive knowledge base exists on the psychological consequences of traumatic experiences for victims, less attention has focused on the enduring psychological consequences for therapists of exposure to the traumatic experiences of victim clients. Persons who work with victims may experience profound psychological effects, effects that can be disruptive and painful for the helper and can persist for months or years after work with traumatized persons. We term this process "vicarious traumatization."
>
> (133)

McCann and Pearlman distinguished their thinking from existing concepts of countertransference and burnout, issues I will examine later, and situated the concept of VT within a constructivist self-development theory, which examines the relationship among traumatic events, cognitions, and our adaptation to the external world. A constructivist foundation to the theory posits that people develop cognitive structures through the process of interpreting their life events. For instance, people are said to develop cognitive structures or schemas that anchor some of their basic beliefs about the world: who can be trusted, what causes what, and one's place in the world. But what if someone's external world is fraught with danger, abuse, and violence? Trauma, these authors argue, disrupts these schemas depending on the saliency of the events for that particular person. For the therapist, exposure to clients' traumatic stories is theorized to disrupt the same schemas related to basic needs of safety, dependency, trust, power, esteem, and intimacy.

Symptomatically, therapists may begin to develop some of the same posttraumatic stress disorder (PTSD) symptoms as their clients. Such disturbances may include intrusive thoughts or images, painful emotional reactions, emotional withdrawal, anxiety, and alterations of their sense of personal safety and trust of others. Pearlman and Saakvitne (1995) outlined five significant areas of impact on the therapist: (a) frame of reference, including alterations in how one sees oneself, one's values, and one's spirituality; (b) self-capacities, or changes in affect regulation, self-soothing capacities, and enjoyment of daily life; (c) ego resources, or "the inner facilities the individual uses to navigate the interpersonal world and to meet his psychological needs"; (d) psychological needs, including safety, trust, esteem, intimacy, and control; and (e) sensory system, or disturbances to memory, imagery, and bodily sensations (66). Importantly, VT is defined as a transformation of the inner experience of the therapist with respect to these areas.

How does VT come about? Pearlman and Saakvitne argued that it is therapists' empathic engagement with clients that creates a vulnerable state for them. The very quality that helps to heal also puts therapists at risk. They described four types of empathic engagement with survivor clients. Cognitive empathy refers to a cognitive understanding of the traumatic events, their meaning, and their effects. Affective empathy suggests that therapists feel some of the client's pain, rage, despair, and other dysphoric affects connected to the client's experiences. In addition, there are temporal dimensions of past and present. Consequently, "there are four realms into which we can enter empathically with our clients: the past cognitive experience, the present cognitive experience, the past affective experience, and the present affective experience" (1995, 297). Pearlman and Saakvitne suggest that the realm of past affective empathic attunement is one that makes therapists most vulnerable to vicarious traumatization. That is to say, a therapist's empathic connection to the client as a child, experiencing the overwhelming nature of powerful affects as they were once felt, moves the therapist deeply. It may force the therapist to challenge cherished beliefs about the world and the goodness of others.

CASE EXAMPLE 1: CHRISTINE

Christine is a thirty-year-old, White, single clinician who works with survivors of violence and sexual abuse. She has been doing this job since graduating with her MSW. She finds the work challenging and rewarding but lately has been questioning her own abilities and motivation for working with this clientele. Daily, she hears stories of physical and sexual abuse from both recent and past experiences. Early on she struggled to "leave work at work," and for a while she thought she was doing better with compartmentalizing. Lately she finds herself thinking more about some clients in the evening. Often thoughts of clients just "pop into her mind" in an intrusive manner, and she can't stop thinking about them. Sometimes these thoughts are accompanied by disturbing imagery—a kind of replay of the therapeutic sessions. She wonders whether she is being helpful to these clients, often remembering moments in the sessions when she wished she had something more soothing or effective to say or do.

Christine grew up the eldest of three in a middle-class family. Both parents were university educated; her father was a high school teacher and her mother a nurse. Her liberal-minded parents instilled in the children the values of social justice and giving to others. Although the family was not actively religious, family vacations were frequently combined with missionary-style work in impoverished countries such as Haiti and Mexico. There she was exposed to severe levels of poverty, but she always came away inspired by the resilient spirit of the people she tried to help. Nothing, however, had prepared her for the horrors of sexual and physical abuse she was to hear in practice. Most disturbing was discovering that some of the men in her community whom she had known in various capacities were the reported perpetrators of such violence. One alleged perpetrator of sexual abuse was her high school teacher, a person whom she had previously admired and from whom she had received an academic reference. It made her wonder whom she could trust. Christine began to sleep poorly, often awakened by disturbing dream content. Gradually she began to withdraw from others, preferring to stay in on the weekends. She had had a few long-term relationships and was interested in a committed relationship but during the past year had stopped dating. Christine pondered changing professions, making occasional inquiries into various MBA programs.

In this case, negative effects of providing trauma treatment were becoming evident in Christine's perception of herself and others and in her behavior. Pearlman and Saakvitne's (1995) model would suggest that Christine is experiencing internal shifts in her cognitive schemas related to basic needs of safety, dependency, trust, power, esteem, and intimacy. Further, she is beginning to experience symptoms of PTSD, in particular intrusive thoughts and nightmares.

COMPASSION FATIGUE

Another way of understanding the effects of working with people who have been traumatized is the concept of secondary traumatic stress (STS)—or what later came to be known as compassion fatigue (CF) (Figley 1995, 2002). Simply put, people who work in caring professions and whose daily tasks involve providing emotional support for clients can frequently suffer psychological distress as a result of those interactions (Bride 2007). CF is defined as "the formal caregiver's reduced capacity or interest in being empathic or 'bearing the suffering of clients'"; it comprises the "natural consequent behaviors and emotions resulting from knowing about a traumatizing event experienced or suffered by a person" (Adams, Boscarino, and Figley 2006, 103). Similar to VT, CF is thought to be a consequence of empathic engagement with trauma clients. The observable negative consequences are comparable to those of VT and include intrusive thoughts, avoidant behaviors, emotional depletion, and feelings of helplessness (Figley 1995). How is CF different from VT? Kadambi and Ennis (2004) offer the following:

> In contrast to vicarious trauma, which is proposed to be an inevitable, irreversible consequence of working with trauma survivors, the experience of compassion fatigue is conceptualized as an expected, yet, treatable and preventable by-product of working with people who are suffering.
>
> (Figley 1995)

The experience of compassion fatigue results from empathizing with those who are experiencing emotional pain and suffering. It is therefore not inextricably bound to the notion that the exposure to descriptions of traumatic events and human cruelty is a necessary condition for the experience of stress symptoms in therapists. Consequently, compassion fatigue is quite applicable to trauma therapists, but is easily generalized to mental health professionals working with a variety of client populations.

(6)

The nursing profession has written extensively about CF. Coetzee and Laschinger (2018) have quite interestingly emphasized a different etiological view of CF, suggesting that "it is not empathy that puts nurses at risk of developing compassion fatigue, but rather a lack of resources, an absence of positive feedback, and the response of personal distress" (14). The organizational factors related to CF are explored later in this chapter.

The idea of CF has a certain "user friendly appeal" as it is intuitively grasped (Bride, Radey, and Figley 2007). Even if we have never worked with trauma survivors, we can imagine the emotional exhaustion of giving of ourselves day after day. If we associate the problem of trauma work with specific settings such as emergency rooms or victim-assistance services, it is easy to minimize the number of trauma histories that are encountered in other populations. In a paper with a highly creative title, "The Unbearable Fatigue of Compassion: Notes from a Substance Abuse Counsellor Who Dreams of Working at Starbuck's," Fahy (2007) described the personal impact of the unique conditions of this work. In the words of one of the therapists interviewed by Fahy:

> How many of my clients have trauma? How about try all of 'em. I've heard it's 80% but I think that it's higher. It's definitely higher in women. I did a women's group once with nine women and all of them had had at least one rape that they remembered. Compassion Fatigue—I don't know what that is but I know I got it. These clients are so needy. Services are being cut and residential beds are evaporating. Sometimes I come home from my job and I just sit and stare. I tell my kids "Mommy can't talk for a while."
>
> (202)

Smith (2007) reflected on the problem of CF as he experienced it and as did graduate students who provided psychotherapy services to people living with HIV/AIDS, a practice area that has received very little attention in this regard. As is true of the clinical population of substance misusers, this service population presented with a significant history of abuse in childhood and adulthood. Indeed, Smith cited evidence that a history of "childhood sexual abuse is a predictor of adult engagement in behaviours that increase risk of HIV transmission" (194). Although his data with respect to CF are descriptive and anecdotal, he provided a compelling argument for the need to research this important area of clinical practice.

Given the definition of CF, it would seem obvious that people who have direct combat-related trauma would be prime examples of those at risk for experiencing the negative effects of secondary trauma. Clearly, the mental health effects of deployment to war zones, such as those in Iraq and Afghanistan, are significant and include a high incidence of PTSD (Hoge, Auchterlonie, and Milliken 2006). Further, the notion of shared trauma has been evoked to capture instances in which clinician and client experience the same traumatic event—for instance, helpers embedded in war zones or directly affected by the terrorist attacks of 9/11.

Sometimes used interchangeably with CF, but incorrectly according to Newell, Nelson-Gardell, and MacNeil (2016), is the construct of secondary traumatic stress (STS). Introduced as a concept by Figley (1995), STS was defined as the "natural and consequential behaviors and emotions resulting from knowing about a traumatizing event experienced by a significant other (or client) and the stress resulting from helping or wanting to help a traumatized or suffering person" (7). The symptoms of STS are thought to mirror those of PTSD, including intrusive thoughts, nightmares, difficulties sleeping and concentrating, fatigue, and hypervigilance.

Although it has become more evident that some therapists will suffer the effects of STS, knowing who may be more susceptible is of particular interest to researchers and clinicians alike. Important in this regard is the question of gender differences. To this end, Baum (2015) conducted a systematic review of gender findings among mental health professionals experiencing secondary traumatization. Baum reported, "The 10 studies that examine STS on the basis of PTSD symptoms show a fairly consistent gender pattern. None of them show greater male susceptibility to STS. Eight of them report greater female susceptibility" (2015, 229). A further challenge in making sense of these findings is distinguishing between primary and secondary traumatization, knowing that the therapists being studied may have had direct exposure to trauma in their own lives. Consequently, more research is required to understand the impact of the client's traumatic experience on the clinician.

BURNOUT

It is important to consider the potential negative effects of trauma work within the context of the external conditions of the clinician's professional environment. As is frequently the case in many agencies, clinicians are faced with increased demands, larger caseloads, higher levels of acuity, less support by way of supervision, greater accountability, and fewer sessions in which to do their work. Not surprisingly, some clinicians experience what has traditionally been referred to as burnout. The term predates the concept of VT, and as is the case with CF, it has wider applicability inasmuch as exposure to trauma clients is not a prerequisite for this "syndrome." The word *burnout* refers to a state of overwhelming exhaustion; feeling depleted, detached, and cynical; and a sense that one's work is lacking in accomplishment (Maslach 1982; Maslach, Jackson, and Leiter 1996). Accordingly, burnout is related intimately to the stress of the modern-day realities of a clinician's work life. Therefore, all clinicians are potentially at risk for experiencing burnout. Fortunately, the effects of burnout, unlike those of VT, are not considered to be long lasting.

Child welfare social workers are at particular risk for burnout given their exposure to traumatized children and heavy workloads. In fact, Leake, Rienks, and Oberman (2017) claim that "of all the helping professions, child welfare workers are considered amongst the highest risk for burnout" (492). Their findings suggest that organizational stressors correlate more strongly to burnout than exposure to children's trauma. Such organizational stressors include "excessively high caseloads, lack of control or influence over agency policies and procedures, unfairness in organizational structure and discipline, low peer and supervisory support, and poor agency and on the job training" (Newell, Nelson-Gardell, and MacNeil 2016, 310). Ben-Porat and Itzhaky (2015) found that trauma social workers who were more susceptible to burnout included younger clinicians and those with a history of trauma.

CASE EXAMPLE 2: JEFF

Jeff is a thirty-eight-year-old supervisor in a large family-service agency. With multiple funders, the agency provides clinical services to a wide range of clients, including survivors of violence against women, sexual assault, and incest. He has been working there for seven years and during the past three has moved into a supervisory role with limited direct clinical responsibilities. He has witnessed significant funding cuts and a corresponding increase in the demand for services. At the same time, the funders require increased accountability via complex and detailed reporting systems. He feels frustrated that much of his time is spent completing paperwork, grant proposals that seem to go nowhere, and bureaucratic "make-work projects." He has little time to support his frontline staff. His long hours at the office do not translate into a sense of productiveness. He constantly feels drained and increasingly bitter over his lack of control of his work life. He dreads falling asleep on Sunday evenings as he knows what is in store for him once he awakens.

Jeff is showing signs and symptoms of burnout. Although he rarely questions his choice of career, he is convinced that work conditions have changed significantly since he entered the profession. When the executive director encouraged Jeff to take a lengthy vacation, he didn't hesitate to comply. Two weeks into a month-long holiday, Jeff began to "feel himself again." His energy and outlook improved, and he looked forward to returning to work. After he had been back at work for two weeks, his holiday seemed like a distant memory.

COUNTERTRANSFERENCE

Countertransference is an inescapable dimension of all clinical practice and indeed a critical element in the therapeutic process with people who have been traumatized. Freud introduced the concept in 1910 as a way to capture the impact of the patient's unconscious on the analyst (Orr [1954] 1988). Freud believed that the analyst needed to recognize these feelings and overcome them in order to properly treat the patient. This classical view of countertransference suggests a phenomenon that is detrimental to treatment. Reich (1951, 1960), a leading proponent of the classical view, warned that emotional intensity on the part of the therapist can suggest unresolved conflicts for him or her. Although this perspective is undeniably valuable, Freud's stance of a hundred years ago stands in contrast with much of the current literature suggesting that countertransference can be more broadly defined to include a full range of subjective experiences a therapist has toward a particular client. For example, Racker ([1957] 1988) showed how countertransference can be used as a tool for understanding a patient's mental processes. He identified two forms of countertransference, concordant and complementary identifications. Concordant identifications are empathic resonating experiences in response to the patient's thoughts and feelings. Complementary identifications imply that the therapist begins to feel as though he or she is some disowned (projected) aspect of the patient's self. For instance, the therapist may begin to feel uncharacteristically punitive or harsh toward the patient. Likewise, Sandler (1976) introduced the concept of "role responsiveness" to capture the dynamic interaction between the patient's transference and the therapist's countertransference, such that pressure is exerted on the therapist to play out a certain role in the relationship. From an intersubjective view the therapeutic process, and indeed countertransference, flows from the interplay of two differently organized subjectivities (Stolorow, Brandchaft, and Atwood 1987). Although the literature on countertransference is vast and beyond the scope of this chapter to review, it is important to emphasize that these various theoretical positions on countertransference have significant implications for treatment. That is, holding either a classical stance (that the countertransference arises from the therapist's own history) or a totalist stance (that the countertransference emerges from a full range of internal and external factors and dynamics) influences understanding and intervention. The limits of both perspectives were pointed out by Tansey and Burke (1989), who stated, "Whereas the classicist may be too quick to attribute an intense personal response to the therapist's exclusively private concerns, the totalist runs the risk of too readily concluding that the countertransference response to the patient constitutes a royal road to the patient's unconscious rather than a detour into his own" (28).

Somewhat more recently, Davies and Frawley (1994), in their work with adult survivors of sexual abuse, articulated eight "relational positions" that are alternatively enacted within four "relational matrices." From a relational perspective, these positions include "the uninvolved non-abusing parent and the neglected child; the sadistic abuser and the helpless, impotently enraged victim; the idealized, omnipotent rescuer and the entitled child who demands to be rescued; and the seducer and the seduced" (167). Davies and Frawley argued that because these positions reflect self and object representations that are often split off from consciousness, they are more accessible through careful attention to one's countertransference.

Pearlman and Saakvitne (1995) recognized the importance of countertransference in their seminal book *Trauma and the Therapist* and devoted considerable attention to its role and relationship to VT. They wrote, "While vicarious traumatization and countertransference are distinct constructs and experiences, they affect one another" (33). The authors also distinguished between these concepts in temporal terms. Although VT is said to be accumulative across many therapies, countertransference is particular to any given therapy. Further, the effects of countertransference are limited in time, whereas the impact of VT is argued to be "permanently transformative." Nonetheless, countertransference and VT are highly interactive.

Indeed, the relationship between the two concepts is such that one can intensify or even set the stage for the other. This is particularly the case when the therapist is unable to hold or contain strong affects that need to be kept outside awareness and consequently outside the treatment process. Pearlman and Saakvitne (1995) offered the following case example:

A therapist was working with a survivor client who had recently suffered a number of significant losses. He was himself anticipating the death of a loved one. Over time, he found himself feeling increasingly unable to maintain hope and a belief in his client's ability to heal from grief. As the client ruminated endlessly on the potential losses and was unable to engage in life, the therapist found himself experiencing the client as physically different: pallid, grey, unappealing, unenlivened. As this perception emerged into the therapist's awareness and he sought consultation, he realized he was engaged in a multi-determined reenactment. He recognized in his perception the repetition of the client's life-threatening illness early in childhood, and the parallel in his response to the client's mother's disconnection and helpless despair. The therapist realized that there was a further parallel in his own history, in his experience of his own mother as helpless in the face of his own childhood medical trauma. As the therapist began to question the effectiveness of this particular therapy process, he became more reactive, less emotionally available, and more withdrawn with all his clients, and specifically less able to tolerate death themes and despair in all therapies. This generalization reflects the impact of the countertransference despair on the hope that maintains therapies, thus creating a vicarious traumatization response.

(319)

Conversely, VT can set the stage for countertransference responses (Pearlman and Saakvitne 1995). Because VT affects the self of the therapist, it would logically hold that changes in one's emotional responsiveness would alter and shape one's countertransference responses. For example, a therapist's reactions to a new traumatic story from a client might be altered if the therapist is feeling depleted, withdrawn, or cynical. In turn, I have suggested that this process, as understood from an intersubjective perspective, would alter the clinical process, shaping and modifying the transference/countertransference process (Rasmussen 2005). Given the mutual, reciprocal, and interactional nature of the therapeutic process, a change in the subjectivity of one participant inevitably affects the other. The following vignette offers an illustration.

CASE EXAMPLE 3: LESLIE AND ANNE

Leslie recently began treating Anne, a White, twenty-nine-year-old, single woman. This is Anne's first experience with therapy. She was sexually abused by her father between ages six and twelve but has talked to no one about the abuse before now. In their early sessions, Anne sketched out for Leslie the "basics" of what happened, but now she is returning to her memories and beginning to divulge more details of the abuse, aspects of which are more horrifying than her earlier reports suggested. On one particular day, the session takes place late in the afternoon. Leslie is tired and depleted, having worked intensely with several clients. Anne has arrived at the session determined to reveal more about her abuse history—in particular, one story that occasionally replays in her mind as a nightmare. At the same time, she is terrified to verbalize the memory. With some encouragement from Leslie, Anne begins to share the story. As she does, she feels an intense wave of fear wash over her. She pauses. She fleetingly makes eye contact with Leslie and notices that Leslie averts her gaze and shuffles in her seat. Leslie says, "Please, go on," in a flat tone. After a lengthy pause, Anne resumes telling the story, only realizing much later in the evening that she left out the most horrific part (Rasmussen 2005, 27).

With this example I shift my analysis of the problem of vicarious traumatization from an intrapsychic problem to a relational one. Changes in the subjective state of the therapist affected the treatment relationship. It is reasonable to assume that clients are perceptive about the subjective states of therapists and adjust their content accordingly (Aron 1991). This perspective suggests that there is no place to hide for therapists and that, for better or worse, "we are in this together" with our clients.

APPLICATIONS TO VARIOUS POPULATIONS

The clinical populations and practice domains relevant to the problem of VT are vast and diverse. What they hold in common is the respective psychological adversity faced by both the survivor and the helper. Here, I will briefly explore some of the practice areas mentioned above in which the clinician is called on to provide assistance and the ways in which these traumas pose psychological challenges to him or her. Pearlman and Saakvitne (1995) focus their writing primarily on psychotherapy with adult survivors of childhood sexual abuse. Their interest in this area is understandable given its prevalence in general populations and its extraordinarily high rate in people with mental health and psychiatric disorders. Further, they argue that this population experiences high levels of symptomatology, requiring a trusting therapeutic relationship with someone willing to hold intense affects, because such clients often evoke complicated and intense countertransference responses that can overwhelm survivor therapists who may have experienced similar traumatic events. Similarly, Herman (1992) has noted how therapists working with this population might be drawn toward a rescuing role and identify with the survivors' feelings of rage and grief. Moreover, therapists working with people who have been sexually traumatized can be overwhelmed by the staggering cruelty inflicted on children. Hearing repeated stories of sexual molestation does make one question basic assumptions about humanity.

Although many therapists work with survivors of sexual assault, others have chosen to work with sexual offenders. The impact on these therapists, who are required to read and hear about sexual offenses in graphic detail, may present different dynamics for therapists who are also expected to maintain an empathic stance with their clients. Although less has been written about these clinicians from a VT perspective, Moulden and Firestone (2007) suggested that there are several factors related to VT in sexual-offender therapists. These factors include client characteristics, therapist characteristics, and therapy characteristics. Some of these therapists are said to report symptoms in the moderate to clinical range. The length of time working with the sexual-offender population is thought to be an important factor—with those early in their careers and those with lengthy service being the most negatively affected. Moulden and Firestone called for "more systematic analyses of the relationship between the contributors and consequences of VT as well as mediators and moderators of this relationship" (78). The call for additional research will be addressed later in the chapter.

Hospital social workers who are indirectly exposed to trauma run the risk of experiencing STS or VT (Badger, Royse, and Craig 2008). Work in these settings is often fast paced and allows for little down time to reflect on feelings or to debrief. Similarly, social work practice in mental health centers (Ting et al. 2005), substance abuse centers (Fahy 2007), and child welfare agencies (Horwitz 2006) is also fast paced, with clinicians exposed to an accumulation of traumatic events. In the latter, child welfare workers are frequently exposed to stories of cruelty and abuse suffered by children of all ages, including infants (Horwitz 2006; Perron and Hiltz 2006). When interventions go badly, child welfare workers are often held accountable, if not blamed outright, for attempting to resolve extraordinarily difficult situations.

The following report of a recurring dream comes from a young, dedicated child welfare worker: "I had this recurring dream for months. . . . In the dream I was always drowning. My head would bob underwater. But in the hand of my one outstretched arm, above the water, was a baby. And I would be screaming, 'Would someone please take this baby!' But no one did and I would wake in a panic" (personal communication).

Given our basic assumptions about VT, it is not surprising that treating torture survivors holds potential for ill effects on therapists. Interestingly, Deighton, Gurris, and Traue (2007) reported that it is not so much the exposure to clients' descriptions that is related to VT symptoms but rather what the therapist does when faced with such exposure. Likewise, mental health professionals working with combat-related trauma are considered to be at high risk for developing CF (Tyson 2007).

Another area of traumatic exposure includes therapeutic response to large-scale disasters, both natural and human caused. On the natural side, such disasters may include earthquakes, floods, tornados, wildfires, and severe storms (Byrne, Lerias, and Sullivan 2006; Leitch, Vanslyke, and Allen 2009). The sheer enormity of the disaster can have an overwhelming effect on a helper responding to it. For example, the emotional contagion evident when large groups of displaced people congregate can be toxic to everyone touched by it. Accordingly, the sense of helplessness, uncertainty, and loss of control is very difficult to soothe. Examples of large-scale disasters of the man-made type include terrorist attacks, school and workplace shootings, and industrial accidents (Naturale 2007).

EMPIRICAL RESEARCH

Research has sought to determine the effects of working with trauma survivors. The body of literature has grown increasingly complex, with new findings leading to more nuanced understandings. What seems clear is that some clinicians treating traumatized individuals will experience symptoms of VT and CF. But the questions of who, how, when, and why have yet to be definitively answered. As Chouliara, Hutchison, and Karatzias (2009) asserted, "While the concept of vicarious traumatisation appears to have been enthusiastically embraced by practitioners, the empirical research remains fragmented and inconsistent and does not yet represent a coherent body of work" (48). In a critical examination of this body of research we must be mindful of the following empirical challenges: (a) differentiating the various conceptualizations of negative impacts of trauma treatment, (b) defining terms as well as operationalizing and validating measures, (c) methodological limitations of recent studies, (d) problems of self-reports, and (e) theoretical limitations of etiological processes. Although mindful of the related concepts of countertransference and burnout, I focus here primarily on the research literature regarding VT and STS. As Kadambi and Ennis (2004) remind us, the field has not "reached a consensus on the identification of a single descriptor that accurately reflects the uniqueness and range of responses to providing trauma therapy" (4).

Research on Vicarious Trauma

An early investigation into VT by Pearlman and MacIan (1995) studied a sample of 188 trauma therapists. Participants were asked to complete questionnaires about their work with trauma survivors and their own psychological well-being. Included in the study was the Traumatic Stress Institute Belief Scale. Results suggested that newer therapists experienced more psychological difficulty, as did therapists who had a history of personal trauma. The findings pointed toward the needs for emotional support for trauma therapists, more training, and more supervision. At the same time, Schauben and Frazier (1995) found that a counselor's history of victimization was unrelated to his or her own level of symptomatology. They did, however, find that counselors who had greater exposure on their caseloads to trauma experienced higher levels of VT. Dane and Chachkes (2001) explored the factors that might lead to VT in hospital social workers. They used focus groups, each comprising twelve participants who worked in various medical specialties throughout a large urban hospital. The four major themes that emerged from the data included (a) organizational stress, (b) guilt, (c) problems with the emotional impact of cases, and (d) social supports. In contradiction to one of the major premises of Pearlman and Saakvitne's work in 1995, these authors concluded that "based on the results of the findings there is no evidence to support the hypothesis that hospital social workers in this study experienced an actual transformation of their inner world resulting from empathic engagement with the patients, which is the hallmark of VT" (45). However, the methodological limitations of the investigation suggest that further study on this question may be useful.

Comparing clinicians who treat survivors of sexual abuse with clinicians who treat sexual offenders, Way et al. (2004) sought to determine the level of VT in both groups as well as the clinicians' methods of coping in relation to the work with differing populations. A total of 347 clinical members (252 working with offenders and 95 treating survivors) responded to a survey that included the Impact of Events Scale and the Childhood Trauma Questionnaire. In particular, the researchers were interested in two factors believed to interfere with trauma treatment: intrusion and avoidance. Interestingly, the findings showed that the two groups did not differ with respect to the levels of VT measured, although the majority of the sample fell within the clinical range for VT. Further, the clinicians treating the survivors were found to use more positive personal and organizational strategies for coping. Consistent with the findings of Schauben and Frazier (1995), the authors did not find that a personal history of trauma was significantly associated with VT.

In a review of the research literature on VT in practitioners working with adult survivors of child sexual abuse, Chouliara, Hutchison, and Karatzias (2009) found that all studies report some degree of negative effects of this specific work on a range of professionals. Some of the studies report high levels of PTSD symptomatology, including disruptions in belief systems, avoidance, intrusive thoughts, and disruptions in trust, intimacy, and safety. However, a clear picture fails to emerge when studies attempt to compare groups of professionals for measures of VT. Accordingly, it is important to establish that VT is intimately related to the effects of trauma work as distinguished from other forms of counseling and therapy. In their review of these studies a worker's personal history of sexual abuse did not show a strong association with higher symptomatology. I'll return a bit later to the methodological limitations of these and other, related studies.

In a study of VT, STS, and burnout by Devilly, Wright, and Varker (2009), the researchers cast similar doubts on what we have assumed about the direct effects of exposure to the traumatic experiences of others. The authors agreed that it makes intuitive sense that exposing oneself to the traumatic stories of others in an empathic context should affect the therapist at an emotional level, whether consciously or unconsciously. But they were also concerned about confusion around the terminology and the difficulty in teasing out significant differences between the constructs. In their study of 152 mental health professionals, all participants completed questionnaires that contained measures of STS, VT, and burnout. In addition, the design included a control group of nontrauma therapists, as it is commonly argued that the trauma work in particular leads to VT and CF, not other variables common to the therapeutic encounter. This research found that "STS, VT and burnout are highly convergent constructs, but the measures for STS and VT do not display construct validity whereas burnout does" (381). Further, the findings led the researchers to conclude that all three constructs appear to measure the same phenomenon. However, an important finding indicates that there were no significant differences in VT or STS for clinicians who were exposed to either high levels or low levels of client trauma. Interestingly, the authors did suggest that the findings point to work-related stressors as the strongest predictors of practitioner stress. This conclusion is in keeping with a commonly heard refrain from clinicians: "It's not the clients that get to you—it's the craziness of working here!"

Research on Compassion Fatigue

Although there are obvious similarities between CF (or STS) and VT, for the purposes of research the definitions reveal an important difference (Baird and Kracen 2006). Figley (1995) defines STS as "the natural and consequent behaviors and emotions resulting from knowing about a traumatizing event experienced by a significant other—the stress resulting from helping or wanting to help a traumatized or suffering person" (7). Although the effects are indirect, the impact of CF bears very close resemblance to symptoms of PTSD. These symptoms include hyperarousal, intrusive imagery, distressing emotions, cognitive changes, avoidance, and functional impairment (Figley 1995, 2002). In measuring CF, several standardized instruments have been developed, including the Compassion Fatigue Test, the Compassion Satisfaction and Fatigue Test, and the Compassion Fatigue Scale (Adams, Figley, and Boscarino 2008). Also included in their discussion of measurements are the Professional Quality of Life Scale, the Secondary Traumatic Stress Scale, the Impact of Event Scale, the Trauma and Attachment Scale, and the World Assumptions Scale. For a full description and discussion of the uses of these tests, see Bride, Radey, and Figley (2007). In a study that sought to determine the psychometric properties of a Compassion Fatigue Scale and its predictive validity, Adams, Boscarino, and Figley (2006) analyzed data taken from a survey of social workers living in New York City following the terrorist attacks of 9/11. Although their conclusions are admittedly tentative, they did find that the Burnout and Secondary Trauma scales "seemed to be quite appropriate assessment tools, either separately or combined into the CF–Short Scale, for identifying caregiving professionals at risk for CF and psychological problems" (107).

But what happens when you survey master's-level social workers who were randomly selected from a large body of licensed professionals? Bride (2007) analyzed data from 294 surveys of social workers who were administered a demographic questionnaire and the Secondary Traumatic Stress Scale. The participants were primarily female, had on average sixteen years of experience, and were engaged in a wide range of service fields, including mental health, health care, child welfare, school social work, and community organizing. Participants were asked to rate the extent to which their client population was traumatized. Some of the interesting findings from this study included the report that 40 percent of respondents found that they had thoughts about their clients without intending to—in other words, intrusive thoughts. Almost 20 percent experienced psychological distress or physiological reactions when recalling their work with traumatized clients, and 27 percent reported irritability and problems with concentration. The authors concluded that social workers engaged in work with traumatized populations are likely to experience at least some of the symptoms of STS, and, important to note, a significant minority (15.2 percent) meet the diagnostic criteria for PTSD.

Critique of the Research

Since the early 1990s, clinicians have been drawn to the idea that therapeutic work with traumatized clients can have a negative effect on themselves as people and therapists. And indeed, some of the early research seemed to support these disturbing contentions. However, more recent research and critiques around conceptual models have stirred debate regarding practically every aspect of this phenomenon and have challenged many to reflect on what has been taken for granted. This is neither a surprising nor an unfortunate development. Research and interest in this complex area were bound to lead to conflicting results and diverging opinions.

First, we can consider the problem and validity of self-reports. Both qualitative and quantitative approaches to understanding this problem area are reliant on therapists' self-reports of subjective states; the history of their own traumatic pasts; previously held beliefs, values, and convictions; and the nature of their work. Here is an important dilemma, although one rarely mentioned in the literature: given that the main avenue by which VT is thought to occur is empathic connection between therapist and client, what therapist would be willing to claim that he or she is unaffected by this work? Who among us would want to be subjected to the implication that he or she is unempathic as a clinician? Some research participants may have been inclined to express negative effects to conform to an internalized and externalized ideal version of the empathic healer. Setting aside the possibility that unempathic clinicians do exist, it seems more likely that other variables (in addition to empathy) play a role in the transmission process.

Much of the current research literature is time limited and cross-sectional in nature. Consequently, there is an important need for longitudinal study of this question. Because VT is thought to alter beliefs, worldviews, and other enduring dimensions of subjectivity, it would make sense for these factors to be explored over a lengthy period of time, such that the hypothesized shifts in the inner world of the therapist could be measured with baselines in mind.

In addition, much of the literature supporting the idea of VT has been generated from studies that have lacked control groups or even comparison groups to help eliminate contributing variables (Chouliara, Hutchison, and Karatzias 2009). This challenges the claim that work with trauma specifically is what affects the therapist. Further study is required of therapists working with trauma survivors as compared to therapists working with clients who are not trauma survivors. In addition, we need to control for the variable of the therapist's own trauma history. Here, the findings have been inconsistent as to predicting VT. Some studies of VT with therapists who have personal trauma histories have found higher levels of traumatic stress (Cunningham 1999; Pearlman and MacIan 1995), whereas Schauben and Frazier (1995) were unable to support this finding. Although intuitively we might surmise that a personal history of abuse would leave one vulnerable to VT, more research is needed to clarify this important concern.

As Kadambi and Ennis (2004) and others (Devilly, Wright, and Varker 2009) have argued, some conceptual limitations constrain the study of VT. For instance, debate surrounds the question of whether VT is a chronic versus acute state among therapists working with trauma survivors. Kadambi and Ennis suggested that "this possibility may provide some insight as to why research investigating vicarious trauma has been characterized by such inconsistency" (15). Further, they concluded, "An often overlooked aspect of much of the research in the area of vicarious trauma is the fact that the majority of professionals providing trauma therapy appear to be coping well with the demands of their work," and consequently, "vicarious trauma as it is currently conceptualized is limited in its ability to account for aspects of providing trauma therapy that are positive and enriching for professionals"

(15). Being able to account in theoretical ways for both negative and positive outcomes is important as we further our understanding of trauma treatment.

Sinclair et al. (2017) offer a forceful critique of the conceptual and research literature informing compassion fatigue, a concept they find "problematic." Although they are careful not to dismiss the stress and suffering reported by health care workers, their review of the literature finds that sympathy, compassion, and empathy are often conflated. Noting this confusion, they conclude that "suggesting compassion is somehow the primary contributor to this phenomena is unfounded" (21), and therefore the concept ought to be critically reexamined.

SELF-CARE

At the outset of the chapter I suggested that trauma-informed therapy could be quite rewarding for the therapist and perhaps even growth enhancing. Indeed, some researchers have recently explored the concept of compassion satisfaction, suggesting that the field needs to understand the positive aspects of caring despite the associated personal risks (Sacco and Copel 2018). Comprehending the nature of such satisfaction is important in understanding the emotional well-being of the clinician. Despite the fact that research shows satisfaction in the work, and that not *all* therapists who engage in trauma treatment suffer ill effects, it does seem prudent to reflect on one's self-care and ongoing emotional health and vitality (Venart, Vassos, and Pitcher-Heft 2007). Decades of research have consistently demonstrated the relationship of a caring and compassionate therapist to positive therapeutic outcomes. The absence of a healthy, emotionally resilient, and attentive therapist is bound to affect both the client and the therapeutic process (Rasmussen 2005).

Here I will explore strategies for therapists to maintain optimal self-care. Many of the recommendations may seem obvious, yet it is surprising how many clinicians struggle to take care of themselves as their first order of business (Kanno and Giddings 2017; Miller et al. 2018). Perhaps as therapists we are inclined to attend to the needs of others before our own. I could speculate as to why—but that would be another chapter.

First is understanding that self-care, as it relates to being an effective therapist, means healing oneself. Very often people who become therapists have experienced many of the same traumas and emotional injuries that their clients have suffered. In fact, the motivation for becoming a therapist may have important unconscious dimensions related to earlier experiences of loss and deprivation (Barnett 2007). The idea of being "triggered" is less abstract when the client's stories resonate loudly within the self, such that the therapist becomes preoccupied by his or her own memories and reflections. This experience can happen in or out of therapy sessions. Although the question of the relationship between the therapist's trauma history and the development of VT requires further study, it seems reasonable to propose that a therapist with a trauma history should seek therapy himself or herself. "Heal thyself" ought to be the first order of business.

Beyond the specific recommendation to seek one's own therapy, the therapist should reflect on a holistic approach to self-care. Such considerations include attention to diet, exercise, sleep, play, and social connections outside work. However, it should be stated that we do not currently have strong empirical evidence to support the idea that traumatic stress can be prevented through specific measures (Kanno and Giddings 2017).

ORGANIZATIONAL RESPONSES

Without question, agencies and organizations that provide services to traumatized people have an obligation to ensure that their settings provide the optimal conditions for therapists to conduct their work (Kosny and Eakin 2008). Given the extensive research literature on VT and CF, it would be reasonable to conclude that providing therapy to traumatized individuals poses a potential occupational hazard. Accordingly, organizations need to be familiar with the latest research and aim to create positive working conditions for their clinicians (Geller, Madsen, and Ohrenstein 2004). Some of the measures that an organization can take to help mitigate the negative effects of trauma treatment include: (a) providing the best possible training and educational opportunities for clinicians, (b) providing clinical supervision and case consultation, (c) providing opportunities for peer support, (d) creating a flexible work environment, (e) balancing the caseload and workload of clinicians, and (f) where possible, supporting a collegial decision-making environment.

CASE EXAMPLE 4: JEN

Early in her MSW program Jen knew that she wanted to work in the field of mental health. She streamlined her course selection to focus on clinical practice, group and family therapy, substance misuse, family violence, and psychopathology. For her two practicums she was placed in nationally recognized treatment facilities, where she received very good clinical supervision and excellent training. When Jen graduated she quickly found a position in a mid-sized agency in a small city, far away from the high-powered university settings to which she had become accustomed. With some background in the area of treating children who had been sexually abused, Jen quickly established a reputation in her community as "the person to refer to" for such cases. She worked independently and with considerable autonomy. At first, she relished the opportunity to experiment with various approaches in treating what became a large caseload almost exclusively made up of sexually abused children. As time went on, however, she began to feel isolated.

She reported to a supervisor who had long before given up psychotherapy and now mostly engaged in administrative duties. Supervision, when it occurred, primarily consisted of issues related to bureaucratic details. When Jen tried to focus on questions of treatment, transference, and countertransference, she quickly realized that her supervisor was largely ineffectual in helping her reflect on her practice and think through treatment options. One time, risking perceptions of incompetence, Jen disclosed that in a recent session with a highly traumatized child, she had frozen and had no idea what to say or do. Her supervisor was surprised by her admission and seemed, in Jen's view, to be disappointed in her.

Moreover, the supervisor and Jen seemed to be talking different languages, each bringing divergent concerns to the table. Jen was concerned that the pressure to focus on immediate symptom relief for the children and reduce her overall number of sessions was interfering with her larger therapeutic goals. Jen's supervisor expressed concern about the lengthening waiting list and the pressure from funders to see more children. Occasionally, Jen would ask to attend a conference or workshop. Her requests were quickly deflected by her supervisor, who said, "We hired you because you were well trained, not thinking that you needed more training."

Jen began to feel trapped and unsupported. Two additional issues added to her frustration. First, her requests to take vacation time on relatively short notice were often refused. And second, her desire to balance her practice week by doing some couple's counseling, another area of strength, was rebuffed. She was told that given the lengthy waiting lists, her work with children was top priority. Jen's input into any administrative decision making was minimal. She left the agency after two years.

Jen's case highlights the ways in which organizational processes, structure, and decision making can negatively affect the well-being of the therapist. Feelings of disempowerment and a lack of support take their toll over time and, in combination with the challenging aspects of trauma treatment, undermine the work of the therapist. Clearly, all therapists need continuing education and advanced training for their specialized work (Phipps and Byrne 2003; Sommer 2008). Further, all clinicians conducting trauma treatment are highly advised to seek some form of clinical supervision (Tehrani 2007; VanDeusen and Way 2006; Wheeler 2007).

In a qualitative study of compassion fatigue, Kapoulitsas and Corcoran (2015) found that "access to and quality of supervision emerged as a common theme during the interviews" (94). Additionally, participants reported positive benefits from debriefing with colleagues. Clinical supervision may take various forms, from one-on-one supervision to peer supervision. Important in any form of supervision is the development of a trusting, supportive relationship. The supervisee has to be able to risk admissions of not knowing, vulnerability, confusion, negative countertransference reactions, and personal weaknesses. As Pearlman and Saakvitne (1995) pointed out, "A trauma therapy supervision or consultation is always a consultation on a therapy relationship, not on the client." In the same spirit, I have argued that clinical supervision should ideally attend to what happens between therapist and client in a dynamic way (Rasmussen 2005). The clinical supervisor is in a position to note the shifts and changes in the supervisee over time. Doing so, in the context of a safe, supportive supervisory relationship, provides the path to personal and professional growth. Concealing one's limitations and vulnerabilities—or as some might say, "Faking it until you make it"—may sound like an adaptive strategy in the short run, but it is a foolish plan in the long run.

Finally, Rasmussen and Bliss (2014) have speculated on some neurobiological factors that may be at play for trauma therapists. For instance, mirror neurons, an overactive amygdala, high levels of cortisol, right-brain functioning, and the fight-flight-freeze response may combine in deleterious ways to impact the therapist's functioning. Taken together, these neurological factors add to a complex biopsychosocial perspective on the potential harmful effects of trauma treatment.

CONCLUSION

The developing literature on the negative impacts of trauma treatment has brought our attention to effects that exposure to other people's trauma might have on clinicians. This body of literature, both conceptual and empirical, has become increasingly complex and nuanced. Indeed, the contradictory results of many of the studies strongly point to the value of further study. Many of the questions posed at the beginning of this chapter cannot be answered conclusively. It seems fair to say that some clinicians working with people who have been traumatized will be negatively affected by such work. But questions such as which therapists, in which ways, and for which reasons cannot be answered with certainty. As Devilly et al. (2009) asserted, "Many simply assume that such traumatization inevitably exists, but there has been some difficulty in building a body of quality empirical support" (373). In addition to understanding the ill effects of trauma treatment, we need to understand how and why so many professionals are coping well with the demands of their work. Kadambi and Ennis (2004) concluded that "shifting empirical focus from mental health professionals' vulnerability to traumatic stress responses, onto their resiliency against it, could serve to identify significant protective or mitigating factors that have yet to be identified" (17). The research literature is still unable to provide adequate answers to these questions.

Besides supporting additional empirical studies into the negative impact of trauma treatment on the therapist, clinicians and researchers should reconsider the conceptual underpinnings of these constructs. In particular, although the idea that empathic immersion in the subjective experience of the traumatized client is central to the etiology of VT, this hypothesis needs to be refined further. What other factors, in what combination, might produce these effects? Could the etiological variables of empathy, a personal history of abuse, and a lack of adequate training combine to provide a stronger explanation? Imagine being a therapist who is overwhelmed by the affect of a client's trauma, triggered by your own traumatic history, and at a loss to know what to say or do to help the client. Imagine such a scenario occurring repeatedly. Of course this is only one possible configuration of interacting variables. Others include issues of gender, culture, and life experiences, to name a few. The important point is that the complexity of the various factors must be accounted for both in the conceptual model and in the research that purports to comprehend it.

That said, we do have enough information and understanding of the effects of providing care to people who have been traumatized to make some broad recommendations. It seems reasonable to suggest that clinicians seek the best available training, supervision, and supportive organizational practices. Many may find it helpful to maintain a balance in the clinical services they offer and also a balance in their personal lives. Finally, therapists who have a personal history of trauma are recommended to seek therapy for themselves. Although answers to maintaining emotional health in the face of the significant challenges posed by trauma treatment are not easy to come by, I suggest that our first order of business ought always to be ensuring our own optimal care. Only then can we optimally care for others.

REFERENCES

Adams, R., Boscarino, J., and Figley, C. (2006). Compassion fatigue and psychological distress among social workers: A validation study. *American Journal of Orthopsychiatry 76* (1), 103–108.

Adams, R., Figley, C., and Boscarino, J. (2008). The compassion fatigue scale: Its use with social workers following urban disaster. *Research on Social Work Practice 18* (3), 238–250.

Aron, L. (1991). The patient's experience of the analyst's subjectivity. *Psychoanalytic Dialogues 1* (1), 29–51.

Badger, K., Royse, D., and Craig, C. (2008). Hospital social workers indirect trauma exposure: An exploratory study of contributing factors. *Health and Social Work 33* (1), 63–71.

Baird, K., and Kracen, A. (2006). Vicarious traumatisation and secondary traumatic stress: A research synthesis. *Counselling Psychology Quarterly 19* (2), 181–188.

Barnett, M. (2007). What brings you here? An exploration of the unconscious motivations of those who choose to train and work as psychotherapists and counsellors. *Psychodynamic Practice 13* (3), 257–274.

Baum, N. (2015). Secondary traumatization in mental health professionals: A systematic review of gender findings. *Trauma, Violence, and Abuse 17* (3), 221–235.

Ben-Porat, A., and Itzhaky, H. (2015). Burnout among trauma social workers: The contribution of personal and environmental resources. *Journal of Social Work 15* (6), 606–620.

Bride, B. (2007). Prevalence of secondary traumatic stress among social workers. *Social Work 52* (1), 63–70.

Bride, B., Radey, M., and Figley, C. (2007). Measuring compassion fatigue. *Clinical Social Work Journal 35*, 155–163.

Byrne, M., Lerias, D., and Sullivan, N. (2006). Predicting vicarious traumatization in those indirectly exposed to bushfires. *Stress and Health 22*, 167–177.

Canfield, J. (2005). Secondary traumatization, burnout, and vicarious traumatization: A review of the literature as it relates to therapists who treat trauma. *Smith College Studies in Social Work 75* (2), 81–101.

Chouliara, Z., Hutchison, C., and Karatzias, T. (2009). Vicarious traumatisation in practitioners who work with adult survivors of sexual violence and child sexual abuse: Literature review and directions for future research. *Counselling and Psychotherapy Research 9* (1), 47–56.

Coetzee, S., and Laschinger, H. (2018). Toward a comprehensive theoretical model of compassion fatigue: An integrative literature review. *Nursing Health Science 20* (1), 4–15.

Cunningham, M. (1999). The impact of sexual abuse treatment on the social work clinician. *Child and Adolescent Social Work Journal 16* (4), 277–290.

Dane, B., and Chachkes, E. (2001). The cost of caring for patients with an illness: Contagion to the social worker. *Social Work in Health Care 33* (2), 31–51.

Davies, J., and Frawley, M. (1994). *Treating the adult survivor of childhood sexual abuse: A psychoanalytic perspective*. New York: Basic Books.

Deighton, R., Gurris, N., and Traue, H. (2007). Factors affecting burnout and compassion fatigue in psychotherapists treating torture survivors: Is the therapist's attitude to working through trauma relevant? *Journal of Traumatic Stress 20* (1), 63–75.

Devilly, G., Wright, R., and Varker, T. (2009). Vicarious trauma, secondary stress or simply burnout? Effect of trauma therapy on mental health professionals. *Australian and New Zealand Journal of Psychiatry 43*, 373–385.

Fahy, A. (2007). The unbearable fatigue of compassion: Notes from a substance abuse counsellor who dreams of working at Starbuck's. *Clinical Social Work Journal 35*, 199–205.

Figley, C. R. (1995). *Compassion fatigue: Coping with secondary traumatic stress disorder.* New York: Brunner/Mazel.

Figley, C. R. (Ed.). (2002). *Treating compassion fatigue.* New York: Brunner/Routledge.

Geller, J., Madsen, L., and Ohrenstein, L. (2004). Secondary trauma: A team approach. *Clinical Social Work Journal 32* (4), 415–430.

Herman, J. L. (1992). *Trauma and recovery: The aftermath of violence from domestic abuse to political terror.* New York: Basic Books.

Hoge, C. W., Auchterlonie, J. L., and Milliken, C. S. (2006). Mental health problems, use of mental health services, and attrition from military service after returning from deployment to Iraq or Afghanistan. *Journal of the American Medical Association 295* (9), 1023–1032.

Horwitz, M. (2006). Work related trauma effects in child protection social workers. *Journal of Social Service Research 32* (3), 1–18.

Kadambi, M., and Ennis, L. (2004). Reconsidering vicarious trauma: A review of the literature and its limitations. *Journal of Trauma Practice 3* (2), 1–21.

Kanno, H., and Giddings, M. (2017). Hidden trauma victims: Understanding and preventing traumatic stress in mental health professionals. *Social Work in Mental Health 15* (3), 331–353.

Kapoulitsas, M., and Corcoran, T. (2015). Compassion fatigue and resilience: A qualitative analysis of social work practice. *Qualitative Social Work 14* (1), 86–101.

Kosny, A., and Eakin, J. (2008). The hazards of helping: Work, mission, and risk in non-profit social service organizations. *Health, Risk and Society 10* (2), 149–166.

Leake, R., Rienks, S., and Oberman, A. (2017). A deeper look at burnout in the child welfare workforce. *Human Services Organizations: Management, Leadership and Governance 41* (5), 492–502.

Leitch, M. L., Vanslyke, J., and Allen, M. (2009). Somatic experiencing treatment with social service workers following Hurricanes Katrina and Rita. *Social Work 54* (1), 9–18.

Linley, A., and Joseph, S. (2007). Therapy work and therapist's positive and negative well-being. *Journal of Social and Clinical Psychology 3*, 385–403.

Maslach, C. (1982). *Burnout: The cost of caring.* Englewood Cliffs, NJ: Prentice Hall.

Maslach, C., Jackson, S. E., and Leiter, M. P. (1996). *Maslach Burnout Inventory Manual.* Palo Alto, CA: Consulting Psychologists Press.

McCann, L., and Pearlman, L. A. (1990). Vicarious traumatisation: A framework for understanding the psychological effects of working with victims. *Journal of Traumatic Stress 3* (1), 131–147.

Miller, J., Donohue-Dioh, J., Niu, C., Shalash, N. (2018). Exploring the self-care practices of child care workers: A research brief. *Children and Youth Services Review 84*, 137–142.

Moulden, H., and Firestone, P. (2007). Vicarious traumatization: The impact on therapists who work with sexual offenders. *Trauma, Violence, and Abuse 8* (1), 67–83.

Naturale, A. (2007). Secondary traumatic stress in social workers responding to disasters: Reports from the field. *Clinical Social Work Journal 35*, 173–181.

Newell, J., Nelson-Gardell, P. and MacNeil, G. (2016). Clinician responses to client trauma. *Trauma, Violence, and Abuse 17* (3), 306–313.

Orr, D. (1988). Transference and countertransference: A historical survey. In B. Wolstein (Ed.), *Essential papers on countertransference* (pp. 91–110). New York: New York University Press. (Original work published 1954.)

Pearlman, L. A., and MacIan, P. S. (1995). Vicarious traumatization: An empirical study of the effects of trauma work on trauma therapists. *Professional Psychology, Research, and Practice 26*, 558–565.

Pearlman, L. A., and Saakvitne, K. (1995). *Trauma and the therapist: Countertransference and vicarious traumatization in psychotherapy with incest survivors.* New York: Norton.

Perron, B. E., and Hiltz, B. (2006). Burnout and secondary trauma among forensic interviewers of abuse children. *Child and Adolescent Social Work Journal 23* (2), 216–234.

Phipps, A., and Byrne, M. (2003). Brief interventions for secondary trauma: Review and recommendations. *Stress and Health 19*, 13–147.

Racker, H. (1988). The meanings and uses of countertransference. In B. Wolstein (Ed.), *Essential papers on countertransference* (pp. 158–201). New York: New York University Press. (Original work published 1957.)

Rasmussen, B. (2005). An intersubjective perspective on vicarious trauma and its impact on the clinical process. *Journal of Social Work Practice 19* (1), 19–30.

Rasmussen, B., and Bliss, S. (2014). Beneath the surface: An exploration of neurobiological alterations in therapists working with trauma. *Smith College Studies in Social Work 84*, 332–349.

Reich, A. (1951). On countertransference. *International Journal of Psycho-Analysis 32*, 25–31.

——. (1960). Further remarks on countertransference. *International Journal of Psycho-Analysis 41*, 389–395.

Sacco, T., and Copel, L. (2018). Compassion satisfaction: A concept analysis in nursing. *Nursing Forum 53* (1), 76–83.

Sandler, J. (1976). Countertransference and role-responsiveness. *International Review of Psycho-Analysis 3*, 43–47.

Schauben, L. J., and Frazier, P. A. (1995). Vicarious trauma: The effects on female counselors of working with sexual violence survivors. *Psychology of Women Quarterly 19*, 49–64.

Sinclair, S., Raffin-Bouchal, S., Venturato, L., Mijovic-Kondejewski, J., and Smith-MacDonald, L. (2017). Compassion fatigue: A meta-narrative review of the health care literature. *International Journal of Nursing Studies 69*, 9–24.

Smith, B. (2007). Sifting through trauma: Compassion fatigue and HIV/AIDS. *Clinical Social Work Journal 35*, 193–198.

Sommer, C. (2008). Vicarious traumatisation, trauma-sensitive supervision, and counsellor preparation. *Counselor Education and Supervision 48*, 61–71.

Stolorow, R., Brandchaft, B., and Atwood, G. (1987). *Psychoanalytic treatment: An intersubjective approach.* Hillside, NJ: Analytic Press.

Tansey, M., and Burke, W. (1989). *Understanding countertransference: From projective identification to empathy.* Hillside, NJ: Analytic Press.

Tehrani, N. (2007). The cost of caring: The impact of secondary trauma on assumptions, values and beliefs. *Counselling Psychology Quarterly 20* (4), 325–339.

Ting, L., Jacobson, J., Sanders, S., Bride, B., and Harrington, D. (2005). The Secondary Traumatic Stress Scale (STSS): Confirmatory factor analyses with a national sample of mental health social workers. *Journal of Human Behavior in the Social Environment 11* (3), 177–194.

Tyson, J. (2007). Compassion fatigue in the treatment of combat-related trauma during wartime. *Clinical Social Work Journal 35*, 183–192.

VanDeusen, K., and Way, I. (2006). Vicarious trauma: An exploratory study of the impact of providing sexual abuse treatment on clinicians' trust and intimacy. *Journal of Child Sexual Abuse 15* (1), 69–85.

Venart, E., Vassos, S., and Pitcher-Heft, H. (2007). What individual counsellors can do to sustain wellness. *Journal of Humanistic Counseling, Education and Development 46*, 50–65.

Way, I., VanDeusen, K. M., Martin, G., Applegate, B., and Jandle, D. (2004). Vicarious trauma: A comparison of clinicians who treat survivors of sexual abuse and sexual offenders. *Journal of Interpersonal Violence 19*, 49–71.

Wheeler, S. (2007). What shall we do with the wounded healer? The supervisor's dilemma. *Psychodynamic Practice 13* (3), 245–256.

SHOSHANA RINGEL, PhD, is an associate professor at the University of Maryland–Baltimore School of Social Work. She is the coauthor of two previous books, *Attachment in Dynamic Practice* (with J. Brandell) and *Advanced Clinical Practice: Relational Principles and Techniques* (with E. Goldstein and D. Miehls), and author or coauthor of nearly fifty refereed journal articles and book chapters. A trained psychoanalyst, Dr. Ringel is also a certified coder on the Adult Attachment Interview and maintains a trauma-focused private clinical practice in Columbia, Maryland. She has presented her work at national and international psychoanalytic conferences.

JERROLD R. BRANDELL, PhD, BCD, is a distinguished professor at Wayne State University School of Social Work, where he has taught since 1992. He has led workshops and lectured widely on clinical topics in the United States, Europe, Asia, and the Pacific Rim. His scholarly interests include theoretical and clinical psychoanalysis, the portrayal of psychoanalysis in the cinema, and psychodynamic supervision. A practicing psychotherapist and psychoanalyst, Brandell has published thirteen books, among them *Attachment and Dynamic Practice* (with S. Ringel), *Psychodynamic Social Work*, and *Of Mice and Metaphors: Therapeutic Storytelling with Children*. Dr. Brandell is the founding editor in chief of the journal *Psychoanalytic Social Work*, which has been published continuously since 1993.

KATHRYN BASHAM, PhD, LICSW, professor, Smith College School for Social Work, Northampton, Massachusetts.

DAVID BYERS, MSW, PhD, assistant professor, Bryn Mawr College Graduate School of Social Work and Social Research, Bryn Mawr, Pennsylvania.

CAITLIN M. CASSADY, MSW, doctoral candidate and adjunct faculty, Wayne State University School of Social Work, Detroit, Michigan.

A. ANTONIO GONZALEZ-PRENDES, PhD, associate professor, Wayne State University School of Social Work, Detroit, Michigan.

JAN GRYCZYNSKI, PhD, senior research scientist, Friends Research Institute, Baltimore, Maryland.

JUN SUNG HONG, PhD, MSW, MA, associate professor, Wayne State University School of Social Work, Detroit, Michigan.

JEOUNG MIN LEE, MA, MSW, doctoral candidate, Wayne State University School of Social Work, Detroit, Michigan.

KERRY HAWK LESSARD, MAA (Shawnee), executive director, Native American Lifelines, Baltimore, Maryland.

LAURA V. LOUMEAU-MAY, MPS, ATR-BC, LPC, art therapist and bereavement counselor, Journeys Program of Valley Home Care, Paramus, New Jersey.

LAVERNE D. MARKS, PhD, LCSW, clinical social worker, Yale Health–Department of Mental Health and Counseling, Yale University, New Haven, Connecticut.

BRIAN RASMUSSEN, PhD, RSW, associate professor, School of Social Work, University of British Columbia, Canada.

STELLA RESKO, Ph.D., associate professor, Wayne State University School of Social Work, Detroit, Michigan.

KAI Z. THIGPEN, MSS, LSW, survivor services therapist, the Joseph J. Peters Institute, Philadelphia, Pennsylvania.

SHELLY A. WIECHELT, PhD, associate professor, University of Maryland, Baltimore County, Baltimore, Maryland.

SARA WOLFSON, MSS, LMSW, clinical social worker, Safe Horizon, Brooklyn, New York.

Note: Figures and tables are indicated by an f or a t following the page number.